Paying for Productivity

THE CENTER FOR ECONOMIC PROGRESS AND EMPLOYMENT

 within the Brookings Economic Studies program is devoted to studies in growth, productivity, and employment opportunities. Its goal is to encourage and coordinate research on these topics in order to inform the policy debate. In addition to the studies listed below, the Center produces an annual Microeconomics issue of the *Brookings Papers on Economic Activity*.

Paying for Productivity

A Look at the Evidence

ALAN S. BLINDER
editor

The Brookings Institution
Washington, D.C.

HD4945
P29
1990

Copyright © 1990 by
THE BROOKINGS INSTITUTION
1775 Massachusetts Avenue, N.W., Washington, D.C. 20036

Library of Congress Cataloging-in-Publication data:

Paying for productivity: a look at the evidence / Alan S. Blinder, editor.
  p.   cm.
  Includes bibliographical references.
  ISBN 0-8157-1000-3. — ISBN 0-8157-0999-4 (pbk.)
  1. Wages and labor productivity.   2. Employee ownership.
  3. Management—Employee participation.   I. Blinder, Alan S.
HD4945.P29   1990
331.2′164—dc20   89-25328
                                                                    CIP

9 8 7 6 5 4 3 2

Set in Linotron Times Roman
Composition by Monotype Composition Co.
  Baltimore, Maryland
Printed by R.R. Donnelley and Sons Co.
  Harrisonburg, Virginia

Foreword

Over the long run, the economic performance of any nation depends on its rate of productivity growth. The more goods and services an economy can produce with a given labor input, the higher the living standards the consumers in the economy can enjoy. The faster labor productivity increases, therefore, the more rapidly living standards improve.

During the last decade, policymakers and academic experts have been wrestling with the difficult challenge of how the United States can raise its disappointing rate of productivity growth. After rising at more than 2 percent a year between 1945 and 1973, annual productivity growth has since slowed to little more than 1 percent.

This book examines one important potential mechanism for increasing productivity growth in the future: tying worker compensation to performance. Many firms, here and abroad, have already experimented with this approach, using different arrangements. Some have shared revenues with employees; some have tied compensation to profits; many have increasingly turned to employee stock ownership plans (ESOPs); and others have given workers an increased voice in firm management.

The authors in this book draw several important lessons from the rich variety of compensation systems in place. A major finding of all the papers in the book—one that was not expected when the book was initially planned—is that whatever compensation scheme is used, meaningful worker participation, beyond labor representation in boards of directors, enhances productivity. With respect to compensation schemes themselves, profit sharing does appear to raise productivity, although it is not clear that the productivity gains are sufficient to pay for profit-based supplements to wage-based compensation. There is much weaker evidence that ESOPs have any material productivity benefits. Gain sharing may be the best system of all for enhancing productivity, but there is insufficient experience with this compensation approach to support any strong judgments.

This book is a result of a conference organized by Alan S. Blinder and held at the Brookings Institution in March 1989. Five papers were commissioned, each prepared by one or more experts on a particular aspect of the compensation-productivity nexus. Each paper was assigned an official commentator, whose remarks and suggestions are included herein, and subjected to vigorous discussion from the floor. Besides many academics, knowledgeable people from government, industry, and organized labor participated in the debate and the papers were revised in the light of this dialogue.

Caroline Lalire and Jeanette Morrison edited the manuscript; Victor M. Alfaro and Roshna Kapadia checked it for factual accuracy; and Susan L. Woollen prepared it for typesetting. Fred L. Kepler compiled the index.

Brookings gratefully acknowledges financial support for its Center for Economic Progress, sponsor of this effort, from the following: Donald S. Perkins, American Express, AT&T, Chase Manhattan Bank, Cummins Engine, Ford Motor Company, Hewlett-Packard, Morgan Stanley, Motorola, Springs Industries, Union Carbide, Warner-Lambert, Xerox Corporation, Aetna Foundation, Ford Foundation, General Electric Foundation, Prudential Foundation, Smith Richardson Foundation, Institute for International Economic Studies, and Alex C. Walker Education and Charitable Trust.

The views expressed here are those of the authors and should not be attributed to the trustees, officers, or staff members of the Brookings Institution.

BRUCE K. MACLAURY
President

December 1989
Washington, D.C.

Contents

Tables

Contents

Figures

Masanori Hashimoto

Introduction

Alan S. Blinder

THERE is little doubt that America's dismal productivity performance during the 1970s and 1980s should be the chief concern of economic policymakers. From 1973 to 1988 output per worker-hour in all U.S. businesses grew at a paltry compound rate of 1.05 percent a year. That is barely more than a third of the growth rate we enjoyed during the halcyon 1947–73 period (2.96 percent a year) and, more important, only about half our long-term historic average. Had U.S. productivity grown at 2 percent since 1973 instead of 1.05 percent, standards of living in the United States would now be about 16 percent higher. If our productivity growth rate remains so depressed for a protracted period of time, America is destined to slip into the second rank of nations in terms of wealth and income, just as the United Kingdom did before us. To most Americans, that is a distasteful prospect.

Suggestions for boosting U.S. productivity are not hard to come by; only *good* suggestions are rare. The best way to raise productivity growth, and perhaps the only way to do so permanently, is to speed up the pace of technological innovation. Unfortunately, no one has a reliable formula for making a society more innovative, although better scientific education and more spending on research and development would presumably help.

By contrast, we know much more—though certainly not as much as we would like—about how to increase the rate of capital formation. Perhaps that is why both economists and policymakers who think about policies to spur productivity keep coming back to incentives for saving and investment. For example, suggestions for various and sundry tax breaks for capital abound.

Unfortunately, the help we can expect from this quarter is likely to be small, and for a simple reason: capital inputs amount to no more than 30 percent of the economy's total costs. A permanent 10 percent increase in the rate of investment, which would eventually raise the nation's

1

capital stock by 10 percent, would be a signal achievement. But with capital accounting for only about 30 percent of total costs, a 10 percent increase in the capital stock would raise labor productivity (output per hour of work) only about 3 percent. And even this small effect would be a long time coming. After five years a 10 percent higher investment rate would be expected to boost labor productivity only 1.2 percent—a mere 0.2 percent a year.[1]

Since labor accounts for at least 70 percent of total costs, it presents a more tempting target. If we could figure out a way to make labor 10 percent more efficient, so that an hour of labor time would accomplish what now takes 66 minutes, output per hour of work would rise by about 7 percent even with no increase in capital. Furthermore, such an increase in labor productivity would soon pull investment along. And if we could accomplish this in a short time, the transitory increase in productivity growth would be impressive.

Once again, a nation has many ways to try to improve the effectiveness of its labor inputs. This book investigates one of them: changing the way labor is compensated for its efforts. If a change in the pay system could indeed raise productivity, it would be a particularly attractive way of doing so, for it would require little or no sacrifice of real resources. By contrast, other (possibly good) ideas for improving work-force quality— such as reducing illiteracy—carry steep price tags.

Yet people who worry about productivity rarely think or write about changing the way we pay labor. It is as if existing institutional arrangements, including the wage system, were part of the natural order of things. In fact, however, a society starting over again to design a pay system to encourage high productivity would be most unlikely to choose the conventional wage system. We now pay workers not for *output* produced, nor even for labor *input* provided, but simply for *time* spent on the job. From what economists and psychologists know about incentives, such a system should not be expected to call forth labor's best efforts. The notion that linking pay to performance might improve productivity is hardly startling.

What is "obvious," however, is not always true, and introspection is a notoriously unreliable guide to empirical magnitudes. Do incentives like piece rates, profit sharing, and gain sharing have important effects on labor productivity? The five papers, with comments, in this book attempt to deal with this and related questions.

1. The calculation assumes a 10 percent annual depreciation rate but is not very sensitive to small variations in this rate.

Alternative Pay Systems:
The Lessons of History

The idea that individual or group pay incentives might motivate workers to higher levels of performance is not new. Piece rates date back to the preindustrial era and were in common use in nineteenth-century manufacturing. Both profit sharing and gain sharing, which means tying wages to some measure of group output or costs, trace their roots back to the nineteenth century.

Daniel Mitchell, David Lewin, and Edward Lawler begin their paper with an informative history of thinking on and experience with alternative compensation systems. Several noteworthy themes emerge. One is that rising and falling tides of interest in the various incentive plans have more to do with changing social, political, and economic fashions than with accumulating scientific evidence on how well the plans work. Another is that advocates of incentives have typically thought of and designed them as add-ons that raise total compensation, not as partial substitutes for straight wages. The authors dub this the "gravy" view.

These lessons of history are extremely timely for two reasons. First, the current surge of interest in profit sharing, employee stock ownership, worker participation, and the like has coincided with unusual wage concessions. It is therefore important to realize that this situation has not been the historic norm. Second, Martin Weitzman has argued on theoretical grounds that profit or revenue sharing can boost employment and mitigate cyclical fluctuations.[2] But his argument is predicated on the idea that sharing substitutes for straight wages. If, instead, workers on profit sharing earn more than workers on straight wages, we should not expect profit sharing to raise employment—unless, of course, it raises productivity sharply, which is the central question of this book.

Mitchell and his coauthors offer several pieces of econometric evidence to support the gravy view. First, they estimate from industry wage surveys covering the years 1979–86 that workers on incentive plans like piece rates or production bonuses earned about 11 percent more an hour than other workers. Second, using data from the 1970s, they estimate that workers who received cash bonuses (including cash profit sharing) were not paid lower straight wages. Third, using data from the 1950s, they estimate that the presence of profit sharing in the compensation package did not reduce other fringe benefits.

2. See Martin L. Weitzman, *The Share Economy: Conquering Stagflation* (Harvard University Press, 1984).

Taken together, these findings invite the interpretation that workers on profit sharing or incentives are more productive than workers on straight wages. After all, if they did not produce more, why would their employers pay them more? But even if workers on profit sharing *are* more productive, two critical questions remain.

The first one is, do profit sharing and incentives actually boost productivity, or do they simply attract the most productive workers to jobs where high productivity is rewarded? As Ronald Ehrenberg notes in his commentary, the regressions cannot answer this question because they lack adequate statistical controls for worker quality. This issue is critical to empirical research on alternative pay schemes. But it may not be critical to a firm deciding whether to institute profit sharing. After all, such a firm cares only *whether* its productivity will rise, not *why*. However, from society's point of view, the source of the productivity gain is crucial. If profit sharing merely shifts workers from one company to another, society as a whole neither gains nor loses. But if profit sharing actually raises the productivity of individual workers, society reaps an important benefit.

The second question is whether profit sharing raises productivity enough to pay for itself. At first blush, the answer seems obvious: if worker productivity goes up and profits are shared, owners of capital must come out ahead. But the issue is more subtle under the gravy view. For example, suppose workers on profit sharing earn, on average, 10 percent more than workers on straight wages. Then if a firm is to benefit from profit sharing, labor productivity must rise at least 10 percent. If it rises only 5 percent, the firm loses money despite the gain in productivity.[3] Given the estimates of the productivity gain from profit sharing in this paper and the next, it is far from clear that profit sharing pays for itself.

The authors briefly survey a wide variety of case study evidence, largely of rather low quality, on the efficacy of profit sharing, gain sharing, and incentive payments. (As the authors note, most case studies "fall more in the realm of magazine reports than research studies.") Most of the evidence is favorable, though that may reflect the natural tendency to advertise success and bury failure. One suggestive finding from the case histories is especially intriguing in view of the evidence in other papers in the book: profit sharing and gain sharing seem to succeed

3. The reader familiar with the theoretical literature on efficiency wages will recognize this as the condition for existence of an equilibrium with an efficiency wage premium: the elasticity of output with respect to the wage must exceed unity over some range.

more often when they are combined with some type of worker participation in decisionmaking.

Near the end of their paper, the authors use a rich new data set on
human resource practices—the Columbia Business Unit data—to estimate the effects of both alternative compensation methods and worker
participation on various measures of firm performance. They find that
employee participation, profit sharing for production workers, and
possibly employee stock ownership plans (ESOPs) have positive effects
on productivity. The estimated average productivity gain from profit
sharing is 8.4 percent—which is sizable. Finally, the authors' regressions
fail to detect the positive interaction between participation and profit
sharing that the case studies suggest.

Profit Sharing and Productivity:
Theory and Evidence

The paper by Martin Weitzman and Douglas Kruse focuses on a
narrow question: whether profit sharing increases productivity. But the
authors paint with a broad, eclectic brush. Their view is that a wide
variety of evidence should be admissible and that an abundance of weak
evidence can add up to a strong case—if it all points in the same direction.
In this instance it does.

Weitzman and Kruse begin with the unremarkable proposition that
paying for performance should elicit better performance than paying just
for time. Thus profit sharing should be superior to straight wages. This
simple intuition seems compelling at first, but it has been open to three
main theoretical objections.

The first might be called the $1/n$ problem. An individual worker in a
firm with many employees gains little if his efforts raise company profits.
Realizing this, he or she may be inclined to shirk. If everyone shirks,
group productivity is low and everyone fares poorly. If everyone works
hard, creating more profits to share, the whole group is better off. But
how can the cooperative equilibrium be sustained when n is large?
Weitzman and Kruse note that this problem is a classic prisoner's
dilemma game—but one that workers play repeatedly, not just once.[4]

---

4. In the classic prisoner's dilemma, the police arrest two suspects who have been
partners in crime. Each knows that the police do not have enough evidence to convict
him unless his partner implicates him. But each also knows that, in the event of a
conviction, he can get a lighter sentence by ratting on his partner. The dilemma is
whether to keep silent (the cooperative solution) or to talk to the police.

Since repeated games admit a multiplicity of solutions, possibly including the cooperative one, Weitzman and Kruse conclude that the $1/n$ problem, though real, is not a decisive objection to profit sharing. But will the cooperative, high-productivity solution actually emerge? The theory is mum on this point. As the authors put it, managers may have to do more than install profit sharing and walk out the door. To garner a productivity bonus, they may have to develop a corporate culture that emphasizes cohesiveness and cooperation.

The second theoretical problem is risk aversion. Linking pay tightly to performance might lead to higher productivity. But it will also give workers more variable income, which they may dislike. Efficient labor contracts must balance these two concerns. Weitzman and Kruse appeal to the literature on the so-called principal-agent problem, which addresses precisely this issue. They conclude that the optimal contract almost certainly mixes some profit sharing with a base wage.

The third issue pertains to the appropriate roles of labor and capital in decisionmaking. Some critics argue that profit sharing leads to demands for worker participation in management, and that such participation necessarily undermines efficiency. Weitzman and Kruse disagree. In theory, efficiency demands that capitalists make all the decisions only if they can supervise and monitor workers costlessly, a situation most unlikely in practice. If, on the other hand, workers can monitor and motivate fellow workers more effectively than managers can, then worker participation may actually raise productivity. The authors suggest, once again, that the optimal labor contract probably has a profit-sharing component.

Economic theory thus modifies and qualifies, but does not overturn, the simple intuition that tying pay to performance should raise productivity. What does the empirical evidence say?

Weitzman and Kruse examine a broad array of evidence. First, looking across countries (both socialist and capitalist) suggests to them that productivity is probably higher when there is a wider constituency for profitability. Second, they echo Mitchell, Lewin, and Lawler's interpretation of the case study evidence as supporting a positive effect of profit sharing on productivity and also suggesting that worker participation helps. The latter, they note, dovetails neatly with the game-theoretic reasoning which suggests that history matters in selecting an equilibrium. Third, opinion polls usually find that both employees and employers believe profit sharing boosts productivity. Fourth, and most intriguing, Weitzman and Kruse marshal the formal econometric evidence in a creative and enlightening way to build a surprisingly strong case for the proposition that profit sharing does indeed raise productivity.

A literature search turned up sixteen studies using forty-two different data samples that estimated the productivity effect of profit sharing. Many of these studies have flaws; none are beyond reproach; several obtain weak results. But the consistency of the disparate results is striking. Of the 218 estimated profit-sharing coefficients, only 6 percent are negative, and none significantly so. By contrast, 60 percent of all the regression coefficients are significantly positive. Using a technique called meta-analysis—which formalizes the commonsense notion that a large number of independent, though relatively weak, results can add up to a strong statistical case—Weitzman and Kruse conclude that the null hypothesis of no productivity effect can be rejected at infinitesimal levels of significance. This, I believe, is the strongest evidence adduced to date that profit sharing boosts productivity.

How large is the estimated productivity dividend? Among the 101 coefficients for which the authors have enough information to answer the question, the median estimate is 4.4 percent and the interquartile range is 2.5 percent to 11 percent.[5] They do not inquire about whether profit sharing substitutes for straight wages or is gravy, and hence do not ask whether a productivity effect of this size is self-financing.

Employee Stock Ownership Plans

Employee stock ownership plans are sometimes confused with profit sharing. In fact, however, they are something quite different—at least in principle.

ESOPs pay benefits in company stock rather than in cash, and the company's contributions need not be tied to profits. However, as Joseph Blasi notes in his commentary, *deferred* profit sharing plans are more like ESOPs, especially when the deferred compensation is held in company stock. And most profit sharing is deferred. ESOPs were accorded special tax status largely as a way to democratize American capitalism by spreading stock ownership, not as a way to improve worker performance. Nonetheless, the argument that tying the fortunes of labor and capital together might improve productivity has been applied to ESOPs, just as it has to profit sharing. In fact, as Michael Conte and Jan

5. The estimates by Mitchell, Lewin, and Lawler, which are part of the Weitzman-Kruse sample, fall neatly within this range.

Svejnar note in their paper, many of the theoretical arguments dealt with by Weitzman and Kruse apply equally well to ESOPs.

ESOPs are highly controversial. Conte and Svejnar conclude from their review of theory and evidence that the plans are neither as wonderful as boosters maintain nor as terrible as detractors claim.

Regarding the latter, ESOPs have been attacked as a raid on the U.S. Treasury. ESOPs are allowed to purchase company stock with borrowed funds. When a firm repays the money that its ESOP has borrowed, both principal and interest are tax deductible. Since only interest, not principal, is deductible in a normal loan, ESOPs are often viewed as a giant tax loophole. But Conte and Svejnar note that, if the money the ESOP used to purchase stock was used instead to pay for another employee benefit (such as health insurance or straight stock bonuses), it would be deductible anyway. So the major alleged tax advantage of ESOPs is illusory—which may explain why only about one-sixth of ESOPs use borrowed funds to purchase stock. Nonetheless, as the authors observe, the 1984 and 1986 tax acts did give ESOPs several tax preferences not enjoyed by other employee benefits, like profit sharing.

The main question for this volume is whether having an ESOP raises productivity. After reviewing the limited number of studies of the question, plus some related studies of European cooperatives, Conte and Svejnar judge the evidence too mixed to support any strong conclusion. No study has found that ESOPs harm either productivity or any other measure of firm performance, and several suggest that they help. But the strong positive effect estimated in the first study of ESOPs and productivity has not been verified by subsequent research. On the other hand, Conte and Svejnar argue that the evidence is much stronger that participatory institutions combined with ESOPs improve performance, a conclusion underscored by Blasi. They believe it is in-plant committees and consultative mechanisms, not voting rights or seats on the board of directors, that help the most.

Appraising Worker Participation

This last finding sets the stage for David Levine and Laura D'Andrea Tyson's thorough examination of worker participation. They begin by repeating two theoretical points made by Weitzman and Kruse: first, that participation can raise productivity if workers monitor other workers better than managers can; second, that workers who play the prisoner's dilemma game repeatedly may select the cooperative, high-effort equilibrium. But *may* is not the same as *will*, so empirical evidence is needed. Levine and Tyson strongly suggest that participatory institutions do indeed foster higher productivity.

Solid empirical evidence on this question is hard to come by, however, because *participation* is a vague term encompassing a wide variety of labor-relations practices, including quality circles, work teams, labor-management consultation, and employee representation on corporate boards. Furthermore, the existing studies use divergent methodologies, and many offer no quantitative measure of the effect of participation on productivity. Nonetheless, Levine and Tyson make a heroic effort to summarize the disparate empirical evidence in their table 1.

If one ignores research on cooperatives—which are special (though often successful) cases—there are twenty-nine studies in all. Of these, only two conclude that participation hurts productivity, whereas fourteen find that it helps notably or in a lasting way or both. The other thirteen offer more ambiguous results; the estimated productivity gains are either small, short lived, or dependent on other factors. This evidence, the authors conclude, makes it much easier to believe that participation helps productivity than to believe it hurts.

Under what conditions do participatory arrangements work best? Levine and Tyson argue that there are four mutually supporting pillars:

—profit sharing or gain sharing, to make workers feel that cooperative behavior is rewarded;

—guaranteed long-term employment, to give workers long time horizons so they do not feel threatened by change;

—relatively narrow wage differentials, apart from those attributable to seniority, to promote group cohesiveness and solidarity; and

—guarantees of worker rights, such as dismissal only for just cause.

The reader will notice a certain similarity to the Japanese industrial relations system—a point to which I will return.

If participation really can raise productivity at little cost to firms, why is it so rare in the United States? Why is it so much more common in some other countries? The authors offer two sorts of explanations.

The first is that the attractiveness of participatory institutions depends on the economic environment within which firms operate. Participation, they argue, works better in countries where average unemployment is low, recessions are mild and infrequent, and providers of capital have long time horizons and close working relationships with the businesses they finance. (According to the authors, the causation works both ways: participation also helps achieve low unemployment and mild recessions.)

These conditions characterize Japan and Sweden, say, much better than the United States.

The second sort of explanation rests on externalities: participatory arrangements work best for one firm when they are also used by others. For example, a firm that pays narrower wage differentials than others may find its best workers quitting, while less-experienced, less-productive applicants flood its personnel office. The problem evaporates, however, if all firms offer the same egalitarian wage structure. Similarly, a firm with a just-cause dismissal policy may find itself attracting inordinate numbers of workers who like to shirk, if competing firms continue to have dismissal at will. But if all firms adopt just-cause, the adverse selection problem disappears. The upshot, Levine and Tyson argue, is that an economy may have two equilibria: a superior one with participation, and an inferior one without.

Worse yet, the participatory equilibrium, if attained, may have a tendency to unravel. Consider wage differentials, for example. If, starting from an equilibrium with narrow wage differentials, one firm begins to offer premium wages to star workers, other firms will find themselves losing their best talent. If they react by widening their own pay differentials, the participatory equilibrium comes apart. Hence a strong social consensus or legislative encouragement may be necessary to achieve and maintain an equilibrium with high levels of participation.

Labor Relations in Japan

Much of Levine and Tyson's analysis sounds like an explanation of why Japan has more, and more effective, worker participation than the United States. But there is one important exception. The authors argue that the most effective forms of participation involve substantive shop-floor decisionmaking, not just labor-management consultation. Masanori Hashimoto takes a different view in his paper.

A few years ago, many Americans thought that the key to Japan's industrial success was more and better capital. Now we are coming to realize that the Japanese edge comes from knowing how to use *people,* not machines. That is certainly Hashimoto's view. He points to nine significant differences between Japanese and American industrial relations systems:

1. Long-term employment is both more prevalent and more formal in Japan, where dismissals and layoffs are extremely rare. So the Japanese

worker has enough job security to identify with the company and to accept industrial change willingly.

2. Wages are tied more tightly to seniority in Japan than in the United States, which Hashimoto interprets as evidence that Japanese firms invest more in firm-specific human capital.[6]

3. Japanese workers receive a substantial share of their compensation in semiannual bonuses. Such bonuses, which are uncommon in the United States, make wages more flexible and might—to the extent that they serve as profit sharing—enhance productivity.

4. Japanese unions are organized along enterprise lines, not along the craft or industrial lines that typify American unions. This creates greater commonality of interests between labor and business leaders and makes it easier for unions to assist in monitoring worker performance.

5. Wage bargaining in Japan is synchronized in the annual spring offensive (*Shunto*). This system helps make wages more flexible than in the United States, where collective bargaining is decentralized and staggered.

6. Japanese labor contracts are brief and sketchy, leaving a great deal to on-the-spot decisions in the workplace arrived at by mutual consent. American labor contracts, by contrast, are long documents that try to spell out everything in writing, thereby rigidifying the employment relationship.

7. Quality control circles are used much more, and apparently more effectively, in Japan.

8. Japanese managers devote much more time and energy to joint consultations with labor than their American counterparts do. These procedures, which are often formalized, facilitate communication, foster harmony, and promote a fair sharing of the gains from innovation.

9. Decisionmaking within Japanese firms is based on consensus building, including the involvement of labor. American management exercises more top-down control.

Hashimoto's list goes well beyond the four factors emphasized by Levine and Tyson. Which are the key ingredients? Hashimoto argues that "joint consultation and consensus-based decisionmaking are the cornerstone of the Japanese industrial relations system." Japanese businesses make enormous investments of time and money in these mechanisms; they must believe that their investments pay off. Why, then, do American businesses not do the same? There are only three

6. Another interpretation, stressed by Levine and Tyson, is that narrow wage differentials, other than for seniority reasons, promote group cohesiveness.

possibilities: American business is underinvesting in participatory mechanisms, or Japanese business is overinvesting, or such investments are
more profitable in Japan than in the United States.

Hashimoto favors the last explanation—which makes him hesitant to
recommend importing Japanese industrial relations practices to America. Specifically, he hypothesizes that the Japanese invest more in the
employment relation because the costs of joint consultation and consensus decisionmaking are lower in Japan, whereas the benefits are more or
less the same in the two countries.

Is the hypothesis true? We do not know. We *do* know that Japanese
managers take more care in screening job applicants. But that just shows
that they do indeed invest more in the employment relation, not that it
is cheaper to do so. Hashimoto suggests that the greater homogeneity of
the Japanese labor force reduces the costs of communication, which is
believable. But the fact that Japanese management techniques seem to
work well in the United States—with *American* workers—gives one
pause.

Levine and Tyson, as noted, emphasize the first explanation—which
leads them to recommend more participation. But the second explanation—that the Japanese overinvest in employee relations—should not
be ruled out. It is well known that upper and middle managers in large
Japanese companies spend many hours after work with employees in
restaurants and bars, at company picnics, and so on. Often the company
picks up the bill. If these hours were counted as part of the workweek,
rather than as leisure time, Japanese labor productivity, as conventionally measured, would be lower than it is.

Thus, though the differences between Japanese and American industrial relations practices are clear, the reasons for them are not. Nor is it
clear that American firms would do better by moving toward Japanese
industrial relations practices—although many people, including myself,
suspect that this is true.

Summary

What, then, do we learn from this important collection of papers?
First, there is good reason to believe profit sharing does indeed raise
productivity, but much less reason to believe ESOPs do so. (Gain sharing
may be the best system of all, but there are too few cases to support any
strong judgments.) The evidence on profit sharing and productivity is
particularly persuasive if one accepts the view that a large number of

weak, but consistent, studies add up to a strong statistical case. However, it is not known whether the productivity dividend is typically large enough to pay for the profit sharing if the profit sharing is given as gravy. Nonetheless, in true Murphy's Law fashion, the U.S. government subsidizes ESOPs, but not profit sharing, with tax breaks.

Second, worker participation apparently helps make alternative compensation plans like profit sharing, gain sharing, and ESOPs work better—and also has beneficial effects of its own. This theme, which was totally unexpected when I organized the conference, runs strongly through all five papers. Weitzman and Kruse explain how "company spirit" can help enforce the cooperative equilibrium where everyone works hard. Mitchell, Lewin, and Lawler point out that case studies find stronger positive effects of profit and gain sharing when there are participatory institutions. Conte and Svejnar tentatively suggest that ESOPs may raise productivity only in a participatory environment. The papers by Levine and Tyson and by Hashimoto put worker participation at center stage and offer evidence that it works.

Which forms of participation raise productivity the most? We do not know. But giving labor a seat on the board of directors may be the least effective form of employee participation. Beyond that, there is controversy—and insufficient statistical evidence to resolve the dispute. Levine and Tyson point to substantive participation in shop-floor decisions; Hashimoto emphasizes joint consultation between labor and management. This is an important question that seems ripe for further research.

So it seems that one can tentatively answer the central question of this book—can American industry raise productivity by changing the way it pays its employees?—in an unexpected way. It appears that changing the way workers are *treated* may boost productivity more than changing the way they are *paid,* although profit sharing or employee stock ownership combined with worker participation may be the best system of all. That answer, and the evidence behind it, should be of intense interest to both policymakers concerned with raising productivity and business executives concerned with raising profits.

Alternative Pay Systems, Firm Performance, and Productivity

Daniel J. B. Mitchell, David Lewin, and Edward E. Lawler III

THE 1970s and 1980s are perceived, with hindsight, as periods of economic change and adjustment. Dramatic shifts occurred in exchange rates, in energy prices, in the rate of inflation and unemployment, and in the extent of government regulation of the product market. It is not surprising, therefore, that words such as *productivity* and *competitiveness* came into vogue during this period. In their separate ways, employers and employees became concerned about their survival and welfare. Given that environment, a willingness to experiment in human resource practices developed, including practices relating to compensation systems.[1]

In this paper we focus on the possible contribution of alternative pay systems applied to nonsupervisory employees—incentive plans, profit sharing, and gain sharing—to microeconomic performance. By design, we do not consider the potentially important area of alternative systems of executive pay. We begin with an analysis of some recent trends in the use and analysis of pay practices. Then we turn to the historical development of these practices. We find that the ebbs and flows in the use of particular pay systems reflect a complex web of social movements, movements in managerial thinking, trends in academic thinking, major economic events (especially the world wars and the Great Depression), and public policies including tax preferences. The ebbs and flows occurred without hard evidence of the productivity effects of alternative pay systems.

Data sets with detailed information on pay and other human resource practices have been scarce. However, we follow the historical analysis with evidence from various data sources. Highlights of the findings are

---

1. The phrase *human resources* has tended to replace the word *personnel* in recent years, except in the economic literature where the phrase *new economics of personnel* is popular. We use the terms interchangeably in this essay but tend to use *personnel* when referring to older practices and literature.

(1) that incentive workers are consistently paid more than time workers, a fact suggesting the former's greater productivity or some cost saving associated with their employment, (2) that profit sharing does not seem to substitute for other forms of pay, a fact relevant to the proposed employment expansion effect of such plans, and (3) that the use of profit sharing was associated with both higher productivity and improved firm performance in the 1980s.

Productivity, Pay Systems, and Human Resource Practices

Economists have long put forward the truism that productivity trends and real wage trends have tended to coincide over long periods.[2] In other words, improvements in living standards depend ultimately on rising productivity. Early investigations of the sources of productivity growth led to the surprising conclusion that much of it could not be explained by such prime candidates as rising capital-to-labor ratios.[3] Yet until measured productivity growth stagnated in the early 1970s, policymakers were usually content to assume that something like a 3 percent productivity increase could be expected annually. Such assumptions were built into the incomes policy experiments of the period.[4]

Although many suggestions have been made to explain the deterioration in productivity performance, interest has grown in exploring the impact of microeconomic-level human resource policies in determining the effective use of employees.[5] Economists have traditionally viewed the price system as a key element in the efficient allocation of resources, on the assumption that people react to incentives. Thus there is a

2. For example, during 1947–87 output per hour in the nonfarm business sector rose at an annual rate of 2.5 percent. Real compensation per hour rose at a rate of 2.4 percent during the same period. *Economic Report of the President, February 1988*, p. 300.

3. Robert M. Solow, "Growth Theory and After," *American Economic Review*, vol. 78 (June 1988), pp. 307–17; and Edward F. Denison, *Trends in American Economic Growth, 1929–1982* (Brookings, 1985).

4. John Sheahan, *The Wage-Price Guideposts* (Brookings, 1967); and Arnold R. Weber and Daniel J. B. Mitchell, *The Pay Board's Progress: Wage Controls in Phase II* (Brookings, 1978), pp. 15–17, 28–54.

5. Harry C. Katz, Thomas A. Kochan, and Jeffrey H. Keefe, "Industrial Relations and Productivity in the U.S. Automobile Industry," *Brookings Papers on Economic Activity, 3:1987*, pp. 685–715; Lester C. Thurow, "Economic Paradigms and Slow American Productivity Growth," *Eastern Economic Journal*, vol. 13 (October–December 1987), pp. 333–43; and Thomas E. Wiesskopf, Samuel Bowles, and David M. Gordon, "Hearts and Minds: A Social Model of U.S. Productivity Growth," *Brookings Papers on Economic Activity, 2:1983*, pp. 381–441.

potential harmony between the view of the human resource professional that incentives can "matter" and economic orthodoxy. But until recently, economists have not sought to explore the effects of alternative pay systems or other human resource practices.[6]

Even before the recent spate of literature on the "new economics of personnel," many had recognized that the employment contract was a complex exchange. Employers want more of their employees than simply time spent at the job. They want loyalty, cooperation, teamwork, or just output (as opposed to input). Yet the conventional time-based wage system pays explicitly only for time on the job. It is not radical to suppose that if the pay system explicitly rewarded desirable behaviors, more such behaviors might be induced; indeed, both economists and psychologists would readily accept this supposition.

New Trends in Human Resources and Industrial Relations

One factor that may have limited the interest of economists in alternative pay systems is the assumption that if such practices were profitable, they would already be in use.[7] However, as will be discussed, pay and other human resource practices have changed over time. Particularly in the compensation area, human resource professionals have begun to show a new interest in systems other than time-based wages.

In the shrinking union sector, the 1980s saw the development of such practices as lump-sum bonuses, two-tier wages, and pay based on product prices or firm profitability. These arrangements were often associated with "concession bargaining" and "givebacks." Precedents for these concession-related features had long existed, but their proliferation was noteworthy. In the nonunion sector pay for performance (rather than for time) became a catch phrase.

Some authors and studies suggested that in both sectors human resource managers were being forced to become more bottom-line

6. For a recent exception, see Ronald G. Ehrenberg and George T. Milkovich, "Compensation and Firm Performance," in Morris M. Kleiner and others, eds., *Human Resources and the Performance of the Firm* (Madison, Wis.: Industrial Relations Research Association, 1987), pp. 87–122.

7. Armen A. Alchian and Harold Demsetz, "Production, Information Costs, and Economic Organization," *American Economic Review,* vol. 62 (December 1972), pp. 777–95.

oriented in implementing their policies.[8] Such pressures could be expected to make these managers consider alternative approaches. Moreover, casual evidence indicates that new entrants to the work force are increasingly interested in monetary rewards.[9] Thus human resource professionals may feel that pay systems which emphasize such rewards will produce better results than they would have produced in the past.

The New Economics of Personnel

We have already alluded to the new economics of personnel that developed in the 1970s and 1980s out of earlier roots.[10] Until this development many economists tended either to ignore the institutional peculiarities of the labor market (such as unemployment) or to simply accept them as given. Although originally a device to explain wage rigidity, the new economics of personnel has opened all human resource practices to scrutiny. Terms such as efficiency wages, implicit contracting, and agency problems have become common in labor economics. Empirical investigations have been undertaken into the duration of the employment contract and the role of seniority in pay status.[11]

To some extent the new economics of personnel can be accused of simply seeking rationalizations of what is observed in terms of standard economic theory. But it also serves to focus attention on what in fact does occur in the labor market. A potential even exists—as occurred earlier in the financial setting—for theorizing to influence practice. So far the chief suggestion in the 1980s to come from economics in the area of pay systems has been based on macroeconomic considerations. However, the growing interest in the economics of personnel may eventually contribute to microeconomic-based suggestions too. But

8. Audrey Freedman, "How the 1980's Have Changed Industrial Relations," *Monthly Labor Review*, vol. 111 (May 1988), pp. 35–38.

9. In the late 1960s and early 1970s, about 40–45 percent of college freshmen identified "being very well off financially" as very important or essential as a life goal. By the mid-1980s the figure had risen to over 70 percent. See Alexander W. Astin, Kenneth C. Green, and William S. Korn, *The American Freshman: Twenty Year Trends, 1966–1985* (Los Angeles: University of California, Graduate School of Education, Higher Education Research Institute, 1987), pp. 23–24.

10. A survey may be found in a symposium on the New Economics of Personnel in the *Journal of Labor Economics*, vol. 5 (October 1987), pt. 2.

11. Katharine G. Abraham and Henry S. Farber, "Job Duration, Seniority, and Earnings," *American Economic Review*, vol. 77 (June 1987), pp. 278–97; and Robert E. Hall, "The Importance of Lifetime Jobs in the U.S. Economy," *American Economic Review*, vol. 72 (September 1982), pp. 716–24.

before that can happen, a better understanding of the empirical reality is needed.

Macroeconomic and Microeconomic
Views of Pay Systems

Before the Keynesian revolution in economic thought during the 1930s and 1940s, economists did not make a clear macro-micro distinction for labor market phenomena or economic performance generally. They largely "explained" unemployment in terms of micro-level wage rigidity; they assumed, therefore, that the solution to the problem in the labor market lay in the labor market's wage-setting arrangements. Keynesian analysis suggested that the labor market's problem could not be solved in the labor market but was more appropriately addressed through fiscal and monetary policies.[12] With the notable exception of the Phillips curve literature, this approach took the attention of economists away from the macro implications of wage systems.

In the mid-1980s, however, the pendulum swung back. Martin Weitzman argued that the problem of the labor market *could* be solved in the labor market through reform of micro-level wage-setting institutions.[13] His solution was not flexibility of the base wage rate, but rather the promotion of widespread use of profit sharing and similar share arrangements. In effect, a shift toward a flexible bonus element of pay would perform the role that flexible wages play in simple models. A change to a share economy, he argued, would have two beneficial macro effects: employment expansion (lower unemployment) and employment stabilization (fewer layoffs in recessions).

Since macro benefits of particular pay systems are inherently external to the firm, not enough such systems will be adopted. But before adding an overlay of external incentives (such as the tax breaks proposed by Weitzman), it is important to explore what private incentives firms have to install arrangements such as profit sharing. In addition, as will be discussed, micro and macro interests may overlap if share pay systems are viewed as ersatz substitutes for flexible wages.

There are, however, potential tensions between the micro and macro views of alternative pay plans. From the micro viewpoint such plans

12. Daniel J. B. Mitchell, "Wages and Keynes: Lessons from the Past," *Eastern Economic Journal*, vol. 12 (July–September 1986), pp. 199–208.

13. Martin L. Weitzman, *The Share Economy: Conquering Stagflation* (Harvard University Press, 1984).

may be seen as desirable if they induce higher productivity, that is, *fewer* workers per unit of output. But from the macro viewpoint the goal may be an *expansion* of employment. This expansion might entail lower measured productivity, since in the Weitzman model firms travel down their marginal product of labor curves as they add employees. Unless the micro influences are sorted out, predictions about the macro responses are perilous.

Weitzman does not predict that all alternative pay systems will have beneficial macro effects. Basically his kinds of plans entail the sharing of profits, value added, or revenues. Simple piece rates and related incentive plans do not meet his objectives. We take up such plans in later sections, however, because at the micro level they are often seen as partial substitutes for share plans. With one notable exception in the later data analysis, we do not include employee stock ownership plans (ESOPs) in our review, since they are dealt with elsewhere in this volume.[14] But it is important to note that much of the empirical work done on alternative pay plans has focused on ESOPs. This bias stems from the considerable tax subsidy provided to ESOPs and the resulting public policy concerns.[15]

Alternative Pay Systems

In reality, many pay systems in use base part of employee compensation on something other than time spent on the job. Even firms that have only time-based pay would usually deny that the eventual rewards to their employees are simply a function of time. They might well argue that subjective merit evaluations and advancements, opportunities for promotion, and so on, make pay ultimately contingent on performance. Our definition of alternative pay systems, however, is confined to programs that have an announced *formula* linking compensation to individual, group, or firm performance. Within that broad criterion three

14. ESOPs in their standard American form do not possess the macroeconomic properties sought by Weitzman, although they may—of course—have desirable microeconomic properties. Meade has proposed an alternative ESOP arrangement under which workers have shares only when employed, thus making the ESOP more like profit sharing. See J. E. Meade, *Alternative Systems of Business Organization and of Workers' Remuneration* (London: Allen and Unwin, 1986), pp. 115–19.

15. See, for example, U.S. General Accounting Office, *Employee Stock Ownership Plans: Little Evidence of Effects on Corporate Performance*, GAO/PEMD-88-1 (October 1987).

major kinds of plans can be distinguished: incentive plans, profit-sharing plans, and gain-sharing plans.

Incentive Plans

Incentive plans, as we define them, link pay to individual or (small) group output. Many kinds of incentive plans exist, but there are three basic types: piece rates, more elaborate incentives, and commissions.

Piece rates essentially make pay proportional to output, though there may be an overlay of minimum guarantees and adjustments to allow for machine breakdowns and other mishaps beyond worker control. Piece rates have a long history in manufacturing and today are often identified with small firms in low-wage industries such as apparel production. But they are found in other industries as well, such as steel, and are sometimes used by firms with sophisticated human resource policies, such as the oft-cited Lincoln Electric Company.[16]

More elaborate incentives are essentially variants of piece rates that depart from proportionality. Typically what is involved is a reward, or an extra reward, above a specified production standard. Names associated with such plans are the Taylor differential piece rate, Gantt task and bonus plans, Halsey and Rowan premium plans, and Bedaux (or Bedeaux) point systems, among others. The idea for a kink in the piece rate goes back to the era of "scientific management" at the turn of the century, and the plans listed here date from that period.[17] Recent surveys of their usage are not available, but as late as the 1950s these turn-of-the-century plans were still reported to be used by employers.[18] However, their usage can be assumed to be declining.

Commissions, unlike other incentive plans, are normally based on a value measure rather than physical output. They are generally used as compensation systems for sales personnel. As with other incentives, commission systems may entail a simple, flat percentage of sales or more elaborate arrangements involving kinks in the reward curve.

16. James F. Lincoln, *Lincoln's Incentive System* (McGraw-Hill, 1946). Additional reference to the Lincoln Electric case will be made later in the text.

17. Modern personnel texts often omit descriptions of these various plans. But they were still described in detail in texts through the 1950s. For information on the various plan formulas, see, for example, William W. Waite, *Personnel Administration* (Ronald Press, 1952), pp. 293–310.

18. Walter Dill Scott, Robert C. Clothier, and William R. Spriegel, *Personnel Management: Principles, Practices, and Point of View*, 6th ed. (McGraw-Hill, 1961), pp. 572–73.

Profit Sharing

As with incentive plans, profit sharing comes in many variants. Some profit-sharing plans provide cash bonuses; others, the more common, take advantage of tax incentives and defer employee receipt of the bonus by placing it into a retirement fund. In principle, firms might pay bonuses on a discretionary basis but link them to profitability as an informal practice. It has been argued, for example, that the cash bonuses paid in Japan constitute a de facto profit-sharing system.[19] But in the United States it is less likely that practices not called profit sharing really are profit sharing than that which is called profit sharing is not.

American firms are prone to call their retirement plans "profit sharing" to take advantage of looser regulatory standards while not necessarily gearing the bonus to profits. In 1986, for example, one survey of a sample of U.S. profit-sharing plans reported that 45.7 percent of the sample based the bonus entirely on employer discretion, and another 9.7 percent relied on a formula along with an additional discretionary contribution.[20] For that reason, our empirical analysis is limited to formula-based plans unless otherwise indicated.

Gain Sharing

Gain-sharing plans entail cash rewards for workers in a plant or other large work unit. The most widely discussed are Scanlon, Rucker, and Improshare plans. However, firms with gain sharing often establish their own customized variants of these plans, such as the much-discussed Kaiser Long-Range Sharing Plan of the 1960s.[21] Except for Improshare plans (which are based on physical output), gain-sharing programs are typically based on a value measure. In the Scanlon plan the formula contains rewards for reductions in the ratio of payroll costs to sales, adjusted for inventory (that is, the gross value of production) relative to

19. Richard B. Freeman and Martin L. Weitzman, "Bonuses and Employment in Japan," *Journal of the Japanese and International Economies,* vol. 1 (June 1987), pp. 168–94. Not all researchers accept the view that the Japanese bonus system produces Weitzman-type macroeconomic effects. See, for example, Sushil B. Wadhwani, "The Macroeconomic Implications of Profit Sharing: Some Empirical Evidence," *Economic Journal,* vol. 97 (Supplement 1987), pp. 171–83.

20. Hewitt Associates, *1987 Profit Sharing Survey (1986 Experience)* (Lincolnshire, Ill., 1987), pp. 12–13.

21. "Long Range Sharing Plan for Kaiser Steel Corp. Employees," *Monthly Labor Review,* vol. 86 (February 1963), pp. 154–60.

a base ratio. The Rucker plan is similar but uses a net value of production (value added) in computing the ratio.

Scanlon plans are usually associated with the union sector. Both Scanlon and Rucker plans (and usually the customized plans) entail mechanisms of "employee involvement." Workers are encouraged to make suggestions for cost reduction and productivity enhancement. Indeed, gain-sharing programs may be regarded as forerunners of the "quality of working life" movement with its quality circles and similar accoutrements that developed in the 1970s. Improshare plans, in contrast, do not emphasize employee involvement systems and stand on the borderline between gain-sharing and group incentive plans.

The Incidence of Alternative Pay Systems

Unfortunately, there are no comprehensive national surveys of the American work force that provide detailed information on the proportion of employees covered by the various pay systems. Two kinds of limited surveys that are available may be distinguished: private surveys and union agreements.

From time to time private researchers or groups undertake studies of employer compensation practices. Often such surveys have a response bias, since firms that view themselves as innovators in the pay area are most likely to provide information. Also, to find out what the innovators are doing, survey researchers deliberately use samples that are biased toward such firms. The American Productivity Center recently undertook a survey of this type.[22] Of the 1,598 responding firms, 32 percent reported having profit sharing, 28 percent reported having individual incentives, 14 percent had small group incentives, and 13 percent had gain sharing. In the last group most of the reported plans were of the customized variety, that is, not specifically of the Scanlon, Rucker, or Improshare models, even though these standard types are the most widely discussed in the human resource literature.

Union agreements provide another source of information on plan usage, although sometimes share plans may not be included in the basic contract. A more serious problem, however, is that by the mid-1980s only one out of seven private wage and salary workers was union-represented. Moreover, the U.S. Bureau of Labor Statistics (BLS) stopped surveying such contracts for budgetary reasons. The final BLS

22. Carla O'Dell and Jerry McAdams, *People, Performance, and Pay* (Houston: American Productivity Center, 1987), p. 8.

survey of "major" union agreements—those covering 1,000 or more workers—found that 2 percent of the contracts and about 1 percent of the workers covered by those contracts in January 1980 had profit-sharing provisions.[23] This survey was taken before the union sector's increased interest in profit sharing associated with concession bargaining.

In the 1980s the principal auto companies alone put about half a million union workers under profit sharing. Profit sharing also extended into other unionized sectors, such as primary metals and telephone communications. If the number of union workers with profit sharing is two-to-three times the number in autos, about 10–15 percent of private sector union workers would be covered by profit sharing. That is a significant increase in coverage since the 1970s. Even so, arguments that "the notion of contingent compensation is sweeping across industrial America" and will soon spill over into nonunion settings seem overblown.[24] The attitude of union leaders toward profit sharing remains skeptical.[25] Worker attitudes have not been adequately surveyed for us to draw any conclusion. We do not know, therefore, whether the concession-era profit-sharing plans will continue over the long haul.[26]

Table 1 summarizes the characteristics of union concession agreements (excluding those in the construction industry) negotiated during 1981–88, where a *concession* has been defined as a first-year freeze or cut in the basic wage. The table shows that the concession situations which resulted in profit sharing were as likely as those which did not to feature a cost-of-living adjustment (COLA) clause in the previous

23. U.S. Bureau of Labor Statistics, *Characteristics of Major Collective Bargaining Agreements, January 1, 1980,* Bulletin 2095 (Department of Labor, 1981), pp. 40–41, 49.

24. The quoted comment, by a management attorney, appears in "Union Input Is Viable Tool in Mergers, Acquisitions, Banker Says," *Daily Labor Report,* June 8, 1988, p. A-3.

25. See, for example, John L. Zalusky, "Labor's Collective Bargaining Experience with Gainsharing and Profit-Sharing," in Barbara D. Dennis, ed., *Proceedings of the Thirty-Ninth Annual Meeting* (Madison, Wis.: Industrial Relations Research Association, 1987), pp. 174–82.

26. To the extent that there has been any survey work, it has tended to investigate stock ownership rather than profit sharing. One study of workers in a concession bargaining situation suggested that they did not put high priority on preserving already existing stock ownership as compared with more traditional wage, benefit, and job security features of their contract. See James B. Dworkin and others, "Workers' Preferences in Concession Bargaining," *Industrial Relations,* vol. 27 (Winter 1988), p. 13. On the other hand, survey data have been cited suggesting that two-thirds of American workers would prefer working at a firm with substantial worker ownership. See Derek C. Jones, "Alternative Sharing Arrangements: A Review of Their Effects and Some Policy Implications for the U.S.," *Economic and Industrial Democracy,* vol. 8 (November 1987), p. 493.

Table 1. Union Concession Agreements, Nonconstruction, 1981–88[a]

Item	Contracts with profit sharing	Contracts without profit sharing
Percent of situations involving COLA	29	28
Percent of COLA situations with		
COLA freeze	29	11
COLA elimination	16	9
Percent of contracts with first-year wage decrease	36	14
Percent of contracts with two-tier wage plan	13	13
Percent of contracts with fixed bonuses	28	42
Number of contracts	133	1,666

Source: Data for this table were drawn by Mitchell from biweekly contract listings appearing in the *Daily Labor Report*, a publication of the Bureau of National Affairs.

a. Concession agreements are defined as those featuring a first-year freeze or cut in the basic wage. A COLA situation is one in which an active COLA clause was negotiated or in which an existing COLA was frozen or eliminated. Profit-sharing contracts include a few gain-sharing plans and plans whereby pay is linked to the product price. The construction industry is excluded from the table because the casual linkage between employer and employee in the industry makes implementation of contractual features such as fixed bonuses and profit sharing difficult. In addition, escalator clauses are comparatively rare in construction.

agreement. But profit-sharing concession contracts were more likely to have frozen or eliminated the COLA than others. Thus one motivation on the employer side in negotiating for profit sharing was to shift from an externally based contingency clause to an internally based system. Specifically, employers felt in the 1970s that the consumer price index had been driven by such factors as energy and agricultural price increases and a peculiar methodology involving mortgage interest rates which had little to do with "ability to pay." By gearing wages to profits, employers could better approximate ability to pay.

Concession agreements containing profit sharing were less likely than others to contain fixed bonuses (lump-sum payments). This characteristic might indicate that the two features were seen as partial substitutes. If that were so, it could be a signal that the United States was evolving to a system whereby so-called fixed bonuses in fact vary with firm profitability. But there is reason to doubt this interpretation. Use of profit sharing is positively associated with cuts in the base wage in the concession sample; use of lump sums is negatively associated with such cuts. Thus the seemingly negative relationship between lump sums and profit sharing may be spurious.[27] Lump sums may yet evolve into a form of profit sharing, but as of the late 1980s there was no clear evidence that they were doing so.

The profit-sharing contracts of table 1 seem to have entailed more

27. Daniel J. B. Mitchell, "Will Collective Bargaining Outcomes in the 1990s Look Like Those of the 1980s?" *Labor Law Journal*, vol. 40 (August 1989), pp. 490–96.

severe concessions than the others. Two forms of wage decreases took place within concession bargaining: two-tier plans and across-the-board cuts. Under the former, pay was cut only for new hires; existing workers were typically spared nominal decreases. Two-tier features were equally likely to occur in profit-sharing and non-profit-sharing concessions. However, as noted, the more drastic across-the-board basic wage cuts occurred more frequently in profit-sharing situations.

It is apparent from the table that the profit sharing negotiated in the union sector in the 1980s reflected a change in bargaining strength and union worker preferences for job security rather than an attempt to motivate employees. Employers were able to shift some risk of demand fluctuations to their unionized work forces and obtained a kind of wage flexibility. Against a background of mass layoffs in the union sector, greater wage flexibility was sometimes traded for job security assurances.

About a fourth of the contracts surveyed by BLS in 1980 had provisions for incentive wages. These contracts covered about a third of the workers in the sample, but not all workers under a contract with provisions for incentive pay were necessarily covered by the pay plan. A survey of union contracts taken in the mid-1980s by a private reporting service found a similar proportion for use of incentives.[28] Fewer than 3 percent of the BLS contracts had commission features.

As noted, there is no comprehensive survey of pay systems for all workers combined, both union and nonunion. The BLS does provide a survey of benefits provided by "medium and large" firms annually. These firms represent almost a third of wage and salary employment in the private, nonfarm sector. Twenty-two percent of the *full-time* workers covered by the survey had profit sharing in 1986. Only 1 percentage point out of the 22 percent had pure cash profit sharing; most had deferred profit sharing or profit sharing with cash and deferred options.[29]

The incidence of incentive plans is picked up in BLS area and industry

28. Bureau of National Affairs, *Basic Patterns in Union Contracts*, 11th ed. (Washington, 1986), pp. 122–23, 125.

29. Bureau of Labor Statistics, *Employee Benefits in Medium and Large Firms, 1986*, Bulletin 2281 (Department of Labor, 1987), p. 81. Some deferred profit-sharing plans may have included contributions to an ESOP. However, because ordinary ESOP plans cover relatively few workers in this survey, most deferred profit sharing can be assumed to have gone into other investment vehicles. (Most of the workers covered by stock ownership plans in the survey were under payroll-based plans—a scheme encouraged by the tax code of that period—which require payments of a small fixed proportion of payroll.)

wage surveys. These surveys, however, do not cover all areas and all workers, and the incentive information is not regularly aggregated. In 1968–70, 14 percent of "plantworkers" in metropolitan areas (20 percent in manufacturing) were paid by incentive methods, down from 20 percent in 1961–63.[30] At least in manufacturing, the declining trend appeared to continue into the late 1970s.[31] Industries with relatively large fractions of incentive workers included apparel, steel, and footwear.

This summary of the incidence of alternative pay systems leaves large information gaps. But it accurately reflects the state of available statistical knowledge. Profit sharing covers perhaps a fifth of the private work force. Incentives—as we have defined them—cover a relatively small fraction of the work force (probably less than a tenth) but are prominent in certain manufacturing industries and (as commissions) in sales work. Gain sharing has attracted substantial academic attention, but as of the late 1970s it seemingly covered very little of the work force and was confined mainly to smaller firms.[32] In the 1980s, however, the gain-sharing idea apparently began to spread to larger firms.

The Early History of Alternative Pay Systems

The payment of workers by other than a time-based wage is hardly a new idea. Even in the preindustrial era such devices as sharecropping might be cited as forerunners of alternative pay systems. In the early nineteenth century piece rates were certainly in use in manufacturing. Miners were sometimes paid according to the price of the ore they produced (a practice that has seen a revival in the 1980s). Examples of profit sharing were developed, with the "first" such plan variously claimed by the United States, Britain, and France.[33] Writing in 1832, the

30. John Howell Cox, "Time and Incentive Pay Practices in Urban Areas," *Monthly Labor Review*, vol. 94 (December 1971), pp. 53–56.

31. Norma W. Carlson, "Time Rates Tighten Their Grip on Manufacturing Industries," *Monthly Labor Review*, vol. 105 (May 1982), pp. 15–22.

32. See U.S. General Accounting Office, *Productivity Sharing Programs: Can They Contribute to Productivity Improvement?* AFMD-81-22 (March 1981).

33. See J. J. Jehring, "The Development of the Profit Sharing Idea in the U.S.," in J. J. Jehring, William J. Howell, Jr., and L. Reed Tripp, *A New Approach to Collective Bargaining?: Progress Sharing at American Motors* (Madison: University of Wisconsin, Center for Productivity Motivation and Industrial Relations Research Center, 1962), pp. 1–23, esp. p. 5; and Labour Department, Board of Trade, *Report by Mr. D. F. Schloss on Profit-Sharing* (London: Her Majesty's Stationery Office, 1894), pp. 25, 161.

pioneering author Charles Babbage proposed wider use of profit sharing:
"It would be of great importance, if, in every large establishment, the
modes of paying the different persons employed could be so arranged,
that each should derive advantage from the success of the whole, and
that the profits of the individuals should advance as the factory itself
produced profit, without the necessity of making any change in the wages
agreed upon."[34]

By the late nineteenth century, several interrelated themes involving
alternative pay systems emerged. One was *social harmony*. Labor and
capital, it was believed, were in actual or potential conflict. A solution
to "the labor problem" was to promote worker ownership of enterprises,
thus merging labor and capital into a single interest. But workers were
often seen as poor candidates to function as managers or entrepreneurs.[35]
Thus social harmonizers in both Britain and the United States (there was
considerable international cross referencing in the literature of the day)
often saw profit sharing as the best option. "There can be no doubt that
the soundest possible solution of the labour question will eventually be
found in such a modification of the terms of partnership as shall bind the
interests of the employer and workman more closely together. Under
such a system the weekly wages would be regarded merely as subsistence
money or advances. . . . The balance . . . would be paid (as) a share of
all surplus profits."[36]

Thus, in the good world to come, workers would see their interests
converge with those of the employer but would not be put in a managerial
role. Social harmonizers often put forward their argument in a moral
context rather than in terms of efficiency or profitability. They advocated
public policies ("wise and permissive laws") that would stimulate profit
sharing, but what exactly those policies would be in an era before
significant direct taxes (and therefore tax incentives) was not clear.[37]
Quaint though the language of nineteenth-century commentators may
seem, the views expressed are still current, though of late they have

34. Charles Babbage, *On the Economy of Machinery and Manufactures* (London: Charles
Knight, 1832), p. 177.
35. Nicholas Paine Gilman, *Profit Sharing between Employer and Employee: A
Study in the Evolution of the Wage System* (Houghton Mifflin, 1891), p. 7; and Francis A.
Walker, *The Wages Question: A Treatise on Wages and the Wages Class* (Henry Holt,
1876), p. 282.
36. W. Stanley Jevons, *The State in Relation to Labour*, 4th ed. (Macmillan, 1910), p.
146.
37. *The First Annual Report of the Commissioner of Labor* (1886), p. 293. Carroll D.
Wright, a noted progressive reformer of the period, was then commissioner.

been presented more forcefully on behalf of employee share ownership plans than on behalf of profit sharing.[38]

Another theme that developed was *union avoidance* or *better union-management* relations, depending on the circumstances. Profit sharing, by creating labor-management harmony, would obviate the need for unions, according to some proponents. Incentive plans would make the worker want to be productive, thus foiling restrictive union work rules and restrictions. Alternatively, other plan proponents argued that the right kind of pay system would foster union-management cooperation.

Finally, among the advocates of alternative pay systems many stressed *efficiency*. Appropriately designed pay systems would automatically overcome the tendency of workers to shirk, thus economizing on supervision. Marx explained piece rates in precisely this fashion: "Since the quality and intensity of the work are . . . controlled by the form of wage itself, superintendence of labour becomes in great part superfluous." In this regard Marx was mirroring Adam Smith, who viewed piece rates as so effective that workers under such plans were likely to overexert themselves and "ruin their health and constitution."[39] But advocates of pay systems for efficiency reasons often had in mind something more elaborate than a simple piece rate. Because they emphasized efficiency and spoke directly to the bottom line, efficiency-oriented advocates had a greater influence in the early part of the twentieth century than the social harmonizers did.

Despite the array of arguments in favor of alternative pay arrangements, skeptics always existed. Their comments ranged from a mild questioning to a complete rejection of basic assumptions. On the mild side the famed British economist Alfred Marshall wondered whether profit sharing was not simply a formalization of practices that existed anyway. Even in a firm without formal sharing, opportunities for employee advancement and job security were inevitably better during periods of profitability and prosperity. Thus workers in such firms received an indirect form of sharing. Although not rejecting all forms of incentives, more severe critics rejected the notion of pay systems based on simple models of "economic man"; according to them, appropriate human relations policies were the best motivators.[40]

38. See, for example, Louis O. Kelso and Patricia Hetter Kelso, *Democracy and Economic Power: Extending the ESOP Revolution* (Ballinger, 1986).

39. Karl Marx, *Capital: A Critique of Political Economy* (Modern Library, 1906), p. 605; and Adam Smith, *An Inquiry into the Nature and Causes of the Wealth of Nations* (Modern Library, 1937), pp. 81–82.

40. Alfred Marshall, *Principles of Economics*, 9th (varorium) ed. (Macmillan, 1961 [1920]),

The Era of Scientific Management, 1880–1929

The writings of Frederick Taylor combined several of the themes just described. Declaring that "the best management is a true science," Taylor found the workplace of his day to be dysfunctional: "A large part of the organization of employers, as well as for employes, is for war rather than for peace." With the proper restructuring of managerial practices, however, including pay practices, "it is possible to give the workman what he most wants—high wages—and the employer what he wants—a low labor cost."[41]

Taylor viewed the elimination of what he termed soldiering by workers (deliberate restriction of output) as the key to his system. The root cause of soldiering lay in the simple piece rates then in use. Employers would periodically cut the rates as productivity rose, thus eventually teaching their workers that extra effort would not be rewarded for long. If rates were set scientifically—by detailed time-and-motion studies rather than by rules of thumb—employees would come to see that the piece rates were objective. Appropriate studies should be undertaken to set the standards; under Taylor's differential piece-rate system, workers who met or exceeded the standard would receive a higher pay rate. That is, the piece-rate function was kinked at the standard.

Taylor did not view his pay system as a substitute for supervision. Indeed, he proposed creating a new overhead "planning department" within the firm to handle the standard setting professionally. The new scientific planners would supplant the existing untrained and arbitrary foremen with "functional foremen," who would be carefully trained to carry out specific tasks, including wise discipline where needed. Using these techniques, firms could transform the "mental attitude" of their workers. Manual jobs would be broken down into relatively unskilled, but efficient, movements; workers would accept the new jobs because they would then be able to meet the standard—and obtain the reward—

vol. 1, pp. 625–26; and Ordway Tead, *Human Nature and Management: The Applications of Psychology to Executive Leadership* (McGraw-Hill, 1929), p. 12.

41. Frederick W. Taylor, *The Principles of Scientific Management* (Harper and Brothers, 1911), pp. 7–10. A sample of writings concerning Taylorism can be found in Clarence Bertrand Thompson, ed., *Scientific Management: A Collection of the More Significant Articles Describing the Taylor System of Management* (Harvard University Press, 1914).

of the differential piece rate. They would therefore feel no need for unions.

Although he recognized early attempts at gain sharing and profit sharing, Taylor found such pay systems inappropriate. Gain sharing required standard setting, but standards were set by unscientific methods and produced the same perverse incentives for workers to obtain too-low standards. Moreover—and very important to Taylor, who was anxious to discourage collective and collusive actions—workers were not rewarded *as individuals* under gain sharing. Profit sharing did not reward individual effort either, though it did avoid standard setting.

Taylor's basic views agreed with the prevailing national enthusiasm for efficiency, the application of science, and the uplift of the working class.[42] Not surprisingly, the Taylorist movement acquired a retinue of disciples, imitators, and consultants, whom one critic termed fakirs.[43] Although Taylor's followers devised a variety of "scientific" pay systems, they gradually began to deemphasize the pay aspects of his ideas and eventually emphasized such features as good planning and record keeping. In a book published in 1915 (the year of Taylor's death), a contemporary observer predicted that the seemingly revolutionary doctrines of scientific management would come to be incorporated into the "general progress" toward better human resource policy.[44] That is precisely what happened.

Incentive Usage in the Era of Scientific Management

It is difficult to measure the exact effect of scientific management on American pay practices. The 1890 Census of Population provided data on the number of reported "pieceworkers" as a proportion of the work force. According to the census, 18 percent of employees were so classified.[45] Although one economic historian (Lebergott) has described the census figures as "reliable data," others have recognized that the 18

42. Samuel Haber, *Efficiency and Uplift: Scientific Management in the Progressive Era, 1890–1920* (University of Chicago Press, 1964).

43. Robert Franklin Hoxie, *Scientific Management and Labor* (Appleton, 1915), p. 117.

44. Horace Bookwalter Drury, *Scientific Management: A History and Criticism* (Columbia University Press, 1915), p. 168.

45. U.S. Census Office, *Report on Manufacturing Industries in the United States at the Eleventh Census, 1890* (1895), pt. 1, pp. 13, 20.

percent number must be a large underestimate.[46] The problem is that the census reporting form asked respondents to classify employees into various occupational categories. Workers were classified as pieceworkers only if they were on piece rates but did not fall into other categories. All we can say is that many workers were paid by the piece in the late nineteenth century and that the 18 percent figure is surely too low.

It does appear, however, that by the 1920s, a period generally viewed as the height of the influence of scientific management, the manufacturing sector's use of incentive pay peaked. A National Industrial Conference Board survey put the proportion of the manufacturing work force under incentives at over 50 percent. Ironically, despite Taylor's call for a move away from simple piece rates, most of the incentive systems in use were piece rates—not the more elaborate type of plan he favored; the more "scientific" schemes with their kinked reward curves were apparently in a distinct minority.[47] Indeed, firms apparently adopted their versions of scientific management in a search for ways of *economizing* on supervisory overhead—not expanding it as Taylor wanted.[48]

Because incentives were so widespread during this period, general notions about how they should be implemented were crystallized. One in particular is important to stress, since it will figure in our later statistical analysis. *It was argued that workers under incentives should usually earn more than what they would have earned under time rates.*[49] That is, the incentive payment should be seen by the worker as "gravy" on top of the regular wage: "Any [incentive] plan to be successful should provide that the sum of the base rate and the incentive pay will be

46. Stanley Lebergott, "The American Labor Force," in Lance E. Davis, Richard A. Easterlin, and William N. Parker, eds., *American Economic Growth: An Economist's History of the United States* (Harper and Row, 1972), p. 200; and John H. Pencavel, "Work Effort, On-the-Job Screening, and Alternative Methods of Remuneration," in Ronald G. Ehrenberg, ed., *Research in Labor Economics*, vol. 1 (Greenwich, Conn.: JAI Press, 1977), p. 229.

47. National Industrial Conference Board, *Systems of Wage Payment* (New York, 1930), pp. 5–9.

48. It has been noted that growth in firm size in the late nineteenth century made direct supervision more difficult. Hence firms sought ways of using the pay system to reduce the need for supervision by providing automatic incentives. That was not exactly what Taylor had in mind, but his early emphasis on the differential piece rate may have suggested that use of any piece-rate system was somehow scientific. See E. J. Hobsbawn, "Custom, Wages and Work Load in Nineteenth Century Industry," in Peter N. Stearns and Daniel J. Walkowitz, eds., *Workers in the Industrial Revolution: Recent Studies of Labor in the United States and Europe* (New Brunswick, N.J.: Transaction Books, 1974), p. 245.

49. Jack E. Walters, *Applied Personnel Administration* (Wiley and Sons, 1931), p. 143.

appreciably above the market rate of the locality for that kind of work."[50] This idea of providing a "gift" of extra pay for extra effort finds resonance in recent theoretical work in the new economics of personnel.[51] However, the personnel literature also recognizes a limit on the extent of the gift; folk wisdom in the field suggests that workers should not be able to increase their pay more than 25–30 percent above their base wage, since such high pay might squeeze the wage hierarchy and demoralize their supervisors.[52]

Profit Sharing in the Era of Scientific Management

As noted, Taylor was not keen on profit sharing as a compensation system. The general view by the 1920s, which is still widely heard, was that profit sharing is too far removed from the worker to provide an incentive.[53] Profits vary for reasons other than worker effort, and the return to individual effort through profit sharing is minuscule.

Profit sharing, however, continued to be a popular discussion point with social reformers, such as those allied with the National Civic Federation.[54] Particularly in the period around World War I, a wave of interest in profit sharing developed. Profit-sharing proponents argued that piece-rate systems might lead to perverse incentives, including an

50. Tead, *Human Nature and Management*, p. 261. This idea remained a constant in the personnel literature. For example, in the immediate post–World War II period, an article on incentives listed elements of good practice. The first question was, "Does your base-wage rate meet standards for the area in which your plant is located, for your industry, for specific jobs?" See "Pay Plans for Higher Production," *Modern Industry*, vol. 11 (April 15, 1946), p. 56.

51. George A. Akerlof, "Labor Contracts as Partial Gift Exchange," *Quarterly Journal of Economics*, vol. 97 (November 1982), pp. 543–69. As George Strauss notes, the gift exchange for employee loyalty need not involve a sharing arrangement; it could simply entail a higher-than-market wage. See his "Participatory and Gainsharing Systems: History and Hope," Organizational Behavior and Industrial Relations Working Paper OBIR-17 (University of California, Berkeley, School of Business, January 1987), p. 16.

52. See George W. Torrence, *The Motivation and Measurement of Performance* (Washington: Bureau of National Affairs Books, 1967), p. 36. A 25 percent rule of thumb also appears in Claude Edward Thompson, *Personnel Management for Supervisors* (Prentice-Hall, 1948), p. 132.

53. Algie M. Simons, *Personnel Relations in Industry* (Ronald Press, 1921), p. 213; and Walter Dill Scott and Robert C. Clothier, *Personnel Management: Principles, Practices, and Points of View* (Chicago: A. W. Shaw, 1923), p. 397.

54. National Civic Federation, *Profit Sharing by American Employers: Examples from England, Types in France* (New York, 1920).

emphasis on quantity over quality, or a waste of raw materials in an effort to exceed production standards. Because incentive-induced poor quality and waste would harm profits, some viewed profit sharing as a better pay system. Some also saw profit sharing as a general tool for building employee loyalty and goodwill, even if it was not a direct motivator.[55]

It was generally thought that profit sharing, like incentives, should be an *addition* to the regular wage, not a substitute for it: "Effective profit sharing must ordinarily presuppose the payment of the full going rate of wages to participants. . . . The object . . . is to induce a special degree of effort, efficiency, cooperation, or some other desirable result, not usually obtainable by the payment of a flat wage. Obviously these special results cannot be expected unless the rewards which call them forth can be counted on to exceed the regular and usual wage."[56]

This position on profit sharing is important in view of the macroeconomic arguments recently made by Weitzman. Weitzman assumes that the expected profit-sharing bonus will substitute for the base wage, thus reducing the marginal cost of hiring to the firm and expanding employment. That is, under the Weitzman proposal, base wages end up lower under profit sharing, leading firms to increase employment. But the conventional view of human resource managers, dating back to the 1920s (if not before), is that profit sharing should be something extra. That notion suggests that wages will not be reduced by adding profit sharing, a point to which we return later.

Profit sharing attracted enough attention in the period around World War I to produce a government study of its usage.[57] A number of large firms at the time had profit-sharing plans, a few dating from the late nineteenth century. However, profit sharing did not cover many workers

55. Arthur W. Burritt and others, *Profit Sharing: Its Principles and Practice* (Harper and Brothers, 1918), pp. 53–60; and Daniel Bloomfield, ed., *Financial Incentives for Employees and Executives*, vol. 2 (H. W. Wilson, 1923), pp. 58–59.

56. Burritt and others, *Profit Sharing*, p. 8. The idea of profit-sharing payments being an amount above the going wage is a continuing theme. For example, a textbook published three decades later says that profit-sharing payments should be "over and above the normal remuneration that would otherwise be paid to . . . employees in the given situation." See Walter Dill Scott, Robert C. Clothier, and William R. Spriegel, *Personnel Management: Principles, Practices, and Point of View*, 4th ed. (McGraw-Hill, 1949), p. 385.

57. Boris Emmet, *Profit Sharing in the United States*, Bulletin 208 (U.S. Department of Labor, Bureau of Labor Statistics, 1917). See also National Industrial Conference Board, *Practical Experience with Profit Sharing in Industrial Establishments*, Research Report 29 (Boston, 1920).

and was often seen primarily as a form of executive compensation. In addition, stock ownership schemes had begun to compete with profit sharing and diverted attention of employers from it.[58]

Union Attitudes in the Era
of Scientific Management

Since piece rates were a common feature in U.S. industry in the late nineteenth century, they were not opposed per se by unions. Unions seemed to have different attitudes, depending on the practices of the trade.[59] But they did oppose scientific management for two basic reasons. First, Taylor explicitly proposed it as a way to eliminate union influence. Second, it was associated with the undermining of skills and the loss of worker autonomy. Time-and-motion analysis in particular was the target of union resentment. Indeed, at one point unions were able to obtain a congressional investigation of the use of stopwatches in federal government establishments. Frictions at nonunion workplaces over the implementation of incentive plans may well have led to union-organizing drives.

A shift in attitude, at least on the part of union officials, occurred in the 1920s. Like the early-to-mid 1980s, the 1920s was a period of declining unionization, employer ascendancy, and sluggish economic conditions in manufacturing. Authors cited a need for labor cost competitiveness, then as in the 1980s: "The policy of demanding higher and still higher wages with little regard for the source whence the wages fund flows will no longer stand the test. If labor is to get greater returns, labor and management must accomplish more. The problem of incentives is now more vital than ever before in the history of industrial enterprise."[60]

As in the 1980s, union leaders seemed to accept this type of criticism and embarked on cooperative experiments with those employers who were willing. The American Federation of Labor (AFL) went through a

58. Sanford M. Jacoby, *Employing Bureaucracy: Managers, Unions, and the Transformation of Work in American Industry, 1900–1945* (Columbia University Press, 1985), pp. 198–99.

59. David A. McCabe, *The Standard Rate in American Trade Unions* (Johns Hopkins Press, 1912).

60. Daniel Bloomfield, ed., *Financial Incentives for Employees and Executives*, vol. 1 (H. W. Wilson, 1923), p. 5.

period of Taylorism and involved itself in time-and-motion studies and related incentive pay systems.[61] However, profit sharing—as opposed to incentives—was never popular with unions, just as it was not with the Taylorites. And, in any case, the era of experimentation in the union sector was ended by the Great Depression.

Alternative Pay Systems, 1930–79

In the period beginning in the 1930s and ending in the 1970s, the various alternative pay systems showed different trends. The use of incentive plans receded during the Great Depression, had a revival during World War II, and then resumed its secular decline. Profit sharing receded during the Depression but then experienced mild waves of increased interest. Participative gain sharing, as represented by the Scanlon plan and its derivatives, was born in the 1930s but never became widespread. Influences on these trends included the Depression itself, the growth of unionization in the 1930s and 1940s, public policy, the human relations movement, changes in technology and the work force, and the increased status and professionalization of the human resource function.

Incentive Plans, 1930–79

One element in the decline of incentive plan usage was the influence of academic research and thinking. Earlier it had been thought that worker restriction of output under piece rates was largely a union phenomenon.[62] The combination of union decline in the 1920s and the use of scientific time-and-motion studies to arrive at work standards surely should have eliminated the problem. Yet pathbreaking research published by Stanley Mathewson in the early 1930s revealed extensive restriction of output among *nonunion* workers:

American industrial managers have in recent years become fully convinced that the output of their employees bears a direct relation

61. Taylor Society, *Scientific Management in American Industry* (Harper and Brothers, 1929), pp. 18–21.
62. Carroll D. Wright, *Regulation and Restriction of Output*, eleventh special report of the U.S. Commissioner of Labor (1904).

to the wages paid and to the methods of payment. As a consequence, "incentive" wage plans in the form of premiums, bonuses, commissions and various kinds of piece rates have spread rapidly throughout our industries. Measured production and payment by results are now generally accepted in management circles as necessary conditions for stimulating wage-earners to put forth their best efforts. In the administration of the various incentive-wage plans, as well as in the principles on which the incentive plans are based, however, wage-earners often find their justification for restriction of output.[63]

Fear of unemployment was cited as a significant motivation for output restriction in the report, a problem that could only intensify during the Depression.

A second wave of research questioned the basic model underlying the use of economic incentives. Critics of scientific management had long argued that the technique ignored the human factor in the workplace. Interest in the use of psychology and mental testing of workers developed in the 1920s.[64] Through these methods, it was argued, workers could be matched with appropriate jobs. Or jobs might be redesigned to interest workers. Some maintained, in terms reflecting a creeping Freudian influence, that workers had a "creative impulse" whose "suppression" was as dangerous as suppression of the sex drive.[65]

Use of psychology in the workplace was not initially taken to mean that incentive pay should cease to be offered; writers of the 1920s, however, viewed psychology as at least a needed adjunct to the pay system.[66] An important variable was the nature of workplace relationships. As one text put it: "The word 'incentive'. . . does not enjoy its full significance if it is restricted to its financial interpretation. Many incentives are of a non-financial nature. Of these, most find their opportunity for expression in the relationship which exists between the worker and his boss."[67]

63. Stanley B. Mathewson, *Restriction of Output among Unorganized Workers* (Southern Illinois University Press, 1969 [1931]), pp. 53–54.

64. Walter Dill Scott and M. H. S. Hayes, *Science and Common Sense in Working with Men* (Ronald Press, 1921).

65. Ordway Tead and Henry C. Metcalf, *Personnel Administration: Its Principles and Practice*, 3d ed. (McGraw-Hill, 1920), pp. 25–26.

66. Tead, *Human Nature and Management*, pp. 242–53.

67. Scott and Clothier, *Personnel Management*, p. 114.

During the 1930s the view of psychology as merely a complement to existing incentive techniques began to change. Incentive plans might appear to work in some cases, but what really mattered was the quality of human relations: "There are many wage-incentive plans that are successful largely because the employers are carrying out the basic principle of consultation with their employees. . . . The plan is working primarily because the employer has as a background the respect and loyalty of the employees."[68] The famous "Hawthorne studies," undertaken by researchers at the Harvard Business School, also seemed to show that incentive systems were unimportant in determining work outcomes. The Harvard researchers argued that personnel managers should be trained in counseling employees and diagnosing social situations in a manner similar to "the doctor-patient relationship."[69] By the late 1930s these ideas from academia found support among professional personnel administrators. As one noted approvingly: "The new theory suggests that it is the emotional factor in human beings which makes for the greatest variation in success and failure."[70] Tools from behavioral science, such as worker attitude surveys, became increasingly in vogue in management circles, especially after World War II.[71]

Union opinions about incentives in the 1930s varied as in previous periods. In the new mass-production industries that were threatened with unionization, however, employers began to see incentives and their associated time-and-motion studies as irritants to the employer-worker relationship. Some companies dropped their incentive systems in an attempt to avoid unionization.[72] And the new left-leaning industrial unions associated with the Congress of Industrial Organization (CIO)

68. Comment by Carroll E. French, reported in Richard Stephen Uhrbrock, *A Psychologist Looks at Wage-Incentive Methods* (New York: American Management Association, 1935), p. 31.

69. Fritz J. Roethlisberger and William J. Dickson, *Management and the Worker: An Account of a Research Program Conducted by the Western Electric Company, Hawthorne Works, Chicago* (Harvard University Press, 1967 [1939]). The studies were undertaken during 1927–32. Although the full report appeared in 1939, earlier summaries of the research were available as early as 1934. See especially pp. 590–604 (quotation on p. 598).

70. Jean L. Shepard, *Human Nature at Work* (Harper and Brothers, 1938), p. 217. The author was a personnel executive at Lord and Taylor.

71. Sanford M. Jacoby, "Employee Attitude Surveys in Historical Perspective," *Industrial Relations,* vol. 27 (Winter 1988), pp. 74–93.

72. Daniel Nelson, "Scientific Management and the Workplace, 1920–30," in Sanford M. Jacoby, ed., *Managing the Workplace: A New Approach to Industrial History* (Columbia University Press, forthcoming).

were not keen on incentives, because they involved managerial discretion in standard setting and variation in worker incomes. Survey evidence suggests a decline in the use of piece rates by the mid-1930s.[73] Still further declines were reported by the end of the decade.[74]

World War II produced a sharp change in union attitudes. Many employers in the 1930s, despite the difficulty they might be having with unions over the issue, believed the use of incentive pay would increase. They argued that firms were being expected to support new social insurance programs and needed more productivity to foot the bill. In addition, workers of the future would be made lazy by New Deal relief programs and would need added incentives.[75] Although such views did not appeal to union officials, once Russia was attacked by Germany left-wing unions decided to cooperate with management in increasing war production, including the implementation of wage incentives.[76]

The war also provided another stimulus to the use of incentive pay rather than time wages. Employers found it easier to circumvent wage controls with incentives because of the periodic need to modify standards.[77] Wage controls authorities could not easily monitor such changes. Proponents of incentives hoped that the wartime experience would usher in a postwar trend toward growth in their use.[78] Hostile union attitudes, they thought, must surely have been altered by the wartime use of incentives: "Wartime experience and modern management methods

73. A survey by the National Industrial Conference Board in 1935 showed about the same percentage (56 percent) of time workers in manufacturing as in 1924. But the proportion of piece-rate workers fell from 37 percent to 22 percent. The big growth was in workers covered by "premium and bonus systems." Although these systems are not clearly defined, they probably often included discretionary rather than formula bonuses. Furthermore, the proportion of time workers in 1935 was higher than in 1928, when it stood at 47 percent. See National Industrial Conference Board, *Financial Incentives: A Study of Methods for Stimulating Achievement in Industry* (New York, 1935), p. 17; and NICB, *Systems of Wage Payment* (New York, 1930), p. 8.

74. A National Industrial Conference Board survey in 1939 found that 52 percent of a sample of companies reported the use of wage incentives for some of their employees, down from 75 percent in a similar survey in 1935. See *Some Problems in Wage Incentive Administration*, Studies in Personnel Policy 19 (New York, 1940), p. 10.

75. National Industrial Conference Board, *Financial Incentives*, pp. 34–39.

76. An example of the union approach to incentives during this period can be found in United Electrical, Radio & Machine Workers of America, *U.E. Guide to Wage Payment Plans: Time Study and Job Evaluation* (New York, 1943).

77. William B. Wolf, *Wage Incentives as a Managerial Tool* (Columbia University Press, 1957), p. 68.

78. J. Keith Louden, *Wage Incentives* (Wiley and Sons, 1944), pp. 9–10.

. . . have dispelled to a great extent labor's fears that wage incentives result in a speed-up.''[79]

Survey evidence suggests that employers did move to "professionalize" the time study function; standards were increasingly set by college-educated engineers, though complaints continued about foremen setting rates without adequate training.[80] Despite the hope of wartime proponents, unions resumed their mixed stance regarding incentives in the postwar era. And even when unions were willing to accept incentives, their new grievance and arbitration mechanisms created a channel for voicing complaints about changes in standards.[81] Employers who used incentives now paid a price in the form of reduced flexibility and possible second guessing by arbitrators.

Thus after World War II the use of incentives resumed its decline.[82] Apart from the union influence, behavioral scientists continued to attack money as a motivator.[83] These views were not the only ones heard, of course. "Practical" observers counterattacked by opposing the overemphasis on "the present-day fashionable chorus of praise for human relations."[84] Postwar books by industrial engineers simply assumed as self-evident the need for direct wage incentive plans.[85] "Nuts and bolts" texts by practitioners also took the use of incentives as a given: "Anyone who believes that incentive systems properly set up and administered are basically unfair to employees and serve management no good purpose

79. "Pay Plans for Higher Production," *Modern Industry*, vol. 11 (April 15, 1946), p. 52.

80. National Industrial Conference Board, *Some Problems in Wage Incentive Administration*, pp. 20–21; and Phil Carroll, *Better Wage Incentives* (McGraw-Hill, 1957), p. 6.

81. Van Dusen Kennedy, *Union Policy and Incentive Wage Methods* (Columbia University Press, 1945), p. 63. See also U.S. Bureau of Labor Statistics, *Incentive-Wage Plans and Collective Bargaining*, Bulletin 717 (Department of Labor, 1942), pp. 9–14.

82. About 30 percent of "plant workers" in manufacturing were reported to be on wage incentive plans during 1945–46. See Joseph M. Sherman, "Incentive Pay in American Industry, 1945–46," *Monthly Labor Review*, vol. 65 (November 1947), pp. 535–38.

83. See, for example, William Foote Whyte and others, *Money and Motivation: An Analysis of Incentives in Industry* (Harper and Brothers, 1955).

84. Malcolm P. McNair, "Thinking Ahead: What Price Human Relations?" *Harvard Business Review*, vol. 35 (March–April 1957), pp. 15–16, 20, 25–34, 39 (quotation from p. 15). See also Robert N. McMurry, "The Case for Benevolent Autocracy," *Harvard Business Review*, vol. 36 (January–February 1958), pp. 82–90.

85. For an example, see Benjamin W. Niebel, *Motion and Time Study*, 4th ed. (Homewood, Ill.: Richard D. Irwin, 1967), pp. 532–34. This text refers to the use of "indirect," that is, discretionary, rewards. But these are described as likely to be ineffective, and the reader is referred to personnel texts should there remain any interest in information about such arrangements.

needs to start his business education all over again."[86] Successful incentive plans merely required knowledge of rules of thumb that had developed over the years; for example, after ten years a plan goes out of date and must be replaced because its standards have become inappropriate.[87]

There was more involved, however, in the decline in incentive use than simply an intellectual debate. Changes in work force composition toward more hard-to-measure white-collar work limited the possibilities of using wage incentives. Even in blue-collar settings, some have argued, as automation turned workers into machine tenders, it became more and more difficult to create effective incentive plans.[88] For example, if the worker's task is to correct machine errors, a reward system based on such corrections would provide a perverse incentive, first to cause errors and then to correct them.[89] In short, the dysfunctions of incentives became better known.

A final factor should be mentioned in accounting for the decline in the use of automatic incentive systems. In the 1930s and 1940s the threatening effect of union growth elevated the status of personnel departments and officials in firms. Employers had to rely on these departments either to deal with unions or to establish policies of union avoidance. This trend toward status elevation was continued, even after union representation of the work force began to decline, by federal regulatory pressures in the labor market and tax-code manipulations of fringe benefits. Expertise in the human resource area was necessary to keep up with, and adjust to, regulations dealing with affirmative action, safety and health, and so forth. During periods of ascendancy of the human resource function, it is likely to assert control over line managers and industrial engineers.

The human resource literature tends to emphasize performance appraisals and discretionary merit awards and bonuses as the proper

86. Theodore A. Toedt and others, *Managing Manpower in the Industrial Environment* (Dubuque, Iowa: W. C. Brown, 1962), p. 719.

87. H. K. Von Kaas, *Making Wage Incentives Work* (New York: American Management Association, 1971), p. 6.

88. Garth L. Mangum, "Are Wage Incentives Becoming Obsolete?" *Industrial Relations*, vol. 2 (October 1962), pp. 73–96. Mangum argued that automation would eventually end wage incentives, but the trend was being slowed by the fact that "the incentive philosophy is deeply ingrained in many industries" (p. 96). Similar views can be found in Robert B. McKersie, Carroll F. Miller, Jr., and William E. Quarterman, "Some Indicators of Incentive Plan Prevalence," *Monthly Labor Review*, vol. 87 (March 1964), pp. 271–76.

89. Martin Brown and Peter Philips, "The Decline of Piece Rates in California Canneries, 1890–1960," *Industrial Relations*, vol. 25 (Winter 1986), pp. 81–91.

way to provide incentives. Texts of the mid-1940s already supported these approaches to providing motivation and differential rewards to employees.[90] Performance appraisal and merit systems are designed and monitored by human resource professionals. Simple incentive systems are often the province of the line manager and the industrial engineer, not the personnel department. As the status of that department rose, it is not surprising that the use of incentive wages declined. Personnel managers argued that wage incentives could cause supervisors to neglect adequate monitoring of subordinates on the assumption that the incentive scheme would automatically produce desired behavior.[91]

Profit Sharing, 1930–79

Although some of the same forces that reduced the use of incentive systems over the long haul also affected profit sharing, there were also counteracting influences. First, some people viewed profit sharing as a device for social betterment. Second, well before the Weitzman proposal profit sharing was seen to have certain features that could benefit macroeconomic performance and employment stabilization. Third, changes in the tax law were implemented to foster profit sharing. Fourth, profit sharing—as a general employee benefit—falls in the province of the human resource function; line managers and industrial engineers have little to do with its design and implementation.

The interest in profit sharing during the period around World War I has already been noted. That period saw an increase in unionization and concerns about industrial strife. Similar concerns were revived in the 1930s as union membership again grew rapidly and strike activity surged. Yet the limited number of profit-sharing plans that existed in the 1920s declined in response to the Depression. With little or no profits to share, and uncertainty over the future course of government policy with regard to pay, firms discontinued or suspended their plans.[92]

Senate hearings were held in the late 1930s with the idea of stimulating profit sharing to reduce labor-management frictions, and to reduce the lure of communism. The tax status of profit-sharing payments was unclear; in the World War I period the U.S. Treasury viewed such

90. Jack E. Walters, *Personnel Relations: Their Application in a Democracy* (Ronald Press, 1945), pp. 144–45.

91. Wilfred B. Brown, *Piecework Abandoned: The Effect of Wage Incentive Systems on Managerial Authority* (London: Heinemann, 1962), p. 26.

92. National Industrial Conference Board, *Profit Sharing* (New York, 1934), p. 28.

payments as gratuities and hence not deductible as business expenses.[93] Certainly, profit sharing was not tax favored.

Testimony from union officials was decidedly unsympathetic to the promotion of profit sharing. John L. Lewis, president of the CIO, complained that management did not provide any opportunity for labor to participate in the managerial decisions that influence profits. Thus workers should not bear the risks of variations in profits due to decisions over which they had no control. Moreover, workers needed stable—not variable—incomes. William Green, president of the AFL, expressed similar views; he also noted that profit sharing had sometimes been used in conjunction with employer-sponsored employee representation schemes to avoid unionization.[94]

Despite such views the Senate subcommittee pursuing the issue reported that profit sharing would increase efficiency, decrease waste and turnover, and "eliminate labor unrest and conflict," among other virtues: "[Profit sharing] makes workers a part of the profit system and by their participation transforms their sentiment from one of antagonism to that of acceptance and defense—the most powerful educational advance that could be devised."[95] To stimulate profit sharing, the subcommittee recommended that payments from deferred profit-sharing trusts to workers (at retirement) be exempt from income taxation. Moreover, the federal government should issue special bonds paying attractive interest rates as investment vehicles for such trusts and to ensure the protection of their asset values.

Although the bond idea never became part of public policy, the government implemented a tax preference (through deferral of taxation rather than total exemption from it) for deferred profit-sharing plans in the 1940s. World War II wage controls further advanced a preference for deferred (rather than cash) profit sharing. During the controls period, creation of new cash profit sharing was virtually banned. Any new plans had to be of the deferred type.[96]

93. Emmet, *Profit Sharing in the United States,* p. 6, fn. 1.

94. *Survey of Experiences in Profit Sharing and Possibilities of Incentive Taxation,* Senate Hearings, November 21 to December 14, 1938, 75 Cong. 3d sess. (Government Printing Office, 1938), pp. 104–09, 189–99.

95. *Survey of Experiences in Profit Sharing and Possibilities of Incentive Taxation,* Report of the Senate Subcommittee of the Committee on Finance, 76 Cong. 1st sess. (GPO, 1939), pp. 129–30.

96. Kenneth M. Thompson, *Profit Sharing: Democratic Capitalism in American Industry* (Harper and Brothers, 1949), pp. 226–27.

The use of profit sharing expanded somewhat in the 1940s.[97] And certainly there was more written about it. Yet profit sharing was not a major force in compensation by any means. As one study noted, "American studies of profit sharing constitute a considerable literature, disproportionate to the insignificant position the movement has attained in industry."[98] Then, as today, the tax incentives for profit sharing were similar to those given to pensions (and now other forms of work-related savings plans). Profit sharing was not really singled out for special tax treatment; deferred pay for retirement was. Thus profit sharing merely competed with pensions (and later other benefit plans) as a retirement practice. While no comprehensive surveys are available, profit sharing in the 1950s seems to have been concentrated in smaller firms.[99]

Although management sometimes used profit sharing as part of a union avoidance policy, employers in the 1950s may have seen it as a two-edged sword, particularly if they were already organized. Unions were at their peak representation of the work force at the time and were considered key players in anything having to do with compensation. Profit sharing, by seeming to legitimate a worker claim on profits, frightened some employers. A 1958 proposal by the president of the United Auto Workers (UAW), Walter Reuther, that the auto industry share profits with stockholders, workers, and customers added to business consternation. Ironically, the proposal may well have been a bargaining and public relations ploy when it was first made.[100]

Whatever its motivation in 1958, the profit-sharing idea was subsequently reflected at American Motors, which implemented "progress sharing" with the UAW in the early 1960s.[101] Bargaining in the early 1960s occurred against a background of sluggish economic performance, a management offensive in bargaining, and the beginnings of foreign competition.[102] Wage negotiations featured wage freezes, work-

97. Jacoby, *Employing Bureaucracy*, p. 266.

98. Bryce M. Stewart and Walter J. Couper, *Profit Sharing for Wage Earners and Executives* (New York: Industrial Relations Counselors, 1951), p. 11.

99. P. A. Knowlton, *Profit Sharing in Practice: Report on Visits to Profit-Sharing Establishments, 1951–52 (Revised)* (New York: Profit-Sharing Research Foundation, 1953), p. 1.

100. For the business reaction, see Chamber of Commerce of the United States, *Reuther's Profit-Sharing Demand* (May 1958).

101. Jehring and others, *New Approach to Collective Bargaining?*

102. The "current emphasis on cost reduction" was cited in the early 1960s as a factor explaining a renewal of interest in alternative pay systems. See Robert B. McKersie, "Wage Payment Methods of the Future," *British Journal of Industrial Relations*, vol. 1 (June 1963), pp. 191–212 (quotation on p. 192).

rule relaxations, and innovative cooperative schemes. The American Motors deal included elements of labor-management cooperation and work-rule revision, thus foreshadowing the concession bargaining of the 1980s.

The Great Depression also spawned—or at least highlighted—some ideas about profit sharing as a device to increase de facto wage flexibility. Conventional economic analysis of the time put great emphasis on the need for wage flexibility to resolve the Depression. Moreover, commentators feared that growing unionization of the work force would lead to increased wage rigidity.[103] But profit sharing could provide a compromise solution by separating compensation into a fixed and a variable element: "Profit sharing [plans act as] . . . a stabilizer of the wage scale by providing a flexible, supplementary payment that will fluctuate with business conditions, and yet also permit the company to control the wage cost so that it will bear a definite relation to company income."[104] By the early 1940s this idea had evolved into a proposal that employment contracts should guarantee job security in exchange for wage variations linked to the firm's gross income.[105]

The possible macroeconomic implications of profit sharing did not become a prominent issue again until the 1980s. However, the microeconomic observation that profit sharing provided the firm with more wage flexibility was often made after the Depression.[106] Indeed, the possibility that simple incentive plans might give employers greater wage flexibility—because of the discretionary element in standard setting—was also noted.[107]

103. Sumner H. Slichter, *Towards Stability: The Problem of Economic Balance* (Henry Holt, 1934), pp. 139–42.

104. National Industrial Conference Board, *Profit-Sharing and Other Supplementary-Compensation Plans Covering Wage Earners*, Studies in Personnel Policy 2 (New York, December 1937), p. 12.

105. Willford I. King, *The Causes of Economic Fluctuations: Possibilities of Anticipation and Control*, rev. ed. (Ronald Press, 1941), pp. 324–30b. King was a well-known business-cycle researcher at the National Bureau of Economic Research and elsewhere. He felt his proposal went further than the standard profit-sharing plans of the period in that he proposed sharing losses as well as gains. The actual distinction is not clear. It might be noted that in the late nineteenth century, Carroll Wright, the first U.S. commissioner of labor, linked profit sharing with employment stabilization, though he did not explain the linkage. See *First Annual Report of the Commissioner of Labor*, p. 281.

106. See, for example, Scott, Clothier, and Spriegel, *Personnel Management*, p. 389; and Kenneth M. Thompson, *Profit Sharing: Democratic Capitalism in American Industry* (Harper and Brothers, 1949), p. 7.

107. William B. Wolf, *Wage Incentives as a Managerial Tool* (Columbia University Press, 1957), pp. 68–69.

Gain Sharing, 1930–79

Gain-sharing plans were known in the nineteenth century, essentially functioning as group piece rates.[108] In the 1930s, however, the development of the Scanlon plan forged a tie between gain sharing and worker participation in decisionmaking. Joe Scanlon, an official of the Steelworkers, devised his plan to rescue a floundering company that had come to the union looking for wage relief.[109] Although, as noted earlier, gain-sharing plans of this type have never covered a large fraction of the work force, they seemed to capture the interest and support of academics.

This academic fascination had two components. First, we have already noted the negative view of simple, individual incentives that came to be held by psychologically oriented behavioral scientists. Even before the Scanlon plan, however, group bonus systems were deemed virtuous in that they were designed to "spur . . . cooperative effort rather than individual self-interest."[110] By promoting gain sharing, post–World War II academics could see themselves as combining the best of economics, behavioral science, and the practical evidence of case studies of gain-sharing usage.[111]

A second appealing feature of the Scanlon plan, in particular, was its emphasis on union-management cooperation. The 1930s and the period immediately after the war had been characterized by industrial strife and turmoil. With its built-in feature of union-management cooperation, the Scanlon plan seemed to be a solution to a major public policy goal—industrial peace. In any event, academic personnel textbooks of the early 1950s held out great promise for the Scanlon approach.[112] Despite the lack of widespread implementation of Scanlon plans—even two decades into the postwar period—the praise continued: "The Scanlon Plan is one of the most promising approaches yet suggested to securing

108. Labour Department, Board of Trade, *Report on Gain-Sharing and Certain Other Systems of Bonus on Production* (London: HMSO, 1895).

109. For a history and background, see Frederick G. Lesieur, ed., *The Scanlon Plan: A Frontier in Labor-Management Cooperation* (Cambridge: Technology Press of Massachusetts Institute of Technology, 1958).

110. Tead and Metcalf, *Personnel Administration*, p. 304.

111. Researchers at MIT, in particular, reported on case studies of use of the Scanlon plan. (Scanlon had become a staff member of the MIT Industrial Relations Section.) See, for example, George P. Shultz, "Worker Participation on Production Problems: A Discussion of Experience with the 'Scanlon Plan,' " *Personnel*, vol. 28 (November 1951), pp. 201–11.

112. Paul Pigors and Charles A. Myers, *Personnel Administration: A Point of View and a Method*, 2d ed. (McGraw-Hill, 1951), pp. 344–49.

widespread employee participation and obtaining industrial peace and higher productivity as well."[113]

The Current View of Pay
for Performance

Our historical survey of the use of alternative pay systems shows that waves of interest and disinterest in these plans occur, linked to social, political, and economic developments. Interest does not necessarily translate into implementation. It seems likely, based on the BLS figures, that the incidence of profit sharing for production workers grew substantially in the 1980s, although for other occupational categories no trend is apparent.[114] The use of gain sharing probably grew among larger firms, but there are no continual surveys on which to base an estimate.

The BLS has not issued any summary reports for trends in simple incentives in the 1980s. The Bureau of National Affairs survey of union contracts showed little change during the 1980s in the proportion of contracts making provision for incentive plan operation.[115] Thus despite the evident growth of discussion and interest in alternative pay systems by personnel practitioners in the 1980s, the only major change has apparently been the increased use of profit sharing in certain unionized industries.

The fact that a practice is being more widely discussed could mean that in the future more implementation will occur. It is therefore useful

113. George Strauss and Leonard R. Sayles, *Personnel: The Human Problems of Management,* 2d ed. (Englewood Cliffs, N.J.: Prentice-Hall, 1967), p. 681.

114. As noted earlier, 22 percent of the full-time work force in medium and large firms had profit sharing in 1986. This proportion was the same for the three occupational categories reported: professional-administrative, technical-clerical, and production workers. Unfortunately, the surveys taken earlier in the decade report coverage by profit sharing in a different way, namely, the percent of full-time workers in establishments in which all workers were covered by profit sharing. This estimate omits workers under plans with less than full coverage. In 1981 the figures for coverage by plans for all workers in the three groups were, respectively, 20 percent, 21 percent, and 13 percent. See Bureau of Labor Statistics, *Employee Benefits in Medium and Large Firms, 1981,* Bulletin 2140 (Department of Labor, August 1982), pp. 39–40. The production worker figure jumped with the 1983 survey, coinciding with the implementation of profit sharing in the auto industry.

115. Twenty-eight percent of the sample had incentive provisions (other than prohibitions and requirements for advance approval by unions) in the 1979 survey as against 29 percent in the 1986 survey. The proportion of contracts prohibiting incentives or requiring advance union approval increased over this period. See Bureau of National Affairs, *Basic Patterns in Union Contracts,* 9th ed. (Washington, 1979), pp. 103–04; and Bureau of National Affairs, *Basic Patterns in Union Contracts,* 11th ed. (Washington, 1986), pp. 122–23, 125.

to consider contemporary views about alternative pay systems. Three viewpoints may be identified: the academic, practitioner, and employee.

Academic Views: Economic Theory

Until recently academic work on pay systems was largely conducted by researchers with a behavioral science bent or by industrial engineers. Economists had little to say about pay systems—especially from a microeconomic viewpoint. But lately both theoretical and empirical work has been done in the economics field.

The theoretical work—part of the new economics of personnel described earlier—accepts the basic neoclassical model but tries to account for types of behavior that did not previously attract the interest of economists. Although this work is still at an evolutionary stage, it has made useful distinctions and raised new issues.

For example, it is important to separate two functions of incentive pay: sorting and motivation. Since incentive systems pay more to more productive workers, workers who are "inherently" more productive will tend to sort themselves toward incentive-using firms.[116] Less productive workers may avoid employers with such systems. Empirical investigations of pay systems may therefore seem to detect a positive motivational effect when what is being observed may be only sorting. At the same time, social forces such as interworker considerations of equity may dampen the link between pay and output. Thus small pay differences may mask larger productivity differentials.[117] Both these observations are useful to keep in mind when considering the empirical evidence presented later.

Some predictions of theory, however, do not accord with empirical observation. The big drawback of incentive rates according to the personnel literature is the restriction of output by workers. Theory suggests that employers might offset such behavior by paying higher pieces rates when workers are first hired than in subsequent periods.[118] Yet such practices are not observed, perhaps because they would require complex, multiperiod individual contracting as employees turned over.

116. Edward P. Lazear, "Salaries and Piece Rates," *Journal of Business*, vol. 59 (July 1986), pp. 405–31.
117. Robert H. Frank, "Are Workers Paid Their Marginal Products?" *American Economic Review*, vol. 74 (September 1984), pp. 549–71.
118. Lazear, "Salaries and Piece Rates," pp. 422–25.

Figure 1. Operation of an Incentive System

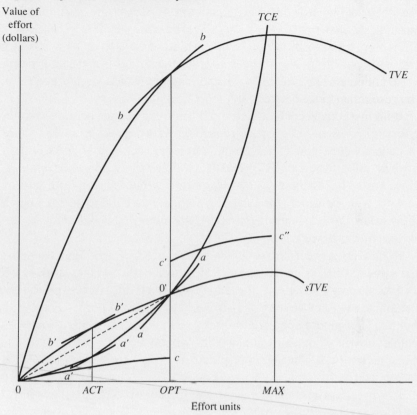

Use of simple theory can illuminate observed behavior. For instance, the "improved" piece-rate systems developed in the era of scientific management had in common the use of kinks in the reward function. Workers who exceeded some output standard received a higher piece rate or bonus. Why should these plan designers all have hit on this approach?

Absent any cost of monitoring, firms would hire effort units, rather than time units, from workers, setting wages so that the marginal value of effort (*MVE*) to the firm was just equal to its marginal physical and psychological cost to the individual worker (*MCE*). On figure 1 the total value of effort (*TVE*) is depicted as a rising curve with diminishing returns that hits a maximum at the point of worker exhaustion (*MAX*) and then turns down. The total cost of effort is depicted as a rising curve that becomes steeper as exhaustion approaches. The optimum level of effort is depicted on figure 1 at effort level = OPT, which occurs where the slopes of the two curves are equal, that is, where lines aa and bb are parallel. At that point $MVE = MCE$. The firm would set a wage per effort unit equal to the slope of $00'$, which depicts total labor costs at alternative effort levels. The earnings of the worker is measured by the vertical distance above OPT to the $00'$ line; the firm's surplus at OPT is the vertical distance between $00'$ and TVE.

With monitoring costs, however, the bargain cannot be transacted in effort units; instead, the worker under simple incentives receives a share of output value (s) in specific or ad valorem terms. He or she will then provide effort where $MCE = sMVE$, which will be *less than optimal,* since s must be less than 1 (unless the firm is prepared to give all returns to workers). Consider, for example, a share system that seems to give the worker the same earnings at OPT that he or she would have under the optimum contract.

If the worker's earning schedule was set at $sTVE$, earnings would be the same at OPT as under the perfect contract. But, in fact, with $sTVE$ as the earnings schedule, the actual point of effort—the point that maximizes worker welfare—is $ACT < OPT$, where $a'a'$ is parallel to $b'b'$. At the same time, once the simple incentive bargain is struck, the employer will want effort consistent with $MVE = 0$, that is, at MAX, since given the scheme's share parameter, the firm's share $(1 - s)$ is maximized at this point.

Put directly, the employer wants the worker to work to exhaustion— an effort level *above that of the optimal contract.* The worker will prefer an effort level *below optimum.* A simple piece rate, therefore, may separate employee and employer interests rather than join them *unless* kinks are included in the schedule around the optimal point where $MCE = MVE$.[119] An earnings schedule $0cc'c''$, for example, will induce the

119. The model suggested here was applied in a different context in Murray L. Schwartz and Daniel J. B. Mitchell, "An Economic Analysis of the Contingent Fee in Personal-Injury Litigation," *Stanford Law Review*, vol. 22 (June 1970), pp. 1125–62; and Daniel J. B. Mitchell and Murray L. Schwartz, "Theoretical Implications of Contingent Legal Fees," *Quarterly Review of Economics and Business*, vol. 12 (Spring 1972), pp. 69–76. It was extended in Kevin M. Clermont and John D. Currivan, "Improving on the Contingent Fee," *Cornell Law Review*, vol. 63 (April 1978), pp. 529–639. Incentive schemes with discontinuities sometimes have desirable properties in other contexts. See Alan S. Blinder and Harvey S. Rosen, "Notches," *American Economic Review*, vol. 75 (September 1985), pp. 736–47. However, the incentive case in the text starts with the assumption of monitoring costs that

worker to supply *OPT* effort units, the optimum result. Such a schedule features a low base wage with a jump (cc') in earnings at the optimum point. Thus one can say that scientific management writers were trying to place kinks at the optimum contract level of effort. But the fact that simple piece rates (without kinks) remained a common form of incentive suggests that identifying the proper kink point remained more elusive than these writers supposed.

Certain ideas in the recent economic literature might be applied to profit-sharing and gain-sharing plans, that is, plans which cover firms or plants rather than individuals or small groups. The issue here is the fostering of teamwork. Theories of altruism in the context of the family developed in the 1970s emphasize that a properly structured family relationship can motivate all family members to act in the collective interest. Specifically, if the family head acts altruistically, sharing family gains in an appropriate manner, other family members—even "rotten kids" who are only self-interested—will nevertheless behave altruistically too.[120] The analogy with the employer who shares gains is evident.

Theory, while suggesting new ways of looking at alternative pay systems, does not necessarily preclude the efficacy of conventional pay-reward mechanisms. For example, within a conventional setting individual employees, especially managers, may be rewarded through promotions and advancements and be encouraged to compete against one another for tournamentlike "prizes" at the workplace. There is no way of saying, based on theory alone, that such a reward system will turn out to be better or worse in practice than some other form of incentive.[121]

Academic Views: Empirical Economics

In recent empirical economic literature there are two strands to alternative pay systems. The first deals with incentives, using informa-

give rise to shirking and contract enforcement problems. In the Blinder-Rosen model the incentive schemes considered (such as tax subsidies to charitable giving) work in the right direction (all encourage more giving), but notch schemes may be more efficient than continuous subsidies. By contrast, the continuous incentive scheme in the text can work in the wrong direction (reduced work effort).

120. Gary S. Becker, *The Economic Approach to Human Behavior* (University of Chicago Press, 1976), pp. 253–81, esp. p. 270.

121. For some empirical evidence, based on sports experience, that tournament-type rewards can be effective in practice, see Ronald G. Ehrenberg and Michael L. Bognanno, "Do Tournaments Have Incentive Effects?" Working Paper 2638 (National Bureau of Economic Research, June 1988).

tion drawn from BLS industry wage surveys. The second concerns use of profit sharing and, to a very limited extent, gain sharing.

INCENTIVE RESEARCH. Users of industry wage surveys in the past noted that incentive workers seemed consistently to earn more per hour than time workers.[122] Of course, productivity and wages are not necessarily the same thing, but the implication seemed to be that incentive workers were more productive. Competitive firms, at least, would have difficulty consistently paying higher wages unless they received something back (in the form of higher productivity or lower monitoring costs) in return. Moreover, in accord with the sorting view, it appeared that individual establishments rarely had both time and incentive workers in a given occupation. That is, they were either under one regime or the other.[123] Indeed, some evidence suggests that when the two pay systems were used in a single establishment for the same occupation, the wage advantage of incentive workers evaporated.[124]

Two studies using 1970s data found significant wage premiums for incentive workers. Seiler obtained detailed data from the mid-1970s for the footwear and men's and boys' suits industries. Using regressions on individuals covered by the surveys (more than 120,000), and standardizing for such characteristics as unionization, he found a wage advantage for incentive workers of roughly 14 percent. He attributed only a small fraction of the overall incentive differential to a risk premium for accepting inherently more variable incentive wages.[125]

122. U.S. Bureau of Labor Statistics, *Effect of Incentive Payments on Hourly Earnings*, Bulletin 742 (Department of Labor, 1943), p. 1; and Wolf, *Wage Incentives as a Managerial Tool*, pp. 21–24.

123. Sandra L. King, "Incentive and Time Pay in Auto Dealer Repair Shops," *Monthly Labor Review*, vol. 98 (September 1975), pp. 45–48. There may be internal equity issues that keep time and incentive workers in separate establishments, apart from the influence of sorting.

124. Pencavel, "Work Effort, On-the-Job Screening, and Alternative Methods of Remuneration," pp. 225–58, esp. pp. 241–48. Pencavel's data were drawn not from BLS industry wage surveys, but from a special survey undertaken by Rees and Shultz in the Chicago area in the 1960s. See Albert Rees and George P. Shultz, *Workers and Wages in an Urban Labor Market* (University of Chicago Press, 1970).

125. Eric Seiler, "Piece Rate vs. Time Rate: The Effect of Incentives on Earnings," *Review of Economics and Statistics*, vol. 66 (August 1984), pp. 363–76. Seiler measures risk by within-firm variance of incentive versus time wages. He regresses the firm wage premium for incentive pay against the difference in the two variances and uses the coefficient of the difference in variance as a proxy for the risk premium. Since these regressions cross occupational lines, questions are raised about the results. He reports that within occupational groups the proportion of the differential attributable to risk rose, but states—without further explanation—that the more aggregated regressions are probably more accurate (pp. 374–75).

Brown also found an incentive differential for the 1970s, using a broader range of industries than Seiler and establishment-level data.[126] He broke down pay methods into standard time rates, time rates with discretionary merit pay, and incentive rates. Dummies for incentives suggested a roughly 10 percent pay premium compared with the time-with-merit systems. Yet standard time rates also had a premium of about 6 percent. It may be—although Brown does not suggest it—that the merit disadvantage reflected a lack of formalized human resource policy; that is, establishments reporting merit use are really saying they do not have standardized pay schedules.[127]

Was the wage premium observed in these studies for incentive workers still present in more recent years? That the incentive pay advantage has been observed for so long would lead one to suspect that it continued to exist into the 1980s. Table 2 provides relevant evidence.

To construct the table, we used data on *average* hourly wages for time and incentive workers drawn from eleven BLS industry wage surveys covering the period 1979–86. We selected those industries whose surveys provided data on time workers compared with incentive workers by occupation and region.[128] A total of 716 occupation-industry-region observation cells were available. A simple regression of the log of hourly wages against regional and industry dummies, the percent of incentive workers in the cell, and the use of an incentive plan suggests a roughly 14 percent wage advantage for workers under incentives. Note that since the regression's point of observation is the occupational wage, standardization for occupation is built into the results. The 14 percent wage advantage result is similar to Seiler's.

126. Charles Brown, "Firms' Choice of Method of Pay," *Industrial and Labor Relations Review* (forthcoming).

127. Brown's finding does not mean that use of a merit system cannot improve employee performance. There is some evidence that employee performance does respond to merit awards and that the response increases with the amount of money placed in the merit program. See Richard E. Kopelman and Leon Reinharth, "Research Results: The Effect of Merit-Pay Practices on White Collar Performance," *Compensation Review,* vol. 14 (Fourth Quarter 1982), pp. 30–40.

128. The industries used were structural clay products, corrugated boxes, motor vehicle parts, men's and boys' suits and coats, boys' shirts and nightwear, iron and steel (gray iron), iron and steel (malleable), iron and steel (foundries), pressed glass (containers), hosiery mills (except women's), and hosiery (women's). Only one wage survey—the latest available—was used for an industry. Hence the industry dummies captured both industry and time. No separate time dummies were included. The regions used were Northeast (New England and Middle Atlantic), Midwest (Middle West, North Central, Great Lakes), South (Border, Southwest, Southeast), and West (Mountain, Pacific).

Table 2. Regression Relating to Incentives and Hourly Wages in Eleven Industries, 1979–86[a]

Dependent varable	Log of hourly wage
Constant	1.76*
	(0.02)
Proportion of workers with incentives	−0.07*
	(0.03)
Incentive plan	0.14*
	(0.01)
Region	b
Industry	c
R^2	0.68
Adjusted R^2	0.67
Number of observations	716

Sources: Data drawn from eleven industry wage surveys for the period 1979–86. See text for details.
*Significant at the 1 percent level.
a. Unit of observation is the average wage in an occupation-industry-region cell. Workers covered are production workers. Incentive plans are piece-work plans or bonus plans geared to exceeding a production quota. Numbers in parentheses are the standard errors. See text and text notes for further details.
b. Includes three regional dummies. Excluded dummy is for Northeast.
c. Includes ten industry dummies. Excluded dummy is for structural clay products.

That the proportion of workers with incentives has a significant negative coefficient suggests that coverage by incentives is associated with worker characteristics which lower wages, even after standardization by occupation, region, and industry. Taken literally, the regression results imply that, other things equal, an occupation with 100 percent incentive coverage would have an average wage about 7 percent lower than one with zero coverage. Even so, incentive workers would have a net wage advantage, because the 7 percent disadvantage would be subtracted from the 14 percent wage premium.[129] Evaluated at the mean proportion of workers with incentives for the regression (36 percent), the net premium for incentive workers is about 11 percent.

We obtained still more detailed information from specially prepared BLS computer files for two industries in 1986—structural clay products

129. It is really not correct to extrapolate the regression coefficients of table 2 to situations with 0 or 100 percent coverage. Our methodology screened out such cases, since we deliberately included only those that had a mix of incentive and nonincentive workers so that a comparison pair could be obtained. It should be noted that the pairing technique means that the incentive plan dummy is orthogonal to all the other independent variables, and hence its coefficient is unaffected by the presence of those variables. However, the coefficient of the proportion of incentive workers is not orthogonal to the region and industry variables, and hence these variables must be included to obtain an accurate estimate of that coefficient.

and furniture—using the individual worker as the unit of observation.[130] Unfortunately, for reasons of confidentiality, workers cannot be identified by establishment; there is no way of determining if any pair of workers had the same employer. Table 3 shows a substantial gross wage advantage of incentive over time workers and, not surprisingly, somewhat greater variation in incentive wages. The table also presents regressions for the two industries of the log of hourly wages against a dummy for large establishments, the presence of union bargaining, location in a metropolitan area, occupational dummies, and a dummy for coverage by an incentive plan. In both industries, after standardization for the other variables, a roughly one-fifth wage advantage accrues to incentive workers. Thus earlier findings of a positive and significant wage advantage for incentive workers apparently continued to apply into the 1980s.

Academic researchers have not done much statistical work on value-based incentives, such as sales commissions. Survey evidence by business-related research groups suggests that commission-paid sales workers also have a history of earning more than time-based sales workers.[131] The differentials seem wide enough to withstand the kinds of standardizing regression analysis that academics have applied to other incentives. But the detailed data needed to confirm this assertion are not available.[132]

PROFIT-SHARING RESEARCH. Statistical research by academics on profit sharing in the United States has been extremely limited. Because of the Weitzman proposal, recent research has tended to focus on employment stabilization and expansion rather than motivation. For

130. We gratefully acknowledge the assistance of Martin Personick and George L. Stelluto of the BLS in obtaining the files.

131. David A. Weeks, *Compensating Field Sales Representatives*, Studies in Personnel Policy 202 (New York: National Industrial Conference Board, 1966), p. 41; and O'Dell and McAdams, *People, Performance, and Pay*, pp. 75–83. Data on hours worked are not available in these studies, so it is not possible to tell whether commissioned sales workers work longer hours than those under time-based pay.

132. In comments on an earlier version of this paper, Ronald Ehrenberg noted that size of employer may play a role in the selection of a pay system and that the O'Dell-McAdams study cited in the previous footnote covered a wage range of employer size categories. Although they do not provide a breakdown by size, O'Dell and McAdams do note (without presenting the data) that there is little difference in the commission-noncommission pay differential between the goods and the service sectors. The service sector is likely to have smaller average firm size than the goods sector, suggesting that the size effect is not prominent in their study. See O'Dell and McAdams, *People, Performance, and Pay*, p. 76.

Table 3. Regressions Relating to Incentives and Hourly Wages in Structural Clay Products and Furniture, 1986[a]

Dependent variable	Log of hourly wage	
	Structural clay products	Furniture
Constant	1.73*	1.48*
	(0.01)	(0.01)
Large establishment[b]	0.03*	0.08*
	(0.004)	(0.003)
Union	0.18*	0.09*
	(0.004)	(0.004)
Metropolitan area	0.02*	0.10*
	(0.004)	(0.003)
Incentive plan	0.21*	0.21*
	(0.005)	(0.003)
Occupation	c	d
R^2	0.37	0.35
Adjusted R^2	0.37	0.35
Number of observations	13,971	39,943
Mean incentive hourly wage (dollars)	8.81	8.06
Coefficient of variation	0.31	0.32
Mean time hourly wage (dollars)	7.22	5.91
Coefficient of variation	0.27	0.29

Source: Data from industry wage survey computer tapes supplied by U.S. Bureau of Labor Statistics.
* Significant at the 1 percent level.
a. Workers covered are production workers. Incentive plans are piece-work plans or bonus plan geared to exceeding a production quota. Numbers in parentheses are the standard errors.
b. Large size is defined as 100 or more employees in furniture, and 250 or more in structural clay products.
c. Includes thirty-four occupational dummies.
d. Includes forty-eight occupational dummies.

example, Kruse finds less cyclical employment fluctuation among profit sharers than among other firms.[133]

Much of the recent statistical research on profit sharing and related plans seems to have been undertaken with European data sets. Thus, using a sample of German metalworking firms, FitzRoy and Kraft find evidence of a productivity-boosting and a profit-boosting effect of profit sharing. A similar finding is made for French worker cooperatives by Defourney, Estrin, and Jones, and for Italian cooperatives by Jones and

133. Douglas L. Kruse, "Profit-Sharing and Employment Variability: Microeconomic Evidence," working paper, Department of Economics, Harvard University, November 1987.

Svejnar.[134] Because of the mix of worker ownership and profit sharing in some of the studies, American readers may be reluctant to apply the findings to simple profit-sharing plans under U.S. institutional arrangements.

Part of the explanation for the limited empirical work on profit sharing is undoubtedly that accessible data sets are not available. The BLS conducted biennial surveys of employer expenditures for employee compensation (EEEC) until the late 1970s but did not explicitly break out profit sharing in these surveys. We will make limited use of this survey later.[135] An annual survey by the Chamber of Commerce of the United States does pick up profit sharing in its questionnaire, though the data have ceased to be separately published. Unfortunately, the chamber refuses to make its data available to outside researchers.[136]

Lack of data has led some researchers to use tax records available from the Internal Revenue Service as a source of information. For example, Kruse used IRS data covering 1971–85 linked to COMPUSTAT estimates of productivity (sales per employee); he found that profit sharing was associated with productivity increases of 2.5 percent to 4.2 percent. In an earlier study using 1981 IRS data, Cheadle concluded that deferred profit sharing was being used by employers as a pension substitute.[137] Using IRS data is a problem because they cover only *deferred* profit sharing (which qualifies for favored tax treatment) and include plans with discretionary as well as formula-based distributions.

134. Felix R. FitzRoy and Kornelius Kraft, "Cooperation, Productivity, and Profit Sharing," *Quarterly Journal of Economics*, vol. 102 (February 1987), pp. 23–35; Felix R. FitzRoy and Kornelius Kraft, "Profitability and Profit-Sharing," *Journal of Industrial Economics*, vol. 35 (December 1986), pp. 113–30; Jacques Defourney, Saul Estrin, and Derek C. Jones, "The Effects of Workers' Participation on Enterprise Performance: Empirical Evidence from French Cooperatives," *International Journal of Industrial Organisation*, vol. 3 (June 1985), pp. 197–217; and Derek C. Jones and Jan Svejnar, "Participation, Profit Sharing, Worker Ownership and Efficiency in Italian Producer Cooperatives," *Economica*, vol. 52 (November 1985), pp. 449–65.

135. Recently a similar survey by BLS has been developed, but it too fails to separate profit sharing from other types of payments. The new survey is drawn from the establishments used to compute the BLS employment cost index. We urge the BLS to consider adding more detailed questions on alternative pay systems to this survey.

136. We urge the chamber to change its policy. Data access need not involve a loss of confidentiality for survey respondents, and outside access would add credibility to the chamber's data.

137. Douglas L. Kruse, "Profit-Sharing and Productivity: Microeconomic Evidence," working paper, Rutgers University, Institute of Management and Labor Relations, August 1988; and Allen Cheadle, "Incentives, Flexibility or ?: Explaining Patterns of Profit Sharing Activity," working paper, University of Washington, Department of Health Services, July 1988.

Under the current regulatory system for pensions and profit sharing, an incentive exists to substitute profit sharing for pensions. Profit sharing gives the firm more flexibility in the size of its annual contribution than a defined contribution pension plan does, and the rules regarding fund investments are looser. However, this usage may be a comparatively recent phenomenon in the history of deferred profit sharing and ought not apply to cash profit sharing in any case.

In the early 1950s the National Industrial Conference Board collected data from employers on fringe benefit packages that also included information on profit sharing. It is possible to construct an index of fringe benefit "richness" from these data. Specifically, the survey indicated the presence of a pension, life insurance, or hospital insurance plan and whether the plan was entirely employee paid, paid by both the employer and employee, or entirely employer paid. Thus each benefit can be coded from 0 (for no plan) to 3, respectively. The indexes for the three benefits can be summed, producing values from 0 (no benefits) to 9 (rich benefits).[138]

There is substantial precedent in the industrial relations literature for the use of indexes of the type just described when groups of human resource practices are involved. Perhaps the most prominent example is in a paper by Kochan and Block, which scored contractual features in union agreements.[139] But some have criticized the index approach, chiefly questioning the robustness of the indexes to alternative defini-

138. The data appear in National Industrial Conference Board, *Fringe Benefit Packages*, Studies in Personnel Policy 143 (New York, 1954). Obviously, the coding scheme, and the equal weighting of the three plans, is somewhat arbitrary. See footnote 142 for additional experiments with the data format. Information on plan details or employer expenditures on them are not available.

139. Thomas A. Kochan and Richard N. Block, "An Interindustry Analysis of Bargaining Outcomes: Preliminary Evidence from Two-Digit Industries," *Quarterly Journal of Economics*, vol. 91 (August 1977), pp. 431–52. Other examples include John C. Anderson, "Determinants of Bargaining Outcomes in the Federal Government of Canada," *Industrial and Labor Relations Review*, vol. 32 (January 1979), pp. 224–41; Paul F. Gerhart, "Determinants of Bargaining Outcomes in Local Government Labor Negotiations," *Industrial and Labor Relations Review*, vol. 29 (April 1976), pp. 331–51; Thomas A. Kochan and Hoyt N. Wheeler, "Municipal Collective Bargaining: A Model and Analysis of Bargaining Outcomes," *Industrial and Labor Relations Review*, vol. 29 (October 1975), pp. 46–66; John C. Anderson, "Bargaining Outcomes: An IR System Approach," *Industrial Relations*, vol. 18 (Spring 1979), pp. 127–43; Peter Feuille, Wallace E. Hendricks, and Lawrence M. Kahn, "Wage and Nonwage Outcomes in Collective Bargaining: Determinants and Tradeoffs," *Journal of Labor Research*, vol. 2 (Spring 1981), pp. 39–53; and Jack Fiorito and Wallace E. Hendricks, "Union Characteristics and Bargaining Outcomes," *Industrial and Labor Relations Review*, vol. 40 (July 1987), pp. 569–84.

Table 4. Regressions Related to Use of Fringe Benefits and Profit Sharing[a]

Dependent variable	Fringe index	Fringe index	Fringe index	Pension index	Pension index	Pension index
Constant	5.87* (0.67)	5.86* (0.67)	5.87* (0.67)	1.39* (0.44)	1.39* (0.44)	1.40* (0.44)
Size of firm	0.29* (0.08)	0.30* (0.08)	0.29* (0.08)	0.30* (0.05)	0.30* (0.05)	0.30* (0.05)
Profit sharing						
All	−0.02 (0.32)	...	...	0.16 (0.21)	...	...
Deferred	...	0.13 (0.40)	...	...	0.14 (0.26)	...
Cash	...	...	−0.06 (0.53)	...	...	0.27 (0.35)
Industry	b	b	b	b	b	b
R^2	0.22	0.22	0.22	0.23	0.23	0.23
Adjusted R^2	0.15	0.15	0.15	0.16	0.16	0.16
Number of observations	419	419	419	419	419	419

Source: National Industrial Conference Board, *Fringe Benefit Packages*, Studies in Personnel Policy 143 (New York, 1954).
*Significant at the 1 percent level.
a. See text for variable definitions. Numbers in parentheses are the standard errors.
b. Includes thirty-four industry dummies.

tions.[140] Among the issues raised is the degree to which aggregation may influence the results. To handle the aggregation issue, we will also present disaggregated results dealing only with the pension component of the fringe index.

Table 4 shows the result of regressions of the fringe index (0–9) and of the pension index (0–3) against a size-of-firm index,[141] industry dummies, and a profit-sharing dummy. We ran separate regressions for the presence of any profit sharing, deferred profit sharing only, or cash profit sharing.[142] As can be seen, in no cases were the profit-sharing

140. Richard P. Chaykowski, "The Empirical Formulation of Nonwage Collective Bargaining Outcomes," *Queen's Papers in Industrial Relations, 1988-8* (Kingston: Queen's University, School of Industrial Relations, July 1988).

141. The index was coded 1 for firms of fewer than 250 employees, 2 for those with 250 to 499, 3 for 500 to 999, 4 for 1,000 to 4,999, 5 for 5,000 to 9,999, and 6 for 10,000 employees and over.

142. Some readers may question the use of ordinary least squares regressions, given the nature of the dependent variables. We experimented with multinomial logit equations and— bifurcating the fringe and pension indexes—with probit. The computer had difficulty converging using logit, but the resulting equations did not show a significant profit-sharing effect. The probit equations also did not show a significant profit-sharing effect.

variables significant. The presence of profit sharing did not reduce the richness of other fringes, as would be true if a substitution effect were occurring. It appears, therefore, that in the early postwar period profit sharing was installed for such reasons as employee motivation or cost flexibility and not as a pension substitute. In that period, it might be noted, the regulatory tilt toward profit sharing and against pensions did not exist.

Table 4 does not reflect the entire compensation package—just the fringe component—so one cannot say for certain that profit sharing did not substitute for cash wages. As described earlier, the Weitzman proposal for profit sharing depends on substitution of the expected profit-sharing bonus for the base wage to obtain the employment-expansion effect. The historical evidence indicates, however, that the folk wisdom surrounding profit sharing is that it is supposed to be installed as something extra (gravy) for employees, that is, not subtracted from other forms of pay. Table 4 suggests that as far as the fringe component was concerned, no evidence of substitution was present. Unless a wage reduction occurred, the profit-sharing payment was gravy.

The EEEC survey by BLS, referred to earlier, included deferred profit sharing with pensions and grouped cash profit sharing with a variety of miscellaneous "nonproduction" bonuses. Pension contributions dwarf those for deferred profit sharing, but cash profit sharing may be a significant component of the bonuses. On that supposition, table 5 presents regressions of total compensation and straight-time wages against the hourly value of nonproduction bonuses (in dollars) and other available variables from a tape containing results of the 1974 survey.[143]

If a substitution effect was occurring for cash bonuses, the bonus coefficient in the compensation regressions should be zero, since bonuses would simply be offsetting some other compensation component. And if the substitution was for wages—as might be expected with a cash bonus—the coefficient in the wage equation should be -1.[144] But if the

143. The other variables were a dummy for the presence of union bargaining, a dummy for location in a metropolitan area, dummies for sixty-seven two-digit industries, four regional dummies (Northeast, North Central, South, and West), and seven dummies for size of firm (fewer than 50 employees, 50–99, 100–249, 250–499, 500–999, 1,000–2,499, and 2,500 or more employees). We did not put compensation variables into these equations to avoid compromising the reduced-form nature of the regressions; other compensation variables might themselves reflect the presence of bonuses, blurring the causal arrows. Data used for the regressions were the basis of tables appearing in Bureau of Labor Statistics, *Employee Compensation in the Private, Nonfarm Economy, 1974*, Bulletin 1963 (Department of Labor, 1977).

144. Since we are using the actual value of the bonus, rather than its expected value, the

Table 5. Regressions Related to Compensation Levels and Bonus Payments, 1974[a]

Dependent variable	Nonoffice workers		Office workers	
	Total compensation per hour	Hourly straight-time wage	Total compensation per hour	Hourly straight-time wage
Constant	5.36*	4.38*	8.29*	7.09*
	(0.47)	(0.38)	(0.77)	(0.68)
Union	1.31*	0.95*	0.44**	0.27
	(0.06)	(0.05)	(0.20)	(0.17)
Metropolitan area	0.35*	0.29*	0.62*	0.58*
	(0.05)	(0.04)	(0.09)	(0.08)
Industry	b	b	b	b
Region	c	c	c	c
Size of firm	d	d	d	d
Bonus payment	1.24*	0.83*	0.39*	0.27*
	(0.24)	(0.19)	(0.05)	(0.04)
R^2	0.60	0.55	0.28	0.26
Adjusted R^2	0.59	0.54	0.27	0.25
Number of observations	3,428	3.428	3,428	3,428

Source: Computer tape from U.S. Bureau of Labor Statistics.
*Significant at the 1 percent level.
**Significant at the 5 percent level.
a. See text for details on variable definitions. Numbers in parentheses are the standard errors.
b. Includes 67 industry dummies.
c. Includes 3 regional dummies.
d. Includes 8 dummies for size of firm classification.

bonus is simply an add-on (gravy), the coefficient in the compensation equations should be + 1 and 0 in the wage equations.[145]

In fact, the bonus coefficient is greater than one in the compensation equations for nonoffice workers and greater than zero in the wage equations for nonoffice and office workers. It is likely that the bonus variable is in part acting as a proxy for some other unspecified pay-raising influence. However, the regressions lend no support to the notion that *cash* profit sharing is offset elsewhere in the pay package. They tend to support the gravy view of cash profit sharing.

---

coefficient should be biased toward zero, that is, somewhat less in absolute value than 1, because of the errors-in-variable effect.

145. It can be (correctly) argued that the use of the bonus variable in the regressions is inappropriate, since the decision to pay a bonus is as endogenous as the decision on the level of compensation or wages. A full model should explain the bonus decision within a simultaneous equation framework. It is possible, for example, that the same forces which raise pay increase the bonus, thus creating a positive correlation between the two that masks a substitution effect. (Similar criticism can be made of the earlier regressions we have presented.) We simply acknowledge this potential weakness in the evidence and note that the available data sets do not provide adequate information for more elaborate models.

Academic Research on Management
Views about Pay Systems

Data sets on the use of particular pay systems are often not linked to any direct performance or outcome measures. Thus the user is forced to infer outcomes from pay differentials. A possible solution is to ask those who are directly affected by alternative pay systems for their attitudes about these plans.

The groups directly affected are employees, union officials, and managers. As noted, information on employee attitudes is usually very limited. In the abstract, workers may believe in "pay for performance." But one recent survey suggests that they are not keen on pay-for-performance systems applied to themselves. On the other hand, if incentives are to be used, employees were reported to prefer individual incentives to profit sharing.[146] There are no comprehensive surveys of the attitudes of union officials. In our review of union attitudes earlier in the paper, we relied on published statements and contract outcomes. That approach is typical of those who have written in this area.

Surveys of managers' views are more common, in part because mailing lists of managers are available from various sources. Thus Voos surveyed managers of unionized firms in Wisconsin about various human resource practices, including profit sharing and gain sharing. The managers who had plans in effect generally believed their plans had improved productivity, quality, and profitability and lowered unit labor costs. There is no way of ascertaining from such survey data whether these managerial impressions are ex post rationalizations of the firm's policy. The managers from firms that discontinued plans were, not surprisingly, less positive in their evaluations, but, again, this raises the issue of a rationalization.[147]

Differences may exist, however, in the perceptions of managers in unionized and nonunionized firms regarding such plans. Managers in unionized firms were found in one study to be somewhat more likely to cite indirect benefits, such as the provision of a retirement plan or an educational effect about the need for profits, than to cite direct benefits

146. "Developments in Pay Systems Are Examined at BNA Conference," *Daily Labor Report*, June 20, 1988, p. C-3.
147. Paula B. Voos, "Managerial Perceptions of the Economic Impact of Labor Relations Programs," *Industrial and Labor Relations Review*, vol. 40 (January 1987), pp. 195–208.

Table 6. Managerial Attitudes toward Alternative Pay Systems[a]

Item	Profit sharing	Gain sharing	Simple incentive
Percent of managers responding that plan best for			
Raising productivity	28(30)	26(59)*	42(55)*
Increasing loyalty	48(49)	18(41)*	15(20)*
Linking labor costs to firm's economic condition	53(56)*	28(57)*	19(23)*
Percent of managers agreeing that plan creates demand for employee participation in management			
Cash bonus	44(39)*	34(69)*	n.a.
Deferred	39(33)*	. . .	. . .
Addendum: percent of respondents with plan	53	6	23

Source: Daniel J. B. Mitchell and Renae F. Broderick, "Flexible Systems in the American Context: History, Policy, Research, and Implications," *Advances in Industrial and Labor Relations* (forthcoming).

n.a. = Not asked in survey.

*Chi-square test on a contingency table indicates that pattern of responses by those with plan was significantly different from those of other respondents at 5 percent level.

a. Numbers in parentheses refer to the responses from individuals whose firms have the plan listed at the column head.

to the firm.[148] A survey of 545 managers by Mitchell and Broderick permitted disaggregation by union status of the respondent's firm and by whether the firm did or did not have a particular pay plan. The survey covered profit sharing, gain sharing, simple incentive plans, ESOPs, and "tax-credit ESOPs."[149] Table 6 summarizes the highlights of the survey for the three types of plans under primary discussion in this paper.

In general, simple incentive plans were most likely to be cited as best for productivity improvement, but least likely to be seen as enhancing worker loyalty or providing labor cost flexibility. This result agrees with the textbook stereotypical view of simple incentives as being direct individual or small-group motivators. It is also in keeping with a New York Stock Exchange survey of managerial attitudes toward alternative pay systems.[150]

Profit-sharing plans were seen as providing an advantage mainly in the areas of loyalty and labor cost flexibility. Unionization made little

148. Laura B. Cardinal and I. B. Helburn, "Union versus Nonunion Attitudes toward Share Arrangements," in *Proceedings of the Thirty-Ninth Annual Meeting* (IRRA, 1987), pp. 167–73, esp. p. 171.

149. Daniel J. B. Mitchell and Renae F. Broderick, "Flexible Systems in the American Context: History, Policy, Research, and Implications," in *Advances in Industrial and Labor Relations* (forthcoming). Tax-credit ESOPs, known as PAYSOPs in their last form, were stock ownership arrangements with lavish tax benefits but tight limits on the value of shares that could be distributed. These plans have been discontinued by changes in the tax code.

150. New York Stock Exchange, *People and Productivity: A Challenge to Corporate America* (1982), p. 47.

difference in these perceptions. But as Voos found, respondents who actually had a plan were more likely to see the plan in positive terms.

Respondents who had profit-sharing plans were less likely to agree than others with the view that the plan created worker demands for participation in management. This finding—when combined with the propensity of managers with plans to say nice things about them— suggests that managers considered such potential demands to be "bad things." It was found that agreement with that view was positively correlated with unionization. Thus managers in the union sector may have been inhibited from using profit sharing from fear that the unions would then provide a voice for participative demands. The small number of respondents with gain sharing were more likely than others to associate participative demands with their plans. However, at least with the Scanlon plan, gain sharing is explicitly linked to participation, and firms that set up such plans have elected to create participative institutions.

The Case Study Approach

Though interesting, surveys of managerial attitudes do not normally provide objective performance measures. Managers may say they think a particular plan increases productivity, but without a productivity index, one cannot be sure an effect really occurs. Thus it is important to consider studies that have tried to measure directly the effect of pay-for-performance systems.

Incentive Plans

Case studies provide a great deal of evidence that individual incentive pay can motivate individual performance; indeed, much of this research is decades old.[151] The case study evidence suggests that gains of 10–25 percent are common when incentive pay is used properly. There is also good reason to believe that incentives can attract and selectively retain good performers because such performers end up being paid more than other workers. Nonetheless, the literature on incentive pay plans is full of vivid descriptions of the counterproductive behavior that piece-rate incentive plans produce.[152] Most of the early accounts are from the

151. Edward E. Lawler III, *Pay and Organizational Effectiveness: A Psychological View* (McGraw-Hill, 1971).

152. William F. Whyte and others, *Money and Motivation: An Analysis of Incentives in Industry* (Harper, 1955).

manufacturing world, but the same kind of issues arise when salespeople and other service personnel are put on incentive pay.

Many case studies have shown that when piece-rate plans are put into place, an adversarial relationship develops between system designers and employees.[153] Employees seek to obtain rates that maximize their pay relative to the amount of work they do. As our historical review showed, case study investigators find that employees work at slow rates to mislead time study experts. They hide new work methods and new procedures. Informal norms develop about just how productive people should be, and workers thus set limits on their own production. Employees who go beyond this limit may be socially ostracized or otherwise penalized.

> Jack warned me that the Methods Department could lower their prices on any job, old or new, by changing the fixture slightly or changing the size of the drill. According to Jack, a couple of operators . . . got to competing with each other to see how much they could turn in. They got up to $1.65 an hour, and the price was cut in half. And from then on they had to run that job themselves, as none of the other operators would accept the job.[154]

Other dysfunctional reactions include producing at extremely low levels when the rates are set at levels that the employees consider too difficult to reach—a kind of quasi strike—and using union grievance procedures to change rates that are too difficult. Employees may also do only what is measured, ignoring other needed activities. For production workers, this may mean not cleaning up and leaving material-handling work undone. For salespeople, it may mean not doing customer service activities.

Since many support jobs and nonproduction jobs do not lend themselves to piece-rate pay, the typical organization that has incentive pay will have only part of the work force on it. This bifurcation has often been found to lead to a we-they split in the work force that can be counterproductive and lead to noncooperative work relationships.[155] Thus positive productivity effects may be offset by intergroup workplace frictions.

Because incentive plans by themselves are relatively complicated and

153. Lawler, *Pay and Organizational Effectiveness*.
154. Whyte, *Money and Motivation*, p. 23.
155. Wolf, *Wage Incentives*, pp. 32–48.

need to be constantly updated, case analysis suggests that a significant number of people are required to maintain them. The problem of maintaining incentive systems is further complicated by the adversarial relationship that develops between employees and management. Since employees try to hide new work methods and to avoid changes in their rates (unless, of course, it is to their advantage), management needs to be extremely vigilant in determining when new rates are needed. Moreover, each time a technological change is made or a new product is introduced, new rates need to be set.

Finally, there is the ongoing cost of computing wages relative to the amount of work and kind of work employees have performed during a particular performance period. These calculations require engineers, accountants, and payroll clerks. Case studies suggest that the support costs of an incentive system are significantly greater than those associated with a straight hourly pay.

The combined effects of dividing the work force into those who are and those who are not on incentive pay and the adversarial process of rate setting can create a hostile, differentiated organizational environment. In particular, incentive-related hostilities have been found to produce an environment of low trust, lack of information sharing, conflict between groups, poor support for joint problem solving, and inflexibility because individuals want to protect their wage rates. In some instances these reactions are caused not so much by the incentive concept itself as by the way it has been managed.

For example, the case literature reports instances in which reducing labor-management frictions has, as a byproduct, eliminated seemingly intractable disputes about incentives. In one instance, the union withdrew a long-standing grievance over incentives after a new contract was signed and a higher level of trust had been established.

For the workers and union leaders, the [grievance] case had symbolized the hatred and distrust they bore toward management. It was evident to them that management was unfair and ruthless. So long as they continued to believe that . . . the case could have no other meaning to them, no matter what logical arguments were brought. . . . But as soon as relations were reorganized so that the hatred and distrust were beginning to be dissipated, there was no longer an emotional need to hold onto that symbol of conflict.[156]

156. Whyte, *Money and Motivation*, p. 114.

Incentive pay clearly fits some organizational situations better than others. It fits situations best where the work is designed for individuals or sometimes for small groups. Management experts find that incentive pay is most suitable for work that is simple, repetitive, stable, and easy to measure comprehensively. More than any other system, it divides the organization, creating isolated individuals or small groups who often feel they are competing with each other. Thus the prevailing view is that it is very important that simple incentives be used only when the need for integration is negligible or when other mechanisms can be used to produce it. Finally, from the management perspective, it helps a great deal if the nature of the work is stable, so that it can be carefully studied and does not require constant revision of standards and payment approaches.

Gain Sharing

There has been a considerable amount of research on gain sharing. Perhaps the most important thing known about gain-sharing plans is that they have often produced desirable results where implemented. Figure 2 lists some of the common positive results found in case studies of gain-sharing plans.[157] Particularly impressive is the finding of the U.S. General Accounting Office that firms with plans in place more than five years averaged an annual savings of 29 percent in labor costs.[158] We know somewhat less about the frequency with which gain sharing is a success, but even here some evidence suggests that it enhances productivity in 50 to 80 percent of the reported cases.[159] Apart from the productivity effect, proponents often claim that gain sharing can produce the other results listed in the figure.

One can easily criticize the research studies upon which the conclu-

157. Carl F. Frost, John H. Wakeley, and Robert A. Ruh, *The Scanlon Plan for Organization Development: Identity, Participation, and Equity* (Michigan State University Press, 1974); Brian E. Graham-Moore and Timothy L. Ross, *Productivity Gainsharing: How Employer Incentive Programs Can Improve Business Performance* (Englewood Cliffs, N.J.: Prentice-Hall, 1983); Carla S. O'Dell, *Gainsharing: Involvement, Incentive, and Productivity* (New York: American Management Association, 1981); Michael Schuster, "Forty Years of Scanlon Plan Research," in C. Crouch and F. A. Heller, eds., *International Yearbook of Organizational Democracy*, vol. 1: *Organizational Democracy and Political Processes* (Wiley and Sons, 1983), pp. 53–72; and J. Kenneth White, "The Scanlon Plan: Causes and Correlates of Success," *Academy of Management Journal*, vol. 22 (June 1979), pp. 292–312.

158. General Accounting Office, *Productivity Sharing Programs: Can They Contribute to Productivity Improvement?* (1981).

159. R. J. Bullock and Edward E. Lawler III, "Gainsharing: A Few Questions, and Fewer Answers," *Human Resource Management*, vol. 23 (Spring 1984), pp. 23–40.

Figure 2. Claimed Effects of Gain Sharing

Coordination, teamwork, and sharing of knowledge are enhanced at lower levels.

Social needs are recognized through participation and mutually reinforcing group behavior.

Attention is focused on cost savings, not just quantity of production.

Acceptance of change due to technology, market, and new methods is greater because higher efficiency leads to bonuses.

Attitudinal change occurs among workers, and they demand more efficient management and better planning.

Employees try to reduce overtime; to work smarter, not harder or faster.

Employees produce ideas as well as effort.

When unions are present, more flexible administration of union-management relations occurs.

When unions support the plan, they are strengthened because a better work situation and higher pay result.

Unorganized locations tend to remain nonunion.

---

sions about the effectiveness of gain sharing are based. Unfortunately, most of the studies do not meet rigorous methodological standards; they fall more in the realm of magazine reports than research studies. Their typical failings include lack of comparison or control sites, measurement of only a few features of the organization, and lack of longitudinal data. The possibility also remains of a tremendous underreporting of negative results, as is true with any literature that relies on case reports. Successful gain-sharing companies, such as Herman Miller, have been featured in the literature for decades and studied many times. But few researchers seem interested in and willing to study the firms that try gain sharing and for one reason or another abandon it after a short trial.

Some important exceptions to the general point about poor research are worth mentioning. Schuster did a longitudinal study of the Scanlon plan, and White analyzed the experience of twenty-two companies with that plan. Goodman and Moore have also done a longitudinal study of the Scanlon plan; Bullock and Bullock have provided longitudinal data on two custom-designed plans; and Jewell and Jewell have compared the performance of a restaurant with gain sharing to similar units in the same chain.[160] The gain-sharing unit outperformed comparable units in

---

160. Michael Schuster, "The Scanlon Plan: A Longitudinal Analysis," *Journal of Ap-*

several areas: gain in number of customers, gain in sales per customer, profit improvement, and employee turnover. Jewell and Jewell attributed these accomplishments both to the gain-sharing plan and the accompanying participative management approach. In general, these better studies are consistent with the more casual reports about the positive effects on productivity of gain-sharing plans.

Bullock and Lawler, in a review of the gain-sharing literature, provided some further data on how plans are structured and installed.[161] They report, for example, that the typical plan pays out monthly, focuses on labor costs, shares over 50 percent of the gain with the employees, and is implemented by a consultant with the involvement of the employees. A more recent study by O'Dell and McAdams (*People, Performance, and Pay*) reports similar findings, as well as data that suggest the typical plan pay bonuses range from 5 to 10 percent of base pay, cover most employees in the organization's unit where they are installed, and are in organizations with fewer than 5,000 employees. Unfortunately, no study has related detailed features of the plan and its implementation to its success. Thus, though we know something about how plans are structured and implemented, little data exist on how these are related to success.

Some case analysis deals with the situational factors that favor gain-sharing plans. For example, it is generally thought that participation and managerial attitudes are critical to the success of such plans. As figure 3 shows (though the literature is biased toward describing successful gain-sharing plans), there have been case analyses and illustrative reports on why gain-sharing plans fail and on which obstacles must be overcome to achieve positive outcomes. An important barrier seems to be lower-level management resistance; gain-sharing plans are often opposed by managers who see their authority and competence challenged and their roles changed in uncomfortable ways.[162]

Relatively little is known about the internal machinery through which

plied Behavioral Science, vol. 20 (February 1984), pp. 23–38; White, "Scanlon Plan," 292–312; Paul S. Goodman and Brian E. Moore, "Factors Affecting Acquisition of Beliefs about a New Reward System," *Human Relations* (June 1976), pp. 571–88; R. J. Bullock and Patti F. Bullock, "Gainsharing and Rubik's Cube: Solving System Problems," *National Productivity Review*, vol. 2 (Fall 1982), pp. 396–407; and Donald O. Jewell and Sandra F. Jewell, "An Example of Economic Gainsharing in the Restaurant Industry," *National Productivity Review*, vol. 6 (Spring 1987), pp. 134–43.

161. Bullock and Lawler "Gainsharing," pp. 23–40.

162. Edward E. Lawler III, *Pay and Organization Development* (Reading, Mass: Addison-Wesley, 1981).

Figure 3. Frequent Problems with Gain Sharing

Formula structure. The formula needs to measure accurately what is going on in the organization. Rigid formulas that do not reflect employee behavior may be developed and lead to failure because employees see no relationship between performance and reward.

Formula change. The formula needs to change as the products, technology, and activities of organizations change. Rigid plans that do not put in place a process to allow for change often fail when change is needed.

Payout level. It is important that some bonuses are paid, particularly at the beginning. Sometimes payments are not made initially because the performance level that must be achieved before a bonus is paid is set too high.

Management attitudes. Unless managers are favorably disposed to the idea of participation, the plan will not fit the management style of the organization. In some organizations, plans have been tried simply as a pay incentive plan without regard to the management style and have failed because of a poor fit.

Plan focus. Many plans focus only on labor savings. This approach presents problems in organizations where other costs are great and are under the control of the employees. It can lead to the other costs being ignored or even increased in order to reduce labor costs.

Communication. For a plan to work, employees must understand and trust it enough to believe their pay will increase if they perform better. For this belief to occur, a great deal of open communication and education is needed. Often this element is ignored and, as a result, plans fail.

Union cooperation. The local union must be supportive. In most of the places where gain sharing has been tried, the local union has supported it. However, some failures have occurred in situations where unions have not supported the plan sufficiently.

Threat to supervisor. Gain sharing changes the roles of supervisors. They are forced to deal with many suggestions, and their competence is tested and questioned in new ways. Unless supervisors are prepared for and accept these changes, the plan can fail. This point goes along with the general point that management must be prepared to manage in a different way.

Participative structure. Gain sharing requires congruent participative structures. Sometimes these are not in place or they are poorly managed; as a result, the plan fails because as an incentive plan gain sharing is a relatively weak intervention.

---

successful gain sharing operates. Proponents of gain sharing cite many mechanisms, including the facts that it works like an effective pay incentive plan, stimulates problem solving, causes people to work smarter, causes social pressures that encourage people to be good performers, causes other organizational changes that contribute to organizational effectiveness, and creates organizational goals that lead to teamwork and cooperation. These may all be ways through which gain-sharing plans work, but at this point little research has been done to document the specifics and identify relative importance. In fact, gain sharing may work for different reasons in different situations. Such factors as technology and organizational size may well influence why and how a plan operates.

Particularly interesting are questions concerning what the bonus formula contributes to participative management and vice versa. The congruence argument, which is largely untested, suggests that economic participation or participation in decisionmaking alone has little effect but that together they are quite powerful. Partial support for this view is provided by data on the institutionalization of gain-sharing plans. Most studies that have reviewed such plans have noted that some survive for many years, in contrast to the relatively short-term effectiveness of participative management programs such as quality circles.

Herman Miller, a furniture company, is perhaps the most widely cited and intriguing gain-sharing case. The company has been rated as one of the ten best-managed U.S. corporations by *Fortune* magazine. Its Scanlon plan, started in 1950, is often considered the source of the firm's success.[163] The plan has been modified to take account of various goals. A highly participative managerial style prevails, and workers are organized into teams that make most operational decisions.[164]

Because of Herman Miller's success, other companies in the industry have sought to adopt gain sharing. However, another leading furniture manufacturer, Knoll, found that installing gain sharing was difficult.[165] Initially the work force voted against installation. After a redesign, the plan reportedly has operated successfully, though it has required modification from time to time. Change in technology and increased understanding of the business by workers both seem to trigger the need for such modification. The Knoll case points to the barriers to adoption of gain sharing. Interested employers must be willing to invest substantial time and effort to launch such programs and keep them in operation.

Profit Sharing

The limited case research on profit-sharing plans suggests that these programs are much less effective than gain-sharing plans in influencing

163. James O'Toole, *Vanguard Management: Redesigning the Corporate Future* (Doubleday, 1985), pp. 87–90.

164. Max DePree, *Leadership Is an Art* (Michigan State University Press, 1987).

165. Bullock and Bullock, "Gainsharing and Rubik's Cube," pp. 396–407. Although this article does not identify the company by name, Edward Lawler was involved in the installation of gain sharing and the subsequent research and thus can identify the firm.

individual or group performance and in producing the kind of social and cultural outcomes listed in figure 2. This result applies particularly to large organizations, where the relation between individual performance and corporate profits is virtually nonexistent. Thus the case analysis research is consistent with the general view of profit sharing expressed throughout this century.

Nonetheless, even a deferred profit-sharing plan in a large corporation can accomplish three things. First, paying people according to organizational performance has some potential symbolic and communications value. It can effectively point out to employees that they are part of the organization and that cooperative effort is needed. Since corporate executives are often paid on the basis of profit sharing, it can also help to ensure some alignment between the rewards received by top management and those received by people throughout the organization. This parallel treatment can help avoid the all-too-common problems that occur when executives receive large bonuses while lower-level employees receive none.[166]

Second, some companies, most notably Hewlett-Packard, seem to have used their profit-sharing plans to educate employees about the financial condition of the business. When employees are actually sharing in the profits, they become aware of what profits mean for the firm and how they are calculated. Thus profit sharing can increase employee interest in learning about profits and organizational effectiveness.

Third, as case analysis suggests, perhaps the most important advantage profit sharing offers is that it makes the labor costs of an organization variable and adjusts these costs to the organization's ability to pay. With profit sharing, a firm can reduce costs significantly without reducing the number of employees or the base wage. This effect has proved to be a particularly desirable feature for organizations that are cyclically sensitive. Without profit sharing, changes in labor costs in these firms would be handled through increases and decreases in the size of the work force, an expensive practice that can lead to the liquidation of valuable human resources.

There are some frequently cited instances in which profit sharing seems to have worked well, perhaps the most famous being the already-

166. For the benefits of a common compensation source to be felt, however, worker and management must be covered by the same profit-sharing formula. Thus at General Motors profit sharing for workers was based on domestic profits and produced little or no bonus payments during the mid-to-late 1980s. In contrast, executive bonuses were geared to worldwide GM profits and were large, creating obvious tensions.

mentioned Lincoln Electric Company.[167] Lincoln Electric combines both piece rates and profit sharing, so that it is difficult to disentangle the two effects. Its profit-sharing component has an unusual merit-rating element: funds based on profits are placed in a bonus pool, and the individual employee receives a bonus from the pool related to his or her merit rating. Lincoln Electric, which was heavily influenced by its founder's philosophy of compensation and employee relations, also features job security and various employee communications mechanisms. Since its shares are closely held, it is able to espouse principles that denigrate shareholder interests without retribution from the financial market.[168]

Success stories like Lincoln Electric, and the more general notion of promoting cooperation through profit sharing, may account for the largely positive views of profit sharing found among managements that use such plans. One survey of 108 companies using profit-sharing plans found that over 50 percent of the company executives surveyed felt the plans improved efficiency, reduced costs, and lowered turnover.[169] Also, studies that compare profit-sharing firms with non-profit-sharing firms have usually found that the profit-sharing ones perform better.[170] Although to attribute causation is difficult with cross-sectional research studies like these, it seems reasonable to conclude that profit-sharing plans can contribute to organizational financial performance.

Linking Pay System Data to Financial Performance

The case study approach provides one route to linking actual outcomes with particular pay systems. It provides more direct information than

167. James F. Lincoln, *Incentive Management: A New Approach to Human Relationships in Industry and Business* (Cleveland: Lincoln Electric Company, 1951); and "The Lincoln Electric Company," in Fred K. Foulkes and E. Robert Livernash, *Human Resources Management: Cases and Text,* 2d ed. (Englewood Cliffs, N.J.: Prentice Hall, 1989), pp. 206–33.

168. "The present policy of operating industry for stockholders is unreasonable. The rewards now given to [the stockholder] are far too much. He gets income that should really go to the worker and the management. The usual absentee stockholder contributes nothing to efficiency. He buys a stock today and sells it tomorrow. . . . Why should he be rewarded by large dividends?" Statement of James F. Lincoln, quoted in "Lincoln Electric Company," p. 227.

169. Bertram L. Metzger, *Profit Sharing in Perspective in American Medium-Sized and Small Businesses* (Evanston, Ill.: Profit Sharing Research Foundation, 1964).

170. "As You Were Saying—Share Profits—Don't Freeze Them," *Personnel Journal,* vol. 54 (January 1972), pp. 54, 62.

managerial attitude surveys. However, individual cases always raise questions about generalization. Another research method is, therefore, to marry data sets dealing with pay plan incidence to others dealing with financial performance. In the past such research has tended to be published under the auspices of plan proponents.[171] But some recent independent research has suggested that particular pay systems do have positive productivity effects.[172]

Isolating the degree to which there are alternatives to flexible pay systems is another way in which detailed information on human resource practices can be helpful. Firms have many practices in place—other than incentive plans, profit sharing, and gain sharing—that are supposed to reward good behavior, such as performance appraisal systems and related merit awards. These programs may substitute for automatic pay system rewards in fostering desirable financial outcomes for the enterprise.

Complementarity is also an issue that regards human resource practices. The literature on sharing arrangements, in particular, often associates economic sharing with sharing of decisionmaking. As noted, managers do not necessarily believe the two forms of sharing must go together. Nonetheless, as a matter of practice, they may tend to go together. If so, disentangling their independent effects becomes important.

Finally, there is a growing body of literature concerned with the link, or lack thereof, between human resource practices and strategic planning of the firm.[173] Human resource managers are being advised that pay systems should be designed to mesh with the organization's design and business objectives.[174] The results may differ depending on such factors as firm size and industry. And the objective may not be an absolute

171. See, for example, Bion B. Howard and Peter O. Dietz, *A Study of the Financial Significance of Profit Sharing* (Chicago: Council of Profit Sharing Industries, 1969). This study used a variety of financial performance measures from COMPUSTAT and compared profit-sharing firms with other firms. Usually the profit sharers were found to exhibit better performance.

172. For example, Shepard reported that in the chemical industry, profit sharing boosts value-added productivity by about one-tenth. He estimated production functions and included profit-sharing variables as inputs. See Edward Morse Shepard III, "The Effect of Profit Sharing on Productivity," Ph.D. dissertation, Boston College, 1986.

173. David Lewin, "Industrial Relations as a Strategic Variable," in Morris M. Kleiner and others, *Human Resources and the Performance of the Firm* (Madison, Wis.: Industrial Relations Research Association, 1987), pp. 1–41.

174. Renae Broderick, "Making Performance Pay," in *Personnel Management: Compensation* (Paramus, N.J.: Prentice Hall Information Services, 1988), pp. 585–90.

performance target; rather, the purpose of a particular pay practice may be to enhance the firm's ability to adapt to change and to share the risks of an unstable environment between shareholders and employee stakeholders.

The Columbia Business Unit Data Set

A new data set pertaining to human resource policies and practices of U.S. private employers has been developed that allows us to examine some of these issues empirically. The data come from survey responses of 495 business units, obtained from a questionnaire originally mailed to more than 7,000 business unit executives by a team of researchers at Columbia University's Graduate School of Business.[175] These units (a more detailed point of observation than the overall firm) were asked to report extensive information on their internal human resource policies for the years 1986–87. The responses were matched to financial performance data contained in the COMPUSTAT file, including information on revenue, profitability, assets, and equity, on an annual basis for the 1983–86 period.

Human resource policy and practice information available from the survey covers eight key areas: human resource planning, job design and analysis, selection and staffing, training and development, performance appraisal, compensation, employee involvement and communications, and employee relations–union relations. The survey instrument used to obtain this information ran twenty-nine pages and is available from the authors of this paper.

Although the Columbia business unit survey provides data for four occupational categories—managers, professional and technical, clerical, and manufacturing production—we limit our analyses to the last two groups. Four business units reported having no significant clerical employment; 100 reported having no manufacturing production workers. The data are available separately for unionized and nonunion business units in each occupational category. Since the point of observation is

175. The survey is discussed more fully in John Thomas Delaney, David Lewin, and Casey Ichniowski, "Human Resource Management Policies and Practices in American Firms," Columbia University, Graduate School of Business, Industrial Relations Research Center, September 1988. An initial response rate of 11 percent was obtained. Eliminating unusable responses brought the rate down to 6.5 percent. Although this rate was low, it was not surprising, because of the extensive information required by the questionnaire. Analysis of the COMPUSTAT information on nonrespondents did not suggest any bias in the sample obtained.

Table 7. Summary Statistics from Columbia Business Unit Survey[a]

	Clerical workers			Manufacturing production workers		
Item	Union	Nonunion	All	Union	Nonunion	All
Percent of business units with						
Profit sharing	15	42	36	18	46	37
Gain sharing	5	3	4	6	5	5
Stock option	12	22	20	9	23	19
ESOP	45	48	47	37	45	42
Incentive or bonus	4	3	3	5	3	4
Mean value of						
ROI (percent)	10	10	10	10	10	10
ROA (percent)	8	8	8	8	8	8
$PROD$ (thousands of dollars)	221	210	212	247	224	235
ROI_T	10	11	11	11	12	11
ROA_T	9	10	9	9	10	10
$PROD_T$	13	13	13	15	14	14
EP (0–5)	1.9	2.6	2.4	2.5	2.7	2.6
$UNION$ (0–1)	1.0	0.0	0.2	1.0	0.0	0.5
NEP (0–18)	10.2	8.3	8.6	9.7	8.6	9.2
LC (0–8)	3.7	3.1	3.2	4.5	3.8	4.2
FBR (0–13)	10.1	10.4	10.3	10.3	10.5	10.4
IS (0–2)	0.9	1.3	1.2	0.7	1.2	0.9
FHR (0–8)	5.2	4.6	4.7	5.9	5.0	5.5
SHR (0–6)	3.8	3.5	3.6	4.1	3.2	3.7
SZ	582	935	884	1,832	1,180	1,520
$PART$ (0–1)	0.45	0.33	0.35	0.47	0.42	0.44
$INFO$ (0–1)	0.62	0.53	0.55	0.62	0.56	0.60
Number of observations	85	406	491	210	185	395

a. For source and variable definitions, see text.

the business unit (or COMPUSTAT business line), rather than the corporate entity or parent company, corporate-parent overhead allocations to business units are not included in the economic performance measures of this data base.

Compensation Policies and Economic Performance

The top part of table 7 provides descriptive statistics pertaining to the businesses' compensation policies and practices for union and nonunion clerical and manufacturing production employees. The differences in the incidence of compensation plans between clerical and production employees are not striking. Consistent with previous information, union workers are less likely to have profit sharing and more likely to have gain sharing than nonunion employees.

Table 7 contains some anomalies that suggest less-than-perfect reporting of plan usage by respondents. The very low rates of usage of incentive and bonus plans (which include piece rates) for manufacturing production workers are inconsistent with other data. Although the proportion of such workers reported as covered by "stock option" plans is low, the figures are surprisingly high for production workers. Such plans were originally designed for executives in high tax brackets at a time when capital gains were given favored tax treatment. Respondents may have mistakenly included various stock *purchase* plans in replying to the survey.

It is likely that the respondents most accurately reported the presence of profit sharing, gain sharing, and ESOPs. Relatively few firms, however, have gain-sharing plans so that the sample provides little information about them. Therefore, any correlations found between economic participation and enterprise performance will probably be dominated by profit sharing and ESOPs.

To explore what relations may exist between performance and economic participation, we first define the economic performance measures that will serve as dependent variables. Then we specify the compensation measure(s) as well as certain control variables that will serve as independent variables in the analysis. We present alternative specifications of both the compensation and control variables.

As measures of economic performance, we use return on investment (*ROI*), the ratio of operating income to equity investment; return on assets (*ROA*), the ratio of operating income to identifiable assets; and productivity (*PROD*), the ratio of net sales revenue to employees.[176] These measures will initially be examined cross-sectionally for the most recent year included in the data base (1986 in most cases). They will then be examined longitudinally, using the 1983–86 percentage growth trend of *ROI, ROA,* and deflated *PROD* as dependent variables.[177] Mean values for the sample are shown in the middle part of table 7.

176. *Net* indicates that revenue from returned or canceled goods and services has been deducted from gross sales in the *PROD* variable. It should be stressed that the denominator for *PROD* is the total number of employees, even in the separate regressions we ran for clerical workers and manufacturing production workers. That is, we did not calculate separate "clerical productivity" and "production worker productivity" variables.

177. The *ROI* and *ROA* variables pose a potential problem for trend analysis since they can be zero or negative in the base period. We set a floor for both variables of 1 percent for

Our interest is in the presence of a compensation system or systems linking an element of compensation to some measure of employer or employee performance. As a measure of the use of such plans, we initially constructed a composite index of economic participation (*EP*), which includes the following items: profit-sharing plan (*PS*), gain-sharing plan (*GS*), stock option plan (*SO*), employee stock ownership plan (*ESOP*), and production incentive or bonus plan (*INC*). This index ranges from 0 (no plans) to 5 (all plans in use) for the business units included in the data base. As we previously noted in discussing table 4, use of such indexes is common in the industrial relations literature. But because of the special interest in pay systems, we also examined the different types of pay plans separately. We also experimented by breaking down the other indexes into their constituent components.[178]

An obvious link to look for is the one between *EP* and the performance variables. With the *ROI* and *ROA* variables, however, a conceptual problem exists. In the long run enterprises should not be expected to make above-normal profits. If the kinds of plans included in *EP* were of value to the firm, the employer should have adopted them. But so should other competitive employers. Thus, even if the *EP* plans were profit enhancing in the short run, there may be no long-run correlation between *EP* and *ROI* or *ROA*. (This problem, of course, plagues all studies that do not have formal modeling of the decision process in choosing compensation systems.) On the other hand, there might be an association

---

1983 and 1986. Thus improvements within the negative range over the period—for example, from − 3 percent in 1983 to − 2 percent in 1986—would be considered as zero changes. (Very few observations were affected by this lower limit.) Percent changes were calculated as $100(dx/x)$, where x is the value of *ROI* or *ROA* in 1983 and dx is the change in *ROI* or *ROA* over 1983–86. Despite the floor restriction, the methodology still counts changes from low bases as larger than those from high bases. Experiments with other formats suggested that the results reported in the text are not very sensitive to the particular trend definition used. Ideally, it would be nice to have separate price deflators for the *PROD* variable for each firm, for regressions involving trends in *PROD*. In the absence of such deflators, however, we used the GNP deflator in the trend regressions. That does not, of course, correct for differential firm inflation rates but simply reduces the magnitude of the trend variable. Unless the rate of firm-specific inflation is correlated with the independent variables, however, the resulting regression coefficients are unbiased estimates of the effect of the variables on real productivity increases.

178. Chaykowski, "Empirical Formulation of Nonwage Collective Bargaining Outcomes," questions the use of constructed contractual variables in analyzing collective bargaining outcomes. It should be noted, however, that our dependent variables are not indexes of the type that concerned Chaykowski. What matters is whether disaggregating the various indexes we did use as independent variables changes the coefficients of the pay plan variables in important ways. The results for the pay plan variables do not seem to be sensitive to the level of disaggregation of the other variables.

between EP and a measure such as $PROD$ that is not directly linked to profits.

Apart from any effect on absolute performance of the enterprise, EP plans may assist the business unit in adapting to volatile economic conditions. The mid-1980s are widely viewed as a period of adjustment for many U.S. businesses. An interesting question is whether the business units in our sample were able to improve their performance during this difficult period.

Although absolute profitability may not be linked to EP for competitive reasons, EP might be associated with trend improvements in the three indexes (denoted ROI_T, ROA_T, and $PROD_T$) during the 1983–86 period for which we have data. Thus, the analysis includes the performance measures both in absolute form and in trend form. Note, however, that even if EP is associated with trend improvements, a causal connection might not exist. It could be, for example, that use of EP is positively associated with the cyclical sensitivity of the firms in the sample—perhaps as a form of risk sharing with employees. If that were so, EP would be positively linked to improved performance in a recovery period such as 1983–86, even if it did not directly contribute to that performance. We cannot rule out such a spurious association, since we do not have a long time series on the cyclical sensitivity of the firms in the sample.[179]

Other Independent Variables

There are likely to be other influences on economic performance besides the pay system. These influences may be correlated with the incidence of particular pay systems. To standardize for such other influences, we included different control variables in the analysis; mean values of these variables are reported in the bottom part of table 7.

A dummy for the presence of a union ($UNION$, where union $= 1$, no union $= 0$) is an obvious control, since many empirical studies provide

179. Note, however, that we have no information to suggest that EP is in fact associated in the sample with cyclical sensitivity. Because we have implicitly treated the EP plans as exogenous variables, along with the other right-hand-side variables described below, it is also possible to object that we have not properly controlled for the influence of the absolute performance variables on the right-hand-side variables (as opposed to the trends). Particularly with regard to EP plans, however, the reverse causal links between the absolute performance measures and the presence of a plan or plans are not evident. Undoubtedly, examples of, say, profit-sharing plans established because firms were profitable can be found. But in the 1980s it is equally possible to find examples of such plans implemented because firms were in economic difficulty, as occurred in various union concession bargaining situations.

a basis for positing a relationship between *UNION* and the economic performance measures. A second independent variable is noneconomic participation of employees (*NEP*), one of a group of controls designed to capture within-firm human resource policies other than pay. The index of *NEP* encompasses eighteen policies: the existence of a formal employee participation program; the extent of issues covered by the participation program, including introduction of new technology, quality of product and service, work unit performance, plant-facility-office layout, supervision, safety, and health, and work flow–work speed; performance appraisals of peers conducted by employees; the existence of a formal information-sharing program for employees; and the extent of issues covered by the information-sharing program, including business conditions, introduction of new technology, work flow, organization, and scheduling, work unit performance or quality data, company investment plans, company marketing plans, compensation in competing firms, and budget-income-financial statements.

The *NEP* index ranges from 0 (no noneconomic participation) to 18 (complete noneconomic participation along all dimensions listed above) for the business units included in the data base. To explore further the effect of noneconomic participation, we also experimented with the different specification of this concept. Employee participation of any type was represented by a dummy *PART* (where 1 = presence of any plan). Information sharing of any kind was represented by a dummy *INFO*.

Earlier we noted that fringe benefits might be substitutes for such plans as profit sharing. Fringe benefits may also have effects on performance by making the outward mobility of employees more costly for them, to the extent that benefits are nonvested or only partly vested. The incidence of fringes may also be an index of paternalistic or other human resource policies. Data available from the survey enabled us to construct as a third control variable an index of fringe benefit richness (*FBR*), composed of thirteen fringe benefits: the provision of day care, health insurance, dental care, eye care, a retirement plan, paid vacation, paid sick leave, tuition reimbursement, paid personal leave, paid legal fees, paternity leave, maternity leave, and employee counseling. This index ranges from 0 (no fringe benefits) to 13 (provision of all the listed benefits) for the business units included in the data base.[180]

180. To the extent that economic participation plans lead to offsetting cost savings through reduced fringe benefits, our entry of *FBR* in the regressions tends to weaken the impact of *EP*.

As noted earlier, incentive pay has sometimes been seen as a substitute for conventional "policing" by supervisors—that is, as a way to reduce shirking. Therefore, as a fourth control variable, it is important to measure the intensity of supervision (*IS*) in examining the relation between the economic participation of employees and the economic performance of businesses. To do so, we constructed an *IS* index that includes the presence of a formal performance appraisal system and the presence of a formal program to train personnel to conduct performance appraisals. This index ranges from 0 (no appraisal system or training) to 2 (use of appraisal and appraisal training).

The human resource management literature contains many concepts and propositions about "good" policies and practices. One way to summarize these is by the formality of human resource practice (*FHR*), where formality presumably reduces arbitrary treatment of employees. The index of *FHR*, used as the fifth control variable, includes these eight elements: the presence of a formal written human resource plan, the presence of a formal job design program, the use of written skill tests in employee selection, the use of written aptitude tests in employee selection, the use of promotion-from-within to fill nonentry job vacancies, the presence of a formal employee training and development program, the presence of a formal grievance or complaint procedure for the unit's nonunion employees,[181] and the conducting of attitude surveys among employees. This index ranges between 0 (no programs of the type listed) and 8 (presence of all of them).

Another dimension of the human resource function is its status, that is, its role in key business decisions. As a proxy for this factor, we constructed a sixth control variable: the status of the human resource function (*SHR*) index, a scaled variable for the involvement of human resource executives in the business planning process. The index runs from 0 (never involved) to 6 (always involved).

The seventh control variable is recent labor cost pressure (*LC*). Our index of this influence has eight elements: the presence of a two-tier pay schedule, the use of lump-sum cash payments to employees, reported increased domestic competition, reported increased foreign competition, reported increased business deregulation, use of pay freezes or reductions, use of fringe benefit freezes or reductions, and use of work force reductions. The index ranges from 0 (no labor cost pressures of

---

181. All business units had some nonunion employees even if they were unionized. Hence a unionized unit could still have a formal grievance mechanism for its nonunion employees.

the type listed) to 8 (all elements of labor cost pressure present). Besides the seven control variables, our regression estimates also include firm size (*SZ*) and industrial classification (*IC*), the latter through the use of industry dummy variables.[182]

Empirical Results

Regression estimates of the economic performance equations using cross-sectional data are shown separately for clerical and production workers in table 8. The composite economic participation variable (*EP*) is positively related to *ROI* and *ROA* for the business units included in this study, but the coefficients are insignificant. In the case of productivity (*PROD*), however, *EP* is significant for production workers.

These results are in keeping with a competitive, long-run equilibrium model. As noted earlier, according to such a model, *EP* and the other control variables may have an effect on the efficiency of the enterprise, but if all competitive enterprises adopt the appropriate policies, there may be no correlation between absolute profitability and the independent variables that measure human resource practices. Of the seven human resource variables in the four regressions involving *ROI* and *ROA,* only one instance of a significant coefficient occurs, a finding that we would prefer not to exaggerate, since it could simply reflect chance. Despite the seeming accord of the *EP* index results with long-run competitive equilibrium, we will show that when *EP* is disaggregated, positive and significant relations between certain components of *EP* and performance emerge.

EP does seem to be positively associated with *PROD* for production workers, along with *UNION* and *NEP*. Because different studies have linked unionization with higher productivity—and because this effect would be enhanced by our lack of control for wage level—this equation seems to us to suggest that *EP* has a productivity-boosting effect, even after standardization for unionization and noneconomic participation. When the *EP* variable is entered in each equation separately for the presence of *EP* by clerical and production workers, *EP* for production workers shows up only as the source of the correlation between *EP* and *PROD*. Clerical *EP* does not seem to be a factor. Since production

182. Industry classifications used for control purposes were agriculture, forestry, fisheries; mining and construction; durable manufacturing; nondurable manufacturing; transportation, communications, utilities; wholesale and retail trade; finance, insurance, real estate; and services.

Table 8. Regressions Related to Economic Performance of Firms and Economic and Noneconomic Participation of Employees, 1986[a]

Dependent variable	Clerical workers			Production workers		
	ROI	ROA	PROD	ROI	ROA	PROD
Constant	7.62*	6.09*	18,023*	7.40*	6.04*	21,162*
	(2.69)	(2.25)	(4,045)	(2.34)	(2.19)	(5,273)
EP	0.89	0.82	691	0.95	0.86	1,788**
	(0.53)	(0.50)	(436)	(0.64)	(0.59)	(827)
NEP	0.87	0.99	10,537*	1.15**	0.95	1,663**
	(0.56)	(0.68)	(4,926)	(0.52)	(0.61)	(798)
UNION	−0.91	−0.74	615	−0.73	−0.80	1,217**
	(0.62)	(0.45)	(437)	(0.46)	(0.50)	(587)
LC	0.71	0.57	846	0.75	0.65	958
	(0.51)	(0.43)	(596)	(0.58)	(0.47)	(654)
FBR	−0.45	−0.31	483	−0.65	−0.51	824
	(0.34)	(0.19)	(321)	(0.47)	(0.38)	(562)
IS	−0.41	−0.34	844	−0.49	−0.42	994
	(0.26)	(0.22)	(535)	(0.34)	(0.31)	(648)
FHR	0.47	0.42	889	0.61	0.54	982
	(0.35)	(0.30)	(582)	(0.41)	(0.34)	(644)
SHR	0.21	0.18	366	0.34	0.27	533
	(0.14)	(0.12)	(231)	(0.20)	(0.19)	(376)
SZ	−0.19	−0.21	345	−0.28	−0.25	497
	(0.12)	(0.13)	(231)	(0.19)	(0.16)	(327)
IC	b	b	b	b	b	b
Adjusted R^2	0.33	0.29	0.36	0.35	0.31	0.37
Number of observations	491	491	491	491	395	395
Interaction analysis, EP, NEP						
EP × NEP	0.62	0.67	820	0.74	0.77	940
	(0.41)	(0.43)	(506)	(0.46)	(0.47)	(613)
EP	0.78	0.75	585	0.88	0.80	1,437**
	(0.47)	(0.46)	(367)	(0.60)	(0.56)	(669)
NEP	0.81	0.92	9,260**	1.10**	0.90	1,413**
	(0.52)	(0.64)	(4,579)	(0.50)	(0.59)	(682)
Expanded EP analysis						
EP-Cler	0.77	0.80	667	0.87	0.81	757
	(0.48)	(0.51)	(432)	(0.54)	(0.57)	(466)
EP-Prod	0.83	0.87	724	0.92	0.84	1,583**
	(0.52)	(0.53)	(458)	(0.58)	(0.59)	(749)

(continued)

Table 8 (continued)

Dependent variable	Clerical workers			Production workers		
	ROI	ROA	PROD	ROI	ROA	PROD
Individual plan analysis, EP						
PS	1.25**	1.03	1,064**	1.38**	1.05	1,965**
	(0.60)	(0.68)	(488)	(0.63)	(0.72)	(914)
GS	0.48	0.41	408	0.43	0.46	882
	(0.32)	(0.29)	(301)	(0.31)	(0.32)	(563)
SO	0.58	0.55	541	0.54	0.51	958
	(0.40)	(0.38)	(335)	(0.37)	(0.35)	(605)
ESOP	0.98	1.01	732	1.04	0.89	1,441**
	(0.62)	(0.65)	(481)	(0.69)	(0.61)	(674)
INC	0.43	0.38	397	0.64	0.60	836
	(0.28)	(0.27)	(233)	(0.42)	(0.39)	(566)
Individual plan analysis, NEP						
PART	0.66	0.61	1.05**	0.71	0.68	1.17**
	(0.51)	(0.45)	(0.49)	(0.59)	(0.52)	(0.53)
INFO	−0.31	−0.29	−0.61	−0.39	−0.26	−0.60
	(0.25)	(0.27)	(0.49)	(0.29)	(0.21)	(0.46)

Source: Columbia University human resource data tapes.
*Significant at the 1 percent level.
**Significant at the 5 percent level.
    a. Coefficients shown for "interaction analysis, EP, NEP" come from equations that also contain all other variables of the basic equations, that is, UNION, LC, FBR, IS, FHR, SHR, SZ, and IC. Coefficients for "expanded EP analysis", "individual plan analysis, EP", and "individual plan analysis, NEP" come from equations that also contain all other variables of the basic equations, that is, NEP, UNION, LC, FBR, IS, FHR, SHR, SZ, and IC. Numbers in parentheses are the standard errors.
    b. Includes controls for eight industries.

workers are closest to the production process, this finding lends intuitive support to the EP-PROD connection. Finally, no special interaction between EP and NEP is indicated. That is, firms can boost productivity by either means, but using the two together does not significantly add to, or subtract from, the effects of either in this sample.

The individual plan coefficients reported on table 8 suggest that most of the explanatory power of the EP variable comes from profit sharing.[183] This part shows the regression coefficients from separate regressions run for each of the EP components separately (along with the other explanatory variables). Not only is profit sharing significant and positive in the PROD equations, but it is also positively and significantly associated with ROI.[184] Our experiment with the alternative specification of

183. The coefficients for PS, GS, SO, ESOP, and INC come from regressions identical to those in the first panel of table 8 except for the use of the pay plan dummies.

184. Since the significance disappears when ROA is substituted for ROI, we are unsure about the interpretation of the result. Apparently there is a more positive association with

Table 9. Regressions Related to Firms' Economic Performance Trend and Economic and Noneconomic Participation of Employees, 1983–86[a]

Dependent variable	Clerical workers			Production workers		
	ROI_T	ROA_T	$PROD_T$	ROI_T	ROA_T	$PROD_T$
Constant	7.39*	6.22*	8.16*	7.82*	6.70*	9.21*
	(2.83)	(2.17)	(3.04)	(2.94)	(2.38)	(2.87)
EP	1.29**	1.20**	1.49**	1.53*	1.39**	2.20*
	(0.60)	(0.54)	(0.67)	(0.50)	(0.64)	(0.83)
NEP	1.37**	1.21*	1.34*	1.47**	1.44**	2.13*
	(0.63)	(0.45)	(0.65)	(0.70)	(0.68)	(0.78)
UNION	−0.67	−0.73	0.84	−0.92	−0.97	2.31*
	(0.43)	(0.46)	(0.57)	(0.62)	(0.65)	(0.86)
LC	1.12**	1.05**	1.17**	1.29**	1.22**	1.59**
	(0.55)	(0.51)	(0.56)	(0.60)	(0.58)	(0.74)
FBR	−0.32	−0.26	−0.34	−0.42	−0.37	−0.61
	(0.20)	(0.17)	(0.22)	(0.29)	(0.24)	(0.45)
IS	0.37	0.25	0.73	0.41	0.35	0.60
	(0.22)	(0.18)	(0.46)	(0.27)	(0.23)	(0.36)
FHR	1.05**	0.89	1.13**	1.24**	0.97	1.33**
	(0.48)	(0.57)	(0.52)	(0.59)	(0.64)	(0.60)
SHR	0.57	0.42	0.30	0.70	0.49	0.72
	(0.39)	(0.25)	(0.19)	(0.45)	(0.33)	(0.47)
SZ	−0.19	−0.23	−1.35**	−0.34	−0.30	−1.55**
	(0.12)	(0.15)	(0.66)	(0.23)	(0.18)	(0.73)
IC	b	b	b	b	b	b
Adjusted R^2	0.36	0.31	0.33	0.37	0.34	0.38
Number of observations	491	491	491	395	395	395
Interaction analysis, EP, NEP						
EP × NEP	0.83	0.87	0.91	0.86	0.93	0.96
	(0.49)	(0.51)	(0.54)	(0.48)	(0.55)	(0.57)
EP	1.16**	1.10**	1.34**	1.41*	1.27**	1.97*
	(0.54)	(0.51)	(0.64)	(0.60)	(0.58)	(0.76)
NEP	1.28**	1.13*	1.26**	1.32**	1.33**	1.99*
	(0.60)	(0.42)	(0.58)	(0.61)	(0.62)	(0.75)
Expanded EP analysis						
EP-Cler	1.19*	1.12**	1.38**	1.40*	1.26**	2.00*
	(0.53)	(0.50)	(0.63)	(0.53)	(0.57)	(0.78)
EP-Prod	1.37**	1.23**	1.47**	1.62*	1.38**	2.31*
	(0.64)	(0.56)	(0.69)	(0.64)	(0.65)	(0.83)

(continued)

Table 9 (*continued*)

Dependent variable	Clerical workers			Production workers		
	ROI_T	ROA_T	$PROD_T$	ROI_T	ROA_T	$PROD_T$
Individual plan analysis, *EP*						
PS	1.52**	1.41**	1.60**	1.62**	1.56**	2.31*
	(0.71)	(0.63)	(0.75)	(0.76)	(0.73)	(0.91)
GS	0.62	0.49	0.60	0.61	0.56	0.81
	(0.43)	(0.35)	(0.39)	(0.43)	(0.39)	(0.55)
SO	0.88	0.75	0.88	0.96	0.81	1.14**
	(0.56)	(0.50)	(0.55)	(0.68)	(0.56)	(0.53)
ESOP	1.36**	1.24**	1.33**	1.25**	1.21**	1.65**
	(0.64)	(0.57)	(0.59)	(0.57)	(0.58)	(0.79)
INC	0.68	0.65	0.74	0.73	0.68	0.76
	(0.48)	(0.53)	(0.45)	(0.43)	(0.41)	(0.44)
Individual plan analysis, *NEP*						
PART	0.73	0.69	1.24**	0.78	0.74	1.44**
	(0.47)	(0.40)	(0.57)	(0.49)	(0.47)	(0.69)
INFO	−0.38	−0.40	−0.73	−0.39	−0.45	−0.81
	(0.29)	(0.26)	(0.44)	(0.26)	(0.32)	(0.58)

Source: Columbia University human resource data tapes.
*Significant at the 1 percent level.
**Significant at the 5 percent level.
a. See note a, table 8.
b. Includes controls for eight industries.

the use of noneconomic participation suggests that the explanatory power comes from employee participation rather than information sharing.[185]

Trend regressions are shown in table 9. One can interpret the regression results reported as providing information about the ability to adapt and adjust in a difficult economic period, though with the caveats already noted. No matter which measure of improved economic performance is used—ROI_T, ROA_T, or $PROD_T$—EP appears as a positive and significant influence, along with *NEP* and *LC*. The finding that labor cost pressures (*LC*) in the 1980s led to steps that improved performance in the 1980s seems in keeping with the popular impressions of the structural changes that took place during this period.[186] Plan-specific coefficients reported

---

the denominator of *ROI* than with *ROA*, which wipes out the significance with the overall ratio. The reason for such a result is unclear.

185. The coefficients for *PART* and *INFO* come from regressions identical to those in the first panel of table 8 except for the use of the *PART* and *INFO* variables.

186. When we broke down the labor cost index into the presence of two-tier pay plans, the use of lump-sum payments, and the use of a wage freeze, all these separate components

on table 9 show that the effect of economic participation is dominated by the profit-sharing and ESOP components of *EP*. We take the link between economic participation and performance trend as a suggestive result, indicating the potential of participative measures, both economic and noneconomic, to assist enterprises in a period of transition.[187] *EP* for clerical and production workers appears to be separately significant in all equations, suggesting that the more extensively the firm used *EP*, the stronger was the enhancement of its transition period adjustment. Again, no interaction effects between *EP* and *NEP* are apparent.

Conclusions

The use of alternative pay systems in the American labor market is a result of a complex set of economic, historical, and institutional forces. A folk wisdom has grown up around the different types of plans. For example, the perils of perverse incentives from simple piece-rate schemes are now well known, and the use of such plans has apparently decreased, so that they are found mainly where the perversities are most controllable or alternatives are not available. Profit sharing is seen as a more general motivator and as a way of making labor costs variable, stabilizing employment, and sharing risks with employees. Gain sharing is the least widely used approach and is often viewed as requiring more elaborate employee decisionmaking participation than the other pay plans.

Our evidence on profit sharing, both from the practitioner literature and the data analysis, suggests that it does not substitute for other forms of pay. This finding, if true, raises questions about a recent macroeconomic argument for profit sharing—that it will increase labor demand—though the labor cost flexibility argument remains. During the difficult transition period of the mid-1980s, firms that featured economic participation for employees seemed to make the adjustment from recession to recovery more easily. Given recent prognostications that firms will be faced with more shocks and greater needs for adaptability in the future,[188]

---

appeared as separately significant in the production worker equations. Results for the separate components were weaker in the clerical equations.

187. When noneconomic participation is broken down into the *PART* and *INFO* variables, only *PART* manages to appear with significance in any of the regressions of table 9. Moreover, *INFO* appears with a negative sign. The *PART* and *INFO* regressions are identical to those in the first panel of table 9 except for the substitution for *NEP*. Similarly, the coefficients for the pay plans taken separately come from regressions identical to the first panel except for the substitution for *EP*.

188. See, for example, Michael J. Piore and Charles F. Sabel, *The Second Industrial Divide: Possibilities for Prosperity* (Basic Books, 1984).

further experimentation with alternative pay systems on the part of U.S.
management and labor is desirable.

Comment by Ronald G. Ehrenberg

In a 1987 paper George Milkovich and I concluded there was very
little empirical evidence available on why corporations choose the
compensation policies they do and on whether these policies have desired
incentive effects at either the corporate or individual level.[1] Given the
importance of these questions for both microeconomic and macroeconomic policies, the virtual flood of research directed toward answering
them during the past two years is not surprising. Besides the activity
generated by this Brookings volume, the Sloan Foundation, the National
Bureau of Economic Research, and Cornell have been jointly supporting
a major two-year project under my direction on the subject Do Compensation Policies Matter? Fifteen papers were presented at our project's
final conference at Cornell in May 1989 and will be published in a special
issue of the *Industrial and Labor Relations Review* in early 1990.

The Mitchell, Lewin, and Lawler paper is a very useful contribution
to the rapidly growing literature on pay systems. The authors begin with
a discussion of the historical evolution of incentive compensation, profit-
sharing, and gain-sharing plans in the United States. They stress, as
their colleague Sanford Jacoby has also recently stressed in a related
context, that "ebbs and flows in the use of particular pay systems reflect
a complex web of social movements, movements in managerial thinking,
trends in academic thinking, major economic events, and public policies
including tax preferences."[2] Put another way, the historical motivation
for the adoption of these policies seems to the casual observer to be
different from what current day analytical labor economists hypothesize.

Of course that does not mean that current day labor economists are
wrong (witness the Lester-Machlup controversy on the relevance of
marginal productivity in the 1940s). Rather, the message I take away
from the authors' observation is that the new economic theories of

---

1. Ronald G. Ehrenberg and George T. Milkovich, "Compensation and Firm Performance," in Morris M. Kleiner and others, eds., *Human Resources and the Performance
of Firms* (Madison, Wis.: Industrial Relations Research Association, 1987), pp. 87–122.

2. Sanford Jacoby, "What Can Modern Labor Economics Learn From the Industrial
Relations Tradition?" unpublished manuscript, 1989.

personnel must provide more than a rationalization for what we already observe. It is incumbent on labor economists to devise tests of their theories based on other predictions the theories may yield.

In fact, though Mitchell, Lewin, and Lawler do not cite them, there is a group of economists involved in such efforts. For example, my colleague Robert Hutchens recently summarized attempts by different researchers to test whether earnings profiles that rise with job tenure reflect human capital investments, deferred compensation arrangements to motivate workers and reduce shirking, or assortative job matching.[3] Similarly, Claudia Goldin used data from the 1890s to test whether monitoring cost arguments explain why female manufacturing workers were more likely to be paid by piece rates than male production workers at the turn of the century.[4]

A large part of the Mitchell, Lewin, and Lawler paper reviews the existing empirical literature on incentive effects of alternative pay systems and then presents some new evidence based on existing Bureau of Labor Statistics and Conference Board data sets, as well as a new Columbia University Business Unit data set. I will focus the rest of my remarks on that part of the paper.

The authors begin with the observation that previous studies, using data from the 1970s, have found significant wage premiums for incentive workers relative to workers paid by the hour. As they note, this may reflect *either* the effects of incentives on worker productivity or the attraction of the most productive workers to firms that offer them the opportunity to earn more. Though presumably either mode of increasing productivity (assuming wages reflect productivity) should be desirable to employers, some evidence shows that changing the nature of incentive plans *can* directly affect the productivity of existing workers. In particular, Andrew Weiss has shown that the shift from an individual to a group incentive plan systematically caused a narrowing in the productivity distribution of a firm's employees (high-productivity people facing diminished incentives reduced effort; low-productivity people now faced with peer pressure improved effort).[5]

3. Robert Hutchens, "Seniority, Wages, and Productivity: A Turbulent Decade," *Journal of Economic Perspectives* (forthcoming).
4. Claudia Goldin, "Monitoring Costs and Occupational Segregation by Sex: A Historical Analysis," *Journal of Labor Economics*, vol. 4 (January 1986), pp. 1–27.
5. Andrew Weiss, "Incentives and Worker Behavior: Some Evidence," in Haig Nalbantian, ed., *Incentives, Cooperation and Risk Sharing: Economic and Psychological*

The authors next present tests in tables 2 and 3 of whether wage premiums for incentive workers continued to exist in the 1980s. In table 2 they use data on an industry-occupation-region breakdown from eleven BLS wage surveys and estimate whether the log of the hourly wage in a cell depends on the existence of, and proportion of workers in the cell covered by, incentive wage plans. They find here that, other things being equal, incentive workers receive about a 7 percent wage premium. Their analyses control, however, only for industry and region of the country. There are no occupational controls, which may be an important omission if occupations have an independent effect on wages and if incentive plans are concentrated among certain occupational groups.

A more general problem with these analyses is that Mitchell, Lewin, and Lawler treat pay system parameters as exogenous. Surely at least economists believe that differences in pay policies may reflect systematic forces. The authors' failure to model the causes of variations in pay policies throughout their paper may bias virtually all their empirical results. Economists like Charles Brown have begun to model empirically why pay policies vary across employers, and Mitchell, Lewin, and Lawler might profitably consult his and other studies.[6]

In their analyses in table 3, using BLS data on individual workers in two industries, they find, after controlling for establishment size, union coverage, metropolitan location, and occupation, that workers covered by incentive plans earn about 21 percent more in each industry. Besides again treating incentive plans as exogenous, the authors do not include establishment dummy variables in the analyses here. It is unfortunate that their data set does not permit them to do so. If it did, they would be able to separate out effects of incentive plans and other omitted establishment policies on wages (for example, work force quality and hourly wage levels).

The authors note in passing that while there has been no statistical work by academics on the effects of sales commissions, surveys by business-related research groups suggest that commission-paid workers are paid more and that these differentials are probably wide enough to withstand the kinds of statistical standardization that academics do. This conclusion seems a bit too uncritical for me. I dug one of the underlying

Perspectives on Employment Contracts (Totowa, N.J.: Rowman and Littlefield, 1987), pp. 137–50.

6. Charles Brown, "Firms' Choice of Method of Pay," *Industrial and Labor Relations Review* (forthcoming).

studies out of the Industrial and Labor Relations library and found that it pertained to 607 employers spread over both manufacturing and other industries.[7] Sales revenue ranged from less than $4 million to greater than $1.7 billion, and sales staff size from fewer than 50 to more than 2,000 for these employers. If one thinks the propensity to have a commission plan varies with firm size or industry, one might question what the raw differential means. Indeed, Charles Brown did find in his paper that the probability of observing that incentive plans exist is positively related to firm size.

It is, however, interesting to note that the study to which the authors referred found that the commission-noncommission differential was less than 3 percent for inside sales workers, about 10 percent for outside sales workers, and about 20 percent for managers of sales. *If* we take these results at face value, the small differential for inside sales workers is consistent with the view espoused by my colleague Bob Frank, that when people work in close proximity, employees' concerns over their and their colleagues' relative earnings are likely to cause employers to moderate productivity-related wage differentials.[8] The larger differential for managers of sales also coincides with the view of many compensation specialists that incentive-type plans are more effective at higher levels in the employment hierarchy.[9]

Mitchell, Lewin, and Lawler's next empirical analyses examine whether profit-sharing plans substitute for, or are add-ons to, other wages and fringes; if profit-sharing arrangements are to induce desirable Weitzman-type macroeconomic effects, the authors argue that substitution must take place. Their analyses, presented in table 4, that use Conference Board data for 419 firms find no substitution of profit sharing for indexes of fringes or pensions. Similarly, their analyses of BLS establishment-level data presented in table 5 do not find a substitution of bonus payments for wages.

In each of these analyses, however, no controls for worker quality are present, and the right-hand-side incentive pay policy variables are again treated as exogenous. The authors are well aware of possible simultaneity problems but nonetheless draw strong conclusions about

7. Carla O'Dell and Jerry McAdams," *People, Performance and Pay* (Houston, Tex.: American Productivity Center, 1987), pp. 75–83.

8. Robert H. Frank, *Choosing the Right Pond: Human Behavior and the Quest for Status* (Oxford University Press, 1985).

9. George T. Milkovich and Jerry M. Newman, *Compensation*, 2d ed. (Plano, Tex.: Business Publications, 1987).

whether profit-sharing arrangements are, in their words, "gravy or add-ons." In fact, similar simultaneity problems have plagued all studies that have sought to estimate compensating wage differentials for favorable or unfavorable job characteristics.[10] I would thus urge the authors to be cautious about drawing conclusions here and would again urge them to try to model the determinants of profit-sharing provisions.

The authors' final statistical analyses involve their use of survey responses from the newly collected Columbia Business Unit data set (henceforth the CBU data) to try to estimate whether pay policies influence productivity and firm performance. At the outset I must note that the 6.5 percent response rate (after eliminating unusable responses) to this survey is dismal and leads one to be concerned about possible sample selection bias. To allay my fears, the authors need more than their present footnote statement: "Analysis of the COMPUSTAT information on nonrespondents did not suggest any bias in the sample obtained." Rather, they should present a formal multivariate analysis of the probability of response and discuss this in the paper. If systematic relationships exist, by now well-known sample-selection bias correction methods can be used.

The CBU data contain information on pay policies for four occupational categories—managers, professional and technical, clerical, and manufacturing workers. Somewhat surprisingly, in light of an extensive literature that deals with the effects of executive pay policies on firm performance, the authors confine their attention to the latter two groups.[11] This seems ill advised for two reasons. First, since the activities of all occupational groups influence aggregate firm performance measures, presumably the pay policies applicable to *all* groups should simultaneously enter the business unit outcome equations. But instead the authors try to estimate the effects of production or clerical groups' policies on business unit outcomes in a separate equation for each group (tables 8 and 9). Second, to the extent that pay policies are correlated (but not perfectly so) across occupational groups within a business unit, unsuspecting readers may draw erroneous conclusions. For example, what they estimate to be the effects of profit sharing for clerical workers on financial variables (table 8) may instead capture the effect of profit

10. Robert S. Smith and Ronald G. Ehrenberg, "Estimating Wage-Fringe Tradeoffs: Some Data Problems," in Jack E. Triplett, ed., *The Measurement of Labor Costs* (University of Chicago Press, 1983), pp. 347–69.

11. Ehrenberg and Milkovich, "Compensation and Firm Performance."

sharing for managers. In this case, a reader might draw the wrong conclusion (in my example, that he or she should institute profit sharing for his or her clerical workers).

Their analyses in tables 8 and 9 relate financial measures of performance and productivity measures (sales revenue per employee), as well as recent changes in these measures, to the existence of profit sharing, gain sharing, or other incentive arrangements and a set of control variables. The latter include measures of unionization, indexes of noneconomic participation of workers, of fringe benefits, of the intensity of supervision, of the formality of human resource practices, of the status of the human resource function, and of recent labor cost pressures, as well as firm size and industry dummy variables.[12]

Their key finding in these tables is that profit-sharing plans seem to be positively associated with financial performance and productivity levels, as well as improvements in the levels. However, as the authors note, their analyses again treat the existence of profit sharing as exogenous. Now *if* profit sharing was instituted primarily when historically high-profit firms were *temporarily* in economic difficulty, one would expect to observe these firms' profits rising to above-average levels in the future independent of the profit-sharing plan. This "regression to the firm's historically mean performance" would lead to a spurious positive correlation, in the years after the plan was adopted, between the presence of profit sharing and the financial and productivity (measured by *sales* dollars) variables and their recent changes. Put another way, their

---

12. This is not the proper forum to criticize extensively the use throughout the paper of the indexes (for example, presence of fringe index in table 4 and all the indexes in tables 8 and 9). Although the authors make reference several times to the precedent in the industrial relations literature for the use of indexes based on the summing of (0,1)— yes/no–type variables, in fact many statisticians, economists, and industrial relations specialists have great problems with the *arbitrary* conversion of various qualitative items to a single quantitative scale. Some difficulties involved in constructing such scales for public sector bargaining laws and nonwage contract provisions are discussed by Reichman and Chaykowski, respectively. Gary Reichman, "The Influence of Public Policy on Fringes and Salaries in the Public Sector," M.S. thesis, Cornell University, 1983; and Richard Chaykowski, "The Empirical Formulation of Nonwage Collective Bargaining Outcomes," *Queen's Papers in Industrial Relations, 1988–8* (Kingston: Queen's University, School of Industrial Relations, July 1988. The authors might turn to these sources for further discussion. Though I do not want to belabor this point, the difference in results they obtain in tables 8 and 9 when *EP* is split into its constituent parts is evidence of the problem of using the constructed index as an explanatory variable. Chaykowski shows how serious problems may arise when such a constructed index is used as a dependent variable.

assertions to the contrary, before one can take their results at face value, the authors need to conduct some analyses that treat the existence of profit sharing (and other incentive schemes) as endogenous.

In concluding my comments, I might note that the authors' extraordinarily comprehensive and useful treatment of incentive pay, profit sharing, and gain sharing and their effects on firm performance and productivity has necessarily omitted some topics. There is no discussion of executive and managerial compensation policies in their paper, nor of how such policies affect firm performance.[13] They do not discuss recent attempts by myself and others to see whether tournament compensation structures influence workers' behavior.[14] Finally, they do not discuss nonwage aspects of the compensation package and how the level and structure of employee benefits may influence worker behavior.[15] There are long empirical literatures in each of these areas to which interested readers can refer.

13. Much of this research is summarized in Ehrenberg and Milkovich, "Compensation and Firm Performance." A series of papers from the Cornell conference, forthcoming in the *Industrial Labor Relations Review*, discusses these topics further.

14. See, for example, Ronald G. Ehrenberg and Michael L. Bognanno, "Do Tournaments Have Incentive Effects?" Working Paper 2638 (Cambridge, Mass.: National Bureau of Economic Research, June 1988).

15. A recent example of this literature is Ronald G. Ehrenberg and others, "School District Leave Policies, Teacher Absenteeism and Student Achievement," Working Paper 2874 (Cambridge, Mass.: National Bureau of Economic Research, March 1989).

Profit Sharing and Productivity

Martin L. Weitzman
Douglas L. Kruse

RECENTLY there has been a strong growth of interest in profit sharing and related forms of pay for group performance.[1] Many reasons undoubtedly exist for this heightened attention. The primary motive probably has to do with the perception that by giving workers a partial stake in their company's performance, profit sharing may, under certain circumstances, lead to desirable outcomes that ultimately increase productivity. If this perception contains an element of truth, widespread profit sharing might conceivably improve national "competitiveness," with consequent policy implications. In such a context, but also for more general reasons, it becomes important to sort out and evaluate as systematically as possible the evidence on a possible link between profit sharing and productivity.

The purpose of this paper is to bring together the partial strands of eclectic evidence from a wide variety of fields and perspectives, including considerations of economic theory, observations from comparative economic systems, industrial relations case studies and surveys of attitudes, and formal econometric investigations. Although we try to be reasonably comprehensive, detached, and objective in this survey, the possible link between profit sharing and productivity is ultimately not the sort of proposition that lends itself to crisp proof or disproof. We cannot honestly give decisive answers and must end up instead with the traditional plea for more research. And more research is genuinely needed in this area. Yet, without denying all that, we think it also fair to conclude that total agnosticism is not warranted. Profit sharing is not as likely to impair as to improve productivity. The weight of the evidence

We would like to thank Andrea Ichino for outstanding research assistance.

1. Throughout most of this paper the term *profit sharing* is used as the generic indicator of group performance, thereby obscuring the distinction with the more narrowly defined *gain sharing* and other such related forms of pay for group performance. The reasons for this uniform treatment is discussed in the section on case studies.

leans toward a positive link. From many different sources there emerges a moderately consistent pattern of *weak support* for the proposition that profit sharing improves productivity. Any one piece of evidence can legitimately be challenged because no single piece is conclusive. But taken as a whole, the many different parts add up to a fairly coherent picture of a weak positive link between profit sharing and productivity.

The paper is organized as follows. In the first section we attempt to use contemporary economic theory to shed light on the possible connections between profit sharing and productivity. Next we try to pull together the admittedly loose evidence that emerges from observing comparative economic systems. We then summarize the relevant findings of the literature, which is also somewhat loose, on case studies, surveys of attitudes, and simple statistical studies. In the following section we survey the existing formal econometric studies. Afterwards, we try to integrate all the disparate pieces, concluding, as already mentioned, that there is consistent, if weak, support for the proposition that profit sharing can improve productivity. Finally, in the last section we speculate on the possible policy implications of that link.

Economic Theory

In general, economic theory can provide a powerful organizing framework for thinking consistently about certain economic issues. And it often suggests the outlines of an answer to some specific question. But pure theory rarely provides a definitive answer. Every model has a counter-model, and judgments about which models apply to which situations are ultimately empirical. The particular issue under examination here—the relation between profit sharing and productivity—is no exception to this generalization. The subject involves a particularly complicated interplay of economic and other motivations that rubs awkwardly against the confines of conventional theorizing. Nevertheless, we think that economic theory can be used here both to frame the main theoretical issues and to offer some explanatory power. We begin with the simplest conventional model and work our way up to more complicated contemporary models that incorporate increasingly sophisticated considerations. Throughout, the emphasis is on talking through a particular application—what the models might say about the real world connection between profit sharing and productivity—not on modeling per se.

The Prototype

The simple one-person case is what most people have in mind as the prototype of the advantages of profit sharing. It illustrates nicely many of the principal issues and can serve as a point of departure for more sophisticated models.

Suppose that a person produces a single output from a single input according to some well-defined production function. The input is most easily thought of as a generic combination of hours of work and effort. The hours part of labor input can be measured, but the effort part largely cannot be. Effort might stand for all sorts of unobservable things like working harder, working smarter, taking initiative, and taking advantage of unforeseen opportunities of time and place. Individual small-scale farming might be a good example of this kind of paradigm, but there are many others.

A "wage system" in the present context would pay the hired farmer-worker a fixed wage in return for a fixed number of hours of labor. The fixed hours, in conjunction with a certain verifiable level of effort set by implicit or explicit standards, would yield some level of output. Unfortunately, there is no guarantee that this output level is efficient. In particular, with effort both unpleasurable and difficult or otherwise costly to monitor (at least beyond a certain point), the wage system would result in too little output being produced relative to what is socially optimal. In other words, a wage system tends to result in low productivity equilibriums, where the marginal value of an extra unit of effort exceeds its marginal cost.

The obvious solution is to pay the hired farmer the value of his output over some fixed amount accounting for economic rent. This kind of profit sharing will automatically guarantee an efficient outcome, where the marginal value of an extra unit of output is equal to the marginal effort-cost of producing it. When the farmer-worker is paid for what he produces, he will automatically adjust his effort to the optimal degree. Here, then, a switch from a wage system to a profit-sharing system would increase productivity.

Such a simple example of a farmer-worker is what most people have in mind when they assume that a profit-sharing system can be expected to increase productivity relative to a wage system. Common sense tells them that a worker will work harder and produce more output under profit sharing than under a rigid wage system because he or she has some stake in the outcome. Even though the basic message of this example can be diluted by more sophisticated formulations, a germ of truth remains. The key insight is that under profit sharing high productivity is rewarded with more pay, so there tends to be *some* pressure to move toward modes of behavior that increase output.

As applied to an individual farmer-worker, the proposition that profit sharing increases productivity is one of the more spectacular examples of simple theory giving an essentially correct insight that is confirmed by experience. One may fairly generalize that throughout the world, other things being equal, agriculture run on a decentralized "responsibility system" with rewards directly linked to output is more efficient than agriculture run on a centralized, labor-for-hire type system with rewards far removed from performance.[2]

This simple model, however, omits certain aspects of reality. In the next three subsections we treat what we consider to be the three most important deviations from the basic model. These are: the free rider problem of individual incentives that become diluted in a group setting where rewards are linked to group effort; risk-bearing issues associated with profit sharing that expose workers to an unacceptable degree of pay variation; and the possible weakening of capitalist property rights under profit sharing through some form of codetermination.

The Free Rider Problem

Some difficult issues are connected with understanding what extension, if any, of the single farmer-worker model applies to a multiworker setting, where profit sharing is naturally tied to group performance. A dilution or free rider problem seems to arise whenever it is hard to monitor a single person's contribution, as is presumably frequently the case. An externality is present because any one person's reward depends on everyone else's effort. With n members of the group, the extra profit-sharing reward associated with marginal effort on any single worker's part is diluted by a factor of $1/n$. The result is an inefficiently low level of effort, which is lower as n is larger. Following the logic of the static Nash equilibrium framework, profit sharing might not have very much effect on a large organization, since every member would hold back effort while trying to free ride off the others.

Such a free rider scenario is often used to argue that group incentives will be ineffective for any reasonably large value of n, and therefore, by

2. Of course there are exceptions that prove the rule, such as, perhaps, some aspects of California agribusiness.

default, relatively greater emphasis should be placed on individual incentives. This argument doubtless has some truth. Yet there is an important caveat. In a repeated game setting the conclusions may be quite different.

The profit-sharing "game" is a form of prisoner's dilemma. All members of the collective are potentially better off if everyone works harder. Yet there is always a temptation for any single individual to shirk, because per capita output and the reward of any member of the group will not be much affected when one person's effort is reduced. (Hence the conclusion in a static context that one-shot profit sharing will not have much effect on effort and output.) But when the game is repeated, which corresponds to a long-term relationship among the workers, a much richer set of strategies emerges in the resulting non-cooperative "supergame." Depending on the specifics of how the technology of observation and production is modeled, workers may punish shirking workers by withholding their own effort or, if feasible, ostracizing the offending antisocial shirkers. In such a setting an enormous number of dynamic equilibrium strategies can exist. Among the equilibria, if the participants' discount rate is sufficiently small, is the cooperative strategy in which all participants choose to work at the socially optimal level. (This is a particular application of the so-called folk theorem of noncooperative game theory.)[3] Thus there is a rigorous sense in which profit sharing *may* defeat the prisoner's dilemma free rider problem and induce greater productivity in a multiperson setting. By contrast, a rigid wage system does not have a chance to improve productivity, because rewards are independent of effort. With profit sharing, as opposed to a rigid wage system, there are modes of behavior that can make everyone better off, and it may be individually rational to pursue such modes for the long-term benefits they yield.

The theory we have outlined—that repetition allows for the possibility of self-enforcing socially desirable outcomes when rewards are linked to group performance—is not without its problems. Profit sharing *may* induce greater productivity, so that the single farmer-worker model can be extended to groups, but other outcomes like narrowly self-interested shirking are possible as well.

Equilibrium is a state of rest from which no agent has an incentive to

3. See Drew Fudenberg and Eric Maskin, "The Folk Theorem in Repeated Games with Discounting or with Incomplete Information," *Econometrica*, vol. 54 (May 1986), pp. 533–54. For a readable account of a broad series of related issues, see Robert M. Axelrod, *The Evolution of Cooperation* (Basic Books, 1984).

deviate, given that all other agents are at equilibrium in the same state of rest. When there are multiple equilibria (in this case an uncountable infinity of them), the relevant equilibrium depends on a complex, typically unspecified interaction between the underlying dynamic process and initial conditions. At present, theory does not offer much guidance on which equilibria are more likely to emerge under what conditions. In a way the theory can be interpreted as highlighting considerations of history, chance, culture, exhortation, institutional detail, and the like.[4]

In the end, repeated game theory delivers a complicated message about the likely effects of profit sharing on productivity in a multiperson organization. It is possible that profit sharing will lead to increased productivity. But it is possible that it will not. The outcome would seem to depend on whether an organization can convince its members that everyone pulling together is essentially a better idea than everyone pulling separately. In some equilibria it may be in my long-term self-interest to pull together because everyone else is pulling together, and if I do not I risk the danger of unraveling the social compact. In some other self-fulfilling equilibria it may not be in my long-term interest to pull together because no one else is pulling together, and I do not think my good behavior is going to influence anyone else.

An attempt to sum up the implications of this particular application of theoretical research to the effect of profit sharing on productivity might go as follows. To some extent the door is open for believing that, by comparison with an unresponsive wage system, a group-based reward system can improve productivity. But it appears to be not enough for management just to install a profit-sharing system and walk out the door. To get the productivity-enhancing effects, something more may be needed—something akin to developing a corporate culture that emphasizes company spirit, promotes group cooperation, encourages social enforcement mechanisms, and so forth.

Risk Issues

Another problem with our original farmer-worker model is that it abstracts away from risk. In a deterministic context, linking a worker's pay to his or her output makes good sense, because it will encourage the

---

4. For related interpretations, see David M. Kreps, "Corporate Culture and Economic Theory," Stanford University, 1984; and Roy Radner, "The Internal Economy of Large Firms," *Economic Journal*, vol. 96 (Supplement, 1986), pp. 1–22.

socially optimal degree of effort. But what happens in the presence of uncertainty? Then the correct contract is not so clear. A higher degree of profit sharing relative to the base wage will elicit more effort from the worker but will also expose him to greater risk. Sometimes this risk-exposure argument is put forth as if it were a compelling reason that workers should be paid only base wages without any profit shares. But on closer examination, the argument is not decisive.

This set of issues has been extensively examined in the theoretical literature under the heading of the so-called principal-agent problem.[5] In the present setting the agent is the farmer-worker, while the principal is the hiring party who is ultimately interested in output. On the one hand, an efficient contract should link the agent's reward closely to output because that will elicit greater, or more attentive, work effort. On the other hand, in a world of uncertainty the agent's pay should be made relatively stable, because the agent is typically more averse to risk than the principal. (A company can diversify risks more easily than a worker, whose pay constitutes the main component of his income portfolio.) The optimal contract balances these two opposing considerations of effort and exposure to risk.

The theory can be used to derive a formula for the optimal mix of base wage and profit share.[6] The formula for the optimal profit share is typically a complicated function inversely related to the degree of risk aversion or the amount of uncertainty and directly related to the elasticity response of output to increased effort. Explicit modeling of risk considerations does not per se eliminate the argument for profit sharing, though it probably lowers the degree of profit sharing in the optimal pay formula (from 100 percent) to soften the exposure to risk. More important, the theory shows that under standard assumptions it is quite difficult to derive a corner solution where the efficient pay contract involves only straight wages and no profit sharing.

An additional consideration in any analysis of the risk aspect of a profit-sharing contract is the effect on employment. Standard principal-agent theory evades this issue. The theory is, in essence, about the individual high-seniority worker who already has job tenure, not about the aggregate of all would-be workers. In a world of sticky pay parame-

5. For a survey see Oliver Hart and Bengt Holmstrom, "The Theory of Contracts," in Truman F. Bewley, ed., *Advances in Economic Theory—Fifth World Congress* (Cambridge University Press, 1987), pp. 71–155, and the references cited there.

6. See, for example, Martin L. Weitzman, "Efficient Incentive Contracts," *Quarterly Journal of Economics*, vol. 94 (June 1980), pp. 719–30.

ters, profit sharing may help to reduce employment fluctuations. If that is so—and this interpretation is controversial—the argument for profit sharing might be somewhat stronger than what is suggested by standard principal-agent theory.[7]

The risk of unemployment is probably the largest income risk faced by labor as a whole, as opposed to the median tenured worker, and it is concentrated on the marginal or outsider worker. If more variable pay for the individual helps to preserve full employment for the group, whereas fixed pay for the individual tends to contribute to unemployment, overall welfare might be improved by having more profit sharing, because of the difference between first-order Okun-gap-type unemployment losses and second-order Harberger-triangle-type random redistribution losses. Of course the insiders, whose pay is made more variable by profit sharing, may resent the sacrifice being extracted on behalf of the outsiders, whose employment is possibly made more secure, and may react adversely. Any attempt to balance this out by side payments from insiders to outsiders could in practice create a serious labor relations problem. (Although there is some overlap, by and large this set of employment-related issues is outside the main scope of our paper.)

Codetermination Issues

The repeated prisoner's dilemma argument previously outlined shows that, other things being equal, profit sharing may improve effort and productivity despite a dilution or free rider problem. In effect, it may be in the self-interest of each member of the work collective to act over time like one artificially aggregated worker, and therefore to work harder under profit sharing. However, this argument neglects one potentially significant element.

If workers share more profits, then capitalists of necessity share less. One must therefore worry about whether diluting the capitalists' incentives might not weaken or fatally compromise their motivation, discretion, power, or authority. For example, increased worker profit sharing may lead to increased worker demands for codetermination in enterprise decisionmaking.

7. For an advocate's argument of this case, see Martin L. Weitzman, *The Share Economy: Conquering Stagflation* (Harvard University Press, 1984); and Weitzman, *The Case for Profit Sharing* (London: Employment Institute, 1986). See Douglas L. Kruse, "Essays on Profit-sharing and Unemployment," Ph.D. dissertation, Harvard University, 1988, for some empirical evidence in favor of this interpretation.

The theoretical arguments, pro and con, on this set of issues are complex because the applicable models are usually concerned only with partial aspects, and in any event they are not fully developed. A complete model would be very messy technically, including as it should considerations of information, monitoring, supervision, dynamic gaming, risk sharing, insider versus outsider workers, and many other issues. At present economists do not fully understand on a theoretical level the possible connection between increased worker profit sharing and increased codetermination in enterprise decisionmaking.

At a practical level, the connection between profit sharing and codetermination is also poorly understood. There are many examples of profit sharing without codetermination. Indeed, that would appear to be the typical pattern in the United States. It seems possible to believe that some profit sharing is basically productive, whereas the more extreme forms of European-style legislated codetermination are essentially counterproductive. Thus we are admittedly on uncomfortable ground in this paper when we try to concentrate on profit sharing per se while blurring the already murky boundary with issues of worker control.[8] The critiques and defenses that have arisen are really of worker management rather than of profit sharing per se. No one, so far as we can tell, has attempted to disentangle the two issues carefully.

In the extreme case of perfectly costless monitoring and supervision, an efficient outcome requires that management be given all the residual claims on profits and all decisionmaking power. This basic insight underlies the claims of some members of the "property rights" school that profit sharing, insofar as it involves worker management, is likely to be inefficient because it diverts vesting of property rights from the capitalist central monitors to individualistically oriented workers whose motivation is diluted by the free rider problem.[9] In this view, profit sharing would be associated with lower productivity because of more shirking, increased enjoyment of on-the-job leisure, slowed or incorrect managerial decisions, a too-short time horizon, an excessively risk-averse attitude due to a nondiversified pay portfolio, and the like. Although there are many variations, the basic theme of the critique of

8. For more on the latter, see the paper by Laura D'Andrea Tyson and David Levine in this volume.

9. See Armen A. Alchian and Harold Demsetz, "Production, Information Costs, and Economic Organization," *American Economic Review*, vol. 62 (December 1972), pp. 777–95; and Michael C. Jensen and William H. Meckling, "Rights and Production Functions: An Application to Labor-Managed Firms and Codetermination," *Journal of Business*, vol. 52 (October 1979), pp. 469–506.

codetermination by the property rights school revolves around the idea that (1) the essence of the firm concerns monitoring because otherwise labor does not work well, (2) capital can effectively monitor labor, and, therefore, (3) efficiency requires that capital be given all residual claims on profits and all decisionmaking power.

The defense of profit sharing and worker participation largely involves challenging the basic assumptions of the property rights school.[10] In less extreme settings than perfectly costless monitoring and supervision, finding the optimal degree of profit sharing becomes an extraordinarily complicated problem in the theory of the second or third best. Some profit sharing may be desirable in a world where workers can sometimes monitor, supervise, and motivate each other more effectively than management can, or where workers are able to provide technical information to management that would otherwise be costly or time consuming to obtain. For what it is worth, the popular literature is full of talk about the importance of corporate culture, cooperative work environments, team spirit, peer pressure, and the like.[11] Proponents of profit sharing and worker participation stress the potential for improved channels of information processing, better conflict resolution, greater possibilities for acquiring on-the-job human capital from other workers, a more positive attitude toward the introduction of new technology, and other good things.

This survey of the worker control issue is a necessarily brief review of some subtle and complicated arguments, whose connection with profit sharing is poorly understood.[12] The main element of the debate seems to center on the appropriate model of monitoring, supervision, and incentives to shirk. Explicit consideration of property rights does not per se eliminate the argument for profit sharing, though it may well affect one's view of the optimal degree of profit sharing. We think the appropriate application of the theory of property rights indicates that quite extreme assumptions are needed to derive a corner solution in which the efficient

10. For well-developed arguments see, for example, Louis Putterman, "On Some Recent Explanations of Why Capital Hires Labor," *Economic Inquiry*, vol. 22 (January 1984), pp. 171–87; and Haig R. Nalbantian, "Incentive Compensation in Perspective," in Haig R. Nalbantian, ed., *Incentives, Cooperation, and Risk Sharing: Economic and Psychological Perspectives on Employment Contracts* (Totowa, N.J.: Rowman and Littlefield, 1987), pp. 3–43.

11. See, for example, Carla O'Dell and Jerry McAdams, *People, Performance, and Pay* (Austin, Tex.: American Productivity Center, 1987); and Rosabeth Moss Kanter, "The Attack on Pay," *Harvard Business Review*, vol. 65 (March–April 1987), pp. 60–67.

12. For more detail see the works cited in notes 9 and 10.

pay contract would consist entirely of base wages, with zero profit sharing. In that sense our conclusions are analogous to those we drew from the principal-agency theory.

Summary

One could go further in applying modern economic theory to analyze the likely effect of profit sharing on productivity, but we believe the main themes have been covered.

If we take all considerations into account, what does contemporary economic theory say about the relation between profit sharing and productivity? The message is complicated and incomplete. Certainly theory does not rule out the possibility that, even in a multiperson context, profit sharing may increase productivity. Whether this happens may depend largely on historical and institutional factors in the workplace. On balance, the theoretical considerations point more toward a positive than a negative effect of profit sharing on productivity. When all relevant considerations are factored in, it seems unlikely that a corner solution consisting of all base wages and zero profit sharing can be an efficient contract. Such an extreme outcome would have a probability measure close to zero, given reasonable probability distributions on underlying model parameters. Although we are far from being able to give an operational formula for the optimal degree of profit sharing, on theoretical grounds alone a value of exactly zero seems implausible. We think that, taken as a whole, economic theory is suggesting the plausible existence of a positive relation between some modest degree of profit sharing and some modest degree of productivity enhancement. But, as usual, theory gives us few hints about quantitative magnitudes.

Comparative Systems

The evidence of a link between profit sharing and productivity gained from studying comparative economic systems is of necessity very loose. The evidence is loose because economic societies have so many differences that it is extremely hard to isolate the pure effects of one particular institution, such as profit sharing, while holding everything else constant. One is forced to fall back on soft, impure arguments by extension and other suspect reasoning that are easy targets for criticism.

It seems fair to say that capitalism, the system that relies primarily on the profit motive, is more productive than socialism, the system that promises full employment to everyone at fixed pay. This sweeping generalization is naturally subject to qualifications, exceptions, and caveats. Nevertheless, we think that the evidence—from specific studies of public enterprises, through observations about bureaucracies and private enterprises, to comparisons of socialist and capitalist experiences—yields as powerful a general message as can be found in economics.[13] Capitalism may not be very good at ensuring economic security or income equality. But it is *relatively* good at delivering efficiency and productivity. Exceptions abound, of course, but this powerful general message remains a broad truth in a world that allows few economic certainties of comparable scope.

Why is a system based on individualistic, decentralized pursuit of the profit motive more productive than a system based on job security at fixed pay? Probably because capitalism embeds in the sociopolitical system a strong local constituency for profitability. Throughout the economy profit-sensitive or profit-directed agents are effectively installed in focal decisionmaking positions. At some point in the capitalist economic hierarchy, an agent who is rewarded by enterprise profitability will put pressure on subordinates to take measures, frequently politically or socially unpopular, to increase profits. This constituency of profit-sensitive agents with decisionmaking power, then, has the authority to make seemingly antisocial decisions in pursuit of its own goals. The essential argument for capitalism is that such a seemingly paradoxical power arrangement works fairly well in practice—compared with the alternatives. The capitalist system automatically delivers efficiency and productivity because that helps the key decisionmaking agents who benefit from the profits. Socialism, in contrast, has a less distinguished record for efficiency and productivity because rewards are not tied closely to performance, and there is no comparable local constituency for profitability to resist more immediately humanitarian aspirations, various "higher goals," bureaucratic inertia, and other features of the system.

From this line of reasoning, one is tempted to conclude, as a kind of heuristic argument by continuous extension, that, other things being equal and within a reasonable range, the broader and deeper the constituency for profitability, the greater the pressure on the system to

13. See, for example, Abram Bergson, "Comparative Productivity: The USSR, Eastern Europe, and the West," *American Economic Review*, vol. 77 (June 1987), pp. 342–57; and Raymond Vernon, *The Promise of Privatization: A Challenge for U.S. Policy* (New York: Council on Foreign Relations, 1988).

increase productivity. The thought goes: "If the profit motive is good for productivity, so is profit sharing." This argument by continuous extension from comparative systems to profit sharing is not rigorous, but it is not implausible either. If the pay of managers as well as owners is linked to profitability, managers have a more direct incentive to be alert to productivity-enhancing measures. If workers, as well as managers and owners, have bonuses linked to profits, they are probably, other things being equal, going to work harder and be more sympathetic to the introduction of new machinery or flexible work rules that increase productivity.

This general line of argument—that to enhance productivity, local agents who care about local profitability must be installed throughout the system—has wide recognition in socialist countries today. Current debate about economic reforms in the Soviet Union, China, and other socialist countries is largely, though not entirely, about linking rewards more closely to performance.[14] Socialist economies often promote meaningful profit sharing in one form or another as a socially acceptable way of creating a broad-based local constituency for profitability that can help to resist the inertia of bureaucratic control. While none of these changes "proves" that profit sharing increases productivity, the beliefs and experiences of socialist reformers seem at least to aim in that direction. Without overdoing the point, it does not seem totally unfair to use a basic empirical generalization from studying comparative economic systems to permit some modest part of the productivity luster of the for-profit system to rub off on profit sharing.

Other suggestive but slightly "cleaner" evidence comes from comparing capitalist countries. Japan, Korea, and Taiwan all have widespread bonus payment systems with strong profit-sharing overtones. (Singapore is now also strongly encouraging the introduction of profit sharing.) In Japan bonuses paid twice a year constitute about 25 percent

14. This includes letting unprofitable enterprises fail, which is just one way in which traditional Yugoslav worker-managed cooperatives have differed from genuine profit-sharing institutions. On economic reform in the Soviet Union, see Ed A. Hewett, *Reforming the Soviet Economy* (Brookings, 1988); Joseph S. Berliner, "Statement," in *Economic Reforms in the U.S.S.R.*, Hearings before the Subcommittee on National Security Economics of the Joint Economic Committee, S. Hrg. 100-749, 100 Cong. 1 sess. (GPO, 1988), pp. 269–85; and Abel G. Aganbegian, *The Economic Challenge of Perestroika* (University of Indiana Press, 1988). On China, see Dwight H. Perkins, "Reforming China's Economic System," *Journal of Economic Literature*, vol. 26 (June 1988), pp. 601–45. For an overview of the socialist reform process in Hungary, see Janos Kornai, "The Hungarian Reform Process," *Journal of Economic Literature*, vol. 24 (December 1986), pp. 1687–1737.

of an average worker's total pay. The ratio of bonus to base wage is statistically significantly correlated with profitability, though the elasticity is much less than one.[15] In Korea and Taiwan the quarterly bonuses constitute about 15 percent of an average worker's total pay and, at least in Korea, there is a statistically significant correlation between the ratio of bonus to base wage and profitability.[16]

An important question is what role, if any, these bonus payment systems play in the remarkable productivity and employment records of the Japanese, Korean, and Taiwanese economies. The question is difficult to answer. Serious research is just beginning. It will probably be hard to reach firm conclusions for all the usual reasons, including the extreme difficulty of disentangling the role of one particular factor in the very complicated set of institutional arrangements we call an industrial relations system.

At the minimum, however, the experiences of Japan, Korea, and Taiwan strongly suggest that bonus payment systems with profit-sharing overtones are not inherently counterproductive. Of course we are not able to say exactly what role the profit-sharing bonus per se plays, since it is so intertwined with other factors. Nevertheless, these three economies are otherwise distinct enough to make the common strand of a meaningful bonus system intriguing. On-the-scene participants and observers in the three countries tend to believe that the bonus system is not just a form of disguised wage, but that it is there for a reason. The reason most often cited follows a familiar story line: a group performance payment mechanism helps to unite the interests of workers and management by giving everyone a stake in the outcome and encouraging positive, flexible, productivity-enhancing workplace behavior.

What emerges from these broad observations of comparative systems is admittedly loose and subject to multiple interpretations. Taken by itself, the evidence is not compelling. Nevertheless, though far from being conclusive, the "big picture" from comparative economic systems at least suggests there is a positive relation between profit sharing and productivity.

15. For a description of the Japanese bonus system (and an attempt at assessing its economic effect), see Richard B. Freeman and Martin L. Weitzman, "Bonuses and Employment in Japan," *Journal of the Japanese and International Economies*, vol. 1 (June 1987), pp. 168–94, and the references cited there.
16. Joon Woo Kim, "Bonuses and Employment in Korea," senior thesis, Harvard University, 1988.

Case Studies

It is hard to summarize accurately the literature on group performance–related pay, in part because of its great diversity. In the next three sections we review several kinds of noneconometric yet systematic attempts to assess the relationship between profit sharing or gain sharing and productivity or other performance measures, in ascending order of methodological rigor. We begin here with the relatively subjective domain of case studies, which are often testimonial and anecdotal.

The industrial relations literature sometimes makes a distinction between gain sharing, defined narrowly, and profit sharing. Gain sharing in that context typically means a group incentive pay system geared to productivity, cost reduction, or something else that may be perceived as less arbitrary and less comprehensive than profitability, which is the basis for profit sharing. Gain-sharing plans come in many forms, including the Scanlon plan, the Rucker plan, and Improshare.[17] Plans are tailored to the individual needs of each particular site, usually consisting of an involvement system and a formula linking pay to performance. The size of the relevant group is designed by the planners, but for very large enterprises it is normally smaller than the entire firm. Each gain-sharing subspecies is enthusiastically promoted by its commercial sponsor, but each seems to differ from the others more in specific details (such as compensation formula, degree of employee involvement, number of participants, and other features that may actually be quite important in practice) than in the general philosophy of why, how, and when it works. From an economic point of view, these various group performance–related pay plans, whether designated as gain sharing or profit sharing, seem generically more similar than different, and we will henceforth blur the distinctions among the varieties of gain sharing and profit sharing.

Two other conceptual issues concern the relationship of profit sharing to employee stock ownership plans (ESOPs) and to unions. A full consideration of these issues is beyond the scope of this paper, but a few brief comments are in order.[18]

The public often thinks of profit sharing and employee ownership as essentially similar, but they are conceptually different. ESOPs have a

17. Bureau of National Affairs, *Labor Relations Week*, vol. 2: BNA Special Report, *Changing Pay Practices: New Developments in Employee Compensation* (Washington, D.C., 1988), pp. 68–74; and Nalbantian, "Incentive Compensation in Perspective."
18. For more about ESOPs, see the paper by Svejnar and Conte in this volume.

profit-sharing component, in that participants (along with outside stock-holders) receive dividends (or share price increases) on stock allocated to their accounts; however, the primary company contributions to ESOPs are not profit based. Profit-sharing plans and ESOPs are some-times used in tandem to motivate and compensate employees, though evidence on U.S. publicly held companies shows that the overlap between profit sharing and ESOPs is not very different from what would be expected by random assignment.[19] The institutional differences between plans are likely to be important, and we do not propose to explore those here. There is a growing empirical literature on ESOPs;[20] a fair generalization is that ESOPs are often associated with better firm performance, but the link is by no means automatic, and it is often weak or nonexistent when adequate controls are applied. In this sense ESOPs differ somewhat from profit sharing. An overview of the empirical literature suggests that the case for a positive link between employee ownership and productivity is weaker (maybe we should say "even weaker") than the case for a positive link between profit sharing and productivity, though probably not to the point of nonexistence.[21]

The relation between unions and profit sharing has attracted little empirical research. Historically, unions have usually resisted profit-sharing plans, and firms have tended to drop profit sharing after becoming unionized.[22] But some unions accepted profit sharing in the 1980s, most notably the United Automobile Workers in their recent contracts with General Motors and Ford. The dynamics of profit sharing under union-

19. Kruse, "Essays on Profit-sharing and Unemployment."

20. This literature is summarized in Joseph R. Blasi, *Employee Ownership: Revolution or Ripoff?* (Ballinger Books, 1988).

21. This conclusion comes out fairly clearly from the econometric studies of cooperatives described later in our paper, which typically show that profit sharing has a more significant effect on productivity than workers' capital ownership or participation. (Coefficients on the latter two variables are often negative or insignificant, or both.) See also Kruse, "Essays on Profit-sharing and Unemployment"; Steven M. Bloom, "Employee Ownership and Firm Performance," Ph.D. dissertation, Harvard University, 1985; Paula B. Voos, "Managerial Perceptions of the Economic Impact of Labor Relations Programs," *Industrial and Labor Relations Review*, vol. 40 (January 1987), pp. 195–208; and U.S. General Accounting Office, *Employee Stock Ownership Plans: Little Evidence of Effects on Corporate Performance*, GAO/PEMD-88-1 (October 1987).

22. Richard B. Freeman and Morris Kleiner, "Union Organizing Drive Outcomes from NLRB Elections during a Period of Economic Concessions," *Proceedings of the Thirty-Ninth Annual Meeting* (Madison, Wis.: Industrial Relations Research Association, 1987), pp. 41–47.

ism, and whether unionism interacts positively or negatively with profit sharing in affecting performance, are interesting questions for which there are currently no clear answers.[23]

As for the case studies proper, they tend to be skewed toward the anecdotal and testimonial side of evidence taking. Even so, we feel this approach can yield some useful information. To give a sense of the vast case study literature, we will summarize the results of what we identified as the major systematic attempts from within the industrial relations community to survey individual case studies on group pay-for-performance plans. We found five such surveys. In addition, we read a great many (although not all) individual case studies from the literature.

Case studies of gain sharing are widely diverse. The first survey, of thirty-three cases, characterized these studies as being of "poor to good" quality.[24] Bullock and Lawler, the authors of the survey, noted that all the cases were "*post hoc* analyses of a single organization"; none "used standard statistical methods."[25] The thirty-three cases were distributed among union and nonunion firms, and among small, medium, and large firms. Gain sharing, it was found, positively influenced organizational effectiveness (productivity, quality, costs, or consumer service) in 73 percent of the cases, and in most of them the quality of work life, innovation, labor-management cooperation, and employee pay improved. Overall, two-thirds of the plans were considered successful. In explaining the successes, the authors observed that "there is surpris-

23. For some attitudinal evidence on unions and profit sharing, see Edwin B. Flippo, *Profit Sharing in American Business: A Study of Methods Used to Maintain and Sustain Profit-Sharing Plans* (Ohio State University, 1955); F. Beatrice Brower, "Sharing Profits with Employees," Conference Board Reports, Studies in Personnel Policy 162 (New York: National Industrial Conference Board, 1957); Opinion Research Corporation, "How Profit Sharing Affects Employee Attitudes," Princeton, N.J., October 1957; I. B. Helburn, "An Analysis of the Industrial Relations Climate in Unionized Profit Sharing Firms," Ph.D. dissertation, University of Wisconsin, 1966; and Laura B. Cardinal and I. B. Helburn, "Union Versus Nonunion Attitudes Toward Share Agreements," *Proceedings of the Thirty-Ninth Annual Meeting*, pp. 167–73. For evidence that profit sharing decreases the probability of union success in representation elections, see Edgar R. Czarnecki, "Effect of Profit Sharing Plans and Union Organizing Efforts," *Personnel Journal*, vol. 49 (September 1970), pp. 763–73. For some interesting reflections on the future of possible "mixed marriages" between unions and profit sharing, see Daniel J. B. Mitchell, "The Share Economy and Industrial Relations," *Industrial Relations*, vol. 26 (Winter 1987), pp. 1–17.

24. R. J. Bullock and Edward E. Lawler, "Gainsharing: A Few Questions, and Fewer Answers," *Human Resources Management*, vol. 23 (Spring 1984), pp. 23–40.

25. Bullock and Lawler, "Gainsharing," pp. 26, 38.

ingly little evidence as to why they work," and speculated that gain-sharing plans "change the culture of the organization" in such a way that employees have a "much broader understanding of and commitment to the total enterprise and its success."[26]

Second, the National Commission on Productivity and Work Quality did a survey of experiences with Scanlon plans.[27] Among forty-four firms with such plans, thirty were considered successful, and fourteen failures. (One suspects that adopted plans may be more likely to be reported as successful than unsuccessful.)

Third, a survey by Katzell and Guzzo of worker productivity experiments covered twenty studies of performance-based compensation; of these, eighteen had found at least one positive effect on an output measure.[28] In addition, seven of nine studies addressing the issue had found that absenteeism or turnover was reduced, and three of four pertinent studies had found improvements in employee attitudes.

Fourth, a 1981 General Accounting Office study investigated thirty-six firms with gain-sharing plans, of which twenty-four provided financial data.[29] In the smaller companies (with annual revenues below $100 million) the average "savings in work force costs" due to gain sharing were calculated as 17.3 percent; in the larger companies the average savings were estimated as 16.4 percent. Level of performance was found to be positively related to the age of the plan.

Fifth, a study of Improshare plans (a form of gain sharing that does not emphasize worker participation in decisions) by Fein found that, among seventy-two firms, the median productivity increase after one year was 19–20 percent.[30]

In addition to (and behind some of) these general surveys are many

26. Bullock and Lawler, "Gainsharing," pp. 36–37.

27. National Commission on Productivity and Work Quality, *A Plant-Wide Productivity Plan in Action: Three Years of Experience with the Scanlon Plan* (Washington, D.C., May 1975).

28. Raymond A. Katzell and Richard A. Guzzo, "Psychological Approaches to Productivity Improvement," *American Psychologist*, vol. 38 (April 1983), pp. 468–72. The authors report that "in some experiments more than one type of program and more than one type of outcome measure were studied" (p. 469), but do not report the number of outcome measures in each study. In interpreting these results, one should remember that a larger number of outcome measures increases the chance of at least one being positive, which is an important caveat for these results.

29. U.S. General Accounting Office, *Productivity Sharing Programs: Can They Contribute to Productivity Improvement?* AFMD-81-22 (March 1981).

30. Mitchell Fein, *Improshare: An Alternative to Traditional Managing* (Norcross, Ga.: American Institute of Industrial Engineers, 1981).

analyses of individual cases.[31] Profit-sharing and gain-sharing plans were found to be basically successful in most of the cases discussed (though it is unlikely that these are representative of all experiments). The tone of the case studies is usually, but not always, favorable to gain sharing. In two cases of failure, Alban and Gray found that profit shares or bonuses were apparently too small.[32] The sharing of monetary gains, it should be pointed out, does not get all the credit in the successful cases; in particular, several authors found that worker participation is an essential component in a successful gain-sharing plan (and may be more important than the monetary incentive taken alone).[33]

The mechanisms translating group incentives into increased productivity are poorly understood. The literature emphasizes such factors as increased worker involvement, more labor-management cooperation, heightened monitoring of fellow workers, more information sharing, working smarter, greater awareness of and interest in the company's profitability, and improved corporate culture.[34] Most observers agree

31. John J. Jehring, "A Contrast between Two Approaches to Total System Incentives," *California Management Review,* vol. 10 (Winter 1967), pp. 7–14; Fred G. Lesieur and Elbridge S. Puckett, "The Scanlon Plan Has Proved Itself," *Harvard Business Review,* vol. 47 (September–October 1969), pp. 109–18; R. B. Gray, "The Scanlon Plan: A Case Study," *British Journal of Industrial Relations,* vol. 9 (November 1971), pp. 291–313; Carl F. Frost, John H. Wakeley, and Robert A. Ruh, *The Scanlon Plan for Organization Development: Identity, Participation, and Equity* (Michigan State University Press, 1974); Ronald Carl Alban, "An Analysis of Companywide Cash Profit Sharing Plans," Master's thesis, Massachusetts Institute of Technology, 1980; Richard D. Rosenberg and Eliezer Rosenstein, "Participation and Productivity: An Empirical Study," *Industrial and Labor Relations Review,* vol. 33 (April 1980), pp. 355–67; R. J. Bullock and Patti F. Bullock, "Gainsharing and Rubik's Cube: Solving System Puzzles," *National Productivity Review,* vol. 1 (Autumn 1982), pp. 396–407; Carl F. Frost, "The Scanlon Plan at Herman Miller, Inc.: Managing an Organization by Innovation," in Robert Zager and Michael P. Rosow, eds., *The Innovative Organization: Productivity Programs in Action* (Pergamon Press, 1982), pp. 63–87; Brian E. Graham-Moore and Timothy L. Ross, eds., *Productivity Gainsharing: How Employee Incentive Programs Can Improve Business Performance* (Prentice Hall, 1983); Linda S. Tyler and Bob Fisher, "The Scanlon Concept: A Philosophy As Much As a System," *Personnel Administrator,* vol. 29 (July 1983), pp. 33–37; and Felix R. FitzRoy and Kornelius Kraft, "Participation and Division of Labor: A West German Case Study," *Industrial Relations Journal,* vol. 16 (Winter 1985), pp. 68–74.

32. Alban, "Analysis of Companywide Cash Profit Sharing Plans"; and Gray, "Scanlon Plan."

33. Frost and others, *Scanlon Plan for Organization Development*; Rosenberg and Rosenstein, "Participation and Productivity"; and Frost, "Scanlon Plan at Herman Miller, Inc."

34. Nalbantian, "Incentive Compensation in Perspective," p. 21; Bureau of National Affairs, *Changing Pay Practices,* pp. 67–94; and General Accounting Office, *Productivity Sharing Programs,* pp. 24–30.

that group performance–related pay plans are more likely to lead to improved productivity than pay plans that are not tied to appropriate performance measures. But it is also a common observation that background organization conditions can significantly influence the pay-performance link.[35]

It is interesting to note how closely the case study observations dovetail with the general conclusions from repeated game theory cited earlier. The usual gain-sharing plan emphasizes employee involvement as well as the group reward structure. Worker participation is generally seen as an essential component in successful Scanlon plans.[36] Practitioners tend to indicate that otherwise well-designed gain-sharing-like plans can fail if trust and cooperation are not generated during the implementation phase.[37] FitzRoy and Kraft, in their West German case study, argue that the traditional division of labor inhibits the worker interaction and collective response that are necessary to produce a positive profit-sharing effect on productivity.[38] Case studies usually conclude that profit sharing can help to improve productivity—in an environment with the appropriate corporate culture.

A current piece of conventional wisdom is that group incentives like profit sharing are productive, whereas individual incentives like piecework are counterproductive. Consistent with this, there has recently been a pronounced growth of group incentive systems.[39] Many observers report that in the rapidly changing work world a great need exists for a highly flexible, cooperative labor force, adaptable to new contingencies and not hampered by rigid work rules. Some assert as an empirical generalization that—especially in the fast-growing service and information sectors—the main potential sources of improved productivity now come from interactive team and collective efforts at the workplace, which are difficult to isolate and encourage with individual incentives. According to this scenario, then, profit sharing, by promoting group values positively related to group productivity, may be becoming an important part of the new work scene.

35. Bureau of National Affairs, *Changing Pay Practices*, pp. 72–75.

36. Frost, "Scanlon Plan at Herman Miller, Inc."; and Frost and others, *Scanlon Plan for Organization Development*.

37. Rosabeth Moss Kanter, "The Attack on Pay," *Harvard Business Review*, vol. 65 (March–April 1987), pp. 60–67.

38. FitzRoy and Kraft, "Participation and Division of Labor."

39. O'Dell and McAdams, *People, Performance, and Pay*, p. 8.

Attitude Surveys

Two broad types of attitude surveys can be distinguished: of employees and of employers. The conclusions based on these surveys are naturally subject to several caveats. First, the initial sample may have an overrepresentation of firms with group incentive systems. Second, there are self-selection biases associated with response to a voluntary survey. Third, organizations or individuals that have adopted a particular plan will normally tend to think well of the plan and to rationalize its existence. Fourth, answers to opinion questions are influenced by the questionnaire design—for this and other reasons the expressed opinions are an imperfect guide to actual behavior or performance. These caveats suggest potential threats to both internal validity (whether the findings represent true performance differences within the sample) and external validity (whether the results can be generalized to larger groups). Nevertheless, it seems plausible that one can obtain useful information from those who have first-hand experience with profit-sharing and gain-sharing plans. Some overall bias probably exists in the survey literature toward finding positive effects for profit sharing. The exact extent of the bias is unknown, but it would most likely not overturn the consistently strong positive findings that emerge.

In this review we have tried to locate all published results of attitude surveys in which employees or employers were asked: (1) questions about performance or motivation, for which the answers could be compared across profit-sharing and non-profit-sharing groups or firms; or (2) direct questions about whether profit sharing has improved performance or motivation.

Employee Surveys

We found six published employee surveys, which are briefly summarized in table 1. As can be seen, employees usually feel that profit sharing and gain sharing are good for personal effort, company growth and productivity, and workplace atmosphere. In the one study that compared answers across profit-sharing and non-profit-sharing employees (Opinion Research Corporation 1957), the former were more likely than the latter to say that they benefit from company growth and that workers get credit for company progress. Also, a majority of profit-sharing employees stated that their interests are not substantially different from those of management (61 percent) and owners (71 percent).

Table 1. Surveys of Employee Attitudes

Authors of the studies[a]	Source of data	Main content of questions asked employees (PS = profit sharing)	Percent of positive answers
Bell and Hanson 1987	2,703 employees of 12 profit-sharing companies (67 percent response rate)	How do you view PS in general?	91
		How do you view PS in your firm?	88
		Does PS improve employee attitudes?	73
		Do you agree or strongly agree that PS:[b]	
		makes people work more effectively?	51
		strengthens loyalty to the firm?	47
		creates a better atmosphere in the firm?	65
		is good for company and employees?	86
		is popular because people like bonuses?	93
		should not be substitute for adequate wage?	96
		can cause disappointment or bitterness because profits can go down?	42
Bureau of National Affairs 1988	1,000 telephone interviews from Omnitel weekly national survey (Bruskin and Assoc.)	Which of the following pay systems do you prefer?	
		company-wide incentive basis?	12
		individual incentive basis?	22
		straight wage salary?	63
Colletti 1969	76 employees at Motorola (36 percent response rate)	Agree that employees gain by cost cutting	80
		Agree that employees share in firm's growth	89
		Is PS an incentive in daily job?	67
		Has PS made you want to do a better job?	72
Jehring 1956	Employees in 202 U.S. companies	Has PS been successful or very successful?	81

National Commission on Productivity and Work Quality 1975	Comparison between 66 blue-collar answers before and after the introduction of a Scanlon plan in one U.S. company	Before the introduction of the plan: would cooperation be better with the plan?	53
		might communication improve?	65
		might participation increase?	44
		After the introduction of the plan: is cooperation better now?	82
		has communication improved?	72
		has participation increased?	71
Opinion Research Corporation 1957	Comparison between two samples of profit-sharing and non-profit-sharing employees	Agree that: employees get their share of company growth?	79 (47)[c]
		employees get credit for company progress?	79 (43)
		employees gain from cost cutting?	60 (40)
		PS cuts down labor-management friction?	32
		employees take it hard if profits go down?	35

a. D. Wallace Bell and Charles G. Hanson, *Profit Sharing and Profitability: How Profit Sharing Promotes Business Success* (London: Kogan Page, 1987); Bureau of National Affairs, *Changing Pay Practices: New Developments in Employee Compensation* (Washington, D.C., 1988); Jerome Colletti, *Profit Sharing and Employee Attitudes: A Case Study of the Deferred Profit-Sharing Program at Motorola, Inc.* (University of Wisconsin, Center for the Study of Productivity Motivation, 1969); John J. Jehring, *Succeeding with Profit Sharing: The Experiences of Profit Sharing Companies in Communicating Their Plans to Their Employees* (Evanston, Ill.: Profit Sharing Research Foundation, 1956); National Commission on Productivity and Work Quality, *A Plant-Wide Productivity Plan in Action: Three Years of Experience with the Scanlon Plan* (Washington, D.C., May 1975); and Opinion Research Corporation, "How Profit Sharing Affects Employee Attitudes," Princeton, N.J., October 1957.

b. These are the answers to a series of five-option questions, ranging from strongly agree to strongly disagree.

c. The numbers in parentheses are percentages for non-profit-sharing employees.

Employees in this sample rated profit sharing as the second most important advantage of working for their companies (second to steady employment and higher than good pay rates and other benefits).

In contrast to the perceived positive effects of profit sharing on effort, growth, and workplace atmosphere, employees apparently dislike the income variability caused by profit sharing. In the Bell and Hanson sample, even though 91 percent of employees supported profit sharing "in general," 42 percent agreed that profit sharing "can cause bitterness or disappointment, because profits can go down as well as up." This is probably the main reason that in the Bureau of National Affairs sample 63 percent of employees stated their preference for a straight wage salary. Consistent with the theory of decreasing relative risk-aversion, low-income workers were more likely than high-income workers to prefer a straight wage salary.

An unpublished employee survey sheds some light on the factors that make employees respond positively to profit sharing. Florkowski surveyed 154 employees in three profit-sharing companies and used several indexes to predict positive responses toward profit sharing.[40] Perceptions of greater pay equity, performance-reward contingencies, organizational commitment, and job satisfaction were correlated with positive attitudes about profit sharing, whereas perceived influence on decisionmaking did not have a strong relationship.

Employer Surveys

We found fifteen published attitude surveys of employers; the thirteen amenable to compression are summarized in table 2. As with employee surveys, the overall result is that employers view profit sharing positively. Between 73 percent and 100 percent agreed with the designation of profit sharing as "successful" or "very successful" in four samples. A majority believed that profit sharing improved employee satisfaction and loyalty.

Mitchell and Broderick's was one of the few samples that included employers without profit-sharing plans. Comparing several types of plans (including ESOPs, gain sharing, and simple incentives), this survey found that 28 percent of all managers viewed profit sharing as the best alternative for raising productivity (second to simple incentives, men-

40. Gary W. Florkowski, "The Organizational Impact of Profit Sharing," Ph.D. dissertation, Syracuse University, 1988.

tioned by 42 percent), and that 48 percent of managers viewed it as the best for increasing loyalty. The survey also shed some light on the question of the relation between profit sharing and participation: 39 percent of managers in cash-profit-sharing companies (and 33 percent in deferred profit-sharing companies) agreed that it creates demands for participation in management.

The American Productivity Center survey (O'Dell and McAdams 1987) found that there has been a striking growth in the number of firms adopting group-based pay for performance systems (more were adopted in the last five years than in the previous twenty years), and that adoption of such plans was higher among firms reporting increased competition. Profit-sharing plans existed in 32 percent of the companies, with "gain sharing" (that is, Scanlon, Rucker, Improshare, or custom plans) in 13 percent and "small group incentives" in 14 percent. Frequent information sharing with employees was found to be more prevalent in gain-sharing and profit-sharing companies (65 percent) than in other companies (37 percent), which suggests that sharing of information may be perceived as an important complement to profit sharing.

The two studies of employer attitudes not summarized in table 2 used attitude measures as dependent variables in formal statistical regressions. Paula Voos analyzed 343 unionized firms in Wisconsin in 1984.[41] Managers were surveyed about their companies' experience with gain sharing, profit sharing, ESOPs, employee participation, and joint union-management committees. Managers were asked to evaluate the effectiveness of the various programs along the dimensions of product quality, productivity, unit labor cost, and profits. The responses were used as dependent variables, with the types of programs used as predictors. The coefficient on gain sharing or profit sharing was always positive and statistically significant at the 5 percent level, with the largest perceived effects on product quality and productivity. The size of the estimates was comparable only to that for employee participation programs (and well above ESOPs), leading Voos to conclude that managers view participation, profit sharing, and gain sharing as the programs most likely to have positive effects on firm performance.

The final employer attitude study analyzed data from the Workplace Industrial Relations Survey, covering 1,266 British establishments in 1984, of which 42.7 percent reported some form of profit-sharing or share

41. Paula B. Voos, "Managerial Perceptions of the Economic Impact of Labor Relations Programs," *Industrial and Labor Relations Review*, vol. 40 (January 1987), pp. 195–208.

Table 2. Surveys of Employer Attitudes

Authors of the studies[a]	Source of data	Main content of questions asked employers (PS = profit sharing)	Percent positive answers
Brower 1957	204 executives of U.S. manufacturing firms	Did the plan improve employee attitudes? Did the plan reduce turnover?	90 77
General Accounting Office 1981	36 companies with gain-sharing plans in action	Did the plan improve labor-management relations? Did the plan reduce grievances? Did the plan reduce absenteeism? Did the plan reduce turnover?	80 47 36 36
Knowlton 1954	300 managers in profit-sharing companies	Was the PS plan very successful? Was the PS plan successful? Was the PS plan disappointing?	32 45 2
Metzger 1966	130 U.S. companies with less than 500 employees, mostly but not necessarily with profit-sharing plans	Was the PS plan very successful? Was the PS plan successful? Did the PS plan improve morale and cooperation? Was the PS plan effective in cutting costs?	26 56 93 64
Metzger 1975	38 U.S. companies with more than $50 million of profit-sharing trust assets in 1971	Was the PS plan very successful? Was the PS plan successful? Was the PS plan disappointing?	53 47 0
Mitchell and Broderick 1987	545 managers out of 6,988 questionnaires sent out (sample heavily biased toward managers knowledgeable about flexible plans)	PS best alternative for:[b] raising productivity increasing loyalty linking labor costs to firm's conditions Agrees that cash PS: raises productivity increases loyalty creates demand for participation is difficult to administer	28 (30)[c] 48 (49) 53 (56) 43 (45) 51 (51) 44 (39)* 50 (57)*

Source	Item	%
Mitchell and Broderick 1987 (*cont.*)	Agrees that deferred PS:	
	raises productivity	32 (32)
	increases loyalty	50 (52)
	creates demand for participation	39 (33)*
	is difficult to administer	43 (54)*
	Agrees that PS in general:	
	links labor costs to firm's conditions	63 (64)
National Commission on Productivity and Work Quality 1975	Comparison between 28 managers' answers before and after the introduction of a Scanlon plan in one U.S. company	
	Before the introduction of the plan:	
	would cooperation be better with the plan?	90
	might communication improve?	79
	might participation increase?	74
	After the introduction of the plan:	
	is cooperation better now?	100
	has communication improved?	93
	has participation increased?	77
New York Stock Exchange 1982	1,158 respondents out of 7,000 U.S. corporations with 500 or more employees	
	Are PS plans successful?	73
Nightingale 1980	86 executives of small Canadian profit-sharing companies	
	Did the plan increase employee satisfaction?	84
	Did the plan reduce turnover?	65
	Did the plan improve morale and cooperation?	72
O'Dell and McAdams 1987	1,598 companies, members of the American Productivity Association	
	PS has a positive or very positive effect on:	
	performance	74
	productivity	65
	quality	70
	turnover	56
Wider Share Ownership Council 1985	Cited by Estrin 1986; and Wadhwani and Wall 1988[d]	
	Did the plan increase productivity?	45
	Did the plan increase loyalty?	77
	Did the plan reduce turnover?	39

Table 2 (*continued*)

Authors of the studies[e]	Source of the data	Main content of questions asked employers	Average rating
Metzger 1975	38 U.S. profit-sharing companies with more than $50 million of trust assets	Employers were asked to rate their plan on a 1 to 3 scale on 9 measures of success; lowest and the highest average ratings were	1.74–2.88
Ruh, Wallace, and Frost 1973	205 managers from 18 U.S. companies that are continuing or have discontinued Scanlon plan	Continuing Scanlon plan companies: average rate on a 1 to 5 scale Discontinuing Scanlon plan companies: average rate on a 1 to 5 scale	4.1 3.7
Smith 1986	303 U.K. profit-sharing companies	Average plan rating on 9 measures of success: scale of 1 to 5	4

a. F. Beatrice Brower, "Sharing Profits with Employees," Studies in Personnel Policies 162 (New York: National Industrial Conference Board, 1957); U.S. General Accounting Office, *Productivity Sharing Programs: Can They Contribute to Productivity Improvement?* AFMD-81-22(1981); Philip A. Knowlton, *Profit Sharing Patterns* (Evanston, Ill.: Profit Sharing Research Foundation, 1954); Bertram L. Metzger, *Profit Sharing in Perspective* (Evanston, Ill.: Profit Sharing Research Foundation, 1966); Bertram L. Metzger, *Profit Sharing in 38 Large Companies: Piece of the Action for 1,000,000 Participants*, vol. 1 (Evanston, Ill.: Profit Sharing Research Foundation, 1975); Daniel J. B. Mitchell and Renae F. Broderick, "Flexible Pay Systems in the American Context: History, Policy, Research, and Implications," paper prepared for the Pacific Rim Comparative Labor Policy Conference, Vancouver, Canada, June 1987; National Commission on Productivity and Work Quality, *A Plant-Wide Productivity Plan in Action: Three Years of Experience with the Scanlon Plan* (Washington, D.C., May 1975); New York Stock Exchange, *People and Productivity: A Challenge to Corporate America* (1982); Donald V. Nightingale, *Does Profit Sharing Really Make a Difference?* (Ottawa: Conference Board in Canada, 1980); Carla O'Dell and Jerry McAdams, *People, Performance, and Pay* (Austin, Tex.: American Productivity Center, 1987); and

Wider Share Ownership Council 1985 (see note d).

b. This study compares managers' attitudes toward the following alternative flexible compensation plans: profit sharing, ESOP, tax credit ESOP, gain sharing, simple incentives.

c. The numbers in parentheses refer to respondents whose firm had a profit-sharing plan in action. A * indicates that the responses of firms with profit sharing are significantly different (5 percent, Chi-square test) from the responses of other firms.

d. Saul Estrin, "Profit Sharing, Motivation, and Company Performance: A Survey," paper prepared for the Employment Institute, June 1986; and Sushil Wadhwani and Martin Wall, "The Effects of Profit-Sharing on Employment, Wages, Stock Returns, and Productivity: Evidence from UK Micro-Data," Working Paper 1030 (London School of Economics, Centre for Labour Economics, 1988).

e. Metzger 1975 (see note a); Robert A. Ruh, Roger L. Wallace, and Carl F. Frost, "Management Attitudes and the Scanlon Plan," *Industrial Relations*, vol. 12 (October 1973), pp. 282–88; and Gillian R. Smith, "Profit Sharing and Employee Share Ownership in Britain," *Employment Gazette*, vol. 94 (September 1986), pp. 380–84.

ownership scheme.[42] Unlike the previously described surveys, this one did not ask managers to evaluate the schemes. Rather, personnel managers were asked whether the company's financial performance was "better than average" compared with the rest of the industry, and this response was coded as a dummy dependent variable for probit regressions. Controlling for size, industry demand, percent labor costs, and unionism, the profit-sharing coefficients in two specifications were positive, with t-statistics of 1.4 and 1.6. Managers in profit-sharing companies were somewhat more likely to report above-average company performance, but the statistical significance was weak.

Unlike the other surveys in our group, which were limited to either employers or employees, a multinational survey conducted by Louis Harris included samples of business executives, trade union leaders, employees, legislators, and members of the public.[43] Of the U.S. employed public, 43 percent felt that "employees getting financial rewards for productivity gains" would increase productivity a great deal; this was the most popular method of raising productivity for the public, business leaders, and congressional members, but not for union leaders. Asked if they were willing to have their salaries linked to productivity if "their sacrifices would provide money needed for investment," 63 percent of U.S. employees answered yes.

To summarize the attitude surveys, while it is clear that potential biases exist, the overall results consistently show that employees and employers view profit sharing and gain sharing as positive influences on productivity and company performance. These positive influences are tempered on the employee side by the risk of fluctuating income.

Simple Statistical Studies

Other evidence on profit sharing can be found in studies that compare profit-sharing and non-profit-sharing companies on measures of financial performance. Almost without exception the six studies summarized in table 3 found that profit-sharing companies have higher mean or median values for performance indexes than non-profit-sharing companies do.

42. D. G. Blanchflower and A. J. Oswald, "Profit Related Pay: Prose Discovered?" London School of Economics, 1987.

43. Sentry Insurance, *A Sentry Study: Perspectives on Productivity: A Global View*, study conducted by Louis Harris and Associates (New York, 1981). The total number of respondents across all samples was 5,098.

Table 3. Simple Statistical Comparisons

Authors of the studies[a]	Source of data	Statistical technique	Principal findings
Bell and Hanson 1987	414 U.K. companies, 113 profit-sharing, 301 non-profit-sharing, 1977–85	Comparisons of 9 measures of performance	Each index had eight years of comparisons. Across 72 points of comparison, profit-sharing firms were superior in 90 percent of the cases. Before and after comparison showed relative improvement in 7 of 9 measures
Howard and Dietz 1969	175 U.S. profit-sharing and non-profit-sharing companies in 9 industries	Comparisons of the median values of 16 indexes of performance in each industry	16 comparisons were made for each industry. Over the 144 points of comparisons profit-sharing firms were superior in 58 percent of the cases and inferior only in 19 percent. In each index considered separately over all industries profit-sharing companies outperformed the others
Howard 1979	202 U.S. profit-sharing and non-profit-sharing companies in 6 industries	Comparisons of the median values of 16 indexes of performance in each industry	16 comparisons were made for each of 6 industries. Over the 96 points of comparisons, profit-sharing companies were superior in 47 percent of the cases and inferior in only 27 percent
Jehring and Metzger 1960	8 U.S. profit-sharing companies and 6 U.S. non-profit-sharing companies	Comparisons with respect to various measures of performance	Profit-sharing companies do better than the others

Metzger and Colletti 1971	8 U.S. profit-sharing companies and 6 U.S. non-profit-sharing companies	Comparisons with respect to 9 measures of performance	With respect to all 9 measures, profit-sharing companies do better than the others, and the superiority gap widens considerably between 1958 and 1969
Metzger 1978	33 U.S. profit-sharing companies, Fortune 500 industrials, and Fortune 50 retailers	Comparisons of median values for 2 indexes of performance	Comparisons were made on return on sales and equities for each year in 1973–76, for both industrials and retailers. Over 16 points of comparisons profit-sharing firms were always superior

a. D. Wallace Bell and Charles G. Hanson, *Profit Sharing and Profitability: How Profit Sharing Promotes Business Success* (London: Kogan Page, 1987); Bion B. Howard and Peter O. Dietz, *A Study of the Financial Significance of Profit Sharing* (Chicago: Profit Sharing Council of America, 1969); Bion B. Howard, *A Study of the Financial Significance of Profit Sharing, 1958–1977* (Chicago: Profit Sharing Council of America, 1979); John J. Jehring and Bertram L. Metzger, *The Stockholder and Employee Profit Sharing* (Evanston, Ill.: Profit Sharing Research Foundation, 1960); Bertram L. Metzger and Jerome A. Colletti, *Does Profit Sharing Pay? A Comparative Study of the Financial Performance of Retailers with and without Profit Sharing Programs* (Evanston, Ill.: Profit Sharing Research Foundation, 1971); and Bertram L. Metzger, *Profit Sharing in 38 Large Companies: Piece of the Action for 1,000,000 Participants*, vol. 2 (Evanston, Ill.: Profit Sharing Research Foundation, 1978).

The five U.S. studies used a variety of financial measures on American firms and found that profit-sharing companies are usually superior.[44] Consistent with these five studies, a British study by Bell and Hanson (1989) found higher growth, profitability, and investor returns among 113 profit-sharing companies than among 301 non-profit-sharing companies. Over the 1977–85 period the cumulative difference in sales growth was 20.3 percent, and the difference in profit growth was 52.8 percent.

An obvious limitation of these studies is the lack of controls for anything other than industry membership. A further limitation is that they used cross-sectional comparisons and did not address the question of causality: it is possible that profit sharing is more likely to be adopted by successful companies. (The one exception to this limitation was Bell and Hanson, who found in a simple longitudinal comparison that mean values increased in seven of nine performance measures after the adoption of profit sharing.) As with the attitude studies, though, the evidence is clearly consistent with the hypothesis of a positive effect of profit sharing on productivity and company performance.

Econometric Literature

After an exhaustive search of the literature we found sixteen formal econometric studies on the relation between profit sharing and productivity, which used forty-two different samples of firms (with several samples analyzed in more than one study). Here we define a formal econometric study as one that uses regression analysis with an objectively measured productivity-like dependent variable, and some type of profit-sharing-like measure as an independent variable. Within this definition the studies vary greatly in data sources, methodologies, and attempts to control for biases. Six of the studies concern cooperatives, in which the authors try to separate the profit-sharing component of the cooperatives from the membership, ownership, and participation components. Two studies cover firms with Scanlon and Rucker plans, and

44. These studies are summarized in Gary W. Florkowski, "The Organizational Impact of Profit Sharing," *Academy of Management Review*, vol. 12 (October 1987), pp. 622–36. The measures include operating income margin, net income margin, return on operating assets, return on total capital, return on common equity, operating earnings per employee, net income to net worth, net income to sales, net worth, company earnings per employee, return on sales, return on equity, sales trend, earnings per share trend, dividends per share trend, and market price per share trend.

one covers firms that voluntarily allow for worker participation. The remaining seven studies cover private or publicly held capitalistic firms. It should be noted that the relation of profit sharing to productivity was not the primary focus of several of these studies.

Salient problems in the estimation of the effect of profit sharing on productivity include all the standard econometric problems of production function estimation, the potential endogeneity of profit sharing, and omitted variable biases due to the unobservable character of managerial quality and other firm-specific variables. Attempts to address these problems will be described briefly.

Generally speaking, the studies use either value added or sales per employee (in logarithm form) as dependent variables; profit sharing is measured as a dummy variable, profit share per employee, profit share as a percentage of compensation, and/or percent of employees covered by profit sharing. The specification is most often based on a Cobb-Douglas production function, though several studies also use the more general constant elasticity of substitution (CES) and translog functions. In the studies that try to control for endogeneity, the most common approach is instrumental variables. (As will be seen, the use of instrumental variables does not change the results greatly relative to the ordinary least squares, OLS, specifications.) Since each econometric study normally includes a number of specifications, it is convenient to have some summary measure of the estimated profit-sharing effect and the significance levels. In this review we present the mean t-statistic on profit-sharing variables, as well as the proportion of profit-sharing t-statistics that indicate statistical significance at the 5 percent level.

The general picture that emerges from the econometric studies is that profit sharing and productivity are positively related. The studies are listed in table 4, with mean t-ratios given and brief notations made on data sources, productivity, and profit-sharing measures. As can be seen, the mean t-ratio is positive in all studies, and greater than two in twelve of the sixteen studies. Of the 226 total profit-sharing coefficients reported (in 216 regressions), 94 percent are positive, and 60 percent have positive t-ratios greater than two. The "grand mean" of all 226 reported t-statistics is 2.46. Only 6 percent of coefficients are negative, and no study reported a t-ratio on a profit-sharing variable that was less than minus two. It is fair to say that no one study yielded convincing evidence on the relation between profit sharing and productivity. However, the similar conclusions that emerge from all sixteen studies taken together provide fairly strong evidence of a consistent pattern.

Table 4. Econometrics Results

Authors of the studies[a]	Source of data	Productivity measure[b]	Profit-sharing measure	Number of regressions reported	Average t-statistic
Cable and FitzRoy 1980	42 West German firms members of the AGB[c] from 1974 to 1976	Value added	Total profits distributed to workers	3	2.45
Conte and Svejnar 1988	40 U.S. firms (period not reported)	Value added	Dummy for firms with profit sharing	6	1.98
Defourney, Estrin, and Jones 1985	440 French cooperatives in 1978; 550 French cooperatives in 1979	Value added	Profits distributed to workers per head	14	2.21
Estrin, Jones, and Svejnar 1987	550 French cooperatives in 1978 and 1979; 150 Italian cooperatives from 1976 to 1980; 50 British cooperatives, 5 year intervals, 1948–68	Value added	Profits distributed to workers per head	11	4.44
FitzRoy and Kraft 1986	61 West German firms in 1977; 62 West German firms in 1979	Profits defined as cash flow divided by assets	Profits distributed to workers per head	2	3.03
FitzRoy and Kraft 1987	61 West German firms in 1977; 62 West German firms in 1979	Total factor productivity (residual of a Cobb-Douglas estimation)	Profits distributed to workers per head	2	3.51

Study	Sample	Dependent variable	Profit-sharing measure	N	Value
Florkowski 1988	3 U.S. profit-sharing companies (monthly data)	Value added per worker	Intercept and slope effects before and after the plan introduction or modification	6	1.69
Jones 1982	From 46 to 30 British cooperatives over the period 1948–68	Value added	Individual bonus to labor	52	2.01
Jones 1987	50 British cooperatives in the retail sector in 1978	Gross margin	Surplus distributed to workers as dividend	2	1.25
Jones and Svejnar 1985	316 Italian cooperatives from 1975 to 1978; 315 Italian cooperatives from 1975 to 1980	Value added	Profits distributed to workers per head	6	6.58
Kruse 1988	2,976 U.S. Compustat firms from 1971 to 1985	Sales per employee	Dummy for firms with profit sharing; percent of employees covered by profit sharing	76	2.41
Mitchell, Lewin, and Lawler 1989	495 U.S. business units, 1983–86	Sales per employee; return on investment; return on assets	Dummy for firms with profit sharing	12	2.09
Shepard 1986	20 U.S. chemical firms from 1975 to 1982	Value added	Dummy for firms with profit sharing; profits distributed to workers per head; ratio of profit sharing to fixed compensation	16	3.41

Table 4 (continued)

Authors of the studies[a]	Source of data	Productivity measure[b]	Profit-sharing measure	Number of regressions reported	Average t-statistic
Schuster 1983	7 U.S. sites with a gain-sharing plan (Scanlon, Rucker)	Employee output per hour	Intercept and slope effects before and after the plan introduction	7	2.97
Schuster 1984	1 U.S. firm with Scanlon plan	Employee output per hour	Intercept and slope effects before and after the plan introduction	2	2.48
Wadhwani and Wall 1988	96 U.K. firms from 1972 to 1982	Real sales	Dummy for firms with profit sharing	1	1.84
Total	...	...	...	216[d]	2.46

a. John R. Cable and Felix R. FitzRoy, "Cooperation and Productivity: Some Evidence from West German Experience," *Economic Analysis and Workers' Management*, vol. 14, no. 2 (1980), pp. 163–80; "Productive Efficiency, Incentives and Employee Participation: Some Preliminary Results for West Germany," *Kyklos*, vol. 33, no. 1 (1980), pp. 100–21; Michael A. Conte and Jan Svejnar, "Productivity Effects of Worker Participation in Management, Profit-Sharing, Worker Ownership of Assets and Unionization in U.S. Firms," *International Journal of Industrial Organization*, vol. 6 (March 1988), pp. 139–51; Jacques Defourney, Saul Estrin, and Derek C. Jones, "The Effects of Worker Participation on Enterprise Performance: Empirical Evidence from French Cooperatives," *International Journal of Industrial Organization*, vol. 3 (June 1985), pp. 197–217; Saul Estrin, Derek C. Jones, and Jan Svejnar, "The Productivity Effects of Worker Participation: Producer Cooperatives in Western Economies," *Journal of Comparative Economics*, vol. 11 (March 1987), pp. 40–61; Felix FitzRoy and Kornelius Kraft, "Profitability and Profit-Sharing," *Journal of Industrial Economics*, vol. 35 (December 1986), pp. 113–30; Felix FitzRoy and Kornelius Kraft, "Cooperation, Productivity, and Profit Sharing," *Quarterly Journal of Economics*, vol. 102 (February 1987), pp. 23–35; Gary W. Florkowski, "The Organizational Impact of Profit Sharing," Ph.D. dissertation, Syracuse University, 1988; Derek C. Jones, "British Producer Cooperatives 1948–68: Productivity and Organizational Structure," in Derek C. Jones

Productivity Effects of Worker Directors and Financial Participation in the Firm: The Case of British Retail Cooperatives," *Industrial and Labor Relations Review*, vol. 41 (October 1987), pp. 79–92; Derek C. Jones and Jan Svejnar, "Participation, Profit Sharing, Worker Ownership and Efficiency in Italian Producer Cooperatives," *Economica*, vol. 52 (November 1985), pp. 449–65; Douglas L. Kruse, "Essays on Profit Sharing and Unemployment," Ph.D. dissertation, Harvard University, 1988; Daniel J. B. Mitchell, David Lewin, and Edward F. Lawler III, "Alternative Pay Systems, Firm Performance, and Productivity" (in this volume); Edward M. Shepard, "The Effect of Profit Sharing on Productivity," Ph.D. dissertation, Boston College, 1986; Michael Schuster, "The Impact of Union-Management Cooperation on Productivity and Employment," *Industrial and Labor Relations Review*, vol. 36 (April 1983), pp. 415–30; Michael Schuster, "The Scanlon Plan: A Longitudinal Analysis," *Journal of Applied Behavioral Science*, vol. 20, no. 1 (1984), pp. 23–38; and Sushil Wadhwani and Martin Wall, "The Effects of Profit-Sharing on Employment, Wages, Stock Returns, and Productivity: Evidence from UK Micro-Data," Working Paper 1030 (London School of Economics, Centre for Labour Economics, February 1988).

b. Measures of productivity used as a dependent variable in the regression.

c. Arbeitsgemeinschaft zur Förderung der Partnerschaft in der Wirtschaft e. V. This is a group of firms that have voluntarily introduced some form of workers'

Studies of Cooperatives

Cooperatives were the focus of analysis in five studies.[45] Specifications based on Cobb-Douglas production functions were used in each study, and translog and CES specifications were also tested in four of the studies. The dependent variable was always value added; the profit-sharing variable was either total shared profits or shared profits per worker. To examine the influence of other features of cooperatives, the studies included the following independent variables: capital ownership by members (all five studies); loan capital and reserves per member (all except Jones 1982); proportion of employees who are members (all except Jones 1987); and worker membership on the board of directors (in Jones 1982 and Jones 1987).

Recognizing the potential endogeneity of the profit-sharing variable, three of these studies (all except Jones 1982 and Jones 1987) used an instrumental variables approach. In addition, the presence of longitudinal variation allowed for the testing of fixed-effects specifications in two studies (Estrin and others 1987; and Jones and Svejnar 1985).

In each of these five studies the large majority of the coefficients showed positive effects of profit sharing on productivity. As seen in table 4, the average t-statistic was always positive and greater than two in three of the studies.[46]

The positive effects of the OLS regressions and of the instrumental variables regressions do not differ much. When using instrumental variables, Defourney and others found positive profit-share coefficients in two regressions, with one significant at the 5 percent level. Estrin and others reported eleven OLS regressions in which the profit-share coefficient was always positive, and nine in which it was statistically significant at the 5 percent level. They found that the instrumental variables estimates were "very similar" to the OLS estimates for the U.K. and Italian samples. The short panel in France, however, allowed for "limited predictive power" of the instrumental variables: five of the six French equations still had positive coefficients but only one was significant at the 5 percent level. Finally, Jones and Svejnar reported

45. Defourney, Estrin, and Jones 1985; Estrin, Jones, and Svejnar 1987; Jones 1982; Jones 1987; and Jones and Svejnar 1985.

46. It should be noted that the sample in Jones 1988 comprised consumer cooperatives in which employees could participate as members and on boards of directors; the sharing of profits with consumers could reasonably be expected to attenuate the productivity effects of profit sharing, which may partially explain the low t-ratios.

that the effect of profit sharing is increased in magnitude by instrumental variables estimates (with *t*-statistics greater than two in both regressions).

A sixth study (Conte and Svejnar 1988) used a sample of forty U.S. firms combining cooperatives with profit-sharing and ESOP firms. Using both OLS and instrumental variables techniques, the authors looked at the effect of participation and profit-sharing variables on productivity. Profit sharing was measured as a dummy variable, and productivity was measured as value added. The profit-sharing coefficients were always positive and were statistically significant at the 5 percent level in two of the six reported regressions (with an average *t*-statistic of 1.98).[47] The magnitude of the coefficients indicates a range of 19–32 percent higher productivity in profit-sharing firms.

Gain-Sharing Plans

Michael Schuster studied Scanlon and Rucker plans, which combine limited forms of employee participation with sharing by employees in the gains from productivity improvement. In his 1983 study he reported results of a longitudinal analysis of four Scanlon plans (one covering two sites) and two Rucker plans. The level of productivity (defined as physical or financial output per worker) increased in six of the seven sites after the implementation of the plans, with statistically significant increases in four of the sites. By contrast, the trend in productivity increased in five of the sites, but only one had a statistically significant trend increase, and one had a significant trend decrease (following a significant level increase).

In the most extensive study by Schuster (1984), which analyzed monthly data over an eleven-year period with a Scanlon plan introduced in the fifth year, he found statistically significant increases in productivity in the manufacturing and repair divisions associated with the adoption of the plan. Also, the growth rate of repair productivity increased by a statistically significant amount, and the growth rate of manufacturing productivity showed an insignificant increase. He also found that no management, organizational, or technological changes occurred at the time of plan adoption, and that employee suggestions apparently played

47. The two significant profit-sharing coefficients occur in equations that include one dummy variable for an employee participation plan; when two dummy variables for participation are included (one for wage decisions and one for production decisions) the profit-sharing coefficients remain positive but are significant only at the 10 percent level.

a role in increasing productivity. Based on his research, Schuster concluded in a 1986 article, "Most firms that introduce gainsharing experience productivity improvements of 5 percent to 15 percent in the first year." He emphasized, consistent with the theory about preconditions for overcoming the free rider problem, that employees "develop positive beliefs about the Scanlon plan when there is organizational trust, group attitudes supportive of the concept, and supervisory acceptance."[48]

Studies of Capitalist Firms

Seven econometric studies have been done on profit-sharing firms other than cooperatives. Three of them analyze West German data. The first, by Cable and FitzRoy (1980), used questionnaire data collected from forty-two firms in 1974–76. These firms were members of a West German association of firms that practice profit sharing or employee shareholding, or both. Using a Cobb-Douglas production function, the authors tested the effects on value added of worker involvement in decisionmaking, individual incentives, worker capital holdings, and total profits distributed to workers. In the sample taken as a whole, the profit-sharing measure is positive but statistically insignificant, but splitting the sample into high-participation and low-participation firms (using an index of worker involvement in decisions) produces a positive and significant coefficient on profit sharing for high-participation firms and a negative but insignificant coefficient for low-participation firms. This result provides some support for the view, discussed in the industrial relations section, that the effect of profit sharing may be conditional on other industrial relations policies.

FitzRoy and Kraft (1986, 1987) used data from sixty-five German metalworking firms from 1977 and 1979 to examine the influence of profit sharing on productivity and profitability. In their 1987 paper the authors regressed total factor productivity (the residual from a Cobb-Douglas estimation) on the profit-share income per employee, with a large number of control variables. In both single-equation and simultaneous-equation estimates, profit-share income coefficients were highly significant (t-values of 3.76 and 3.26, respectively). The coefficient sizes indicate that the mean value of profit-share income per employee is associated with a 3 percent higher productivity relative to no profit sharing. Interestingly,

48. Michael Schuster, "Gainsharing: The State of the Art," *Compensation and Benefits Management*, vol. 2 (Summer 1986), pp. 285–90.

the age of the profit-sharing plan was a strong predictor of profit-share income, which "suggests that a significant learning process is indeed involved in encouraging cooperative behavior through group incentives" (p. 31). The authors noted that the results were very robust but that there was an unavoidable lack of information on managerial quality as a possible omitted variable.

In their 1986 paper FitzRoy and Kraft analyzed the effect of profit sharing on profitability (measured as the ratio of cash revenues to assets), with simultaneous estimation of an equation for the amount of profit sharing. They found strong positive effects of profit sharing on their measure of profitability, but no feedback from profitability to profit sharing (though the cross-sectional sample limited their efforts to untangle the problem of causality). Both of the coefficients on profit sharing were positive and statistically significant at the 5 percent level.

British publicly traded companies were the subject of a study by Wadhwani and Wall (1988). Their sample included ninety-six firms over the 1972–82 period, of which eighteen had a profit-sharing plan at some point in the period. Using sales as the dependent variable, with firm-specific dummies and measures of employment and capital stock (both instrumented to help control for endogeneity), the authors estimated the effect of a profit-sharing dummy and a profit-sharing dummy interacted with the capital stock. Both profit-sharing variables have positive coefficients, with t-statistics of 1.53 and 2.16, respectively. The coefficient on the profit-sharing dummy indicates an increase of 2 percent in real sales associated with profit sharing (not counting the effect through the interaction term, which could not be calculated from the reported results).

Four econometric studies have been done on U.S. firms other than cooperatives. Since the Mitchell, Lewin, and Lawler study appears in this volume, it will not be described here. A study by Shepard (1987) examined twenty chemical firms with publicly traded stock during 1975–82, of which nine had profit-sharing plans. Using a production function framework with value added as the dependent variable, he concluded that the profit-sharing firms had 9–10 percent higher value added than the others, and that the elasticity of value added with respect to the profit-sharing to compensation ratio was 0.3 (using two-stage least squares to control for endogeneity). Of the fourteen regressions reported, thirteen had positive profit-sharing coefficients significant at the 5 percent level, with an average t-statistic of 3.41. Interestingly, by using an approximated CES production function to estimate whether profit sharing was labor augmenting or capital augmenting, Shepard found that profit sharing influences productivity "principally through the effect upon labor effort" (p. 100). Since no firms switched profit-sharing status over the time period studied, fixed unobservable characteristics could not be controlled.

Florkowski (1988) conducted detailed case studies of four U.S. profit-sharing firms, with productivity data available from three. He measured productivity as value added and used an ARIMA interrupted time-series design to examine changes in levels or trends after changes in profit-sharing status. In the two companies that adopted profit sharing within the sample period, productivity trends increased in both cases, whereas productivity levels increased in one case and decreased in the other (none significant at the 5 percent level). But Florkowski noted that a comparison with three-digit (standard industrial classification) industry data suggests that profit sharing did spur productivity improvement in one company. In a third company, which changed the profit-sharing formula in the sample period by funding a pension plan out of the profit shares (thereby forcing employees to defer the benefits), there was a large and statistically significant decrease in the trend of productivity (with a small insignificant increase in the level). This evidence is consistent with the idea that cash plans are better motivators than deferred plans; however, for this third case Florkowski noted that the formula change coincided with a competitor's product breakthrough that strongly affected sales and value added. He concluded that the introduction of profit sharing coincided with productivity improvement in one firm but had no effect in another; in a third firm a shift in the profit-sharing formula toward deferred payments coincided with decreased productivity.[49]

Finally, Kruse (1988) analyzed a large sample of U.S. publicly traded firms. The sample was drawn from the CompuStat files and matched to the federal government's private pension data base, which provides information on whether a firm had a deferred profit-sharing plan and indicates the year in which the plan was begun. Out of 2,976 firms, 1,198 (40.3 percent) were found to have a profit-sharing plan in 1984, and about half had been adopted since the beginning of the sample period (1971). Kruse used three types of estimation: cross-sectional by year, first-

49. In the firm that apparently experienced increased productivity, measured quality decreased and absenteeism increased after the introduction of profit sharing, suggesting that these were not the mechanisms of productivity improvement (although industry comparison data were not available).

difference over long periods (ten or fourteen years), and panel regressions using both first-difference and firm-intercept specifications. Here we focus on the panel regressions, since they use the most information. (The cross-sectional and long-period regressions yielded similar results.) The dependent variable was revenues per worker, and profit sharing was alternatively measured as a dummy variable and as the proportion of a firm's employees who participate in profit sharing. Controls were included in all regressions for capital stock, employment, and industry effects. It should be borne in mind, however, that the profit-sharing plans examined in this study were all deferred-payment plans (as opposed to immediate cash-payment plans), since these are the only plans that must be reported to the federal government (where they are collected in the data base). That is a potential weakness of the study, since we are not exactly sure to what extent it picks up genuine profit sharing.

The firm-intercept and first-difference panel regressions showed consistently positive and statistically significant increases in productivity associated with the adoption of profit-sharing plans, with a range of 2.8–3.6 percent for manufacturing firms and 2.5–4.2 percent for nonmanufacturing firms. The t-ratios ranged from 2.25 to 3.5. The estimated effect was stronger when profit sharing was measured as the proportion of employees covered: a plan covering all workers was estimated to have an 8.0–8.9 percent effect on productivity in manufacturing, and a 10.3–11.0 percent effect in nonmanufacturing (again, with high significance levels). When trend terms were included to capture the effect of profit sharing over time, these were close to zero and insignificant, showing there was no tendency for productivity either to increase or to decrease with the age of the profit-sharing plan.

Kruse used several methods to try to control for the potential endogeneity of profit sharing: (1) addition of a prior productivity growth variable, to control for the possibility that growing firms may establish profit sharing to attract new employees; (2) restriction of the sample to consistent taxpayer firms, to control for the possibility that only consistent taxpayers adopt profit sharing to reduce tax liabilities; (3) restriction of the sample to firms with pension plans, to control for the possibility that the existence of pension plans, rather than profit sharing per se, increases productivity; and (4) restriction of the sample to firms that adopted profit sharing within the sample period, again to control for the possibility that these were quickly growing firms that had large productivity increases throughout the period. The results were unchanged by restrictions 1 and 2 and only slightly weakened in size and significance by restrictions 3 and 4.

As mentioned, omitted variables bias is a potentially important issue. An attempt was made to control for fixed unobservable characteristics of firms through the use of firm-specific intercepts and first-difference specifications, but the adoption of profit sharing could also be associated with changes in management or other personnel policies. The study reported on a special survey of manufacturing firms that gained additional information on their personnel policies and management changes. Of the fifty-eight profit-sharing managers who were asked whether profit sharing had been adopted following a change in management, only two responded affirmatively. As for the adoption of other personnel policies (quality circles, individual bonus systems, job rotation plans, other group bonus systems, and regular employee surveys), very few managers reported that these were adopted within two years before or after the start of profit sharing. The inclusion of these personnel policies in productivity regressions did not change the profit-sharing adoption coefficients. It therefore seems unlikely that the strong positive coefficients on profit-sharing adoption are due to simultaneous new management teams of higher quality or to the concurrent adoption of other personnel policies.

Summary

The consistently positive results from the econometric evidence are striking. Across all studies, with a total of 226 reported profit-sharing coefficients (in 216 regressions), only 6 percent of the coefficients on profit-sharing variables are negative, and not one of the negative coefficients is statistically significant at conventional levels ($t < -2$). Positive coefficients appear in 94 percent of the regressions, and 60 percent of all the regressions have positive coefficients statistically significant at the 5 percent level ($t > +2$). Twelve of the sixteen studies have average t-statistics greater than two, and the lowest average t-statistic reported by any study is 1.25. The grand mean of all 226 reported t-statistics is 2.46. In the studies that tried to account for the possible endogeneity of profit sharing, the results were not greatly changed by adding endogeneity controls.

If all studies used identical methods and data, the results would be more suspect (since they could all share common defects). The variety of specifications employed, as well as the diversity of data sources, lends greater credibility to the findings. We have performed several standard statistical tests developed under the name meta-analysis, a set of techniques used to analyze combined results from secondary sources.[50] Not surprisingly, because the present survey covers forty-two presumed independent samples in sixteen studies, the probability derived from meta-analysis is essentially infinitesimal that the null hypothesis of an underlying profit-sharing coefficient of zero or less is true. Although any one study has definite limitations, the evidence from all the studies taken together provides a quite strong indication that profit sharing and productivity are positively related.

A further question is the magnitude of the relation between profit sharing and productivity—if profit sharing does have an effect, is this effect large or small? The size of the effect almost certainly varies with the circumstances in which profit sharing is implemented. Point estimates of the size of the profit-sharing effect must be viewed with caution, since the estimates come from varying industries, time periods, sizes of firms, and so forth. To gain a rough idea of the size of the profit-sharing effect on productivity, we derived estimates from the regression coefficients of the various studies where sufficient information was provided. The mean estimated effect of profit sharing on productivity for "average" amounts of profit sharing (as measured by the mean values of profit-sharing variables within profit-sharing firms) is 7.4 percent, with a median estimate of 4.4 percent (and lower and upper quartiles of 2.5 percent and 11.0 percent).[51] Such estimates strike us as reasonable—they are neither

50. We used eight methods for analyzing significance levels across studies: the Fisher combined test, the method of adding t's (Winer test), adding probabilities, adding z's (Stouffer test), adding weighted z's, mean p, mean z, and the binomial sign test. All results overwhelmingly reject, at the highest levels of significance, the null hypothesis of a true underlying profit-sharing coefficient of zero or less. The methodology of meta-analysis, which has so far been used primarily in the psychometrics literature, is described in Robert L. Bangert-Drowns, "Review of Developments in Meta-Analytic Method," *Psychological Bulletin*, vol. 99 (May 1986), pp. 388–99; Frederic M. Wolf, *Meta-Analysis: Quantitative Methods for Research Synthesis* (Sage Publications, 1986); and Robert Rosenthal, "Combining Results of Independent Studies," *Psychological Bulletin*, vol. 85 (January 1978), pp. 185–93.

51. These estimates are based on 101 coefficients from twelve of the sixteen studies; excluded are 12 coefficients representing trend effects, 55 coefficients with insufficient information to calculate effects, and the 58 coefficients that were not based on panel data in Kruse 1988. (The 18 panel coefficients were judged to be better estimates of the "true" effect of profit sharing; when Kruse's nonpanel coefficients are included, the overall mean effect is 8.2 percent and the median 6.4 percent.)

Where profit sharing was measured as a dummy variable, the percentage effect size

so small as to be negligible, nor so large as to be implausible when adjustment costs are included.

A limitation of the econometric studies is that they shed little light on the mechanisms through which profit sharing may affect productivity. As discussed in the theory and industrial relations sections, productivity gains may come from many different sources, including more effort, greater quality, freer information flow, and increased acceptance of technological change. An important item on the research agenda is to gather data on these mechanisms and examine their relative contributions, since this knowledge is potentially important for managerial and public policy.

Conclusions and Implications

The available evidence on the connection between profit sharing and productivity is not definitive. Yet it is also not neutral—many sources point toward a positive link; the only quarrel seems to be over magnitudes. The firm-level econometric studies can perhaps be considered the most rigorous tests, and these studies taken together provide the strongest evidence that profit sharing and productivity are positively related. From the industrial relations literature, most case studies show improved performance when there is profit sharing or gain sharing (though a strong theme of that literature is that the success of these plans often depends on the conditions under which they are implemented). Attitude surveys indicate that employers and employees usually feel that profit sharing helps improve company performance. Considerations of economic theory and observations from comparative economic systems, though at best suggestive, are generally supportive of a positive link between profit sharing and productivity.

If one were tentatively to accept this evidence as showing that profit sharing has positive effects on productivity, what would be the policy

---

was estimated as $[exp(coefficient) - 1] \times 100$. Where profit sharing was measured as a continuous variable, the percentage effect size was estimated as $[exp(coefficient \times mean) - 1] \times 100$, where *mean* is the mean of the profit-sharing variable. In Jones 1982 profit sharing was measured in logarithmic form in the majority of the specifications, so that the coefficient represents an elasticity; there the rough estimate of the percentage profit-sharing effect is simply the coefficient times 100. When the dependent variable was not in logarithmic form, the percentage effect was estimated as $[(coefficient) \times (profit\text{-}sharing\ variable\ mean)] \div (dependent\ variable\ mean)$. In Schuster 1983 the percentage effect was estimated as the immediate change in the level of productivity, divided by the current level (ignoring the productivity trend change, which was positive in four of the six cases).

implications? Because productivity gains from profit sharing would seem to accrue largely to the firm, in principle there should be a firm-level incentive to adopt such plans and no public policy as such is needed. This observation may well contain a large measure of truth, but in practice, we feel, the issue is not settled. There could be many reasons why profit sharing is not more widespread even though it may basically be a good idea. The gains are probably modest, and perhaps it is a difficult change to engineer. A society's labor payment system seems to be one of the more likely candidates for historical inertia, institutional rigidities, and imitation effects. The profit sharing–productivity link is obviously complicated and depends on different environmental factors, some of a public-goods nature. Possibly, information gathering, exhortation, financial incentives, or other forms of social encouragement may be warranted. At this stage, it seems premature to speculate much further in such directions. More basic, empirical, data-oriented research is needed so that we can better understand the productivity effects of profit sharing and other group incentives.

Comment by David Card

Weitzman and Kruse's paper is remarkable for the breadth of evidence brought to bear on the question of profit sharing and productivity and for the exhaustive survey of previous empirical studies. Their reading of the evidence is that profit-sharing plans are associated with higher productivity. I have no quibble with this important conclusion. Nevertheless, as I read the paper several points occurred to me that deserve further consideration.

First, one should keep in mind that the productivity effects of a profit-sharing plan are likely to be once-for-all effects associated with the adoption of the plan. There is little presumption that profit sharing can lead to long-run changes in productivity *growth* .[1] Yet it is the growth

---

1. It is sometimes asserted that profit-sharing plans increase the incentives of employees to devise and suggest productivity-improving innovations. See, for example, Sumner H. Slichter, James J. Healy, and E. Robert Livernash, *The Impact of Collective Bargaining on Management* (Brookings, 1960), esp. pp. 851–75. If this assertion is correct, it implies that a correct empirical specification relates the level of productivity to the number of years of operation of the plan.

rate of productivity, rather than its level, that is the focus of many policy discussions.

Second, I find the dismal calculus of $1/n,$ associated with the free rider problem in group incentive schemes, rather more compelling than Weitzman and Kruse do. They argue that $1/n$ is overcome in a repeated game setting. In the absence of a clearer mapping between the game theory and the plans themselves, however, I remain skeptical that simple economic models of individual self-interest can usually explain the effects of profit sharing. It is true that cooperative behavior can be induced in multiperiod games by dynamic punishment schemes and the like. But what role is played in these games by profit-sharing plans that link current compensation to current profits? I would underscore the authors' conclusion that more research is needed on the mechanism by which profit-sharing plans elicit individual effort. Empirical work on this question would be aided by a clear statement of the theoretical linkages suggested by the more complicated multiperiod models.

A third comment pertains to the "meta-analysis" underlying table 4. The authors note that of 216 regressions reported, only 6 percent of the estimated profit-sharing coefficients are negative, and none are significantly negative at conventional levels. If these were unfiltered reports of 216 independent trials, that would be an impressive record. Unfortunately, there are important biases that can lead to a preponderance of positive coefficients even if the true coefficient is zero. The biases (or prior beliefs) of the authors of these studies are likely to lead to stopping rules for their specification searches that make positive coefficients more likely to turn up.[2] These biases are accentuated by the publication process, which makes it more likely for significantly positive results to appear in the literature.[3] In spite of these biases, however, several of the individual studies are carefully done, and taken with the rest, lead to a presumption of a positive effect.

2. See Edward E. Leamer, *Specification Searches, Ad Hoc Inference with Nonexperimental Data* (Wiley and Sons, 1978).
3. This publication bias is highlighted in a recent meta-analysis of cancer treatments. See Jesse A. Berlin, Colin B. Begg, and Thomas A. Louis, "An Assessment of Publication Bias Using a Sample of Published Clinical Trials," *Journal of the American Statistical Association,* vol. 84 (June 1989), pp. 381–92.

The Performance Effects of Employee Ownership Plans

Michael A. Conte and Jan Svejnar

EMPLOYEE ownership received much attention in Western economies in the 1970s and 1980s. In the United States the principal vehicle has been the employee stock ownership plan (ESOP); elsewhere other forms have been stressed (for example, cooperatives in Italy and France). This paper focuses on the effect on economic performance of employee ownership in the United States; in this context we mainly discuss ESOPs. But to provide a balanced view, we also discuss results from other countries.

Employee stock ownership plans are defined in sections 401(A) and 4975(E) (7) of the Internal Revenue Code and in section 407(D) (6) of the Employee Retirement and Income Security Act (ERISA). These and all other federal laws mentioning ESOPs treat them as employee benefit plans. However, the original promoters of ESOPs did not intend them to serve primarily as such. The 1976 annual report of the Joint Economic Committee described the intended purposes of ESOP incentives as follows: "to provide a realistic opportunity for more U.S. citizens to become owners of capital, and to provide an expanded source of equity financing for corporations."[1]

A subsequent congressional report acknowledged that "ESOPs share certain characteristics with other employee benefit plans—profit sharing, thrift and savings, and stock purchase or bonus plans."[2] But the differences between ESOPs and other employee benefit plans were again stressed, particularly the potential use of ESOPs as a technique of corporate finance. The report also stated that ESOPs "may . . . enhance

We thank Alan Blinder, Joseph Blasi, and Corey Rosen for their comments on an earlier version of the paper.

1. U.S. Congress, Joint Economic Committee, *1976 Joint Economic Report*, S. Rpt. 94-690, 94 Cong. 2 sess. (Government Printing Office, March 1976), p. 100.

2. U.S. Congress, Joint Economic Committee, *Broadening the Ownership of New Capital: ESOPs and Other Alternatives*, Committee Print, 94 Cong. 2 sess. (GPO, June 1976), p. 4.

employee motivation which in turn increases productivity." It was intended that widespread adoption of ESOPs would increase both the incomes of individuals in adopting companies and the level of the gross national product.

In this paper we discuss the reasonableness of these objectives and review the available empirical evidence on the extent to which ESOPs have stimulated economic performance. First, we describe the structure of ESOPs and the tax incentives that have been provided to encourage them. We then report some of the available descriptive statistics regarding the extent of ESOP adoption in the United States, the characteristics of the ESOPs adopted, and the extent of stock ownership and voting power resulting from ESOP adoption. Next we outline the theory underlying the possible effect of ESOPs on performance, then report the available evidence on the extent of such an effect. Afterwards, we briefly review some results from studies of employee ownership companies abroad. ESOPs have until recently been peculiar to the United States; it is unclear whether employee ownership of the kinds found in Europe has had the same effects on performance as employee ownership in America. Nevertheless, the results from the European studies seem to be consistent with the ESOP findings for the United States, and they also aid in interpreting some of the findings about ESOPs. Finally, we provide some concluding remarks.

ESOP Structure and Tax Incentives

In this section we compare ESOPs with other employee benefit plans and describe the central ESOP incentives that have been adopted by Congress. We note that, though the extent of tax incentives for leveraged ESOPs has been overstated in the popular literature, important incentives for adoption of leveraged ESOPs have been passed since 1984, accounting for the relatively explosive growth since then.[3]

Structure

The three main types of employee benefit plans are defined benefit pension plans, profit-sharing plans, and stock bonus plans.

Defined benefit pension plans (DBPPs) guarantee prespecified distri-

---

3. For a detailed discussion of ESOP legislation, see Joseph R. Blasi, *Employee Ownership: Revolution or Ripoff?* (Ballinger, 1988).

butions to employees upon their meeting certain conditions, such as reaching retirement age and terminating employment. As with all the other deferred compensation plans discussed here, DBPPs function through a trust containing an accumulation of plan assets at each point in time. Company contributions to the trust are based on the amounts needed to meet actuarially projected future plan distributions. These future distributions depend on the provisions of the plan; DBPPs usually award benefits to employees on the basis of the wages and salaries they earn in current service. The investment strategy of pension trusts is governed by law, the principal restriction being that no more than 10 percent of a defined benefit pension trust may be invested in the stock of the employer.

In contrast, defined contribution pension plans, such as *deferred profit-sharing plans* and *deferred stock bonus plans*, do not guarantee specific amounts for future distribution. Once a company contribution is made, resulting distributions depend on the investment performance of the trust. Because profit-sharing and stock bonus trusts are not designed to provide predictable future benefits, they are less highly regulated than pension trusts and may invest to any degree in the stock of the employing company.

Until 1986 contributions to deferred profit-sharing plans were required to be tied to the employer's accounting profits, at least insofar as there could be no contributions to the plan if the firm earned no profits during the year. However, the Deficit Reduction Act of 1984 removed even this minimal required relationship between profit-sharing contributions and accounting profits. Hence there is little left to distinguish a profit-sharing plan from a stock bonus plan.

Deferred stock bonus plans may contribute to a trust on any basis, and the trust may be fully invested in employer stock (although no investment in employer stock is necessary). The main distinguishing feature of a stock bonus plan is that employees have the right to insist on distributions in the form of employer stock—a right that employees do not have under pension or profit-sharing plans.

Both defined benefit and defined contribution pension plans are subject to many restrictions and regulations designed to protect employee account values. Over and above the limitation imposed on defined benefit plans regarding investment in employer securities, the main restrictions are that contributions cannot exceed 15 percent of total employee compensation, that the trust cannot engage in any financial relationship with the employer except to receive contributions, and that the trust may not borrow money. Even though *employee stock ownership plans* have many features in common with other deferred employee benefit plans, none of these restrictions apply to ESOPs. But certain other restrictions do apply. The central restriction on ESOPs is that the trust, called an employee stock ownership trust (ESOT), be invested primarily in the employer's stock. The word *primarily* is usually interpreted to mean 51 percent. Note that this level of investment in employer securities is permitted to employee stock bonus plans and to profit-sharing plans; however, it is *required* of ESOPs.

What makes ESOPs unique among all employee benefit plans is that the trust may engage in financial interactions with the company (for example, by buying stock of a closely held company) and may borrow money. The General Accounting Office refers to an ESOP with a borrowing provision as "leverageable." Note that a leverageable ESOP need not actually be leveraged; nevertheless, the leveraging feature was promoted as one of the most desirable aspects of the ESOP tax incentives.

Initially, ESOP contributions were governed by the same 15 percent (of total employee compensation) rule governing all other employee trusts. But in 1981 this ceiling was raised to 25 percent, because the 15 percent limitation made it difficult to amortize a loan for an employee buyout over a reasonable period of time.

In brief, then, an ESOP is a stock bonus plan that is required to invest primarily in employer securities and that may be leveraged. Also, as in any stock bonus plan, the value of distributions from an ESOP is determined by the performance of the trust, and employees may insist on distributions in the form of employer stock.

An additional feature that differentiates ESOPs from other employee benefit plans is that plan participants must be permitted to vote the securities allocated to their accounts if the securities are registered on a national exchange. Furthermore, as will be discussed next, several tax incentives for ESOP adoption passed in the 1980s have increasingly served to differentiate ESOPs from other employee plans.

ESOP Tax Incentives

There are two principal types of ESOP: tax deduction and tax credit.[4] Incentives to form tax credit ESOPs (TRASOPs or PAYSOPs) were

4. Additional concepts like the GESOP (government employees stock ownership plan) and the CSOP (consumers stock ownership plan) have been proposed, but we are not aware of any examples of these variations.

discontinued in 1986, and none have been formed since then. For this reason we limit discussion of tax credit ESOPs to the appendix. Here we discuss only tax deduction ESOPs and refer to them simply as ESOPs.

Under ERISA, ESOPs were primarily designed to engage in the following transactions: an employee stock ownership trust borrows money and uses it to purchase employer stock;[5] the ESOT may purchase treasury stock from the company or preexisting shares available on public markets or direct from previous owners. The trust then holds these shares as its chief investment. Repayment of the principal and interest of the loan is guaranteed by the company, which makes cash contributions to the ESOT according to the loan repayment schedule. Under this scenario the repayment of both the principal and the interest is tax deductible because they are portrayed as ESOP contributions. In comparison, under a conventional loan only the interest payment is tax deductible. The deductibility of the principal of a loan has been extensively cited as a central ESOP tax incentive.

In fact, however, no extra tax deduction is associated with this element of the ESOP transaction. Richard Musgrave and W. Gordon Binns were among the first to note that, for tax purposes, the above transaction is equivalent to forming a regular stock bonus trust; that is, borrowing money directly from a bank and repaying the loan while simultaneously making equivalent contributions of stock to the trust.[6] Under the stock bonus plan approach the stock contribution is deductible; under the ESOP, however, it is treated as a sale and is therefore nondeductible. Total deductions are the same in either case. As a result, an ESOP is an extremely expensive form of corporate finance unless the company planned on providing company stock to employees in any event. The company must either part with treasury stock, thus diluting the interest of preexisting shareholders, or donate the entire loan amount to employees in the form of shares purchased from preexisting owners. Dilution occurs in the second instance as well, even though there is no

5. If the ESOP buys treasury stock, this provides the company with cash and accounts for the view that the ESOP is a technique of corporate finance. In addition, legislation subsequent to ERISA introduced new corporate finance elements, discussed later in the text. But in many cases ESOPs have bought preexisting shares, which implies that the financial purpose was not to obtain cash. Estate planning and takeover defense are typical motives in such cases.

6. Musgrave submitted a statement to the 1976 Joint Finance Committee hearings, and Binns submitted a statement after the Joint Economic Committee hearings on ESOPs in the same year. See *Broadening the Ownership of New Capital*, p. 41.

expansion in the number of shares outstanding, because the donation reduces net assets. (Of course, any increase in earnings resulting from increased productivity would counteract the dilution effect in both instances.) Hence, though ESOPs do provide an additional technique of corporate finance, the cash that a leveraged ESOP can bring is not necessarily inexpensive.

If the company plans on donating shares to employees even without an ESOP, using an ESOP in a leveraged transaction may be more costly than taking out a conventional loan, since the tax deduction occurs only as the loan is repaid. If instead of using an ESOP the company donated the loan proceeds to a stock bonus trust to purchase stock on the market or from close holders, the full amount of the donation would be immediately deductible. It is therefore inappropriate under any scenario to view the ESOP provisions of ERISA as offering an inexpensive source of corporate finance. Although it is true that (if the ESOP buys treasury shares) the cash available to the company before distributions from the trust is greater than the cash available from conventional financing of the same magnitude,[7] the company would nonetheless be better off using conventional financing if cash was the only goal of the transaction and regular financing was available. This explains why up until the last few years the number of ESOP adoptions using a leveraged transaction was limited.

Several subsequent rules and tax incentives have made ESOPs considerably more attractive than they initially were. In 1981 the Economic Recovery Tax Act (ERTA) raised the limit on deductible contributions to an ESOP trust from 15 percent to 25 percent; the limit for all other kinds of employee trusts remained at 15 percent. This change increased the attractiveness of ESOPs primarily when employees were acquiring a complete or other large interest in the company, since it permitted a repayment schedule of shorter duration.

The Deficit Reduction Act of 1984 (DEFRA) included four additional incentives:

—*Tax-free rollover on sale to employees.* This permitted the tax-free rollover of the proceeds from the sale of a business to an ESOP or to a

---

7. Consider company A, which borrows a given sum through conventional financing, and company B, which borrows the same amount through the ESOP transaction. Of course, both A and B initially have this amount to use for the purpose of the loan. However, A's repayment is not tax deductible, whereas B's is; therefore, before distribution of any proceeds from the trust, cash available to B is greater than that available to A.

worker-owner cooperative, provided the proceeds were reinvested in the securities of another business within one year and provided the ESOP or cooperative, after the sale, held at least 30 percent of the employer securities.

—*Assumption of estate tax liability*. ESOPs or worker co-ops could assume the estate tax liability of a business estate in return for a stock contribution worth at least as much as the tax liability.

—*Deduction for dividends paid on ESOP stock*. This allowed a corporate deduction for dividends paid on stock held in an ESOP, provided the dividends were paid out to employees in the same year.

—*Partial exclusion of interest earned on ESOP loans*. This permitted banks, thrifts, insurance companies, and certain other commercial lenders to exclude 50 percent of the interest received on loans to ESOP companies from their taxable income, provided the loan proceeds were used to finance an ESOP's acquisition of company stock. As of this writing, the IRS is expected to rule that it will allow ESOPs to publicly sell bonds to finance their stock purchases and that these bonds will be governed by the interest exclusion (provided they are purchased by a commercial lender). The creation of a public market in tax-favored ESOP debt is expected to lead to an even greater mushrooming of ESOPs in the near future.[8]

Finally the Tax Reform Act of 1986 increased ESOP incentives in two important ways:

—*The elimination of the special tax treatment of long-term capital gains*. This increased the tax savings associated with the tax-free rollover provision of DEFRA.

—*A 50 percent exclusion on estate taxes when stock is sold to an ESOP*. This was intended to encourage owners of controlling interests in closely held companies to turn over their interest to their employees after death. However, this provision contained an unintended loophole: in effect, anyone could purchase the stock of an ESOP company in the open market, sell that stock to the company's ESOP, and avoid paying taxes. This loophole, which was actually used by several publicly held companies, threatened to eliminate estate taxes in the United States. It has now been closed by the IRS. But the provision as originally intended still provides a major ESOP incentive.

In addition, the 1986 act extended the deductibility of interest on ESOP loans to mutual funds and permitted corporations to take a tax

8. Matthew Winkler, "IRS Approves Public ESOP Bond Sales," *Wall Street Journal*, June 2, 1989, p. C1.

deduction for borrowing that is coordinated with the contribution of stock to a nonleveraged ESOP as long as the stock is allocated to employees in the same year. Note that the new maximum corporate tax rate of 34 percent (down from 46 percent) reduced the incentive associated with ESOP tax deductions; on balance, however, the 1986 act significantly increased the benefits of ESOP adoption.

Basic ESOP Statistics

Descriptive information on ESOPs is relatively sparse, since no government agency is charged with compiling summaries of information about employee plans on a continual basis. Two private organizations, the National Center for Employee Ownership (NCEO) and the ESOP Association, have conducted various studies. But most of the current publicly available descriptive information comes from a series of four reports issued by the General Accounting Office in response to an extensive information request from Senator Russell Long in 1984. The information we present here is primarily drawn from those reports and concerns the number of companies that have ESOPs and the main characteristics of their ESOPs: type, extent of ownership, availability of voting rights, and extent of other forms of nonmanagerial participation in decisionmaking.

A 1986 GAO study estimated that 4,174 ESOPs were active in the United States as of January 1983. Rosen, Klein, and Young estimated that in 1985 the number of firms with tax-qualified ESOPs was about 4,000, covering approximately 7 million participants. The National Center for Employee Ownership has since estimated that there were "8,777 ESOPs and similar plans at the end of 1987," covering about 7 million employees.[9] (These figures include stock bonus plans that are not qualified ESOPs as well as stock bonus plans that are part of an ESOP.) Although by these estimates the number of ESOPs and ESOP-like plans is small compared with the number of profit-sharing plans (about a hundred thousand) and pension plans (several hundred thousand), they reflect a fifteenfold increase in ESOPs since the ERISA

9. General Accounting Office, *Employee Stock Ownership Plans: Benefits and Costs of ESOP Tax Incentives for Broadening Stock Ownership*, GAO/PEMD-87-8 (December 1986); Corey M. Rosen, Katherine J. Klein, and Karen M. Young, *Employee Ownership in America: The Equity Solution* (Lexington Books, 1986); and "ESOP Growth Strong in 1987," *Employee Ownership Report*, vol. 8 (September–October 1988), p. 1.

legislation.[10] Thus the growth of ESOPs has been rather strong since they were officially sanctioned by mention in the tax code.

The GAO estimated in 1985 that 26 percent of the ESOPs active in 1983 were of the tax credit type (TRASOPs or PAYSOPs). The remaining 74 percent were of the tax deduction type, of which 51 percent (two-thirds of this group) were leverageable and 16 percent had used the leveraging provision.[11] This small fraction of leveraged ESOPs is consistent with the idea that ESOP loans are not an inexpensive source of corporation finance. Note that, according to a later GAO report, a stated reason for ESOP formation in about 4 percent of cases was to "save a failing company" and in about 5 percent to make the company "less vulnerable to hostile takeovers."[12] The leveraging provision of ESOP is useful in such cases, but not because of the associated cost of funds. If the ESOP mechanism did provide an inexpensive source of corporation finance, it would be used much more frequently to finance investment in real assets.

Overall, 90 percent of all ESOP participants were in TRASOPs or PAYSOPs because large companies tended to form those kinds. Tax credit ESOPs were approximately 3.2 times the size of tax deduction ESOPs in total dollar value; however, tax deduction ESOPs had substantially more assets per participant—$7,759 as against $2,968. PAYSOPs offered a virtually token employee benefit when measured by yearly contribution and provided employees with a very small stake in their company's performance: they were limited to a contribution of 0.5

10. Using data from the employee plan master file, compiled jointly by the Internal Revenue Service and the U.S. Department of Labor, Bloom estimated that only 310 plans with "ESOP features" existed in the year 1973, that is, two years before ERISA. Steven M. Bloom, "Employee Ownership and Firm Performance," Ph.D. dissertation, Harvard University, 1985. There is disagreement, however, about whether it is appropriate to use the term employee stock ownership plan to refer to employee plans that existed before ERISA. Many legal experts argue that the formation of an ESOP was illegal before ERISA, though the Regional Rail Reorganization Act of 1973 had mandated a study of the use of ESOPs to reorganize several northeastern railroad companies into what eventually would be called Conrail. This piece of legislation was largely supervised by proponents of ESOPs, who felt that prior law permitted such plans to operate. The legitimacy of establishing an ESOP at Conrail before ERISA was never tested for two reasons: first, though the study recommended that Conrail adopt an ESOP, it did not do so; second, ERISA followed soon on the heels of the rail act.

11. General Accounting Office, *Initial Results of a Survey on Employee Stock Ownership Plans and Information on Related Economic Trends,* GAO/PEMD-85-11 (September 1985).

12. General Accounting Office, *Employee Stock Ownership Plans: Benefit and Costs of ESOP Tax Incentives for Broadening Stock Ownership,* GAO/PEMD-87-8 (December 1986), p. 20.

percent of employee wages and salaries each year. In contrast, surveys by Feldman and Rosen found that contributions to tax deduction ESOPs average about 10 percent of salaries and wages each year, implying that workers at the 1983 median wage level of $18,058 would amass about $31,000 in their ESOP account after ten years of participation in the plan.[13]

Only about 24 percent of firms with ESOPs were publicly traded in 1983, though 65 percent of tax credit ESOPs were sponsored by publicly traded companies. Again this reflects the large-firm phenomenon. Privately owned firms operated 94.4 percent of all ESOPs that had a leveraging provision and 84.7 percent of all ESOPs that were actually leveraged. In general, these percentages reflect the limited availability of financing and outright sale opportunities for privately held compared with publicly held firms. Even though ESOP financing is costly in the long run, it does provide a temporary cash advantage over conventional borrowing, which may prove attractive to a financially strapped private company. Additionally, what has come to be called the estate motive for ESOP financing applies primarily in private companies. These are situations in which an owner wishes to divest shares and for one of several reasons wants to sell them to employees of the company. The tax-free rollover provision of the 1984 tax bill permits doing so when at least 30 percent of the company is owned by employees, a difficult quota to achieve in publicly traded companies.

The typical ESOP owns a relatively small percentage of the corporation's stock. In 1986 the GAO estimated that the median percent of stock owned by ESOPs was 10 percent. As might be expected, however, this percentage varied greatly by type of ESOP: tax credit ESOPs owned a median of 2 percent of employer stock, whereas leveraged ESOPs owned a median of 20 percent.[14]

Ownership need not imply voting strength. Nearly 70 percent of ESOPs hold employer stock with voting rights, but for several reasons ESOP participants may actually exercise very little voting strength. First, ESOPs that have voting stock may also have some stock which either does not have a vote or may not be voted by the participant. That situation is most common in leveraged ESOPs, in which employees may not vote shares that have not been allocated; allocation occurs only as

13. Jonathon Feldman and Corey Rosen, "Employee Benefits in Employee Stock Ownership Plans: How Does the Average Worker Fare?" National Center for Employee Ownership, Oakland, Calif., September 1985.

14. GAO, *Employee Stock Ownership Plans: Benefits and Costs*, p. 39.

the loan is paid down. Second, though all ESOPs since 1978 have been required to own classes of stock with (the best) voting rights, privately held corporations need not pass these rights through to participants except on supermajority corporate issues. Hence even 100 percent employee ownership can involve little actual employee voting power.

A related but separate issue is the extent of nonmanagerial employee involvement in decisionmaking. Many of the arguments for expecting an effect of employee ownership on productivity depend on the ability of employees to bring about organizational change of some type— perhaps by better monitoring of fellow employees (as will be discussed). In 1986 the GAO found that managers in 27 percent of all ESOP firms reported an increase in nonmanagerial employee involvement in company decisionmaking since ESOP adoption. This percentage varied very little across types of ESOP companies; there was, however, a substantial difference across types in the percent of companies reporting that increased participation occurred in formal structures like committees or task forces. Of the companies with leveraged ESOPs reporting an increase in nonmanagerial employee participation, 27 percent indicated that participation was through a formal structure, but only 3 percent of those with tax credit ESOPs reported the existence of such structures.[15] This fact is significant because, as will be seen, research has shown that participation through committees and the like affects performance positively, whereas increases in employee voting strength and board membership do not have a measurable effect.

Employee Ownership and Productivity

Since the Industrial Revolution, business firms have experimented with many compensation schemes in which employees share in the variability of earnings. The first such type of plan to be tried on a broad basis was profit sharing, which creates a link between group performance and individual pay as well as a commonality of goals between labor and management. It has long been argued that this link provides an incentive for increased employee work effort and that the accompanying commonality of interest within the company decreases labor-management tensions, thereby promoting better company performance.

The incentive argument has been applied to all schemes in which a link exists between an outcome of importance to the firm and an outcome of importance to the individual. Employee ownership, however, may

15. GAO, *Employee Stock Ownership Plans: Benefits and Costs*, p. 41.

actually be a better application of the argument than profit sharing, because it is not always in the interest of the firm (that is, all shareholders) to increase current profits. This is true, for example, when a firm needs to invest heavily in new technology in the present to ensure future profitability. In the early years of such an investment program, a profit-sharing plan may provide few benefits to employees because accounting profits are low (owing to accelerated depreciation). By contrast, in an efficient market (one that captures the effect of future profits in present stock prices), such an investment program should increase stock prices in the early years, thereby providing "correct" incentives to employees. By itself, the incentive argument is not very compelling because of the classic free rider problem: all employees, whether or not their effort levels are high, share in the reward. The situation may be regarded as a prisoner's dilemma: an individual has an incentive to shirk, but all employees would be better off if all agreed to work hard. In the absence of possibilities for enforceable agreements among employees over individual levels of effort, the incentive to exert effort is only $1/n$ of the result of that effort, where n is the number of persons sharing in the reward. If employees could achieve a cooperative solution wherein enforceable agreements about effort levels could be made, the group reward would be a much greater motivator. The issue then comes down to the possibilities for drawing up agreements and for enforcing them once made.

Other arguments for the existence of both positive and negative productivity effects are more compelling; these involve employee self-selection, investment in firm-specific human capital, and monitoring and information costs.

The self-selection argument is that employees who desire to be paid according to their own performance are themselves likely to be more productive persons and will be drawn to firms that have performance-dependent compensation systems. Therefore, the existence of an employee ownership program as part of the compensation structure might aid managers in selecting a high-quality work force. This does not mean that aggregate productivity will be higher with ESOPs, but it is an important estimation issue. It implies that empirical analyses should control for the quality of the work force. And if self-selection occurs, there is an obvious implication for management. (It should start ESOPs to attract good employees. Of course, this is a zero-sum game.)

As for the next argument, the vesting provisions of all employee plans lead to the possibility of increased average job tenure. Vesting of employee accounts usually takes several years, which makes the quit decision a relatively costly one. As a result, average tenure with the firm will probably increase in firms whose plans have these features, with an accompanying increase in firm-specific human capital.

A monitoring cost argument developed by Jensen and Meckling can be used to support either a positive or negative productivity effect. The authors later used this approach to argue for a negative productivity effect, citing added monitoring costs in employee-owned firms.[16] This view assumes that employee-owners have greater latitude in their daily tasks as a result of a deemphasis on hierarchical structure within the firm. However, Fitzroy and Kraft argue that monitoring costs in employee-owned firms are lower than in conventionally owned firms because "horizontal monitoring" is possible. And Bradley and Gelb provide evidence from the Spanish Mondragon group of cooperatives that employee-owners do monitor each other.[17] That is clearly less costly than hierarchical monitoring, and it makes the cooperative solution to the prisoner's dilemma game a more likely outcome.

Information costs may also be lower in employee-owned firms because managers and employees will have more interests in common. Asymmetry of information is a well-documented source of productive inefficiency, and various types of employee involvement programs, such as Scanlon plans, labor-management committees, and quality circles, have been developed to address that issue. Besides providing information to management, such groups promote formal and informal information sharing among employees, which again permits the achievement of a cooperative solution. On the other hand, employee ownership may raise desires for information and participation in decisionmaking on the part of employees. If those desires are frustrated, employee turnover may increase and work effort diminish.

Empirical Results Relating to ESOPs

An ideal experimental design would include imposing a characteristic of interest randomly on a sample of subjects, observing the subjects over

16. Michael C. Jensen and William H. Meckling, "Theory of the Firm: Managerial Behavior, Agency Costs and the Ownership Structure," *Journal of Financial Economics*, vol. 3 (October 1976), pp. 305–60; and Jensen and Meckling, "Rights and Production Functions: An Application to Labor-Managed Firms and Codetermination," *Journal of Business*, vol. 52 (October 1979), pp. 469–506.

17. Felix FitzRoy and Kornelius Kraft, "Profitability and Profit-Sharing," *Journal of Industrial Economics*, vol. 35 (December 1987), pp. 113–30; and Keith Bradley and Alan Gelb, "Motivation and Control in the Mondragon Experiment," *British Journal of Industrial Relations*, vol. 19 (July 1981), pp. 211–31.

time, and comparing the change in performance of the "treated" group with the change in performance of the "nontreated" group. This purity of design is unachievable in the social sciences except in experimental settings that abstract from the complexity of a natural environment. As a result, almost all studies of how characteristics of firms affect their performance are subject to selection (endogeneity) bias.

None of the ESOP studies to date have adequately dealt with the potential estimation bias due to endogeneity. Nonetheless, several of the studies have addressed the problem explicitly, with dramatic changes in results in some cases. The availability of better data in the future will permit better control to be made for self-selection. Here we report the most important results achieved so far and indicate the conclusions that we feel are safe to make at this stage of the research effort.

Conte and Tannenbaum

This was the earliest published study of the effect of employee ownership on company performance.[18] The authors used survey data from ninety-eight companies that had been identified as being at least partly employee owned either through an ESOP or through direct share ownership. They took the ratio of pretax profits to sales as a basis for gauging performance; this ratio was divided by the corresponding industry ratio as reported in Robert Morris Statement Studies for companies in the same size group and in the same industry. Profit data were supplied by thirty companies.

Conte and Tannenbaum adjusted the accounting statement of profit for five of the companies in which employees had complete discretion in wage setting and in which, to avoid taxes, part of the profit was regularly distributed as wages. The average profit ratio for the thirty companies after this adjustment was 1.7, implying that the employee-owned companies had (adjusted) profit-to-sales ratios 70 percent higher than their industry counterparts. (The average unadjusted profit ratio was 1.5.) Because in-sample profitability had a high variance and the number of cases was relatively small, the 70 percent differential was not statistically significant. Nonetheless, this high ratio suggested that there might be a large difference between the performance of employee-owned and non-employee-owned companies. An ordinary least squares (OLS) regression analysis was therefore performed to assess which features of

18. Michael Conte and Arnold S. Tannenbaum, "Employee-Owned Companies: Is the Difference Measurable?" *Monthly Labor Review*, vol. 101 (July 1978), pp. 23–28.

Table 1. Regression Results from the Conte and Tannenbaum Study

Independent variable	Profitability		Productivity	
	Coefficient	Standard error	Coefficient	Standard error
Constant	0.57	1.10	−0.40	0.25
Types of ESOP	0.94	0.97	0.20	0.21
Assets per participant	0.00	0.00	−0.00	0.00
Percent owned by ESOP	−0.02	0.03	−0.00	0.01
Full voting rights	−0.24	0.91	0.21	0.20
Level of participation	−0.87	0.97	0.52[a]	0.21
Change in participation	−1.22	0.83	0.25	0.18
Industry	0.58	0.74	0.24	0.17
Size (revenues)	−0.00	0.00	−0.00	0.00
R^2	0.07	3.10	0.23	0.49
Number of cases	80	. . .	47	. . .

Source: Michael Conte and Arnold S. Tannenbaum, "Employee Owned Companies: Is the Difference Measurable?" *Monthly Labor Review*, vol. 101 (July 1978), pp. 23–28.
a. Significant at the 0.02 level.

employee ownership, if any, caused the sample companies to apparently differ in profitability from the norm. The predictors used were

—form of ownership (direct ownership = 1, ESOP = 0);

—percent of employees participating in plan;

—percent of equity owned internally (by both managers and nonmanagers);

—percent of equity owned by nonmanagerial employees only;

—whether worker representatives sit on the board of directors (yes = 1, no = 0);

—whether employee stockholders vote (yes = 1, no = 0).

The reason for including two measures of inside ownership (total internal ownership and ownership by nonmanagers only) was to test for the effect of specifically nonmanagerial employee ownership.

The regression results are reported in table 1. Interestingly, the only significant predictor of adjusted profitability (relative to the industry average) was the percent of equity owned by nonmanagerial employees, which had a coefficient of 1.02, implying that a 1 percent increase in nonmanagerial employee ownership increases profitability by 1 percent—a very large effect. The percent of equity owned internally and the percent of employees participating in the plan had relatively large negative, but insignificant, coefficients. The two participation variables, worker representatives on the board and employee share vote, had small negative and insignificant coefficients.

On the surface these findings mean that nonmanagerial employee ownership increases profitability and that other aspects of employee ownership, such as managerial employee ownership and nonmanagerial participation in decisionmaking, either contribute negatively to profitability or do not matter. The authors cautioned, however, that any conclusions should be tentative because "the companies that provided profit data may be select, and the analyses are based on correlations that illustrate association among variables—they do not prove causation."[19] Moreover, since the analysis was not based on a model explaining the adoption of employee ownership, endogeneity problems exist.

Aside from these technical issues, the Conte-Tannenbaum study results raise at least two important institutional questions. Why would nonmanagerial employee ownership have a positive influence on company performance when other internal ownership exerts a negative or negligible influence? And do the variables "whether worker representatives sit on the board of directors" and "whether employee stockholders vote" accurately and adequately measure nonmanagerial employee participation in decisionmaking? As will be discussed, these are important issues that have been addressed in subsequent studies.

Livingston and Henry; and Brooks, Henry, and Livingston

These two studies also tried to shed some light on the relation between ESOPs and profitability.[20] The authors used data on the annual profits of fifty-one firms with employee stock ownership and compared them to data from fifty-one firms without employee ownership, matched to the first group by industry and size. However, since the plans included in this sample were initiated between 1916 and 1966, they are unlikely to have been ESOPs. According to the General Accounting Office, they were actually stock purchase plans. If that is true, then the results of these two studies are not relevant to ESOPs. But their conclusion is worth mentioning; it is as important for the attending caveat as it is for our knowledge about the relationship between employee stock ownership and firm performance. By using a univariate comparison of means and a multidimensional discriminant analysis, Livingston and Henry

19. Conte and Tannenbaum, "Employee-Owned Companies," p. 27.
20. D. Tom Livingston and James B. Henry, "The Effect of Employee Stock Ownership Plans on Corporate Profits," *Journal of Risk and Insurance*, vol. 47 (September 1980), pp. 491–505; and LeRoy D. Brooks, James B. Henry, and D. Tom Livingston, "How Profitable Are Employee Stock Ownership Plans?" *Financial Executive*, vol. 50 (May 1982), pp. 32–40.

found that profitability ratios are significantly different for ESOP and non-ESOP firms, with the ESOP firms having lower profitability. (The Brooks, Henry, and Livingston results were similar.) The authors note that "one important and possible explanation for this difference in profits may be that less profitable firms formed ESOPs in an attempt to improve their competitive position by using the plans as employee motivators."[21] This is the endogeneity issue mentioned earlier.

The findings of these two studies on the profitability effects of employee ownership hence conflict with those of Conte and Tannenbaum. That study was analytically more sophisticated because in its multivariate regression analysis it controlled for the profitability effect of a number of factors. One might therefore argue that its results are more credible; however, the univariate analyses in the other two studies depended on a larger data base and as such they potentially contain more information. Since estimates in all three studies may suffer from the endogeneity of regressors and selectivity biases, it is hard to assess which set of findings is more credible.

Bloom

In his 1986 doctoral dissertation Steven Bloom used a production function approach at the company level and could therefore investigate the effect of ESOPs on a true measure of productivity.[22] He worked with two kinds of publicly available data: (1) data about ESOPs from the employee plan master file (EPMF), a unique data base compiled from information returns to the Internal Revenue Service and the Department of Labor, and (2) Standard and Poor's Compustat primary, supplementary, tertiary, and over-the-counter data bases, which contain operating data for many public companies. Bloom included in his analysis all firms represented in both data sets, that is, primarily large and exclusively publicly traded firms.[23]

The median plan contribution per active participant in Bloom's ESOP firms was $578, or about 2.2 percent of the median total labor expense

21. Livingston and Henry, "Effect of Employee Stock Ownership Plans," p. 502.

22. Bloom, "Employee Ownership and Firm Performance."

23. The employee plan master file is based on form 5500 information returns, which are required of companies that have employee plans with 100 or more participants. These data of course bias the sample toward larger companies, which were more likely to have tax credit ESOPs (TRASOPs or PAYSOPs) than small companies. The bias against small companies is increased by the matching with Compustat data, which primarily include public companies with "significant investor interest."

per employee (salaries and wages, pension benefits, and other fringe benefits), which Bloom reported to be $26,700. Therefore, employees in most of the ESOP firms in this sample did not receive a substantial fraction of their income from the ESOP and did not have ESOP accounts that were large relative to their income. (The median assets per active participant in Bloom's sample of firms was $1,926, or about 7.2 percent of median labor cost.) The reason is probably that Bloom's data were biased toward large companies, which were likely to have TRASOPs. As discussed in the appendix, per-participant contributions to TRASOPs were usually low relative to contributions to tax deduction ESOPs. Also, a majority of Bloom's ESOP firms were in capital-intensive industries, particularly utilities, which were most inclined to adopt TRASOPs.[24]

These relatively small contribution levels suggest that there should not be much difference, *on average,* between the performance of Bloom's ESOP sample and his non-ESOP sample after controlling for other factors. That is basically what Bloom found in his first approach, which used a cross-sectional regression on one year of data (1981). Regressing the log of per-employee sales on a constant and an ESOP dummy variable (coded 1 when the company had an ESOP in 1981 and 0 otherwise) was positive and highly significant, but the significance of the ESOP dummy disappeared when gross plant per employee and total employment were included in the equation. Such great sensitivity to model specification is clearly related to the fact that Bloom's ESOPs were primarily TRASOPs, clustered in capital-intensive industries and providing little ownership to employees.

Bloom discussed several problems arising from the simple cross-sectional methodology, principally the problem of endogeneity (self-selection) in the sample of ESOP firms. For various reasons one can expect that firms which adopt ESOPs are different from firms which do not. For example, firms which are highly profitable have a greater financial incentive to adopt plans that reduce their corporate profit tax. Assuming that productivity and profitability are positively correlated, this tax-avoidance behavior could result in a positive estimated productivity effect even if ESOP adoption has no effect on either productivity

24. The TRASOP tax benefit was in proportion to the capital investment of the company. That, combined with economies of scale in plan administration, led to a preponderance of large capital-intensive companies with TRASOPs. Smaller or less capital-intensive companies found that the benefit-cost ratio worked against establishing a TRASOP.

or pretax profitability, or it could result in "no effect" when the effect may actually be negative.

As another example of possible endogeneity bias, assume that ESOP adoption does enhance productivity by some percentage, say X. Wise managers will realize this and implement an ESOP, whereas less apt managers will not. Suppose that good management increases productivity by Y. A regression in which a dummy variable for ESOP adoption is included, but the quality of management is not controlled for, may well impute the amount $X + Y$ to the ESOP dummy variable, thereby overstating the amount of the productivity increase due to ESOP adoption. This example is not fanciful because, contrary to popular belief, only about 5 percent of ESOPs have been formed in troubled companies. If there is a positive ESOP effect, some of the measured effect probably reflects farsighted management.

In general, if ESOP adoption is endogenously determined, productivity differentials may be correlated with, though not caused by, the presence of ESOPs. Bloom tried several approaches to ameliorate the self-selection bias. First, the regression equations were reestimated in a time-series setting. Then the cross-sectional and time-series regressions were reestimated for a within-sample cut of the data and for a cut that used data only from companies with positive tax bills.

In general, the various approaches had about the same results. The ESOP effect was measured fairly consistently as positive but insignificant. The main exception was the within-sample approach; there ESOP was measured not by the use of a dummy variable, but rather with two variables measuring ESOP size: fraction of employees owning ESOP shares (FRACPART) and fraction of company shares owned by the ESOP (FRACSHARES). In most of the regression specifications on the within-sample data the coefficient on FRACPART was insignificant, though in some cases it was negative. The coefficient on FRACSHARES was also insignificant throughout, but it had a relatively large negative value for some of the regressions, indicating that "productivity falls by between 5 and 8 percent for every additional 10 percent of stock owned by the employees."[25] Bloom surmises that this negative coefficient may itself have resulted from a simultaneity issue of a different sort,[26] and

25. Bloom, "Employee Ownership and Firm Performance," p. 186.

26. According to Bloom, "Apparently this variable is picking up financially-troubled companies who adopted ESOPs as a matter of survival, making a determination of a positive productivity effect of ESOPs ever more unlikely" (p. 186).

concludes that ESOPs have had little effect on any of the variables of interest.

The findings of the Bloom study hence fall between the positive effects found by Conte and Tannenbaum and the negative effects detected by Livingston and Henry, and Brooks, Henry, and Livingston. Apart from explaining the behavior of sales rather than of profits, the Bloom study differs from the other two by using a much larger sample of firms and undertaking a more in-depth analysis of the data. The unfortunate characteristic of Bloom's data set is that the sampled firms show low levels of employee stock ownership and little variation in its extent. Because of this and because the sample was probably composed largely of TRASOPs, which no doubt involves a selection bias of its own, a spurious finding of no significant effect of ownership on productivity can result.

Quarrey

This unpublished study was the first to pay close attention to the participation variable.[27] Michael Quarrey used three alternative approaches to measuring employee participation in decisionmaking. The first measured formal decisionmaking power: whether employees have voting stock and whether employee representatives sit on the board of directors. The second approach measured managers' perceptions. Managers were asked to indicate how much influence workers have over seven areas: social events; working conditions; the way workers perform their own jobs; pay and other compensation; hiring, firing, and other personnel decisions; selection of supervisors and management; and company policy. Possible answers ranged from (1) "workers have no say" to (5) "workers decide alone." The company's score was the average response to all seven items. Finally, the third approach measured the existence of working groups or committees dealing with seven substantive areas.

Besides measuring participation, Quarrey tried to measure awareness of employee ownership. A simple scale measured the number of different ways in which the company communicated information to its employees about the ESOP.

For his study Quarrey gathered data from 45 ESOP firms and 292

27. Michael Quarrey and Corey Rosen, "Employee Ownership and Corporate Performance," National Center for Employee Ownership, Oakland, Calif., October 1986.

matched non-ESOP firms (at least 3, and an average of 5.3, per ESOP company). The data for the ESOP firms were available for periods both before and after ESOP adoption, thus permitting before-after comparisons.

The performance measures used in the study (the rate of sales growth, the rate of employment growth, and the rate of growth of the ratio of sales to employment) are only weakly related to productivity or profitability. The results were nonetheless instructive. Quarrey calculated the average difference in performance between the ESOP and non-ESOP companies, both for the postadoption years and for the preadoption years. He found that the postadoption average employment growth difference was 6.52 percent higher than the preadoption difference, and the postadoption sales growth difference was 7.09 percent higher than the preadoption difference. Both these differences (of differences) were significant at the 99 percent confidence level. However, the analysis did not control for self-selection, and therefore no causal inference can be made. It is possible, as with the Bloom study, that additional analysis controlling for preadoption characteristics would diminish the power of these results.

Quarrey also carried out several correlation analyses within the ESOP sample. Of greatest interest is the finding that in a multiple regression model estimated with OLS, using the variables management philosophy, perceived employee influence, existence of participation groups, number of years for 100 percent vesting of employee accounts, the existence of share voting rights in the ESOP, board representation, and company size, the only variables that were significant at the 0.1 level of confidence were perceived influence and existence of participation groups. Moreover, perceived influence was significant at the 0.1 level for only one of the three dependent variables used in this analysis (employment growth, sales growth, and growth in the ratio of sales to employment), while existence of participation groups was significant at the 0.05 level for two of these regressions and at 0.1 for the third.

Note that extent of employee ownership was not included in the regressions because it was shown not to have even a simple correlation with the performance variables. Note also that neither voting rights nor board representation was correlated with any of the performance measures, though "participation" was strongly correlated. Clearly, voting rights and board representation do not guarantee a participative environment, whereas participation groups do. This fact may explain Conte and Tannenbaum's result on voting and board representation (no impact).

Furthermore, if companies with employee ownership also tend to have participation groups, then the Conte-Tannenbaum result may be driven by the (unmeasured) existence of participation groups in the highly employee-owned companies in their sample.

General Accounting Office

The GAO has conducted the only study of ESOP profitability and productivity effects based on tax return data.[28] It identified a representative national sample of about 1,100 ESOP firms and collected tax data for 414 of these firms that established their ESOPs in the 1976–79 tax years. (These dates ensured that there would be two years of pre-ESOP and three years of post-ESOP data available for the analysis.) Six consecutive years of tax returns were obtainable for 111 of the ESOP firms. The GAO matched these firms by industry and gross revenue to non-ESOP firms and then analyzed those firms for which data were complete for all six years (106 for the analysis of profitability and 45 for the productivity analysis). Since most of the data used in the analysis were supplied compulsorily (to the IRS), the response bias problem was small, though the potential for a significant survival bias remained. (The data included ESOP firms that survived until 1985 as against non-ESOP firms that survived until 1982.) In addition, data were available on both a time-series and matched cross-sectional basis, and the sample represented the national mixture of ESOP firms for the most important characteristics (industrial classification, firm size, ESOP type, and ESOP size). Hence the data base was perhaps the best yet available to study performance effects of ESOPs.

One problem the sample design could not address was the selection bias discussed earlier. The GAO tried to control for that bias by using analysis of covariance (ANCOVA). In its analysis the GAO sought to identify whether the rate of growth of profitability or labor productivity, or both, was greater after the adoption of ESOP than before, as compared with the performance of a matched sample of non-ESOP firms in the same years. (The purpose of the matching was to control for any profitability and productivity growth that may have been due to national economic conditions rather than to ESOP adoption.) The ANCOVA compared each of the post-ESOP years' profitability and productivity

28. General Accounting Office, *Employee Stock Ownership Plans: Little Evidence of Effects on Corporate Performance*, GAO/PEMD-88-1 (October 1987).

performance with the average of the pre-ESOP years, implicitly controlling for performance levels in the pre-ESOP years. The analysis found profit performance in the second post-ESOP year, but not in the third year, to be significantly greater than in the average of the pre-ESOP years. This reflected either a transitory profitability gain or a spurious correlation. The ANCOVA-estimated productivity effects were all insignificant, and results from a multivariate analysis of variance (MANOVA) were similar. As a result, the GAO concluded that ESOP adoption did not affect profitability or productivity in the adopting firms.

In an accompanying regression analysis, the GAO was able to test for the performance effect of a number of ESOP features rather than accomplish only a simple before-after performance comparison. With both profitability and productivity as dependent variables, their regressors, estimated coefficients, standard errors, and significance levels were as given in table 1. These regression results seem to confirm the conclusion from ANCOVA and MANOVA that neither the extent nor the type of employee ownership affects performance levels. Note, however, that this regression model is very rigid; it imposes a linear form on the ESOP performance effect, implying that this effect increases (or decreases) steadily as the percent of employee ownership increases. If this assumption is incorrect and, say, the true performance impact was nonlinear, perhaps resembling an inverted U, the estimated coefficient in a linear equation might take on any sign or be insignificant.

The only coefficient that was significant at normal confidence levels was that on "level of participation" in the productivity equation. The coefficient of 0.52 implies that, other things being equal, firms in which nonmanagerial employees participate in company decisions have a 52 percent more rapid rate of productivity growth than firms in which they do not. (This does not imply that the former are 52 percent more productive, but nonetheless the implied participation effect is very large.) This result must be interpreted with great care; if it is true, it remains unclear whether such a large differential could be sustained over a long period, and it also remains unclear how the result relates to employee ownership. The result is, however, consistent with Quarrey's finding about the effect of nonmanagerial employee participation in decision-making and also with Conte and Tannenbaum's finding. (Table 1 shows that full voting rights—the participation measure used by Conte and Tannenbaum—have no significant effect on either profitability or productivity. Apparently, voting rights do not themselves guarantee that participative decisionmaking will take place. But when it does take place, the evidence is that it affects company-level productivity positively and rather strongly.)

Conte and Svejnar

These two companion studies are based on an unbalanced panel of 40 U.S. firms with varying degrees of worker ownership, profit sharing, participation in management, and unionization.[29] In particular, 21 of the 40 firms have an ESOT plan, 21 have a profit-sharing plan, 12 display direct ownership of capital by workers, and 13 operate a worker participation scheme. The two studies were the first to take into account the effect of all these variables on enterprise performance simultaneously. The ability to do so is important because omitting an important scheme from the analytical framework may result in a biased estimate of the effect of the other schemes.

The aim of the two studies was to estimate the impact of worker ownership, profit sharing, participation, and unionization on the total factor productivity (productive efficiency) of the firms. The 1987 Conte and Svejnar study carried out the analysis within a Cobb-Douglas production function framework, whereas their 1988 paper cast the analysis within a broader translog form. In both studies the authors tested a variety of specifications and generated estimates both by OLS and instrumental variable techniques. Their approach was to augment the standard input function by the relevant measures of the extent of worker ownership, profit sharing, participation, and unionization.

The results show that the various schemes systematically influence productive efficiency but that the estimates are sensitive to both the regression specification and the estimating technique. As for the effect of ESOPs on productivity, the studies suggest that it is positive at low and moderate levels of ownership but diminishes at high levels. To illustrate, the authors found that an ESOT which holds the sample mean fraction of company stock (12 percent) raises productivity 9 percent above what it would be in the absence of an ESOT.

29. Michael A. Conte and Jan Svejnar, "Productivity Effects of Worker Participation in Management, Profit-Sharing, Worker Ownership of Assets and Unionization in U.S. Firms," *International Journal of Industrial Organization,* vol. 6 (March 1988), pp. 139–51; and Conte and Svejnar, "The Effects of Worker Participation in Management, Profits and Ownership of Assets on Enterprise Performance," paper presented at a conference on New Developments in Labor Markets and Human Resource Policies, Massachusetts Institute of Technology, June 11–12, 1987.

Summary of Findings on U.S. Data

The principal studies based on U.S. data offer some contradictory results and some consistent ones. The main contradictions concern the effect of ownership per se. Conte and Tannenbaum found a large positive and significant ownership effect when no control was exerted for participation; Conte and Svejnar found that the ownership effect may be nonlinear but still significant and, on average, positive when controlling for participation. The other studies have usually found the partial employee ownership effect to be negligible. Although Quarrey showed that ESOP companies outperform non-ESOP companies, the GAO study seriously undermines the view that this better performance is caused by ESOP adoption. Obviously the final word on the partial effect of employee ownership is not yet in; it awaits somewhat better data and somewhat more sophisticated research designs than have yet been implemented.

Perhaps the clearest evidence concerns the effect of participation in employee-owned companies. The evidence shows that participation groups improve company performance in an employee ownership setting, though share voting and board representation do not. It remains to be seen how participation and employee ownership relate to each other; that is, would participation in decisionmaking have a significant effect, or as large a one, in a non-employee-ownership setting? A related interesting question is whether employee ownership is responsible for the existence of participation groups in companies that have both.

Empirical Results Relating to Non-ESOP Worker Ownership

A number of studies have examined the effect of worker ownership on performance in other (non-ESOP) contexts. These studies deal mostly with non-American cases, and as such they are not the main focus of our paper. But since the evidence on ESOPs is still limited and the information from other countries is complementary, we briefly review the principal findings of these studies.

Cable and Fitzroy

The authors sampled 42 out of more than 700 West German firms that operated profit-sharing and worker ownership of enterprise capital schemes in the 1970s.[30] They obtained three annual observations on each firm and tested different hypotheses, including whether employee stock ownership systematically affects productive efficiency. Their approach was to fit an augmented Cobb-Douglas production function, with the extent of worker ownership of capital being one of the included variables. Their OLS estimates show that the productivity effect of capital ownership is insignificant in the sample as a whole. However, when they divided the sample into firms with high and low degrees of worker participation in management, Cable and Fitzroy found that the effect was significantly positive in the high-participation firms and significantly negative in those with little participation.

This result clearly helps in interpreting some of the results for U.S. ESOP companies discussed earlier. It implies that there may be an interaction between employee ownership and participation, which possibly explains the presence of an ownership effect in the Conte and Tannenbaum study—in which participation was measured only by voting rights—and the absence of an independent ownership effect when participation was measured well (by Quarrey and the GAO).

Jones and Svejnar

This study analyzes the largest and fastest growing system of producer cooperatives in industrialized Western economies—the Italian co-ops.[31] It covers a sizable 1975–80 panel of data on 134 co-ops in manufacturing and construction. The data show considerable variation in the extent of worker ownership of capital, with some firms having almost none and some significant amounts. The sample thus lends itself to a test of the impact of worker ownership on performance, though it has a drawback in that no traditional (non-co-op) firms are included.

The study estimates the effect of worker ownership on productivity within a number of specifications of production functions. The specifications best supported by the data are selected and used in drawing empirical conclusions. The results suggest that individual worker own-

30. John R. Cable and Felix R. FitzRoy, "Productive Efficiency, Incentives, and Employee Participation: Some Preliminary Results for West Germany," *Kyklos,* vol. 33, no. 1 (1980), pp. 100–21; and Cable and FitzRoy, "Cooperation and Productivity: Some Evidence from West German Experience," *Economic Analysis and Workers' Management,* vol. 14, no. 2 (1980), pp. 163–80.

31. Derek C. Jones and Jan Svejnar, "Participation, Profit Sharing, Worker Ownership and Efficiency in Italian Producer Cooperatives," *Economica,* vol. 52 (November 1985), pp. 449–65.

ership (that is, ownership of negotiable shares by individual workers) has significant positive productivity effects in manufacturing and either insignificant or positive effects (depending on the functional form used) in construction. In contrast, capital owned collectively by all workers (that is, retained earnings without claims by individual workers) has a negative productivity effect in both sectors. The latter result replicates Jones and Bakus's earlier finding for British footwear cooperatives.[32]

Defourney, Estrin, and Jones

Methodologically this econometric study is similar to the previous one by Jones and Svejnar.[33] But it examines 1978–79 data from 541 cooperatives in France and so provides evidence on the effect of worker ownership in a different socioeconomic setting. Although the results vary by industry, the principal finding is that the extent of individual worker ownership (measured by the proportion of individually owned assets that are in the hands of workers) has a significant positive effect on productive efficiency.

Estrin, Jones, and Svejnar

This study uses a common set of proxies for the variables measuring worker ownership (as well as other variables), and it carries out a set of tests on the aforementioned Italian and French co-op data as well on a data set of twenty-four British co-ops during five-year intervals between 1945 and 1968.[34] The study therefore enlarges the data base and ensures

32. Derek C. Jones and David K. Backus, "British Producer Cooperatives in the Footwear Industry: An Empirical Evaluation of the Theory of Financing," *Economic Journal*, vol. 87 (September 1977), pp. 488–510. The coefficient on the collective ownership variable in this study was significant only at the 0.2 level of confidence. Moreover, the authors found the opposite (positive) sign when estimating the same production function on the large firms in their sample. Taken together with the Jones and Svejnar findings, these results indicate that the efficiency effects of collective ownership remain unclear. Because there are few examples of collective employee ownership in the United States, we do not discuss this phenomenon or the associated regression results in detail here.

33. Jacques Defourney, Saul Estrin, and Derek C. Jones, "The Effects of Workers' Participation on Enterprise Performance: Empirical Evidence from French Cooperatives," *International Journal of Industrial Organization*, vol. 3 (June 1985), pp. 197–217.

34. Saul Estrin, Derek C. Jones, and Jan Svejnar, "The Productivity Effects of Worker Participation: Producer Cooperatives in Western Economies," *Journal of Comparative Economics*, vol. 11 (March 1987), pp. 40–61.

that cross-country differences in findings are not due to different mea-
surements of the relevant variables. The analysis indicates that the
effects of worker ownership vary from one setting to another and that
the effect of worker ownership on productivity ranges from positive to
insignificant. The statistically insignificant effect is found most notably
in the British sample.

Estrin and Jones

In a recent study Estrin and Jones reexamined the French co-op data
to assess simultaneously the determinants of worker ownership, co-op
membership, and productive efficiency.[35] Unlike the earlier studies,
which merely controlled for the fact that the extent of worker ownership
of capital may be endogenous (that is, determined jointly with production
and other decisions), this study tried to model the complex relationship
between the ownership and productivity variables in greater depth. The
principal finding is that the effect of ownership on productivity remains
positive and statistically significant.

Lee

In her 1988 dissertation Barbara Lee examined the issue of productivity and employee ownership in Sweden.[36] In addition to theoretical
modeling, Lee used a 1983–85 panel of data from fifty employee-owned
and fifty-one matching nonemployee-owned firms to test the hypothesis
that employee ownership affects productivity. Lee tried a number of
specifications of total factor productivity and production function models.
Her overall findings show that worker ownership does not significantly
affect total factor productivity in Swedish industry.

Conclusions

Although the evidence on the performance effects of ESOPs is still
limited and the results achieved to date are somewhat contradictory,
one may still draw some preliminary conclusions. First, ownership does

35. Saul Estrin and Derek Jones, "Workers' Participation, Employee Ownership
and Productivity: Results from French Producer Cooperatives," London School of
Economics, Department of Economics, and Hamilton College, Department of Economics, November 1988.
36. Barbara W. Lee, "Productivity and Employee Ownership: The Case of Sweden,"
Ph.D. dissertation, Uppsala University, Sweden, 1988.

not decrease the level of company performance, as suggested by Jensen and Meckling. Not one study of U.S. firms found a negative performance effect. Jones and Svejnar found a negative performance effect for collective ownership, but this type of employee ownership is rare in the United States; it bears little relation to employee ownership through ESOPs. Cable and Fitzroy found a negative performance effect for employee ownership when participation was lower than normal. It may be true that splitting U.S. ESOP samples into high- and low-participation groups would have the same effect (namely, that the negligible results would turn into strong positive and strong negative results for the high- and low-participation groups, respectively). That remains to be seen, and in general raises the question of an interaction between ownership and participation. No U.S. studies have explicitly tested for such an interaction.

Second, whether employee ownership through ESOPs aids company performance remains unclear. As Bloom's work shows, the estimated effects depend crucially on research design and equation specification. What is needed is to develop a sufficiently large and varied data set capable of supporting estimation of a detailed simultaneous model.

Finally, it seems clear that participative institutions within firms lead to heightened performance levels when combined with employee ownership. However, the participation measures most commonly associated with ESOPs—voting rights and board representation—seem to have little or no performance effects either on their own or when combined with ownership. Future research should investigate the linkages, if any, between employee ownership and bona fide employee participation in decisionmaking.

Appendix

Under the Tax Reduction Act of 1975 companies were permitted to take an extra 1 percent investment tax credit if the full amount of the additional 1 percent was contributed to a tax reduction act stock ownership plan, commonly known as a TRASOP. This program was a pure subsidy from the U.S. treasury to companies and their employees for the purpose of broadening stock ownership. In 1976 TRASOP incentives were expanded by providing a tax credit for an additional 0.5 percent of capital outlay for employers who contributed an additional full percent in stock to employees. In 1983, because the incentive as originally passed favored capital-intensive companies, the basis of contributions was changed from investment in capital equipment to covered payroll; as a result, the tax-credit ESOP came to be referred to as the PAYSOP (payroll-based employee stock ownership plan). The idea remained the same, however; the federal government subsidized the transfer of stock to employees at a 100 percent rate for the first 1 percent of covered payroll, and at 50 percent for an additional 1 percent.

The tax incentive for companies to form TRASOPs or PAYSOPs was quite high. For small companies, however, the cost of setting up such a plan and applying for tax qualification was large even in relation to the offered tax credit. Most traded companies did adopt TRASOPs or PAYSOPs, or both. But because of the high cost of this form of ESOP to the federal treasury, the PAYSOP tax credit was discontinued, effective December 31, 1986, by the Tax Reform Act of 1986.

Comment by Joseph Raphael Blasi

My comment focuses on four issues central to the economic performance effects of employee ownership: (1) distinguishing between employee ownership and profit sharing; (2) clarifying the implications of trends in ESOP diffusion on this question; (3) understanding the limits of current studies and developing a strategy for useful research; and (4) deciding whether a rational analysis of this material supports ESOPs, profit sharing, or labor-management problem solving separately or together as a national policy objective. In discussing these issues, I will respond to the useful summaries of research found in Michael Conte and Jan Svejnar's paper and address some limitations to that paper.

Distinguishing between Employee Ownership and Profit Sharing

The fact that Conte and Svejnar and other contributors to this volume use employee ownership and profit-sharing plans to refer to two different kinds of labor sharing creates serious problems. Most of what researchers call profit-sharing plans are really deferred profit-sharing trusts that have sizable amounts of employee ownership of employer securities. Of the approximately half-million profit-sharing plans in the United States 96 percent are deferred profit-sharing trusts. An additional 3 percent are a combination of a deferred trust and cash profit sharing.[1]

There are different ways to estimate how much employee ownership is being masked as deferred profit-sharing plans. The crudest estimate is based on the total amount of employer securities held by ESOPs and deferred profit-sharing trusts. In 1983 ESOPs held almost nine-tenths of 1 percent of all corporate stock outstanding in the United States, whereas deferred profit-sharing trusts held 1.2 percent. (Other defined contribution plans, such as savings plans and 401(k) plans, which are both payroll-based savings plans with employer and employee contributions, held 0.9 percent.) Thus in 1983 deferred profit-sharing trusts were responsible for 25 percent more employee ownership than employee stock ownership plans in total; if all defined contribution plans (excluding ESOPs) are counted, they are responsible for almost two and one-half times more employee stock ownership than ESOPs.[2]

Several studies show that private and public company deferred profit-sharing trusts hold substantial assets in employer securities. Various estimates based on public company surveys indicate that 12–20 percent of public companies have deferred profit-sharing plans. Plans with more than $10 million in assets tend to hold 34 percent of those assets in company stock. Nineteen percent of the Fortune 1,000 firms have profit-sharing plans that hold 10 percent or more in company stock. About 50–70 percent of large manufacturing and nonmanufacturing firms have savings or thrift plans; in one sample 41 percent *required* investment in employer stock. And company stock is offered as an investment option in many 401(k) plans; 51 percent of those plans have an investment option for employer securities. A 1981 study found that in nine out of the seventy-nine deferred profit-sharing trusts in the Fortune 500 companies employee benefit plans were the largest stockholder. These firms held an average of 13.1 percent of the company's stock. It is significant to note that very few of the trusts were ESOPs.[3] A 1988 survey of largely private corporations showed that 17 percent of them put part of the fund

1. Joseph R. Blasi, *Employee Ownership: Revolution or Ripoff?* (Ballinger, 1988), p. 12.

2. Blasi, *Employee Ownership*, p. 11.

3. Joseph R. Blasi, *Employee Ownership through ESOPs: Implications for the Public Corporation,* Work in America Institute Studies in Productivity (Pergamon Press, 1987), p. 10.

in employer securities. Among these, 18 percent invested more than 50 percent of total plan assets, 41 percent invested 10–50 percent, and 41 percent invested less than 10 percent of total plan assets.[4]

Aside from the 1,500–2,000 ESOPs that own a majority of their corporation's stock, the General Accounting Office estimates that 75 percent of ESOPs own less than 25 percent of the company. One way to consider the real extent of the employee ownership of deferred profit-sharing trusts is to ask how *small* it must be to surpass the employee ownership in ESOPs. If more than 2 percent of the half-million deferred profit-sharing plans—namely, 10,000 companies—owned more than 20 percent of their employer's securities, then these trusts would represent a larger number of companies with sizable employee ownership than contained in the whole ESOP sector, which in 1989 included only about 10,000 firms.[5]

More systematic data will probably conclude that the distinction between "profit sharing" and "employee ownership" is largely bogus, the result of a massive disguising bias. And since over 96 percent of profit-sharing plans are of the deferred type, all comparisons and other discussion of employee ownership and profit sharing in this volume partake of that bias. Both ESOPs and deferred profit-sharing trusts provide the economic incentive to employees after a long period of employment. Only comparisons between ESOPs and cash profit-sharing plans, or *perhaps* deferred profit-sharing plans without employer securities, really segment the two kinds of labor involvement. Comparative studies of the performance effects of ESOPs and deferred profit-sharing trusts stumble over whether the employee ownership is profit sharing or the profit sharing is employee ownership! The usefulness of the Conte-Svejnar perspective, as well as that of profit-sharing researchers, is limited by these considerations.

Implications of the Trends of ESOP Diffusion

Since the economic performance studies of ESOPs reviewed by Conte and Svejnar have been completed, a major change in ESOP distribution has taken place. The authors rightly note that ESOPs in publicly held companies tended to be small tax credit plans holding very little company

4. Hewitt Associates and Profit Sharing Council of America, *1988 Profit Sharing Survey* (Chicago, 1988).
5. Blasi, *Employee Ownership*, pp. 100–05.

equity, and that Steven Bloom's study of public company ESOPs and economic performance, while significant in method, looked at this least relevant group of ESOPs. In fact, the tax credit ESOP was terminated by the Reagan tax reform. Aside from Bloom's, most studies of ESOP economic performance have examined privately held corporations. Now, however, ESOPs involve large numbers of public corporations with sizable employee ownership.

Approximately 250 publicly held corporations have set up ESOPs in the last two and one-half years, putting several tens of billions of dollars of corporate equity in the hands of employees. For the first time in U.S. economic history there is sizable broad-based employee equity in these companies, and it is expanding by the week.[6]

Typically, a company borrows funds that are used to purchase convertible preferred shares for the employee stock ownership plan (a leveraged ESOP). The ESOP usually ends up owning 12–20 percent of the company. Many companies have coordinated this transaction with a stock buyback that uses the new funds made available by the ESOP to support the stock price of the firm and prevent any dilution to shareholders.

The ESOP, especially in Delaware corporations (and states that follow the Delaware takeover statute), is perceived as an efficient anti-takeover defense.[7] A hostile raider must gain more than 85 percent of the company's disinterested shares in a tender offer, so that an ESOP of more than 15 percent would seem to make that impossible.

Companies are also restructuring their retirement or health benefits by substituting ESOPS for defined benefit plans (which have unpredictable costs), for commitments to pay post-retirement health benefits, and for defined contribution plans holding other than employer securities. My initial analysis shows that as many as 20 percent of these new ESOP adoptions entail replacing other benefits with the ESOP, so it is unclear that the ESOP represents a new compensation incentive.

As Conte and Svejnar discuss, ESOPs offer substantial tax advantages for public companies. Because dividends paid on the stock are also

6. These preliminary findings are based on the monitoring of the Dow Jones News Service throughout this period. *Business Week* recently highlighted this surprising development. Christopher Farrell and John Hoerr, "ESOPs: Are They Good for You?" *Business Week*, July 10, 1989, pp. 56–62. For a detailed study, see Joseph R. Blasi, "ESOPs in the Publicly Traded Corporate Sector," Rutgers University, Institute of Management and Labor Relations, 1989.

7. C. Berger, *Memorandum Opinion, Civil Action No. 10,075, Shamrock Holdings, Inc v. Polaroid Corp.* (Court of Chancery of the State of Delaware, 1988).

deductible for the company over and above the normal ESOP deduction limits, preferred shares with a high yield can thus substantially increase a public company's annual deduction.

Corporations are moving toward a flexible compensation system that replaces the fixed wage system, and many like the idea of tying part of pay to the performance of the company. A few firms see employee ownership as a sensible addition to their employee system either because they want to integrate employee and shareholder interests or because they want to complete an already progressive approach to labor-management relations. Polaroid, Procter and Gamble, and Weirton—three firms that emphasize participative management—are the prominent and possibly the only examples of public corporations that have announced this intention. Finally, some corporations are using the ESOP in novel financial transactions such as restructuring, cashing out large shareholders, refinancing debt, and recovering excess pension assets.[8]

Economic researchers need to focus their attention on this important sector. ESOPs in public companies are and will continue to be responsible for over 90 percent of the public tax expenditures on ESOPs. Also, unlike private companies, public companies by law must pass through voting rights on employee-owned shares. And unlike most private corporate ESOPs, the ESOP in a public company, with 12–20 percent of the firm's equity, is usually the largest shareholder.

Limits of Current Studies and Strategy for New Research

A review of economic performance studies of ESOPs that generally concurs with and supplements the Conte and Svejnar material has appeared elsewhere.[9] The evidence shows that employee ownership in ESOPs is not bad for companies and has a positive effect on productivity if combined with formal, organized labor-management problem solving in participation groups. The amount of equity owned by the ESOP and the presence of voting rights or board-of-director seats does not automatically change this situation.

In most cases unionized and part-time employees in the firm are excluded from the ESOP; employees are given stock according to relative incomes, with huge premiums for higher-paid employees. Normally, the

8. Blasi, "ESOPs in the Publicly Traded Corporate Sector."
9. Blasi, *Employee Ownership*, pp. 220–38.

company gives employees little or no detailed information on the employee ownership or the company's operations, and it may convert or terminate other benefits to make room for the ESOP. Employees have no voting rights on either allocated or unallocated stock nor have they any board representation or say about who the trustee is. The annual stock allocation frequently is a very small percentage of the employee's annual compensation, dividends are seldom paid to employees, and most ESOPs do not have cash profit sharing or gain sharing in addition to the ESOP. Since these elements are widespread,[10] and since employee involvement is only thinly sprinkled among thousands of ESOPs, the finding that ESOPs *improve* economic performance only when combined with true employee involvement should not be surprising.

Many surveys and field studies of ESOPs show that employee ownership increases the employee's identification with the company.[11] Then, consistent with the Conte-Svejnar point of view, management must create an environment of cooperative problem solving that engages this identification and does something with it. Indeed, a number of case studies demonstrate that the expectations raised by this increased identification may result in a worsening of labor-management relations if practical forms of information sharing and involvement are not developed.[12]

What should the future research strategy be? Economists will be tempted to create yet another perfect statistical study of thousands of ESOPs without ever entering a corporation. They will try to control for the economic performance effects of the self-selection of ESOP firms and other factors that may explain improved performance, such as capital intensity or market conditions or industry specificity. I believe, however, that the main questions require more subtle approaches.

First, samples of the most participatory ESOPs firms should be intensively studied, including far more detailed and varied measures of productivity, profitability, and participation. Ethnographic descriptions of corporate culture and participatory mechanisms should be completed for each firm, and exhaustive steps taken to rule out various reasons for improved economic performance when these firms are compared with non-ESOP, nonparticipatory firms. Although this strategy magnifies selection bias of a certain kind, it will probably lead to greater under-

10. Blasi, *Employee Ownership*, pp. 31–62, 121–220.
11. Blasi, *Employee Ownership*, pp. 275, 286.
12. Blasi, *Employee Ownership*, pp. 189–220.

standing than repeated statistical tinkering with large public data sets whose narrow usefulness is now receding. The exception to this is that statistical studies of the new ESOP public sector are needed.

Second, intensive longitudinal studies of individual firms are necessary to monitor closely how employee ownership and participation interact over time. The productivity and profitability of such individual firms should be compared with comparable non-ESOP firms in their industry. That will require camping out in some firms to explore how, where, when, and why information sharing, problem solving, monitoring, and cooperative agreements to reduce the free rider problem occur. Since economic researchers know that many productivity increases are the result of capital investment, technological development, and improvements in specific human capital, particular attention should be paid to how labor and management identify such critical areas and cooperate to take effective action on them. The notion that having shares of stock makes people work harder or become less resentful is an outmoded but unfortunate presence in many studies relating capital acccumulation plans to firm performance. Only thicker ethnographic description and careful internal investigation can clarify these issues.

Much productivity improvement can result from soundly analyzing capital investment needs, eliminating unnecessary level of management, reducing overhead, controlling workers' compensation and health costs, putting the customer first by emphasizing quality and service, and expanding volume by entering the right markets at the right time. Economic researchers on ESOPs have provided little insight to help real managers sort out these issues or understand how to design a work culture that effectively distinguishes between employee involvement in peripheral, insignificant solutions to problems and employee involvement in information gathering and problem solving connected to the core puzzles that really determine a firm's improvement.

Finally, several crucial questions need more explicit answers. What are the relative incentive effects of ESOPs of different sizes in proportion to base compensation? Researchers have put too much emphasis on the percentage of the company owned by the employees as a whole and the dollar amount of the worker's stake while giving too little guidance to corporate managers on what percentage of base salary gets employees' attention. Is there a size of the ESOP incentive so large and powerful that it motivates employees to get more involved in the success of the company without management initiating a participatory environment in the first place? In other words, would an annual ESOP stake of 20 percent of base wage in a firm with comparable industry wage scales and benefits lead to worker-initiated involvement? What does the incentive literature have to teach us about this issue? Conversely, how important is organizational innovation in tapping the ESOP incentive, given that increased work effort is an unimportant factor in many capital- and knowledge-intensive firms?

Conte and Svejnar speak about the interaction effect between ownership and labor-management problem solving which raises some specific questions. Common sense suggests that employee ownership means the majority employee owned firm, but researchers should explore how *little* employee ownership would be enough, and under what circumstances, to create an identification between employees and the firm and serve to motivate labor-management problem-solving teams. This is especially relevant since ESOPs owning 15–30 percent of the stock of publicly traded corporations will probably constitute the main ESOP sector, and these firms will want to know how to benefit from employee ownership without being fully "employee-owned" or losing their public status.

A key problem is whether employee ownership is irrelevant to and labor-management problem solving is sufficient for economic performance. Work innovation researchers have found that employee involvement programs without some form of ownership or gain sharing leads either to employee apathy (because workers have no incentive to participate) or to management apathy (because a hierarchical corporate culture without extensive labor participation on many levels will resist real change). This problem needs to be systematically studied; we need to know under what conditions employee involvement can work without any special productivity incentives and, specifically, what role employee ownership plays in the puzzle.

Policy Recommendations

One goal of the Brookings conference and research review was to clarify where public policy should go in using compensation incentives to increase national productivity. My analysis raises many questions but does suggest a few answers for policymakers and corporate and labor leaders and consultants.

First, given the paucity of cash profit-sharing plans, the distinction between public policy support for ESOPs and for profit-sharing plans is artificial, both because ESOPs share many deferred and defined contribution plan structural features with profit-sharing plans and because deferred profit-sharing trusts share much employee ownership with ESOPs. Every employee benefit plan that has certain employee ownership characteristics, no matter what it is called, should be given the same tax incentives and regulated similarly. The focus needs to be on unitary policy measures for this whole category of capital accumulation plans.

Second, deferred ESOP trusts and deferred profit-sharing trusts both have a common problem: they do not give employees any immediate economic reward connected to firm performance. It is reasonable to assume that such compensation would clearly and explicitly link pay to performance. The federal government should consider providing extra tax incentives to firms that combine capital accumulation plans, such as ESOPs, deferred profit-sharing trusts, or any defined contribution plan holding a certain amount of employer securities, *with* a cash profit-sharing or gain-sharing plan.

Third, future research might still conclude that annual employee ownership stakes or profit-sharing payments representing a large proportion of base pay lead to behaviors that affect firm performance without management-initiated participatory innovations. But such a finding is not expected, or at least the ability of many companies to jack up their bonuses this high is probably unrealistic. Thus a reasonable direction for companies would be to combine labor-management problem solving and employee involvement programs with capital accumulation plans that are structured to provide employees with an opportunity to improve productivity.

For almost a decade and a half the importance of labor-management cooperation has been stressed as central to U.S. competitiveness and productivity improvement. Two recent *Business Week* cover stories have usefully documented how difficult it is for management and labor to engage in joint problem solving, information sharing, and power sharing in both ESOP and other kinds of companies.[13]

Individual states, alone or together with Congress, should establish a special labor-management cooperation-training tax credit for firm expenditures that exceed defined amounts on labor-management problem solving. Abuse of this credit would be reduced by making it available only to firms that have these characteristics: (1) an ERISA-qualified plan holding at least 15 percent of the securities of the company with voting stock; (2) an employee relations committee representing all salary levels of the company elected on a one-person one-vote basis; (3) a cash profit-

13. Farrell and Hoerr, "ESOPs"; and John Hoerr, "The Payoff for Teamwork," *Business Week*, July 10, 1989, pp. 56–62.

sharing or gain-sharing plan that pays 10 percent or more of W-2 compensation annually; and (4) a written formal dispute resolution procedure made available to all employees.[14] Thus reasonable conclusions emerge, and both companies and the government can engage in some initial experimentation to link pay and performance.

14. I am indebted to David Levine and Douglas Kruse for jointly developing this proposal with me.

Participation, Productivity, and the Firm's Environment

David I. Levine
Laura D'Andrea Tyson

How does employee participation in decisionmaking affect firm performance? Intense interest in this question among American managers, unions, and workers has been spurred by the competitive assault on U.S. companies from Japanese and other foreign companies with more participatory industrial relations systems, by the skill and organizational challenges of new production technologies, and by the disappointing productivity of American companies. As a result, many firms are experimenting with various forms of worker participation in firm profits, decisionmaking, and ownership. Experiments include quality circles, employee stock ownership plans (ESOPs), team production techniques, employee representatives on company boards of directors, and profit- and gain-sharing schemes.

This paper focuses on the effects of participation on productivity. We begin with an exploration of what economic theory has to say about the relation between productivity and participation. Our basic conclusion is that there is no simple theoretical link: whether participation has a positive effect on performance is finally an empirical question, not a theoretical one.

And, for reasons detailed below, it is an empirical question that is dauntingly difficult to answer. Nonetheless, the literature we review yields a fairly consistent set of conclusions. Participation usually has a positive, often small, effect on productivity, sometimes a zero or statistically insignificant effect, and almost never a negative effect. The size and significance of the effect are contingent on the type of participation involved and on other aspects of the firm's industrial relations environment. Participation is more likely to have a positive long-term effect on productivity when it involves decisions related to shopfloor

Pei-Hsiung Chin has provided expert research assistance. Alan Blinder, Jennifer Halpern, Derek Jones, Doug Kruse, Jonathan Leonard, George Strauss, and Oliver Williamson made useful comments on earlier versions of the paper.

daily life, when it involves substantive decisionmaking rights rather than purely consultative arrangements (for example, quality circles), and when it occurs in an environment characterized by a high degree of employee commitment and employee-management trust.

If employee participation often has positive effects on productivity, why don't we see more of it? This question is the focus of the second half of the paper. We examine how the firm's external environment—the labor, capital, and product market conditions in which it functions—affects its industrial relations system.

On the basis of several successful participatory arrangements, including those in large Japanese and Swedish firms, in producer cooperatives in Mondragon, Spain, and elsewhere in Europe, and in large U.S. companies with "high-commitment" work forces (such as Hewlett-Packard and the New United Motor Manufacturing Inc., a joint-venture between Toyota and General Motors), we identify four features of a firm's industrial relations system needed to maintain employee support for participation. These features are gain sharing, long-term employment relations, measures to build group cohesiveness, and guaranteed individual rights for employees. Whether a firm has these features will affect how participatory arrangments influence its productivity over time.

We argue that whether a firm chooses to introduce such features depends in part on the environment in which it operates. In particular, we demonstrate that the firm's choice is sensitive to certain characteristics of its product, labor, and capital markets. Since these characteristics vary widely across economies, it is not surprising that industrial relations systems also differ significantly.

Moreover, since industrial relations systems differ in their effects on productivity, it is possible that an economy will be trapped in a socially suboptimal position. Each firm takes its environment as given and chooses a privately optimal system. The sum of all these private choices, in turn, creates the environment for each individual firm. If the choice of work organization at one firm affects other firms, then the resulting outcome may not be efficient.

We demonstrate our arguments about the interaction between the firm's environment and its industrial relations system with evidence from Sweden and Japan. Finally, the paper spells out some implications of our arguments for the development of successful participatory systems in the United States.

The Theory of Participation

Two basic economic approaches to the effects of participation can be distinguished. The first approach focuses on how participation coupled with gain sharing and worker-worker monitoring can increase productivity in a firm with long-term employment relations. The second approach focuses on how participation influences worker motivation and, through motivational changes, how it affects worker effort and productivity.

The first perspective on participation is a logical extension of agency theory. In neoclassical theory, the decisionmaking rights of the firm are vested in its owners. These owners usually delegate some of their rights to appointed agents or managers to act in their behalf.

The problem confronting the owners is how to develop an incentive contract for the managers in order to guarantee that they will use their superior access to information to act in the owners' interests. This incentive problem gives rise to so-called agency costs—the costs the owners must pay to motivate the managers to act in their behalf, and the reduction in the value of the firm that results from the inevitable slippages and imperfections in the motivational arrangements adopted.

From an agency perspective the delegation of at least some decisionmaking rights by managers to workers is likely to have negative effects on firm performance from the owners' point of view. Agency theory postulates that as the number of decisionmakers or agents increases, the costs of monitoring increase.[1] This postulate has led scholars working in the agency framework, such as Jensen and Meckling, to conclude that participatory arrangements are inevitably inefficient. A similar conclusion has been suggested by Williamson, who stresses the greater transactions costs of making and carrying out decisions when many people participate in decisionmaking.[2]

1. In addition, the firm's residual loss is also likely to be greater if the delegation of decisionmaking rights is accompanied by profit sharing to motivate the participating workers. Residual loss increases because the greater the number of persons with contractual rights to sharing in the firm's residual income, the smaller will be the incentive for each to undertake the effort and stress associated with creating these gains.

2. Michael C. Jensen and William H. Meckling, "Rights and Production Functions: An Application to Labor-Managed Firms and Codetermination," *Journal of Business*, vol. 52 (October 1979), pp. 469–506; and Oliver E. Williamson, *Markets and Hierarchies: Analysis and Antitrust Implications—A Study in the Economics of Internal Organization* (Free Press, 1975), chap. 3.

Working within an agency or transactions cost framework, however, one can identify circumstances in which participatory arrangements can improve firm efficiency and profitability. For example, if workers have knowledge that managers lack about the workplace and the behavior of fellow workers, then participatory arrangements that motivate workers to use such information in their jobs or to communicate it to the managers can improve the firm's performance. Such arrangements can actually increase managerial control over the workplace, although they may appear to dilute traditional managerial discretion.

Team production techniques and quality circles are two types of participation that are most likely to have the beneficial effects on organizational efficiency suggested here. The postulated link between participation and improved efficiency is one of information—participation leads to an increase in productivity because it enhances the flow and use of information in complex organizations. From an economic perspective this line of reasoning begs the question of motivation—what motivates workers to use their superior information in the firm's interests? Psychologists and sociologists who stress the potential benefits of participation often overlook this motivational question, perhaps because of experimental evidence suggesting that good work is often its own reward. To an economist it should not be surprising to find that participatory arrangements, such as quality circles, that are designed to elicit better information from workers without offering any stake in the returns to such information are usually short-lived.

Thus we are left with the question of how to motivate workers. Economic theory suggests that the firm can be thought of as a group of individuals involved in a profit-sharing game that takes the form of a prisoner's dilemma. All members of the firm are potentially better off if everyone works hard and the firm pays high wages. Yet there is always a temptation for any single person to shirk because his reward will not be much affected as long as other members continue to work hard. The result is a noncooperative solution in which effort will be withheld to the degree allowed by monitoring. This noncooperative solution is privately rational for each person, but it is not optimal for the firm or for workers as a group.

An alternative to this inefficient noncooperative solution is a cooperative strategy in which all firm members choose to work at the socially optimal level. Game theory demonstrates that such a strategy is one possible outcome if the "game" is repeated many times. The game-theoretic approach seems to suggest that whether the cooperative outcome is realized depends on whether an organization can convince its members that everyone pulling together is essentially a better idea than everyone pulling separately. But how can the firm build such a conviction among its members?

This is where participation comes in. Participation can support the cooperative strategy when there is group interaction and peer pressure. Suppose workers are divided into work groups or teams on the basis of the interdependence of their work, pay is based on team output, and the teams help organize their work. By working together, team members recognize their mutual interests and observe how shirking by one can hurt the group. Shirking or free riding now imposes an observable cost directly on all co-workers, so that social sanctions may be rationally applied against workers who deviate from the cooperative work norm.

In this case participation supports the cooperative solution when it is accompanied by the right group incentive scheme. This is a simple extension of traditional economic reasoning, augmented by worker-worker monitoring and sanctioning.

Psychologists, other behavioral scientists, and some economists stress a complementary link between participatory arrangements and cooperative behavior among firm members. This link focuses on the possible effects of participation on such factors as the workers' commitment to the firm's goals, their trust in the firm's managers, and their sense of goodwill toward other firm members. One broad interpretation is that participation may actually change the goals of the workers so that they more closely conform to the goals of the firm.[3]

A related connection between participation and performance is that the increased commitment, trust, and goodwill resulting from partici-

3. Chester I. Barnard, *The Functions of the Executive* (Harvard University Press, 1938); James V. Clark, "Motivation in Work Groups: A Tentative View," in Robert A. Sutermeister, ed., *People and Productivity* (McGraw-Hill, 1969), pp. 461–80; George C. Homans, "The Western Electric Researches" [1941], in Sutermeister, ed., *People and Productivity*, pp. 73–81; Raymond A. Katzell and others, *Work, Productivity, and Job Satisfaction: An Evaluation of Policy-Related Research* (New York: Psychological Corp., 1975); Richard T. Mowday, Leyman W. Porter, and Richard M. Steers, *Employee-Organization Linkages: The Psychology of Commitment, Absenteeism, and Turnover* (Academic Press, 1982); Charles O'Reilly, "Corporations, Culture, and Commitment: Motivation and Social Control in Organizations," *California Management Review*, vol. 31 (Summer 1989), pp. 9–26; and Jaroslav Vanek, *The Participatory Economy: An Evolutionary Hypothesis and a Strategy for Development* (Cornell University Press, 1971).

patory arrangements may increase worker morale and job satisfaction and reduce the disutility of effort, and these in turn may result in greater worker effort and productivity.[4]

When economists model the effects of participation on worker goals, morale, and satisfaction, they are leaving the traditional economic theory of motivation, which takes individual utility functions as given and emphasizes monetary rewards and the disutility of effort. Such economic modeling strategies fall back on work done by behavioral scientists who have looked at the effects of participation on worker motivation. Their results suggest that the links between participation and such factors as worker satisfaction, commitment, and loyalty are quite sensitive to the type of participation involved and to the industrial relations environment in which it is introduced.

In particular, other social scientists have found that participation does not always lead to higher morale and satisfaction. Furthermore, there is no predictable link between morale or satisfaction on the one hand and increased worker productivity on the other.

The conclusion emerging from both economic reasoning and other social science research is that there is no simple link between participation and productivity. Whether participation has a positive effect is an empirical question, not a theoretical one—and as the next section discusses, the impediments to measuring this effect are substantial.

The Empirical Evidence

This section reviews some empirical evidence on the productivity effects of participation. We begin by describing various types of participation, then summarize the evidence on the performance effects of each.

Typology of Participation

Participatory arrangements can be described according to several different characteristics, including whether such arrangements involve direct or indirect channels for participation, the extent to which they involve real influence over firm decisions, and the content of the decisions involved. Direct participation entails decisionmaking by the workers themselves, while indirect participation entails some form of employee representation. The extent of influence in participation varies along a

4. Edward L. Deci, *Intrinsic Motivation* (New York: Plenum Press, 1975).

continuum from arrangements that promote information exchange and communication to arrangements that give employees formal rights to vote on or otherwise influence corporate decisions. The content of decisions may vary from routine personnel functions and work organization to such companywide policies as layoffs, profit sharing, and investment.[5]

Three broad types of participatory arrangements stand out: consultative participation in work and workplace decisions, substantive participation in work and workplace decisions, and representative participation. In the interests of drawing conclusions from the empirical literature, we have consolidated many distinctive forms of participation into each of these broad categories.

Typically, *consultative participation* allows employees to give their opinions, but final decisions are still made by management. Most such arrangements focus on workplace organization and other shopfloor and personnel issues important to workers and about which they often have significant information not readily available to management. While worker suggestions are solicited, workers are not permitted to *decide* how to solve problems, and often they do not even implement those of their suggestions that are accepted by management.

In the United States quality control circles (QCs) are the most common form of consultative participation. Quality circles usually consist of small voluntary groups of employees from the same work area who meet together on a regular basis to identify and solve quality, productivity, and other problems. Typically about 25 percent of a firm's workers participate in voluntary quality circles. Members of quality circles often receive special training in such subjects as group dynamics and problem solving. Despite their name, quality circles frequently deal with subjects other than quality, for example, work flow, productivity, safety, and employee welfare.

Substantive participation in work and workplace decisions includes formal, direct participation schemes, such as work teams. Usually

5. These characteristics of participation have also been identified and discussed in the organizational literature by, among others, Locke and Schweiger, and Cotton. See Edwin A. Locke and David M. Schweiger, "Participation in Decision-Making: One More Look," in Barry M. Staw and L. L. Cummings, eds., *Research in Organizational Behavior: An Annual Series of Analytical Essays and Critical Reviews*, vol. 1 (JAI Press, 1979), pp. 265–339; and L. Cotton and others, "Employee Participation: Diverse Forms and Different Outcomes," *Academy of Management Review*, vol. 13 (January 1988), pp. 8–22. All the empirical evidence discussed in this section involves formal participation schemes. Participation may also be informal, of course.

substantive participatory arrangements concentrate on the same kinds of issues as consultative arrangements—the difference is not in the content of the decisions, but in the degree of worker influence.

For example, members of work teams are given wide discretion in organizing their own work and operate with little supervision. Typically, these groups make their own work assignments and determine their own work routines, subject to overall workflow requirements.

Work teams have been given responsibility for developing relations with vendors, for determining which operations can be handled individually and which by the group as a whole, for setting the work pace (perhaps fast in the morning and slow in the afternoon), for training new employees, and even for keeping financial records. Sometimes team members serve in roles normally reserved for staff personnel or supervisors: chairing the plant safety committee, redesigning work equipment, or troubleshooting customers' problems. At some locations the job of supervisor is rotated among members of the group. For example, when the new General Motors' Saturn plant opens up, first-line supervisors will be elected by their subordinates.

Representative participation includes workers' councils, joint labor-management consultation committees, and employee representation on company boards of directors. Representative arrangements differ significantly from both consultative and substantive arrangements in the extent of employee influence and the content of the decisions involved. For example, workers' councils and joint labor-management consultation committees often serve as purely advisory or informational channels with no direct employee influence. Although similar to consultative arrangements in terms of employee influence, representative arrangements encompass a wider range of issues, including investment policy, technology, and corporate-level strategy. Employee representation on company boards of directors can be purely advisory or informational or can involve influence in the form of voting rights. Because the number of employee positions on such boards is small, however, their influence is usually quite limited.

Evidence on the Effects of Participation

Table 1 contains a survey of empirical studies that evaluate the effects of these three types of participation on productivity.[6] We limit our

6. The idea for this table comes from Cotton and others, "Employee Participation." Similar reviews are found in Katherine I. Miller and Peter R. Monge, "Participation,

coverage to studies measuring productivity specifically, instead of broader notions of performance.

These studies vary widely in their methodologies, including econometric tests, field experiments, and case studies (identified by $e, f,$ and c in table 1). Survey articles, laboratory experiments, and case studies that provide a qualitative rather than a quantitative assessment of the effects of participation on productivity are excluded from the table.

Whenever possible, each study is also classified according to the type of participation on which it focuses. When a study examines the effects of more than one form of participation, it is classified according to the form that appears to be the most prevalent in its sample.

To some extent this classification scheme is artificial, since successful participation may involve the interaction of several formal participation schemes. For example, shopfloor participation may be most effective when there are representative participatory bodies to handle issues spanning work groups and to arbitrate shopfloor disagreements between workers and supervisors.

We confronted two difficult problems in classifying the empirical literature we surveyed. First, some studies use indexes of participation that encompass a broad range of participatory arrangements differing in form and content. We classified such studies as substantive participation, because the arrangements they examined included more than consultative and representative participation.

Second, few empirical studies provide quantitative assessments of the effects of substantive participation in work teams on productivity. Most studies of work teams yield qualitative assessments of their effects in particular cases. Quantitative evaluations are extremely difficult to make because teams are usually associated with several other important changes in the workplace, including new technology, more training, new

---

Satisfaction and Productivity: A Meta-Analytic Review," *Academy of Management Journal,* vol. 29, no. 4 (1986), pp. 727–53; Edwin A. Locke, David M. Schweiger, and Gary P. Latham, "Participation in Decision Making: When Should It Be Used?" *Organizational Dynamics,* vol. 14 (Winter 1986), pp. 65–79; and John A. Wagner III and Richard Z. Gooding, "Shared Influence and Organizational Behavior: A Meta-Analysis of Situational Variables Expected to Moderate Participation-Outcome Relationships," *Academy of Management Journal,* vol. 30, no. 3 (1987), pp. 524–41. Several of these include laboratory and qualitative case studies that we exclude. Their conclusions are broadly consistent with our own. For an excellent overview of much of the empirical literature, see also Raymond Russell, "Forms and Extent of Employee Participation in the Contemporary United States," *Work and Occupations: An International Sociological Journal,* vol. 15, no. 4 (1988), pp. 374–95.

Table 1. Studies Evaluating the Productivity Effects of Participation

Type of firm and form of participation	Positive		Evaluation Neutral, short-lived, or not significant		Negative		Contingent	
	Type of study		Type of study		Type of study		Type of study	
Conventional firms								
Consultative workplace	f	Marks and others, 1986	c	Accordino, 1989	e	Katz and others, 1985[a]	e	Katz and others, 1983
	f	Schuster, 1983	c	Cammann and others, 1984			f	Griffin, 1988
Substantive workplace participation	e	Cable and FitzRoy, 1980	e	Katz and others, 1987	. . . . . .		f	Faxen, 1978[b]
	f	Coch and French, 1948	f	Latham and Yukl, 1976			f	Latham and Yukl, 1975[c]
	f	Fleishman, 1965	. . . . . .					
	c	Krafcik, 1988						
	e	Mitchell and others, 1989						
	f	Morse and Reimer, 1956						
	f	Neider, 1980						
	f	Rice, 1953						
	f	Trist, 1977						
Representative participation	e	Morishima, 1988	c	Rosenberg, 1980	e	FitzRoy and Kraft, 1987	. . . . . .	
			e	Svejnar, 1982[d]				

Firms with worker ownership

Employee stock ownership plans

Participation effects	c GAO, 1987 c Quarrey and Rosen, 1986	. . . . . .	. . . . . .
Ownership effects	c GAO, 1987 e Kruse, 1988 c Quarrey and Rosen, 1986	. . . . . .	. . . . . .

Worker cooperatives

Participation effects	c Bellas, 1972 e Ben-Ner and Estrin, 1988 e Conte and Svejnar, 1988[f] c Jerovsek, 1978 e Jones, 1982 e Jones, 1987	c Conte and Tannenbaum, 1978	e Jones and Svejnar, 1985[e]
Ownership effects	c Berman, 1976 e Conte and Tannenbaum, 1978 e Defourney and others, 1985 e Estrin and Jones, 1987 e Estrin, Jones, Svejnar, 1987 c Long, 1980 c Thordarson, 1987	. . . . . .	e Conte and Svejnar, 1988[g] e Jones, 1982[h] e Jones and Svejnar, 1985[i]

Type of Study: c = case study; e = econometrics study; f = field experiment.

Table 1 (*continued*)

a. Participation in suggestion programs has significant positive effects on direct labor efficiency, while the effect of quality-of-work-life program involvement (including, for example, quality circles) is statistically insignificant.

b. Capital intensity and machine dependence seem to affect the productivity effects of employee participation in the studied Swedish firms. Those branches with low capital intensity and machine dependence tend to have a significant positive productivity effect, while other branches have insignificant or negative effects.

c. For a sample of low-educated logging crews, the condition with a goal set participatively had higher productivity than the assigned goal and "do your best" conditions. No significant differences among conditions were found for the educated sample, although this may have been because of problems in implementing the goal-setting program with this sample.

d. The study estimates the impact of codetermination on productivity in the Federal Republic of Germany. The results suggest that the introduction of employee participation through the 1951 Codetermination Law and the 1952 Works Constitution Act had no significant effect on productivity. The produc-

tivity effect of the 1972 Works Constitution Act is found to be either insignificant or mildly negative.

e. Participation, defined as the ratio of the number of cooperative members working in the firm to the total number of workers including hired labor, has significant positive effects in manufacturing cooperatives, but insignificant ones in construction cooperatives.

f. The forty companies in the sample include profit-sharing companies, companies with employee stock ownership plans, and producer cooperatives in construction cooperatives.

g. The impact of employee ownership depends on the amount of ownership. This fact implies that there is an "optimal" amount of nonmanagerial employee ownership (if the goal is solely technical efficiency).

h. Increased ownership enhances productivity when participation is high and reduces productivity when participation is low.

i. The average ownership of worker-members has significant positive effects in manufacturing cooperatives and either positive or insignificant effects in construction cooperatives.

Studies

Accordino, John. "Quality of Working Life Systems in Large Cities: An Assessment." *Public Productivity Review*, forthcoming.

Bellas, Carl J. *Industrial Democracy and the Worker-Owned Firm: A Study of Twenty-One Plywood Companies in the Pacific Northwest*. Praeger, 1972.

Ben-Ner, Avner, and Saul Estrin. "Unions and Productivity: Unionized Firms versus Union Managed Firms." Working Paper 88-01. Industrial Relations Center, University of Minnesota. August 1988.

Berman, K. "Comparing Productivity in Worker-Managed Cooperative Plywood Plants and Conventionally Run Plants." University of Idaho, 1976.

Cable, John, and Felix R. FitzRoy. "Cooperation and Productivity: Some Evidence from West German Experience." *Economic Analysis and Workers' Management*, vol. 14, no. 2 (1980), pp. 163–80.

Cammann, C., and others. "Management-Labor Cooperation in Quality of Worklife Experiments: Comparative Analysis of Eight Cases." Report prepared for the U.S. Department of Labor. Institute for Social Research, University of Michigan, 1984.

Coch, Lester, and John R. P. French. "Overcoming Resistance to Change." *Human Relations*, vol. I (1948), pp. 512–32.

Conte, Michael, and Arnold S. Tannenbaum. "Employee-Owned Companies: Is the Difference Measurable?" *Monthly Labor Review*, vol. 101 (July 1978), pp. 23–28.

Conte, Michael, and Jan Svejnar. "Productivity Effects of Worker Participation in Management, Profit-Sharing, Worker Ownership of Assets and Unionization in U.S. Firms." *International Journal of Industrial Organization*, vol. 6 (March 1988), pp. 139–51.

Defourny, Jacques, Saul Estrin, and Derek C. Jones. "The Effects of Workers' Participation on Enterprise Performance: Empirical Evidence from French Cooperatives." *International Journal of Industrial Organization*, vol. 3 (June 1985), pp. 197–217.

Estrin, Saul, and Derek C. Jones. "Why Workers Want Participation and Ownership and Their Effects upon Productivity." Working Paper 87/10. Department of Economics, Hamilton College. New York, 1987.

Estrin, Saul, Derek C. Jones, and Jan Svejnar. "The Productivity Effects of Worker Participation: Producer Cooperatives in Western Economies." *Journal of Comparative Economics*, vol. 11 (March 1987), pp. 40–61.

Faxen, Karl-Olof. "Disembodied Technical Progress: Does Employee Participation in Decision Making Contribute to Change and Growth?" *American Economic Review*, vol. 68 (May 1978, *Papers and Proceedings*, 1977), pp. 131–34.

FitzRoy, Felix R., and Kornelius Kraft. "Cooperation, Productivity, and Profit Sharing." *Quarterly Journal of Economics*, vol. 102 (February 1987), pp. 23–35.

Fleishman, Edwin A. "Attitude versus Skill Factors in Work Group Productivity." *Personnel Psychology*, vol. 18 (Autumn 1965), pp. 253–66.

Frank, Linda L., and J. Richard Hackman. "A Failure of Job Enrichment: The Case of the Change That Wasn't." *Journal of Applied Behavioral Science*, vol. 11 (December 1975), pp. 413–36.

Griffin, Ricky W. "Consequences of Quality Circles in an Industrial Setting: A Longitudinal Assessment." *Academy of Management Journal*, vol. 31, no. 2 (1988), pp. 338–58.

Jerovsek, Janez, and Stane Mozina. "Efficiency and Democracy in Self-Managing Enterprises." In *Workers' Self-Management and Organizational Power in Yugoslavia*, edited by Josip Obradovic and William N. Dunn. University Center for International Studies, University of Pittsburgh, 1978.

Jones, Derek C. "British Producer Cooperatives, 1948–68: Productivity and Organizational Structure." In *Participatory and Self-Managed Firms: Evaluating Economic Performance*, edited by Derek C. Jones and Jan Svejnar. Lexington Books, 1982.

———. "The Productivity Effects of Worker Directors and Financial Participation by Employees in the Firm: The Case of British Retail Cooperatives." *Industrial and Labor Relations Review*, vol. 41 (October 1987), pp. 79–92.

Jones, Derek C., and Jan Svejnar. "Participation, Profit Sharing, Worker Ownership and Efficiency in Italian Producer Cooperatives." *Economica*, vol. 52 (November 1985), pp. 449–65.

Juralewicz, Richard S. "An Experiment of Participation in a Latin American Factory." *Human Relations*, vol. 27, no. 7 (1974), pp. 627–37.

Katz, Harry C., Thomas A. Kochan, and Jeffrey Keefe. "Industrial Relations and Productivity in the U.S. Automobile Industry." *Brookings Papers on Economic Activity*, 3:1987, pp. 685–715.

Katz, Harry C., Thomas A. Kochan, and Kenneth R. Gobeille. "Industrial Relations Performance, Economic Performance, and the Quality of Working Life Efforts: An Inter-plant Analysis." *Industrial and Labor Relations Review*, vol. 37 (October 1983), pp. 3–17.

Katz, Harry C., Thomas A. Kochan, and Mark R. Weber. "Assessing the Effects of Industrial Relations Systems and Efforts to Improve the Quality of Working Life on Organizational Effectiveness." *Academy of Management Journal* vol. 28 (September 1985), pp. 509–26.

Krafcik, John F. "Triumph of the Lean Production System." *Sloan Management Review* (Fall 1988), pp. 41–52.

Kruse, Douglas. "Profit-Sharing and Productivity: Microeconomic Evidence." Rutgers University, June 1988.

Latham, Gary P., and Gary A. Yukl. "Effects of Assigned and Participative Goal Setting on Performance and Job Satisfaction." *Journal of Applied Psychology*, vol. 61 (April 1976), pp. 166–71.

———. "Assigned versus Participative Goal Setting with Educated and Uneducated Woods

Workers." *Journal of Applied Psychology*, vol. 60 (June 1975), pp. 299–302.

Long, Richard J. "Job Attitudes and Organizational Performance under Employee Ownership." *Academy of Management Journal*, vol. 23 (December 1980), pp. 726–37.

Marks, M. L., and others. "Employee Participation in a Quality Circle Program: Impact on Quality of Work Life, Productivity, and Absenteeism." *Journal of Applied Psychology*, vol. 71 (February 1986), pp. 61–69.

Mitchell, Daniel J. B., David Lewin, and Edward E. Lawler. "Alternative Pay Systems. Firm Performance, and Productivity." In this volume.

Morishima, Motohiro. "Information Sharing and Firm Performance in Japan: Do Joint Consultation Committees Help?" Simon Fraser University, British Columbia, Faculty of Business Administration, December 1988.

Morse, Nancy C., and Everett Reimer. "The Experimental Change of a Major Organizational Variable." *Journal of Abnormal Psychology*, vol. 52 (January 1956), pp. 120–29.

Neider, L. L. "An Experimental Field Investigation Utilizing an Expectancy Theory View of Participation." *Organizational Behavior and Human Performance*, vol. 26 (December 1980), pp. 425–42.

Quarrey, Michael, and Corey Rosen. *Employee Ownership and Corporate Performance.* Oakland, Calif.: National Center for Employee Ownership, October 1986.

Rice, A. K. "Productivity and Social Organization in an Indian Weaving Shed." *Human Relations*, vol. 6, no. 4 (1953), pp. 297–329.

Rosenberg, R. D., and E. Rosenstein. "Participation and Productivity: An Empirical Study." *Industrial and Labor Relations Review*, vol. 33 (April 1980), pp. 355–68.

Schuster, Michael. "The Impact of Union-Management Cooperation on Productivity and Employment." *Industrial and Labor Relations Review*, vol. 36 (April 1983), pp. 415–30.

Svejnar, Jan. "Codetermination and Productivity: Empirical Evidence from the Federal Republic of Germany." In *Participatory and Self-Managed Firms: Evaluating Economic Performance*, edited by Derek C. Jones and Jan Svejnar. Lexington, Mass.: Lexington Books, 1982.

Thordarson, Bodil. "A Comparison of Worker-Owned Firms and Conventionally Owned Firms in Sweden." In *Advances in the Economic Analysis of Participatory and Labor-managed Firms*, edited by Derek C. Jones and others. Vol. 2. Greenwich Conn.: JAI Press, 1987.

Trist, Eric L., Gerald I. Susman, and Grant R. Brown. "An Experiment in Autonomous Working in an American Underground Coal Mine." *Human Relations*, vol. 30 (March 1977), pp. 201–36.

U.S. General Accounting Office. *Employee Stock Ownership Plans: Little Evidence on Effects of Corporate Performance.* GAO-PEMD-88-1. Washington, 1987.

team or group reward structures, and greater representative participation. Most of the available empirical studies do not distinguish the effects of teams from the effects of these other workplace innovations.

Table 1 also classifies studies according to whether they examine firms in which workers have partial or full ownership rights. We make this distinction because firms with employee ownership often have a wide variety of mechanisms through which employees as employees and employees as owners participate in firm decisions.

Shortcomings in the empirical evidence on the links between participation and productivity are numerous. For one thing, there are the usual difficulties encountered in measuring productivity. For another, because participation takes many forms, there are major difficulties not only in defining but in measuring the kinds of participation involved in any given arrangement. The empirical literature relies on several different measures, including the existence of a quality circle, work team, or works council, the number of workers participating in such groups or serving on company boards of directors, and the extent of employee financial stakes in the firm. All these measures are only indirect indicators of the actual extent of employee participation and influence in different types of decisions.

There is often a dynamic to participation schemes—a firm may begin cautiously with a quality circle and move gradually to more substantive arrangements in which workers have real decisionmaking power. Moreover, some evidence shows that participatory arrangements that increase productivity are sometimes terminated because of managerial opposition. Causality is also an issue. Does participation increase productivity, or do high productivity and the profits it generates allow the firm to improve working conditions by introducing participatory mechanisms favored by its workers? Furthermore, successful participatory schemes are probably more often reported in the empirical literature than are failures. Another concern is that, for reasons discussed below, the large body of econometric work on the links between participation and productivity in worker cooperatives may have limited applicability to more traditionally organized firms.

Finally, firms with high levels of participation often have other distinctive features, such as gain sharing and employment security. Ideally, we want to understand how participation interacts with these other features. In practice, this correlation is usually impossible to do. Much of the empirical work has focused on case studies in unique circumstances that cannot be easily replicated. Despite these difficulties, the studies summarized in table 1 suggest several general conclusions.

FIRMS WITH WORKER OWNERSHIP. The first row of table 1 includes several studies that measure the effects of *consultative participation,* specifically quality circles, on productivity. Marks and others, for example, compared the productivity of manufacturing plant employees who volunteered to participate in the quality circle program with that of nonparticipants over a twenty-four-month horizon. While the two groups had similar demographic characteristics and almost identical initial productivity, the productivity of the nonparticipants rose less than 10 percent, while the productivity of the participants increased by more than 20 percent during the course of the study.

Although this study finds a significant positive impact of quality circles, most other empirical studies do not. The most important evidence on the long-run effects of quality circles comes from studies that do not directly measure their performance but measure their longevity. Most studies find that the half-life of quality circles is under three years. The studies of consultative participation in table 1 support a general consensus emerging among scholars that quality circles and other purely advisory shopfloor arrangements are not likely to achieve sustainable improvements in productivity. Such improvements require work reorganization and a broadening of employee participation in decision-making.[7]

On substantive participation, the evidence included in table 1 suggests two main conclusions. First, substantive participation in shopfloor decisions usually has a positive effect on productivity. Second, an increase in worker participation tends to be associated with an improvement in productivity.

7. Lawler and Mohrman; Kochan, Katz, and Mckersie; Kochan, Cutcher-Gershenfeld, and MacDuffie; and Gershenfeld all provide case evidence supporting this conclusion. See Edward E. Lawler III and Susan A. Mohrman, "Quality Circles: After the Honeymoon," *Organizational Dynamics,* vol. 15 (Spring 1987), pp. 42–54; Thomas A. Kochan, Harry C. Katz, and Robert B. Mckersie, *The Transformation of American Industrial Relations* (Basic Books, 1986); Thomas Kochan, Joel Cutcher-Gershenfeld, and John Paul MacDuffie, "Employee Participation, Work Redesign and New Technology: Implications for Public Policy in the 1990's," report prepared for Commission on Workforce Quality and Labor Market Efficiency, U.S. Department of Labor, March 1989; and Joel Gershenfeld, "Tracing a Transformation in Industrial Relations: The Case of Xerox Corporation and the Amalgamated Clothing and Textile Workers Union," Bureau of Labor-Management Relations and Cooperative Programs, Department of Labor, 1988.

The studies by Mitchell and others (1989) and by Cable and FitzRoy (1980) suggest that more participation in the sense of more channels for participation and coverage of a broader range of issues leads to higher productivity. This conclusion is supported by other studies in table 1, including those by Rosenberg and Rosenstein (1980), Bellas (1972), Jerovsek (1978), Quarrey (1986), the GAO (1987), and the econometric studies of the European producer co-ops by Defourney and others (1985), Estrin and Jones (1987), Estrin, Jones, and Svejnar (1987), and Jones and Svejnar (1985).

The study on "Alternative Pay Systems, Firm Performance, and Productivity," by Mitchell, Lewin, and Lawler in this volume constructs an index on the number of decision areas in which employees participate. Regression results show that the participation index is positively related to the productivity of both clerical and production workers, and that participatory arrangements rather than information-sharing arrangements are responsible for this positive relationship.

Two studies by Cable and FitzRoy examine a group of West German "industrial partnership" firms that provide both profit sharing and participatory rights for their workers. They construct an index of participation based on managers' perceptions of worker participation in various areas. The index rises as the extent of worker participation rises from no participation to purely advisory participation to active influence, and as the number of issues on which workers participate expands. Their regression results show that as the index rises, value-added rises for constant amounts of labor and capital inputs. They also present results based on a dichotomization of their sample into "low" participation and "high" participation firms. On average the high-participation firms outperformed the low-participation firms by 15 percent, 177 percent, and 33 percent in terms of output per worker, output per unit of capital, and profitability (rate of return on capital employed).[8]

Even in firms with substantive participation, empirical research indicates that productivity increases do not follow automatically. For

8. John R. Cable and Felix R. FitzRoy, "Cooperation and Productivity: Some Evidence from West German Experience," *Economic Analysis and Workers' Management,* vol. 14, no. 2 (1980), pp. 163–80; John R. Cable and Felix R. FitzRoy, "Productive Efficiency, Incentives, and Employee Participation: Some Preliminary Results for West Germany," *Kyklos,* vol. 33, no. 1 (1980), pp. 100–21. In a more recent article Cable presents some criticisms of the methods used to define and measure the participation index in these studies. See J. Cable, "Some Tests of Employee Participation Indices," in Derek C. Jones and Jan Svejnar, *Advances in the Economic Analysis of Participatory and Labor-Managed Firms,* vol. 2 (JAI Press, 1987).

example, the studies by Krafcik (1988) on the automobile industry suggest that team production techniques, which are an integral part of the Japanese automobile production system, have a positive effect on productivity in Japanese plants. But these plants also have several other unique features of Japanese industrial relations, and the studies do not distinguish the effects of work teams from the effects of these other factors on productivity.

Many observers attribute the success of Nummi, the joint General Motors–Toyota venture, to substantive participation via work teams. The old General Motors plant was plagued with drug abuse, absenteeism, and poor labor relations. Largely using the same technology and the same workers as in the old plant, and with the same union in place, Nummi has reduced by 40 percent the number of labor hours required for each car, has zoomed to the top of U.S. auto plants in quality, and has the lowest absenteeism rate in the U.S. auto industry.[9] At Nummi work teams are responsible for planning job rotation, balancing work assignments to equalize work loads, and engaging in what Toyota calls *kaizen* (continuous job improvement). Team leaders, who remain union members, are selected on the basis of recommendations of a joint union-management committee.

There is widespread agreement that team production has played a major role in Nummi's superior productivity performance. But Nummi, like other Japanese-owned plants, has several additional unique features that have affected productivity, including just-in-time inventory and production techniques, job security, and union-management consultation committees at every level of the organization. To date, the research on Nummi does not allow one to isolate the productivity effects of these features from the productivity effects of team production.

In contrast, recent econometric work on a U.S. auto plant by Katz and others (1988) distinguishes the productivity effects of work teams from the productivity effects of other forms of substantive and consultative participation in technology and work group decisions. The results suggest that team production techniques, by themselves, lower labor productivity and quality, while substantive participation in work groups, coupled with substantive participation in technology-related decisions, increases labor productivity and product quality. The statistical associations between the measures of participation and plant performance,

9. Clair Brown and Michael Reich, "When Does Union-Management Cooperation Work? A Look at NUMMI and GM-Van Nuys," *California Management Review*, vol. 31 (Summer 1989), pp. 26–37.

however, are weak (many of the estimated coefficients are not statistically significant at even the 10 percent level).

These results and the results of other empirical studies by Kochan and his co-workers suggest that team production techniques accomplish little unless they are integrated with broader changes in the firm's industrial relations environment, including changes that facilitate greater employee participation in higher-level decisionmaking.[10] This conclusion is buttressed by qualitative evidence from case studies showing that team production yields sizable improvements in both organizational performance and the quality of working life when accompanied by such organizational changes as increased worker participation in business strategy decisions, job-security programs, and group pay reward structures. As we argue in the second part of this paper, such broader organizational changes seem to be essential to the long-term viability and performance of substantive employee participation.

The available empirical literature suggests that various forms of representative participation can improve performance when they are part of a package of participatory policies; taken alone, they may improve labor-management relations, but have little effect on productivity.

In an empirical study of West German codetermination laws requiring worker representatives on company boards of directors, Svejnar (1982) finds that the introduction of codetermination had either no significant productivity effect or a mildly negative one. Similar results are found for mandated works councils.[11]

Representative participation appears to be more important when it is only one of several channels for employee participation and only one of several distinctive features of the firm's industrial relations system. For example, in a recent study on British retail cooperatives, Jones (1987) finds that the presence of worker representatives on the board of directors had a positive but modest effect on productivity.

A recent econometric study by Morishima (1988) examines the

---

10. Kochan and others, *Transformation of American Industrial Relations*.

11. Jan Svejnar, "Codetermination and Productivity: Empirical Evidence from the Federal Republic of Germany," in Derek C. Jones and Jan Svejnar, eds., *Participatory and Self-Managed Firms: Evaluating Economic Performance* (Lexington, Mass.: Lexington Books, 1982). Strauss surveys the case study evidence; FitzRoy and Kraft provide econometric support. See George Strauss, "Workers' Participation in Management: An International Perspective," in Barry M. Staw and L. L. Cummings, eds., *Research in Organizational Behavior*, vol. 4 (JAI Press, 1982), pp. 173–265; and Felix R. FitzRoy and Kornelius Kraft, "Cooperation, Productivity, and Profit Sharing," *Quarterly Journal of Economics*, vol. 102 (February 1987), pp. 23–35.

productivity effects of joint consultation committees (JCCs), a form of representative participation characteristic of Japanese companies. JCCs are corporate-level bodies that deal with business strategies and plans pertinent to the entire company. Such committees serve two main functions: sharing of business information with employees, and prior consultation by the management with employees on upcoming business decisions. Morishima's econometric results show a strong and sizable positive association between an index of information sharing and three performance indicators—firm profitability, employee productivity, and labor costs.

PARTICIPATION AND PRODUCTIVITY IN EMPLOYEE-OWNED FIRMS. Most employee stock ownership plans have little or no employee participation and have no measurable effects on productivity. The studies by Quarrey (1986) and the GAO (1987) cited in table 1 indicate that ESOP firms that give employees additional opportunities for participation in decisionmaking are significantly more likely to outperform conventionally owned firms than ESOP firms that fail to offer such opportunities. Furthermore, of the various forms of participation, those that reach closest to the shopfloor have the largest productivity effects, while stock voting rights or employee representation on company boards of directors have insignificant productivity effects.[12] These findings for ESOPs are consistent with the findings for conventionally owned firms discussed earlier.

There is an extensive empirical literature on the performance of worker-owned firms and cooperatives in the United States and abroad.[13] Much of this literature is discussed in detail in the chapter in this volume by Conte and Svejnar. Here we summarize only the main conclusions about the effects of participation in worker-owned firms.

Table 1 divides the empirical studies on worker-owned firms into two

12. Only 4 percent of firms with ESOPs elected union or other representatives of nonmanagerial employees to serve on company boards of directors. See General Accounting Office, *Employee Stock Ownership Plans: Little Evidence of Effects of Corporate Performance*, GAO-PEMD-88-1 (Washington, October 1987). For more detail on this conclusion, see the discussion of employee stock ownership plans in the chapter by Conte and Svejnar in this volume.

13. For excellent reviews of the empirical findings on the performance of worker-owned firms, see John Bonin, *Economics of Cooperation and the Labor-Managed Economy* (New York: Harwood Academic Publishers, 1987); and Derek C. Jones and Jeffrey Pliskin, "The Effects of Worker Participation, Employee Ownership and Profit Sharing on Economic Performance: A Partial Review," in V. Rus and R. Russell, eds., *International Handbook of Participation in Organization*, vol. 2 (Oxford University Press, forthcoming).

parts: studies that look at how the extent of employee participation affects productivity in such firms, and studies that examine how ownership per se affects productivity in such firms. Most of the studies suggest that both participation and ownership have positive effects on productivity. For example, the studies by Conte and Svejnar (1988), Defourney and others (1985), Estrin and Jones (1987), and Estrin, Jones, and Svejnar (1987) conclude that the extent of employee ownership of the firm's capital—measured as the share of the firm's equity owned by employees or the share of the firm's employees who choose to become firm owners by buying the minimum capital contribution required for doing so—has a significant positive effect on the firm's productivity. In a similar vein, the studies by Berman (1976), Long (1980), and Thordarson (1987) find the productivity performance of worker-owned firms superior to that of conventionally owned companies that are otherwise similar.

None of these studies directly measure the productivity effects of the participatory arrangements that usually accompany significant employee ownership or distinguish these effects from the productivity effects of employee ownership per se. Moreover, several of the studies interpret their ownership variables as proxies for the extent of employee participation in decisionmaking.[14] Such variables are obviously imprecise proxies that provide no information about the actual form and content of participation.

Studies—such as those by Bellas (1972), Ben-Ner and Estrin (1988), Conte and Svejnar (1988), Jerovsek and Mozima (1978), Jones and Svejnar (1985), and Jones (1982, 1987)—that specifically examine the effects of participation on productivity in worker-owned firms usually find these effects to be positive as well.[15]

14. The European producer co-ops have several distinguishing features: employees can become firm members by buying into the firm; worker-members participate in management; control is usually on the basis of one member, one vote and may be exercised indirectly on most matters through an elected board of directors; and worker-members and often non-worker-members share in the firm's profits. Workers have to buy into membership in these firms. They receive only limited returns on their capital contributions (returns that are below returns on alternative assets), and they cannot sell their shares back to the firm or on the secondary market as long as they remain employees.

15. A similar conclusion is supported by empirical research on the Mondragon producer cooperatives in Spain. Studies of the Mondragon co-ops suggest that they have higher productivity than comparable conventional firms operating in the same economic environment. See, for example, Henk Thomas and Chris Logan, *Mondragon: An Economic Analysis* (London: Allen and Unwin, 1982); and Keith Bradley and Alan Gelb, "Motivation and Control in the Mondragon Experiment," *British Journal of Industrial Relations*, vol. 19, no. 2 (1981), pp. 221–31.

Overall, empirical research on employee-owned firms suggests that within companies of this kind, employee participation is positively associated with productivity. As argued earlier, however, such firms almost always have several other characteristics that distinguish them from conventionally owned firms. For example, the European worker co-ops, which have been the subject of extensive empirical inquiry, typically have managements committed to employee ownership and representation, job security, compressed status and compensation differentials, and guaranteed worker rights. As a result, it is dangerous to draw general conclusions about the effects of employee participation on productivity from the experience of these firms. For the reasons discussed in the second half of this paper, it is quite likely that such effects will be much smaller in conventionally owned and organized firms without such characteristics.

While table 1 summarizes the empirical research on the productivity effects of participation, in fact there is a much larger empirical literature examining how participation affects more easily measured outcomes such as turnover, absenteeism, and worker satisfaction. In general the results have been more consistently favorable for these other performance measures. In most reported cases the introduction of substantive shopfloor participation (job redesign and participative work groups) leads to some combination of an increase in satisfaction, commitment, quality, and productivity, and a reduction in turnover and absenteeism—at least in the short run.[16] In almost no cases does participation make things worse. Most studies suggest that the changes in productivity caused by participation tend to be less dramatic than the changes in satisfaction.[17]

CONCLUSIONS FROM THE EMPIRICAL LITERATURE. Our overall assessment of the empirical literature from economics, industrial relations, organizational behavior, and other social sciences is that participation *usually* leads to small, short-run improvements in performance and *sometimes* leads to significant, long-lasting improvements in performance. There is usually a positive, often small, effect of partici-

16. Cotton and others, "Employee Participation"; Ricky W. Griffin, "Consequences of Quality Circles in an Industrial Setting: A Longitudinal Assessment," *Academy of Management Journal*, vol. 31, no. 2 (1988), pp. 338–58; M. L. Marks and others, "Employee Participation in a Quality Circle Program: Impact on Quality of Work Life, Productivity, and Absenteeism," *Journal of Applied Psychology*, vol. 71, no.1 (1986), pp. 61–69; Miller and Monge, "Participation, Satisfaction, and Productivity"; and Wagner and Gooding, "Shared Influence and Organizational Behavior."

17. In contrast to the findings in Cotton and others, "Employee Participation."

pation on productivity, sometimes a zero or statistically insignificant effect, and almost never a negative effect. The size and strength of the effect are contingent on the form and content of participation. Participation is more likely to produce a significant, long-lasting increase in productivity when it involves decisions that extend to the shopfloor and when it involves substantive rather than consultative arrangements.

Finally, the productivity effects of participation are contingent on characteristics of the firm's broader industrial relations system. In the second half of this paper, we identify four characteristics that are important for successful employee participation, and we look at how the firm's external environment affects whether it adopts these features.

Employee Participation and the Firm's External Environment

The empirical literature strongly suggests that employee participation, correctly done, has positive effects on productivity. For economists, this leads naturally to the question: Why don't we see more of it? There are several ways to approach this question. One approach would emphasize such noneconomic factors as habit, history, and culture as possible barriers to participation. Studies of organizational design that concentrate on the role of management styles or personalities or on the role of cultural values exemplify this approach.

Another approach would emphasize how production technologies affect a firm's organizational and incentive structure. When tasks are routine and easily monitored, the improvement in productivity from participation is likely to be minimal. In contrast, when technology requires a considerable degree of worker flexibility, when tasks are complex and involve broad worker discretion, and when monitoring of individual effort is costly, theory suggests that employee participation is more likely to have significant beneficial effects. Researchers working within the agency, property-rights, and transaction-costs approaches to organizational design have investigated how monitoring problems and technologies affect the relations between employee participation and the firm's profitability.[18]

A third approach to understanding why employee participation is not

18. See, for example, Jensen and Meckling, "Rights and Production Functions"; and Oliver E. Williamson, "The Organization of Work: A Comparative Institutional Assessment," *Journal of Economic Behavior and Organization*, no. 1 (March 1980), pp. 5–38.

more widespread focuses on how the firm's external environment affects its organizational design and incentive structure. This is the approach we explore in the remainder of this paper.

Four Characteristics of Successful Participatory Systems

We have identified four characteristics of a firm's industrial relations system that are likely to influence how employee participation affects productivity over time. These are some form of profit sharing or gain sharing; job security and long-term employment relations; measures to build group cohesiveness; and guaranteed individual rights. This set of characteristics is frequently observed in both foreign and domestic firms with employee participation. Table 2 describes three foreign cases (large firms in Sweden and Japan, and the Mondragon cooperatives) and one representative American case (Hewlett-Packard) in terms of these four characteristics and in terms of their employee participation schemes. Although the table contains only four cases, there are numerous other participatory firms that exhibit the same four characteristics. Important cases include other "high-commitment" U.S. firms, such as IBM, Nummi, Xerox, and the Topeka Dog Food plant, and other worker-owned firms, such as plywood cooperatives in the Pacific Northwest, the Israeli kibbutzim, and most European cooperatives.

As table 2 demonstrates, our four characteristics of participatory firms are quite broad and vary across the cases we examine. For example, gain sharing in large Swedish firms differs from annual bonus payments in large Japanese firms. And there is considerable variation in the mechanisms used to build group cohesiveness as well as in participatory arrangements. Finally, the Mondragon co-ops have several unique features reflecting the fact that they are fully owned by employees.

Despite their important differences, however, the firms described in table 2 share one basic feature that explains their similarities: in the words of Masahiko Aoki, "The body of employees is, together with the body of shareholders, explicitly or implicitly recognized as a constituent of the firm, and its interests are considered in the formation of managerial policy."[19]

To be sure, many other factors affect the success of participation.

19. Masahiko Aoki, "The Japanese Firm in Transition," in Kozo Yamamura and Yasukichi Yasuba, eds., *The Political Economy of Japan*, vol. 1: *The Domestic Transformation* (Stanford University Press, 1987), pp. 263–89, quotation, p. 265.

Table 2. Characteristics of Participatory Employment Systems, Four Cases

Item	Japanese primary firms	Mondragon co-ops	Swedish auto industry	Hewlett-Packard
Decisionmaking participation: shopfloor	Widespread quality circles with the power to change the deployment of workers within workshops and the way jobs are conducted.[1]	Experiments with shopfloor redesigns, small work teams, and quality circles along Japanese and Swedish lines are being diffused among the co-ops.[2]	Workers design and organize their own jobs within a team framework to accomplish their common assignment. The design of the factory supports their self-paced team work.[3]	700 quality circles at peak. Implementing self-directed work teams. Cooperative product design.[4] Quality program.[5]
Decisionmaking participation: intermediate forms	Widespread consultation mechanism between management and labor in which managerial policies are discussed.[6] The *ringi* system diffuses participation and responsibility to lower echelons of the management hierarchy.[7]	Each cell of ten workers elects a representative to the Social Council, which serves in an advisory capacity to management and the board.[8] Participation mainly reactive rather than proactive.[9]	Employer obligated by law to negotiate with workers on major issues including closure, reorganization, expansion, and employee transfer.[10]	HP participatory management. Open door policy. "Management by wandering around."[11]
Decisionmaking participation: board of directors	No worker representatives in the boardroom. Little divestiture of formal top management authority.[12]	Elected on a one-man one-vote basis by the General Assembly, of which all cooperateurs are members.[13]	Minority worker representation on the board of directors backed by strong central unions.	No worker representation in the boardroom.
Profit sharing or gain sharing	Annual bonuses of about two months' salary, determined by profitability and collective bargaining.[14] Wages rise with firm growth.[15]	Surplus based on profitability, distributed mainly to individual accounts in proportion to labor and interest income.[16]	Gain-sharing bonus system, calculated by multifactor productivity indexes.[17]	Cash profit-sharing plan under which the company distributes to employees 12 percent of pretax profits.[18]

Ownership of assets	De facto capital participation due to seniority wage system and the investment of pension reserves in the employing firm.[19]	Capital contribution equivalent to about one year's pay required upon entry. Shares may not be sold; voluntary departure involves penalty.[20]	No substantive ownership of assets.	Stock purchase program under which as much as 10 percent of salary can be used to buy company stocks.[21,22]
Team production techniques	Organization structures, such as broad job specification, group responsibility, and job rotation, promote and require team work.[23]	Experiments with small work teams, and quality circles along Japanese and Swedish lines are being diffused among the co-ops.	Self-directed assembly groups with frequent job rotation and enrichment.	Units are kept small. Communication emphasized. Participative decisionmaking practiced. Implementing self-directed work teams in new factories.
Long-term employment relations	Lifetime employment in general, internal transfer often used for short-term adjustment, early retirement often used for contractions longer than one year.[24]	Lifetime employment expected. Some redeployment between cooperatives. Little use of casual labor.	No layoffs at Volvo since company began in 1929. Company redeploys workers within the firm.[25] Government subsidizes in-plant training as an alternative to layoff.[26]	Corporate strategy stresses employment commitments.[27] Employees have accepted shortened work weeks during recessions. No layoffs in company history.[28]
Group cohesiveness measures	With subcontracting hierarchy and seniority-based wage and promotion system, wage differentials are modest within the cohorts.[29]	Wage differential limited by the group rules. Maximum spread until 1980 of 1:3 later raised to 1:4.5.[30]	Wage differential limited by bargaining policy.	By industry standard, top managers moderately paid; workers at the lower end of the wage scale well paid.[31] Adjustment burdens borne by all, including top managers.[32]
Guaranteed individual rights	Unions guarantee just-cause dismissal protection.	Just-cause protections.	Just-cause protections required by law.[33]	Non-union grievance procedure.[34]

Table 2 (*continued*)

1. Kazuo Koike, "Human Resource Development and Labor-Management Relations," in Kozo Yamamura and Yasukichi Yasuba, eds., *The Political Economy of Japan*, vol. 1: *The Domestic Transformation* (Stanford University Press, 1987), pp. 289–330; and James R. Lincoln and Kerry McBride, "Japanese Industrial Organization in Comparative Perspective," *Annual Review of Sociology*, vol. 13 (1987) pp. 289–312.

2. Accounting for the slow progress of work redesign, Bradley and Gelb consider that "apart from technical advantages there is less incentive for such experiment in Mondragon. Worker ownership provides an alternative means to generate consensus and integrate the workforce." Keith Bradley and Alan Gelb, *Cooperation at Work: The Mondragon Experience* (Heinemann Educational Books, 1983), p. 36. Whyte and Whyte, on the other hand, emphasize incidental external economic pressures that divert management's efforts and implementation problems due to inexperience. William Foote Whyte and Kathleen King Whyte, *Making Mondragon: The Growth and Dynamics of the Worker Cooperative Complex* (Ithaca, N.Y.: ILR Press, 1988), pp. 125–27.

3. Berth Jönsson and Alden G. Lank, "Volvo: A Report on the Workshop on Production Technology and Quality of Working Life," *Human Resource Management*, vol. 24 (Winter 1985), pp. 455–65.

4. Thomas J. Peters and Robert H. Waterman, Jr., *In Search of Excellence: Lessons from America's Best-Run Companies* (Harper and Row, 1982), p. 137.

5. Peters and Waterman, *In Search of Excellence*, pp. 175–77.

6. Koike, "Human Resource Development," pp. 319–21.

7. Lincoln and McBride, "Japanese Industrial Organization," p. 300.

8. Bradley and Gelb, *Cooperation at Work*, p. 16.

9. For a comprehensive discussion of worker participation in Mondragon, see Whyte and Whyte, *Making Mondragon*, pp. 113–27 and 209–13.

10. Lennart Forseback, *Industrial Relations and Employment in Sweden* (Stockholm: Swedish Institute, 1980).

11. Richard O. von Werssowetz and Michael Beer, "Human Resources at Hewlett-Packard," Case Study 9-482-125 (Harvard Business School, 1982).

12. James R. Lincoln and Arne L. Kalleberg, "Work Organizations and Workforce Commitment: A Study of Plants and Employees in the U.S. and Japan," *American Sociological Review*, vol. 50 (December 1985), pp. 738–60.

13. Keith Bradley and Alan Gelb, "Cooperative Labour Relations: Mondragon's Response to Recession," *British Journal of Industrial Relations*, vol. 25 (January 1985), pp. 77–97.

14. Kazuo Sato, "Saving and Investment," in Kozo Yamamura and Yasukichi Yasuba, eds., *The Political Economy of Japan*, vol. 1: *The Domestic Transformation* (Stanford University Press, 1987), pp. 137–85.

15. Rodney Clark, *The Japanese Company* (Yale University Press, 1979).

16. Bradley and Gelb, *Cooperation at Work*, p. 34; Bradley and Gelb, "Cooperative Labour Relations," pp. 88–90.

17. Warren C. Hauck and Timothy L. Ross, "Sweden's Experiments in Productivity Gainsharing: A Second Look," *Personnel*, vol. 64 (January 1987), pp. 61–67.

18. Robert Levering, Milton Moskowitz, and Michael Katz, *The 100 Best Companies to Work for in America* (Addison-Wesley, 1984), p. 144.

19. Masahiko Aoki, "The Japanese Firm in Transition," in Kozo Yamamura and Yasukichi Yasuba, eds., *Political Economy of Japan*, pp. 263–88.

20. Bradley and Gelb, "Cooperative Labour Relations," p. 18.

21. Levering and others, *100 Best Companies*, p. 144.

22. "The company had distributed $64 million in cash profit-sharing bonuses in the previous five years, and about half the employees were participating in a stock-purchase program." Roger M. Atherton and Dennis M. Crites, *Hewlett-Packard Company (A): Problems of Rapid Growth*, Case 0208 (Dover, Mass.: Lord Publishing, 1976), p. 7.

23. Lincoln and McBride, "Japanese Industrial Organization," pp. 296–97.

24. Koike, "Human Resource Development," pp. 308–09.

25. Volvo personnel department, personal communication, February 1989.

26. Bo Jangenäs, *The Swedish Approach to Labor Market Policy* (Stockholm: Swedish Institute, 1985).

27. "Rather than run the risk of 'big' layoffs, Hewlett-Packard has declined to bid on short-run government contracts. It has also avoided getting into product lines where there are wide fluctuations in sales volume, such as in many consumer products." "Since the company had policies of keeping employment steady and operating on a pay-as-you-go basis, both Hewlett and Packard believed minimal debt would be more consistent with these policies and the weakening U.S. economy." "Their financial strategy has been to use profits, employee stock purchases, and other internally generated funds to finance growth. They have avoided long-term debt and have resorted to short-term debt only when sales growth exceeded the return on net worth." Atherton and Crites, *Hewlett-Packard*, pp. 7, 4, 4.

28. William G. Ouchi, *Theory Z: How American Business Can Meet the Japanese Challenge* (Addison-Wesley, 1981), p. 118.

29. Koike, "Human Resource Development," pp. 319–21; Jacob Mincer and Yoshio Higuchi, "Wage Structures and Labor Turnover in the United States and Japan," *Journal of the Japanese and International Economies*, vol. 2 (June 1988), pp. 97–133.

30. Bradley and Gelb, *Cooperation at Work*, p. 17.

31. "Even though their individual stock holdings in 1975 were worth some $700 million, Hewlett and Packard still ran an egalitarian company. They drew salaries of only $156,000 each, and few top officers made more than $100,000." Atherton and Crites, *Hewlett-Packard*, p. 7.

32. K. K. Wiegner, "John Young's New Jogging Shoes," *Forbes*, November 4, 1985, pp. 42–44.

33. Guy Standing, *Unemployment and Labour Market Flexibility: Sweden* (Geneva: International Labour Office, 1988).

34. Wiegner, "John Young's New Jogging Shoes."

Successful participatory schemes must maintain the support of supervisors, higher management, and (when organized) union leaders.[20] In addition, the culture, history, laws, and traditions of particular firms and particular national environments will influence work organization. We acknowledge the importance of these other factors, but do not discuss them here.

PROFIT SHARING OR GAIN SHARING. Some form of profit sharing, broadly defined, is a key element of participatory systems, and is observed in all of the cases discussed in table 2. Profit-sharing arrangements characteristic of participatory systems, such as those of the Japanese and Swedish firms in table 2, provide for a base wage, often in excess of the reservation wage of current employees, plus some variable reward based on a specified measure of profitability or group productivity.[21]

One can imagine profit sharing without participation and vice versa, but in fact the two are likely to go together in successful participatory systems. In the short run, participation may be its own reward for many employees. In the long run, however, sustained, effective participation requires that employees be rewarded for the extra effort which such participation entails, and that they receive a share of any increased productivity or profits. Workers feel that it is unfair if they do not share in the benefits generated by their cost-saving ideas. Group-based gain sharing gives workers incentives to maintain norms of high effort, to monitor each other, and to sanction workers who are shirking. More positively, group-based pay also gives workers incentives to cooperate, and not to try to advance at the expense of their colleagues.

Just as participation can lead to demands for profit sharing, profit sharing can lead to demands for participation. When there is profit sharing, workers' incomes depend on the decisions of the firm, and workers want to have a say in these decisions.[22]

20. David I. Levine and George Strauss, "Employee Participation and Involvement," report prepared for the U.S. Department of Labor, Commission on Workforce Quality and Labor Market Efficiency, 1989.

21. It is important to emphasize that profit sharing as used here is different from Weitzman's version of profit sharing in The Share Economy, which is any scheme where compensation per employee automatically falls when the number of workers employed by the firm increases. Such schemes are obviously at odds with usual notions of fairness and with the objective of building the commitment of employees to the firm.

22. This situation is an instance of the more general result from property-rights economics that residual claimants should have some control rights over the firm. See Eirik G. Furubotn and Svetozar Pejovich, eds., The Economics of Property Rights (Ballinger Publishing, 1974).

Moreover, there is growing evidence that profit sharing and participation interact positively, implying that the combination is more potent than the sum of its parts.[23] A recent study concludes, "The available evidence is strongly suggestive that for employee ownership, including profit-sharing and ESOP programs, to have a strong impact on performance, it needs to be accompanied by provisions for worker participation in decision making."[24]

LONG-TERM EMPLOYMENT RELATIONS. All the participatory systems included in table 2 have implicit or explicit long-term employment contracts with their workers. There are several distinct but related reasons why job security and long-term employment relations are needed for participation to work.

Most directly, workers are unlikely to cooperate in increasing efficiency if they fear that by so doing they jeopardize their jobs. Guarantees of job security reduce fears that higher productivity will lead to layoffs.[25]

Workers with job security have a longer time horizon and are more likely to forgo short-term gains to build a more effective organization. To the extent that participation relies upon work group cooperation and employees monitoring one another, long-term employment relations are essential. The longer an employee expects to be in a work group, the more effective are group-based rewards and sanctions as motivators. Long-term employment relations also alleviate many of the problems of a gain-sharing system, since a worker or work group that is shortchanged in one time period knows that there will be other chances for future rewards.

Finally, participatory firms often need to make large investments in the selection, socialization, and training of workers. From the firm's

23. See the evidence in the Weitzman and Kruse paper in this volume. See, for examples, General Accounting Office, *Employee Stock Ownership Plans*; Michael Quarrey and Corey Rosen, *Employee Ownership and Corporate Performance* (Oakland, Calif.: National Center for Employee Ownership, October 1986); and Richard J. Long, "Worker Ownership and Job Attitudes: A Field Study," *Industrial Relations,* vol. 21, no. 2 (1982), pp. 196–215.

24. Jones and Pliskin, "Effects of Worker Participation," p. 26.

25. Worker restriction of output to save jobs has been observed at least since Mathewson, and Roethlisberger and Dickson. Stanley B. Mathewson, *Restriction of Output among Unorganized Workers* (New York, 1931; reprinted Southern Illinois University Press, 1969); and Fritz J. Roethlisberger and William J. Dickson, *Management and the Worker: Technical vs. Social Organization in an Industrial Plant* (Harvard University Press, 1939). Many cases have been reported in which fear of layoffs has inhibited the success of participation. See Thomas Kochan, Harry Katz, and Nancy Mower, "Worker Participation and American Unions," in Thomas A. Kochan, ed., *Challenges and Choices Facing American Labor* (MIT Press, 1985), p. 290.

point of view, long-term employment relations are needed to recover the higher investment in human resources that usually accompanies participation.

MEASURES TO INCREASE GROUP COHESIVENESS. A feature of the participatory systems in table 2 is that they reduce pay and status differentials among employees, particularly between workers and managers, relative to those observed outside. There are three related reasons why smaller differentials are associated with participation.

First, narrow differences in wages and status help develop an atmosphere of trust and confidence between workers and management, and so reinforce the atmosphere of participation. There is evidence that large differences in status can inhibit participation.[26]

Second, bonuses based on group output give workers incentives to work for group goals and provide incentives for workers to monitor and sanction free riders. On the other hand, large wage differences and competition for promotions can reduce cooperation, as workers try to win the bonus or promotion "tournament."[27]

Group-based pay, almost by definition, reduces individual pay differentials. According to Morton Deutsch, who has been studying the relationship between egalitarianism and productivity for over forty years, when "efficiency requires efficient cooperation, almost any movement towards a democratic egalitarian structure increases effectiveness." Numerous laboratory experiments have found that narrow wage dispersion increases worker cohesiveness and increases productivity.[28]

26. George Strauss, "Participatory and Gainsharing Systems: History and Hope," Organizational Behavior and Industrial Relations Working Paper OBIR-17 (University of California, Berkeley, Center for Research Management, January 1987); and Irving Bluestone, "Comments on Job Enrichment: Long on Theory, Short on Practice," Organizational Dynamics, vol. 2 (Winter 1974), pp. 46–47.

27. Ronald A. Dye, "The Trouble with Tournaments," Economic Inquiry, vol. 22 (January 1, 1984), pp. 147–49; and Edward P. Lazear, "Pay Equality and Industrial Politics," Journal of Political Economy, vol. 97 (June 1989), pp. 561–80.

28. Quotation from Morton Deutsch, "Is There a Tradeoff between Economic Efficiency and Equity?" Asilomar Conference, April 17, 1988. And see Morton Deutsch, Distributive Justice: A Social-Psychological Perspective (Yale University Press, 1985); and Karen S. Cook and Karen A. Hegtvedt, "Distributive Justice, Equity and Equality," Annual Review of Sociology, vol. 9 (1983), pp. 217–41. Pages 296–98 of Albert J. Lott and Bernice E. Lott, "Group Cohesiveness as Interpersonal Attraction: A Review of Relationships with Antecedent and Consequent Variables," Psychological Bulletin, vol. 64, no. 4 (1965), pp. 259–309, review the early literature on this subject. See also William J. Goode, "The Protection of the Inept," American Sociological Review, vol. 32

Finally, participation may extend into the realm of compensation. To the extent that the median employee exerts influence on the firm's compensation policy, there is likely to be pressure to reduce high-end wages, thereby compressing wage differentials.

Regardless of the theoretical rationale, in practice most participatory workplaces, including worker-owned firms in the United States and abroad—the large Japanese and Swedish firms described in table 2 and successful participatory firms in the United States—tend to pay relatively egalitarian wages, largely to induce cohesiveness within the work force. Personnel research in support of these findings includes John Witte and Katrina Berman on U.S. participatory firms, Keith Bradley and Alan Gelb on foreign cooperatives, and William Ouchi, Thomas Rohlen, and Ezra Vogel on Japanese companies. Edward Lawler, and Michael Beer and others, have turned this finding into prescription, recommending that participatory firms should rely heavily on group-based compensation and narrow wage differentials.[29]

GUARANTEED INDIVIDUAL RIGHTS. Participatory systems usually have rules and procedures to safeguard employee rights.[30] To participate effectively, people need "the assurance that they will not be penalized for their participation. Such acts as criticizing existing proce-

---

(February 1967), pp. 5–19; and Ivan D. Steiner, ed., *Group Process and Productivity* (New York: Academic Press, 1972).

29. John F. Witte, *Democracy, Authority, and Alienation in Work: Workers' Participation in an American Corporation* (University of Chicago Press, 1980), p. 162; Katrina Berman, "The Worker-Owned Plywood Cooperatives," in Frank Lindenfeld and Joyce Rothschild-Whitt, eds., *Workplace Democracy and Social Change* (Boston: Porter Sargent Publishers, 1982), pp. 161–76, esp. p. 171; Keith Bradley and Alan Gelb, *Cooperation at Work: The Mondragon Experience* (London: Heinemann Educational Books, 1983). On Japan, see William Ouchi, *Theory Z: How American Business Can Meet the Japanese Challenge* (Avon, 1981); Ezra Vogel, *Japan as Number One* (Harper and Row, 1979), pp. 120, 140–41; and Thomas P. Rohlen, "The Company Work Group," in Ezra F. Vogel, ed., *Modern Japanese Organization and Decision-making* (University of California Press, 1975). See also Edward E. Lawler III, *Pay and Organizational Development* (Reading, Mass.: Addison-Wesley, 1981), p. 225; and Michael Beer and others, *Managing Human Assets* (Free Press, 1984), p. 145. A more detailed review of the evidence is found in David I. Levine, "Cohesiveness, Productivity, and Wage Dispersion," Working Paper 14 (University of California, Berkeley, Institute of Industrial Relations, January 1989).

30. For examples, see Strauss, "Participatory and Gainsharing Systems"; Lindenfeld and Rothschild-Whitt, eds., *Workplace Democracy and Social Change;* Shoshana Zuboff, *In the Age of the Smart Machine: The Future of Work and Power* (Basic Books, 1984); Fred K. Foulkes, *Personnel Policies in Large Nonunion Companies* (Prentice-Hall, 1980), pp. 63, 90, and chap. 15.

dures or opposing proposed policy changes could invite reprisals from management."[31] Personnel systems governed by the rule of law are perceived as more legitimate and fair than systems in which decisions are at the discretion of supervisory personnel.[32]

Guaranteed rights increase worker trust in the firm. Several studies indicate how high-trust environments depend on employee perceptions of due process. Such environments facilitate employee participation and better performance, creativity, and communication.[33]

Guaranteed individual rights are an important part of long-term employment relations, since workers have an alternative to quitting if they are unhappy about an aspect of their jobs. Richard Freeman and James Medoff have surveyed the evidence relating individual rights ("voice") and performance. They conclude that union workers with guaranteed individual rights have higher productivity and lower turnover rates than other similarly paid workers.[34]

A just-cause dismissal policy is a critical right for participation.[35] In contrast to just-cause dismissal policies, at-will dismissal policies mean that employment can be terminated by the firm at any time "for good cause, for no cause, or even for cause morally wrong."[36]

When firms guarantee individual rights, such traditional motivators as fear of dismissal become less effective. In most successful participatory firms, however, workers are motivated by group rewards, peer

31. Paul Bernstein, *Workplace Democratization: Its Internal Dynamics* (New Brunswick, N.J.: Transaction Books, 1980), p. 75.

32. See James N. Baron, "The Employment Relation as a Social Relation," *Journal of the Japanese and International Economies*, vol. 2 (December 1988), pp. 492–525.

33. See Mowday and others, *Employee-Organization Linkages*, pp. 33, 34, on how guaranteed individual rights increased commitment. On the relation of trust and performance, see Frank Friedlander, "The Primacy of Trust as a Facilitator of Further Group Accomplishment," *Journal of Applied Behavioral Science*, vol. 6 (October 1970), pp. 387–400; Dale E. Zand, "Trust and Managerial Problem Solving," *Administrative Science Quarterly*, vol. 17 (June 1972), pp. 229–39; Richard J. Klimoski and Barbara L. Karol, "The Impact of Trust on Creative Problem Solving Groups," *Journal of Applied Psychology*, vol. 61 (October 1976), pp. 630–33; and Charles A. O'Reilly III and Karlene H. Roberts, "Information Filtration in Organizations: Three Experiments," *Organizational Behavior and Human Performance*, vol. 11 (April 1974), pp. 253–65.

34. Richard B. Freeman and James L. Medoff, *What Do Unions Do?* (Basic Books, 1984).

35. George Strauss, "Managerial Practices," in J. Richard Hackman and J. Lloyd Suttle, eds., *Improving Life at Work: Behavioral Science Approaches to Organizational Change* (Santa Monica, Calif.: Goodyear Publishing, 1977), pp. 297–363, esp. pp. 307–11.

36. Jack Stieber, "Employment-at-Will: An Issue for the 1980s," *1983 Industrial Relations Research Association Proceedings* (1984), p. 2.

pressure, and so forth—not by traditional fear of punishment. The evidence suggests that the gains in perceived fairness and in workers' willingness to participate outweigh the losses of guaranteed individual rights for participatory firms. The fact that high-commitment firms such as Hewlett-Packard have voluntarily adopted just-cause policies and guaranteed many other employee rights implies that the firm anticipates net benefits from such constraints on managerial actions.

The Interaction of Participation and the External Environment

Many economists have concluded that the low incidence of participatory arrangements in market systems implies that such arrangements are inefficient—for if participation were a good idea, then the market would favor companies with participation. Here we argue that evolutionary forces may fail to select for potentially efficient work organizations. Despite the potential efficiency of participatory workplaces, conditions in product, labor, and capital markets can discourage firms from adopting the four characteristics we have identified as necessary for successful participation. Specifically, stable aggregate demand, low unemployment, wage and status compression, universal just cause, and long investor time horizons affect the relative costs of different types of industrial relations systems.

We make our arguments using a parable of two fictitious nonunion auto plants.[37]

The first plant, Munni (Manufacturing by United Nifty Neighbors, Inc.), uses a highly participatory work organization. It has the four characteristics necessary for successful participation: gain sharing, long-term employment relations, narrow wage and status dispersion to increase group cohesiveness, and guaranteed individual rights. Its competitor in the auto industry is Farmingham, one plant of Motors Gigantium (MG). The Farmingham plant uses a traditional labor relations system with none of these four characteristics.

The Effects of Product Market Conditions

At both Farmingham and Munni, nominal wages are set once a year. Farmingham lays off workers whenever there is a downturn in demand.

37. All our arguments can be formalized and are subject to empirical test—work which we and others are currently carrying out.

Munni, on the other hand, has long-term employment relations and a no-layoff policy. During downturns Munni trains workers, freezes hiring, transfers workers within the firm, and ultimately hoards excess labor.

Farmingham's use of layoffs is relatively cheaper when recessions are frequent and deep, while Munni's no-layoff pledge and long-term employment relations are relatively cheaper when recessions are shallow or infrequent. As a result, Munni will flourish if its product market is characterized by lower probabilities of declines in demand; that is, the lower the variability of industry and aggregate demand, and the higher the average growth rate of the industry and the economy.[38]

There is also feedback from the firm's employment system to the macroeconomy. Recessions are deeper when many firms have layoffs (Farmingham style).[39] Layoffs lead to lower spending on consumer goods by Farmingham workers, resulting in further layoffs at stores in the Farmingham area, and eventually affecting producers around the world. On the other hand, recessions are shallower when many firms avoid layoffs (Munni style).

Since the costs of running participatory systems increase as the variability of product demand increases, policies that reduce this variability will tend to encourage such systems.[40]

The Effects of Labor Market Conditions

We discuss three facets of the labor market that work to the advantage of participatory firms: low unemployment, narrow wage dispersion, and universal just cause.

38. Robert J. Gordon, "Productivity, Wages, and Prices Inside and Outside of Manufacturing in the U.S., Japan, and Europe," *European Economic Review,* vol. 31 (April 1987), pp. 685–733. There is evidence that economic crises can prod management, workers, and unions to *initiate* participatory experiments; nonetheless, demand stability reduces the costs of *maintaining* participation.

39. This result assumes that workers are often short of liquid assets, and that temporary layoffs reduce consumption expenditures. There is growing evidence of liquidity constraints among workers. See, for example, Marjorie Flavin, "Excess Sensitivity of Consumption to Current Income: Liquidity Constraints or Myopia?" Working Paper 1341 (Cambridge, Mass.: National Bureau of Economic Research, May 1984); and Fumio Hayashi, "The Permanent Income Hypothesis: Estimation and Testing by Instrumental Variables," *Journal of Political Economy* (October 1982), pp. 895–916.

40. This result is an extension of an earlier observation by Michael Piore that aggregate stabilization policies permit the primary sector to expand. Michael J. Piore, "Perspectives on Labor Market Flexibility," *Industrial Relations,* vol. 25 (Spring 1986), pp. 146–66.

Because Farmingham's disciplinary system is based on fear of dismissal, it is relatively inexpensive when unemployment is high.[41] Whenever unemployment drops, however, Farmingham suffers an increase in absenteeism and turnover and a decrease in productivity and quality. On the other hand, Munni's motivational system is based on participation, gain sharing, worker-worker monitoring, and so forth. Correspondingly, when unemployment is low, Munni and other participatory firms gain in relative productivity.

If most firms have the Farmingham system, the macroeconomy tends to generate a high average unemployment level. If unemployment temporarily drops to a low level, wages and costs increase and profits and investment decline; both developments lead to lower labor demand. This outcome is the basic result of efficiency-wage models: if firms require unemployment to motivate workers, the macroeconomy will endogenously create unemployment.[42]

If all firms use participation, then low unemployment and tight labor markets are sustainable. Since motivation does not depend on the threat of dismissal, tight labor markets will not inevitably lead to declines in profits and investment coupled with increases in wages and turnover. While participation does not ensure full employment (other macroeconomic policies may be needed), participation may be necessary to sustain low levels of unemployment.[43]

41. The results of this section are elaborated in David Stern, *Managing Human Resources: The Art of Full Employment* (Boston: Auburn House Publishing, 1982).

42. The results of this paragraph are derived formally in many efficiency-wage models, such as Carl Shapiro and Joseph E. Stiglitz, "Equilibrium Unemployment as a Worker Discipline Device," *American Economic Review,* vol. 74 (June 1984), pp. 433–44; and Samuel Bowles, "The Production Process in a Competitive Economy: Walrasian, Neo-Hobbesian and Marxism Models," *American Economic Review,* vol. 75 (March 1985), pp. 16–36.

43. Samuel Bowles, David M. Gordon, and Thomas E. Weisskopf, *Beyond the Waste Land: A Democratic Alternative to Economic Decline* (Anchor Press/Doubleday, 1983), p. 303. Beer and Driscoll note how "high rates of turnover or absenteeism, high grievance rates, sabotage, complaints and hostility, and labor problems can create *internal* pressures for improving the quality of work life." Michael Beer and James W. Driscoll, "Strategies for Change," in J. Richard Hackman and J. Lloyd Suttle, eds., *Improving Life at Work: Behavioral Science Approaches to Organizational Change* (Santa Monica, Calif.: Goodyear Publishing, 1977), pp. 364–453.

The situation with high unemployment and use of traditional monitoring techniques will be stable only if participatory firms are constrained to pay wages that are comparable to market wages. Otherwise, participatory firms will open up paying low wages, hire the unemployed, and put traditional firms out of business. Since participatory firms

Thus there can be two stable economy-wide equilibria: a "Farmingham" equilibrium, in which firms motivate workers with fear of dismissal, and the average unemployment rate is high; and a "Munni" equilibrium, in which firms motivate with participation, and the average unemployment rate is low. A new auto plant built in an economy with a Farmingham equilibrium would find Farmingham-style arrangements profit maximizing—with many unemployed workers, there is no need to use participation to motivate. On the other hand, a new auto plant built in an economy with a Munni equilibrium would find Munni-style arrangements profit maximizing—with low unemployment, the firm would be encouraged to use participation to motivate.

As this parable of multiple macro equilibria demonstrates, the choice of work organization by new firms will depend partly on how tight the labor market is. When average unemployment rates are low for sustained periods, participatory work organizations become more attractive as ways to motivate and retain workers.

In Sweden, for example, the government has consistently held the unemployment rate below 3 percent. This situation has increased rates of turnover and absenteeism in monotonous jobs to the point that job redesign has become vital for Swedish managers.

At Farmingham, wage and status differentials are important motivators.[44] In contrast, Munni reduces status and pay differentials to increase worker cohesiveness. There are no reserved parking places, no executive dining rooms, and so forth. In fact, there are not even any "workers," only "associates."

Munni also has lower wage differentials. Promotions are based largely on seniority, and promotions for star workers are less rapid than at Farmingham. This policy promotes cooperation for group goals and reduces individual efforts for self-promotion. The extensive use of group-based pay, not individual incentives, also promotes cooperation and worker norms of high effort.

Munni's policies of narrowing differentials occur partly by increasing pay for the bottom of the wage distribution, with the increase paid for

---

require that workers feel they are treated fairly, and since they have high costs of employee turnover, it is plausible that they cannot provide their workers with below-market utility levels.

44. The argument in this section is elaborated in David I. Levine, "Cohesiveness, Productivity, and Wage Dispersion."

by the increase in productivity from participation. Thus low-end workers at Munni receive wages above the market rate. This above-market wage is not "taken into account" by the market when judging which firms make sufficient profits to survive; therefore, the market will supply inefficiently few firms paying rents to low-wage workers.[45]

For example, assume that Munni increases cohesiveness by raising low-end wages $1.10 an hour, and productivity increases $1.00 an hour. Productivity increases (that is, more output is produced with identical physical inputs), but profits fall by 10 cents per hour per low-wage worker. Because profits are lower, the market selects against Munni, even though productivity is higher than at other firms. A subsidy of 10 cents an hour would raise GNP by $1.00 an hour.

In addition to raising low-end wages, part of the narrowing in differentials occurs at the expense of high-wage workers. Thus Munni has trouble keeping "stars" and high-skill workers. If stars and high-skill workers are needed for production, Munni's compensation policy will be costly in the presence of firms with wide wage dispersion.

On the other hand, if Farmingham and all other firms had narrow wage and status differentials, Munni could keep its stars, and all firms could enjoy the efficiency gains of participation. Such an economy-wide equilibrium, however, is not usually stable. Starting from a position where all firms pay narrow wage differentials, Farmingham can hire away other companies' star employees by bidding up their wages. The star employees who move will earn higher wages, and Farmingham will make higher profits. Farmingham's policies will make paying narrow differentials difficult for all firms. Thus the gains of participation will be lost for all firms, and for all nonstar employees. (We discuss below some of the special circumstances that permit Japanese firms to pay narrow wage differentials in order to promote cohesiveness.)

Farmingham relies upon the threat of dismissal to motivate its workers and dismisses employees at will (that is, it does not need to demonstrate a reason to dismiss a worker).[46] Munni has a just-cause policy and must justify any dismissal. Munni management is concerned that its workers feel that personnel policies are fair and that criticisms will not lead to

45. In this model, participatory firms pay efficiency wages to low-end workers. As in other efficiency-wage models, the market leads to too few workers receiving the relatively high wage.

46. The results in this section are elaborated in David I. Levine, "Just Cause Employment Policies in the Presence of Worker Adverse Selection," University of California, Berkeley, School of Business Administration, November 1987.

dismissal. Munni uses internal motivation and worker-worker monitoring, not fear of dismissal; its dismissal rate is only 10 percent of Farmingham's.

Because only Munni has just-cause dismissal, many of the less-motivated workers at Farmingham want to work there. This is especially the case for workers who are talented at putting forth little effort without providing enough evidence to be dismissed; at Munni, they can enjoy a lengthy on-the-job vacation. Even if these talented shirkers make up a low proportion of the population, their concentration in Munni's applicant pool will vastly increase Munni's screening costs.

On the other hand, if just cause were universal, then these poorly motivated workers would be distributed evenly across firms, without concentrating at Munni. Under these circumstances, the efficiency gains of just-cause policies are more likely to outweigh the burden imposed by shirkers.

Externalities from just-cause dismissal policies, therefore, are a second reason that multiple equilibria are possible—one can imagine a Farmingham equilibrium in which at-will dismissal policies are the rule, and the costs of introducing just-cause policies are very high for individual firms; and an alternative Munni equilibrium in which just-cause policies are the rule, and each firm finds that the benefits of just cause outweigh the costs.

In the former economy, firms with just cause will have to bear significant screening and monitoring costs to counter their adverse selection problem. Even in an economy where just cause is the rule rather than the exception, however, firms will have to develop systems for monitoring workers so that just cause can be demonstrated in dismissal decisions. Thus it is not surprising to find that the participatory systems described in table 2 have elaborate screening procedures for hiring new workers and elaborate horizontal and vertical monitoring devices for current workers.

Capital Market Conditions

Just as the success of participation depends on product and labor market conditions, it also depends on capital market conditions. Munni faces three problems: capital markets are inherently biased against the hard-to-monitor human capital and trust that are prerequisites for participation; takeovers that result in companies reneging on their commitments "can in the long run result in deterioration of trust necessary for the functioning of the corporation"; [47] and transaction costs can be larger for participatory firms. All these problems are less severe when firms have close long-term relations with their banks and equity holders.

Both Farmingham and Munni face imperfect capital markets. In perfect markets all investments with positive present values are under-taken. When information is imperfect, however, there will be inefficiently little investment in hard-to-monitor projects. Banks, stockholders, and the central headquarters of multidivisional firms all prefer investments in tangible assets. They fear that when managers claim to be investing in intangibles (reputations with workers, research and development, and so forth), they might really (1) be using the resources to cover up their own incompetence; (2) be purchasing on-the-job amenities and leisure; or (3) be increasing current reported performance at the expense of investments that pay off in the future. [48]

This general bias of capital markets is especially severe for Munni, since its participatory style requires high levels of investment in human capital and in worker commitment—investments that are very difficult to monitor.

Munni's investment in human capital and in worker-firm trust is also made more expensive because of reputational externalities. Such in-vestment pays off only in the long run, and only if the firm's promises are credible. Every time a firm reneges on its promises, the faith that Munni workers have in their company's promises will be diminished. Recent takeovers, leveraged buyouts, mergers, and restructuring are often designed to yield short-run gains. Typically, they lead to the rapid dismantling of human organizations and the rapid erosion of human capital. Takeovers whose profits come from reneging on promises to

47. Andrei Shleifer and Lawrence H. Summers, "Breach of Trust in Hostile Takeovers," Working Paper 2342 (Cambridge, Mass.: National Bureau of Economic Research, August 1987).

48. Reason (1) concerns adverse selection. Reason (2) concerns manager moral hazard. Reason (3) concerns managerial "signal jamming," where managers have no easy way to signal that current low earnings are due to high investment in invisibles, not from bad news about the firm. It is discussed in Jeremy C. Stein, "Efficient Capital Markets, Inefficient Firms: A Model of Myopic Corporate Behavior," Harvard Business School, 1988. John Grant Rhode, Edward E. Lawler III, and Gary L. Sundem, in "Human Resource Accounting: A Critical Assessment," Industrial Relations, vol. 15 (February 1976), pp. 14–15, discuss proposals to make human resource investments more visible.

workers make it harder for remaining high-commitment strategies to work.[49]

Participatory firms, in addition, face higher transactions costs for raising equity and loans. Farmingham's owners have all rights to the profits of Farmingham and have complete legal control over decision-making. Munni's owners, in contrast, share profits and decisionmaking rights with Munni employees. Thus all other things being equal, Munni will confront a higher cost of equity capital than Farmingham.

While Munni is disadvantaged in the equity market, it cannot survive solely on loans.[50] In a world with asymmetric information, firms (whether they are participatory or not) can borrow more and at a lower rate if they have more equity.[51] A firm that tries to rely exclusively on debt financing will find that it faces higher costs of funds than does a firm with partial equity financing. This line of reasoning suggests that the higher the debt-equity ratio firms can support without encountering an increase in their capital cost, the more supportive capital market conditions are for participatory firms.[52]

Although these problems are serious, Munni can succeed under certain conditions. Suppose, for example, that Munni relies on investors, such as banks or other firms, that have long-term interests in the firm and extensive communication links with it. Further, assume that Munni borrows from banks with which it has close, continuous relationships. These investors, in turn, have detailed information about Munni and its

49. Shleifer and Summers, "Breach of Trust in Hostile Takeovers." See also Philippe Aghion and Benjamin Hermalin, "The Value of Legalizing the Right to Breach Contracts," University of California, Berkeley, September 1989.

50. See, for example, the proposal by McCain, Putterman, and others that the participatory firm be financed by external debt finance, including so-called risk-participation bonds that differ from ordinary equity only in that their owners have no voting control over enterprise decisions. Roger A. McCain, "On the Optimum Financial Environment for Worker Cooperatives," Zeitschrift fur Nationalokonomie, vol. 37, no. 3–4 (1977), pp. 354–84; and Louis Putterman, "On Some Recent Explanations of Why Capital Hires Labor," Economic Inquiry, vol. 22 (April 1984), pp. 171–87.

51. Joseph E. Stiglitz and Andrew Weiss, "Credit Rationing in Markets with Imperfect Information," American Economic Review, vol. 71 (June 1981), pp. 393–410.

52. Munni cannot raise all its funds through employee ownership; internal self-finance reduces workers' diversification and limits the amount of equity finance available in accordance with the wealth constraints of firm employees. Wealth constraints are quite severe: in 1985 the median U.S. family had financial assets of only $3,500, far below the mean of $27,365. U.S. Department of Commerce, Statistical Abstract of the United States (Washington, 1986), p. 465, table 780. Munni would have more success relying on employee equity if the wealth distribution were less skewed.

investments over a substantial period. As a result of such relationships and of the investors' and creditors' information, Munni will have access to finance at favorable rates to finance its investments, including its investments in human capital and corporate culture. In this case, the suppliers of finance are likely to be more willing to share their income and control rights, because their information about the firm reduces their risks and monitoring costs.

In contrast, if Munni has arm's-length relationships with its investors, it will face a higher cost of capital. Stock market investors with limited access to information about the firm's performance will rely on the information that can be effectively summarized in short-term fluctuations in the firm's stock price. Banks will use the price and period of loan payoff as the main decision criteria. Such investors will be much less willing to share their income and control rights with firm employees. Moreover, when Munni encounters financial difficulties, it may be forced by its creditors to cut back first on its human resource investments, even though to do so may quickly harm the trust and legitimacy on which the firm's participatory system depends.

In sum, capital market arrangements that allow high debt-equity ratios without increasing the cost of capital, that lengthen the time horizon of investors, and that broaden and improve the flow of information between a firm and its investors are likely to be relatively more favorable to participatory firms.

These arguments are important for understanding the borrowing practices of participatory American firms such as Hewlett-Packard. Hewlett-Packard has relied heavily on retained earnings and employee stock purchases and has avoided long-term debt. These policies are explicitly designed to promote investment in hard-to-observe human capital and R&D, and to remove obstacles to the firm's job security policy.[53] As the following discussion demonstrates, very different solutions to capital market imperfections have been an important factor behind the growth of participatory firms in Japan.

Japanese Participatory Firms

The labor-relations system characteristic of Japan's large firms has been the subject of extensive scrutiny, in part because of Japan's

---

53. Roger M. Atherton and Dennis M. Crites, *Hewlett-Packard Company (A): Problems of Rapid Growth,* Case 0208 (Dover, Mass.: Lord Publishing, 1976), p. 4; and Roger M. Atherton and Dennis M. Crites, *Hewlett-Packard: A 1975–1978 Review,* Case 0209 (Lord Publishing, 1980), p. 5.

dramatic and persistent productivity gains, and in part because of Japan's low unemployment rate. There is a vast and growing literature identifying the distinguishing features of this system and speculating about its causes and effects.[54] Many of the conclusions of this literature support our ideas about the likely features of participatory systems and about the effects of product, labor, and capital markets on the development of such systems.

An estimated 30–40 percent of Japan's work force is employed in firms that exhibit our four defining characteristics for participatory firms. Most of these workers are employed in large Japanese companies (1,000 or more employees). The apparent positive correlation between company size and participation may seem surprising at first, but sociological evidence from several organizations suggests that commitment structures are more easily realized in large firms than in small ones.[55] And for a variety of reasons noted below, the product, labor, and capital market conditions facing Japan's large companies are particularly supportive of participatory arrangements.

Participation channels in Japanese firms take three main forms: quality circles and team production at the shopfloor level, formal plant or company-level organizations for joint consultation between management and labor (including the joint consultation committees discussed earlier in the paper), and the *ringi* system. Quality circles are widespread and are generally evaluated as successful in supporting real participation by workers in decisions about shopfloor organization. This success is attributed to the skill and knowledge of Japanese workers, resulting from frequent job rotation; substantive participation via team production methods; and extensive on-the-job training. Workers have the knowledge about shopfloor operations required to make meaningful suggestions, and they have the power to change work methods in accordance with their suggestions.

Formally, there is no legal framework for worker participation in management decisions in Japanese firms, but workers are extremely

54. See, for example, Kazuo Koike, "Human Resource Development and Labor-Management Relations," in Yamamura and Yasuba, eds., *Political Economy of Japan*, pp. 289–330; Robert E. Cole, *Work, Mobility, and Participation: A Comparative Study of American and Japanese Industry* (University of California Press, 1979); and Taishiro Shirai, ed., *Contemporary Industrial Relations in Japan* (University of Wisconsin, 1983).

55. See, for example, Baron, "Employment Relations"; and James R. Lincoln and Arne L. Kalleberg, "Work Organization and Workforce Commitment: A Study of Plants and Employees in the U.S. and Japan," *American Sociological Review*, vol. 50 (December 1985), pp. 738–60.

vocal about management issues, and joint consultation between labor unions and the company at the enterprise and plant level is widespread. Through joint consultation committees, employees participate with management in forming high-level strategic plans and general firm policies.[56] Unions also bargain on worker issues, such as wages and working conditions. Some have argued that the extensive communication between management and unions in Japanese firms is helped by the fact that many high-level firm managers served as union leaders during their rise through the company.

Besides worker-management communication channels, the *ringi* system of decisionmaking within the managerial ranks promotes the flow of information through all levels of the firm. In the *ringi* system, proposals originate with lower-echelon employees and are communicated to higher-ranking officials for their approval after a long process of consensus-seeking discussion and modification in which virtually everyone affected is involved.[57] The *ringi* system combines a high degree of centralization of formal authority for plant- or firm-level decisions in top executive positions with high levels of actual or informal participation by employees of widely differing rank.

Participation in Japanese firms is supported by extensive profit sharing. On average, about a third of the total annual compensation of employees is in the form of bonus payments.[58] Bonuses are mainly proportional to base wage compensation for all employees, and there are only minor adjustments for individual performance. Empirical work by Freeman and Weitzman indicates that bonus payments vary with profits as one would expect in a profit-sharing system of compensation, although far less than a third of compensation actually fluctuates proportionally with profits.[59] Firms also often set up group-level competitions, implying group gain sharing.[60]

Japanese organizations rely heavily on job rotation and team production techniques. Such techniques allow workers to gain extensive on-

56. This point is made by Taishiro Shirai, "A Theory of Enterprise Unionism," in Shirai, ed., *Contemporary Industrial Relations,* pp. 117–44.

57. Lincoln and Kalleberg, "Work Organization and Workforce Commitment."

58. Chalmers Johnson, "Japanese-Style Management in America," *California Management Review,* vol. 30 (Summer 1988), pp. 34–45; and James C. Abegglen and George Stalk, Jr., *Kaisha, the Japanese Corporation* (Basic Books, 1985).

59. Richard B. Freeman and Martin L. Weitzman, "Bonuses and Employment in Japan," *Journal of the Japanese and International Economies,* vol. 1 (June 1987), pp. 168–94.

60. Rohlen, "Company Work Group."

the-job training, which adds to their skills and allows them to work up the internal job promotion ladder as their years with the firm increase.

In addition, team production methods provide effective horizontal monitoring devices for individual worker effort. Such methods also allow a great deal of flexibility in how each work group is organized, and there is substantial evidence that teams take advantage of this flexibility to organize production differently than in the United States.[61] Finally, team production methods serve an important integrating function, fostering participation, trust, and cohesiveness among team members.[62]

Cohesiveness is also encouraged by the compensation policy of Japanese firms. Individual compensation is tightly linked to employee seniority. As Koike has pointed out, the Japanese seniority system covers not only white-collar workers, for whom seniority and pay are positively related in most of the advanced industrial countries, but blue-collar workers as well.[63] An implication of this compensation system is compression of wage and status differentials, especially between blue-collar workers and white-collar employees.

There are many studies demonstrating that the earnings distribution is more compressed in Japanese firms than in American firms of comparable size. For example, Andrew Weiss has studied wages of male university graduates in a large Japanese electronics company. He reports that, controlling for age, the top decile earned 50 to 60 percent more than the bottom decile. Not controlling for age, the maximum differential is about four to one. In the United States, pay differentials within a firm are typically two or three times as large as in a Japanese firm. Age-corrected differentials in U.S. firms—the correct measure of inequality over a worker's lifetime—are perhaps 500 percent as large as those in a Japanese firm.[64]

As many observers have noted, in Japanese firms the differentials in nonpecuniary status symbols are also compressed, especially between workers and management.[65] Japanese firms are also noted for their long-

61. Koike, "Human Resource Development."
62. Lincoln and Kalleberg, "Work Organization and Workforce Commitment"; and James R. Lincoln, Jon Olson, and Mitsuyo Hanado, "Cultural Effects of Organizational Structure: The Case of Japanese Firms in the United States," *American Sociological Review*, vol. 43 (December 1978), pp. 829–47.
63. Koike, "Human Resource Development"; and Kazuo Koike, "Internal Labor Markets: Workers in Large Firms," in Shirai, ed., *Contemporary Industrial Relations*, pp. 29–62.
64. Andrew Weiss, "Incentives and Worker Behavior: Some Evidence," Working Paper 2194 (Cambridge, Mass.: National Bureau of Economic Research, March 1987).
65. Vogel, *Japan as Number One;* Rohlen, "Company Work Group"; Ronald P.

term employment commitment to their workers (at least their full-time male workers). Such a commitment does not mean that Japanese firms are never faced with the need to reduce their work force, although the mechanisms for handling them when they are necessary have distinctive features. Japanese firms react differently to short-term cyclical reductions in product demand and to long-term reductions that are perceived to be permanent. In the face of cyclical disturbances, Japanese firms use several mechanisms to maintain the employment of their regular employees, including hoarding of labor (often performing maintenance or training activities), layoffs of temporary (largely female) workers, less subcontracting of work to other firms, intrafirm transfers of workers from declining product lines to other product lines with stable or increasing demand, and transfers of workers to other firms.[66]

Intrafirm transfers are smooth because the enterprise union structure and seniority pay scheme pose few barriers to the movement of workers from one job to another, even when the transfer is across plant lines. Such transfers are also more feasible in large firms with several product lines—hence one of the advantages of size in maintaining a participatory system. Interfirm transfers are eased by the fact that most large Japanese firms are either members of business alliances or work closely with a group of affiliates and subcontracting firms. These networks of firms are held together in several ways, including mutual shareholding arrangements, long-term supply and customer relationships, and links to common banks and trading companies.

In the face of a sustained reduction in demand, all these measures may prove insufficient to the size of the employment adjustment required, and the firm may be forced to cut its long-term work force. In such cases, the firm tends to rely to the extent possible on attrition and special retirement allowances to encourage the early retirement of its senior workers. Under such circumstances, the firm can often draw on resources from the government if it can demonstrate that it is in a declining

---

Dore, *British Factory, Japanese Factory: The Origins of National Diversity in Industrial Relations* (University of California Press, 1973); Baron, "Employment Relations"; Abegglen and Stalk, *Kaisha,* chap. 8; Arne L. Kalleberg and James R. Lincoln, "The Structure of Earnings Inequality in the United States and Japan," *American Journal of Sociology,* vol. 94 (Supplement, 1988), pp. S121–53.

66. Such instances of transfer of workers to related firms are mentioned by Michael Gerlach, "Business Alliances and the Strategy of the Japanese Firm," *California Management Review,* vol. 30 (Fall 1987), pp. 126–42; Abegglen and Stalk, *Kaisha,* chap. 8; and Koike, "Human Resource Development."

industry.[67] Finally, Japanese firms have just-cause dismissal policies as part of an elaborate structure of regulations that provide the foundation for firm legitimacy.

When we examine what product, labor, and capital market conditions shaped firm structure in Japan, we find that Japan's participatory firms arose in a high-growth environment, characterized by relatively small cyclical disturbances.[68] Because of rapid, stable growth, such firms operated in tight labor markets, in which there was strong competition for the best available employees. These external conditions meant that it was in the individual firm's interest to build labor-relations systems that would attract and keep the best workers. Such conditions also lowered the costs of maintaining these systems, especially the adjustment costs associated with cyclical declines in demand. And rapid growth allowed the firm to offer its workers quick promotion opportunities in return for their commitment to the firm's success. Slow growth would have been detrimental to the firm's seniority compensation system and its elaborate internal promotion ladder, both of which supported the commitment and cohesiveness of its permanent work force.

That most large Japanese firms opted for similar participatory systems meant that the cost of such a system to any one of them was lower than it would have been otherwise. In particular, the adverse selection problem associated with just-cause dismissal policies was less severe because such policies were also offered by other firms competing for workers. Nonetheless, the possibility of adverse selection is probably one of the reasons that Japanese participatory firms engage in substantial screening of new employees. In this they are helped by the competitive tracking characteristic of Japan's educational system: the large firms recruit from the very best schools, and they draw from a labor pool that has already been significantly screened and has a high level of general educational attainment.

The compression of differentials in large Japanese firms is possible largely because their average compensation exceeds that of smaller firms. Frustrated good workers who believe that their relative pay and

67. For more on the declining-industry law and the benefits it offers to maintain employment or ease transition, see Jimmy W. Wheeler and others, *Japanese Industrial Development Policies in the 1980s: Implications for U.S. Trade and Investment—Final Report* (Hudson Institute, 1982), chap. 7.

68. Gordon, "Productivity, Wages, and Prices."

status position should be higher cannot find attractive compensation opportunities outside the primary sector of the economy.

But why aren't the best workers hired away by other large participatory firms that are willing to pay them more? There are several answers. First, the high investment in firm-specific human capital made possible by long-term employment relations makes it difficult for outsiders to be as productive as insiders. Second, firms pay extremely steep wage profiles to workers, so young workers are relatively cheap and older workers are relatively expensive. Furthermore, firms that hire new employees at high levels would reduce the number of promotions available for lower-seniority workers, thus reducing their motivation. Any new firm that entered and tried to hire from existing firms would face problems establishing a reputation as a good employer. There also appears to be a cultural element that discourages job changing for senior male employees, though this element may be declining over time.

Finally, the capital market environment in which large Japanese firms operate has supported the development of their unique industrial relations system. Because of close long-term relationships with their banks and institutional shareholders, large Japanese companies can sustain high debt-equity ratios without incurring a cost-of-capital penalty. In addition, external suppliers of capital have a variety of means to monitor the behavior of the firms to which they lend, including regular meetings between firm management and representatives of banks and other large companies who are significant institutional shareholders. This situation makes it easier for Japanese firms to obtain external finance for long-term investment in such intangibles as human capital and research and development.

The extent and methods of control over firm decisionmaking by external suppliers of finance in Japan seem to be significantly different from those in the United States. Most institutional investors in large Japanese firms are large banks and other large companies, often businesses that have close ties in product or input markets. These institutional investors tend to have long-term associations with the firms in which they hold significant equity. Hostile takeovers are largely unheard of— indeed many observers see the system of reciprocal shareholding by large companies as a means to ward off such takeovers.

Moreover, the income and control rights of these large institutional investors—and of smaller private investors as well—appear to be much more limited than those of significant holders of equity in the U.S. capital market. In particular, the shareholders in large Japanese companies behave more like long-term investors and less like controllers.[69] Company boards of directors are composed almost entirely of inside members of the company, chosen by management. Many of these inside members are ex-officials of company unions. The directors appointed by outside shareholders are almost never a majority of the company board, nor are such directors truly "outsiders," since they are usually appointed by the large banks and businesses with which the company has extensive, ongoing financial and product relationships.

This system insulates management from external control to a considerable extent and allows for significantly more participation by insiders in decisionmaking. Of course, the downside, as Aoki and others have noted, is that there is a real possibility that managers, relatively free of control by external suppliers of capital, will fail to take actions in their interests. In such an environment, the neoclassical assumption that the firm acts to maximize its value in the interests of its shareholders seems inappropriate.

A more appropriate model developed by Aoki sees the Japanese firm as a quasi-permanent organization representing the interests of its stockholders and its employees. Firm behavior is the outcome of a cooperative game between these two groups, and the role of managers is to estimate the relative bargaining power of these two groups and to formulate the firm's policy to lead to an organizational equilibrium of this power. The outcome of this game should lie somewhere between maximization of value in the interests of the shareholders and maximization of income per worker in the interests of the firm's employees.[70]

Capital market imperfections have also been less severe for Japanese firms than for American firms because of the methods by which participation was introduced. As Robert Cole has emphasized, a key player in the dissemination of quality circles in Japan has been the Japanese Union of Scientists and Engineers (JUSE). JUSE is a highly respected professional association, with credibility in the business community. Thus a company that invests in JUSE-sponsored training for its members is making a more tangible, credible investment than a U.S. firm that spends investor resources experimenting with participation. Finally, knowledge is a classic public good, and the costs of disseminating knowledge about

69. This point is made by Abegglen and Stalk, *Kaisha;* Aoki, "Japanese Firm in Transition"; and Gerlach, "Business Alliances and the Strategy of the Japanese Firm."

70. Masahiko Aoki, *The Economic Analysis of the Japanese Firm* (Amsterdam: North Holland, 1984).

successful participation have been lowered because JUSE has acted as a clearinghouse.[71]

We do not mean to attribute all aspects of the Japanese industrial relations system to the environmental characteristics we describe; Japan's specific history played a large role in shaping its industrial relations system. In addition, the Japanese model has numerous "losers," including women, foreign workers, and workers trapped at the bottom of the secondary sector. Nonetheless, the success of Japan highlights how an economy with favorable product, labor, and capital market features can more easily develop participatory workplaces.

Swedish Participatory Firms

Over the past twenty years, Sweden has paid more attention to workplace participation than has any other nation. This section will first examine the unique "Swedish model" of industrial relations, focusing on how its full employment policies contributed to the spontaneous growth of participation. We will then discuss the more recent Swedish experience; a decline in labor demand has slowed the spontaneous growth of participation, although legally required participation has expanded.

The Swedish model is based on the Social Democratic Party (SDP) and the labor movement working together to maintain full employment and moderate inflation. Unionization in Sweden is almost complete: 95 percent of the blue-collar workers are members of the largest labor organization (the LO), and 75 percent of white-collar workers are members of three smaller federations.

The SDP ruled Sweden from 1932 until 1976, and has been in power again since 1982. Since its inception, the SDP has been closely allied with Swedish unions. The key to SDP-union cooperation remains the government focus on full employment. Since 1952 the Swedish unemployment rate has never risen above 3 percent. The SDP has also worked to equalize incomes and to build a strong social welfare system.

During the 1950s and 1960s, Swedish wage bargaining was highly centralized: the LO and a federation of private sector employers met to determine the overall wage increase for much of the economy. During this era, the other union federations followed the LO's lead, and no union had to worry that its workers were losing relative to other Swedish

71. Robert E. Cole, *Strategies for Learning: Small-Group Activities in American, Japanese, and Swedish Industry* (University of California Press, 1989).

workers. Since the LO was closely associated with the ruling SDP, the union took into account the government's inflation goals when it made its wage bargains.

Partly through design, and partly through luck, the pieces of the Swedish model fit together rather well.

Under centralized bargaining, low-productivity firms paid the same wages as high-productivity firms. This policy also increased efficiency by forcing low-productivity firms out of business and shifting workers to firms where productivity was higher.

Such a strategy of letting plant closures redirect labor would have been inhumane, except that it occurred in an environment of full employment. Labor market boards made up of union, government, and management representatives coordinated information, easing the movement of workers to new jobs. Firms informed the boards (to some extent) of their hiring and layoff plans, facilitating planning.

The government sponsored extensive retraining for workers who lost their jobs, focusing on occupations with labor shortages. A displaced worker was also eligible for moving assistance, including funding of job searches in other regions and new house financing.

Full employment was maintained also by subsidizing private investment during recessions. In addition, local governments kept a list of projects that needed to be carried out, and during times of weak labor demand the national government subsidized employment for these projects. Unemployment benefits were generous, if little used. Thus full employment was reached, not primarily by holding on to old jobs, but by making it easy for people to move into new jobs.

Most progressive and left-wing governments find that their efforts to maintain full employment are hindered by the ability of firms to stop investing. As far back as 1938, the SDP and LO reached an agreement with employers to ensure that productivity would be high enough to offset high wages and redistributive social policies. Thus many government policies that help workers (for example, retraining) are also intended to help firms (workers are trained for jobs that firms are having difficulty filling). Moreover such aspects of the social welfare system as day care, an excellent education system, and a socialized health system increase the quantity and quality of workers that are available, and do so with no direct payments by firms.[72]

By the late 1960s the environmental conditions for firms in Sweden

72. The Swedish model has its difficulties. For example, when unions vie for increases in relative wages, inflation can accelerate rapidly.

were similar to those we described above as fertile grounds for participation. Almost complete unionization led to universal guarantees of
worker rights and just-cause protection within firms. The narrow wage
differentials and egalitarian ideology of the ruling party promoted worker
cohesiveness, while the excellent educational system led to a work force
qualified to make decisions.

Egalitarian wage policies, while they promote cohesiveness, often
reduce labor demand for young workers. In Sweden, there were high
levels of education, high levels of labor demand, and grants for in-plant
training—all of which encouraged companies to hire young workers.

Product market conditions were also consistent with participation, in
that the government was committed to stabilizing aggregate demand.
Sweden was enjoying the worldwide prosperity of the late 1960s, and
Swedish workers knew that government commitment to full employment
was credible. The reduced fear of layoff increased each worker's
expected tenure at his or her current employer, and made workers more
open to innovation and technological change. The combination of low
unemployment, government-sponsored retraining, and narrow wage
differentials reduced workers' fears of overproduction, since job loss
would not entail either a long spell of unemployment or a deep cut in
pay.

Most important, the tight labor market was making rigidly hierarchical
and divided jobs unsustainable. In 1969 a major strike—rare for a nation
where labor peace is the rule—by mine workers achieved nationwide
support in its demands for a more humane and democratic workplace.
At the same time, assembly lines were suffering turnover rates of 50
percent a year, and absenteeism ran rampant.

Called "the most innovative European company in matters of work
organization,"[73] Volvo, the Swedish car and truck manufacturer, was
led into spontaneous experiments with job rotation, work redesign,
autonomous teams, and related developments at numerous sites by the
tight labor market of the 1960s.

Volvo was sufficiently encouraged by the successes of these un-
planned experiments that it decided in the early 1970s to integrate their
lessons into its new Kalmar auto plant. Not surprisingly, the Kalmar
plant exhibits the four conditions described above: gain sharing, long-

73. David Jenkins, "Quality of Working Life: Trends and Directions," in Harvey
Kolodny and Hans van Beinum, eds., The Quality of Working Life and the 1980s
(Praeger, 1983), p. 18.

term employment relations (Volvo has never had a layoff), measures to increase group cohesiveness, and guaranteed individual rights.

While a traditional assembly line has repetitive work with little room for employee discretion, the Kalmar plant separates the work into a series of production stations. At each station, a team of workers performs all jobs associated with a stage in production: the team inspects incoming materials, does its own quality control, performs maintenance on machinery, and so forth. Workers have significantly more control than in a typical plant over the pace and order of work, and are able to work ahead to take breaks.[74]

There are usually about seven workers in a team. Jobs are rotated, and each group of two or three teams receives a proportion of its pay based on group performance.[75] Further steps are being implemented, with teams participating in production planning, hiring procedures, and technological development.[76]

The Kalmar plant has generally been a success. Labor finds its work more meaningful and satisfying, yet there has been "no sacrifice of efficiency, profitability, or competitiveness."[77] Nine Volvo plants finished since Kalmar have incorporated many features of this innovative plant.

The capital market difficulties that many firms face when introducing participation were ameliorated by the special conditions in Sweden. Volvo's introduction of participation was highly visible, largely because the innovations were heralded by Volvo's president in literally worldwide publicity. Volvo's size (the largest company in Sweden) made it much easier to build a reputation for high investments in workers. Swedish macroeconomic policies also helped, since the need to borrow to finance labor hoarding was reduced by government-assured full employment and by countercyclical investment subsidies.

The innovations at Volvo are not unique in Sweden: more than a thousand firms have experimented with changes in work organization.[78]

74. Berth Jönsson and Alden G. Lank, "Volvo: A Report on the Workshop on Production Technology and the Quality of Working Life," *Human Resource Management*, vol. 24 (Winter 1985), pp. 455–65.
75. Warren C. Hauck and Timothy L. Ross, "Sweden's Experiments in Productivity Gainsharing: A Second Look," *Personnel*, vol. 64 (January 1987), pp. 61–67.
76. Jönsson and Lank, "Volvo."
77. Jönsson and Lank, "Volvo," p. 459.
78. Cole, *Strategies for Learning*, p. 31, citing D. Gunzburg and O. Hammarström, "Swedish Industrial Democracy, 1977," in International Council for the Quality of

Again, the structural conditions of fairly stable product demand, full employment, cohesive wage policies, and universal just-cause dismissal policies reduced the costs of introducing participation.

As in Japan, a well-respected management organization lowered the costs of introducing participation. In Sweden the organization was the Technical Department of the Employers' Federation, which acted as a clearinghouse for information and as a consultant for firms. Thus firms were acquiring a known product when they introduced participation with the help of the Technical Department. Furthermore, information about successful innovations was disseminated more quickly, and the risks of modifying the organization of work were lower. In addition, innovations that were sponsored by the Technical Department were more "tangible" to creditors monitoring the performance of a firm— reducing the importance of capital market imperfections.[79]

The Swedish model served the economy well until the second half of the 1970s. Sweden, as a heavy user of energy, was hit harder than most countries by the 1974 and 1979 jumps in oil prices. At the same time, competition from Korea and Japan was devastating Sweden's major heavy industries of steel and shipbuilding. By 1977 Sweden was trapped with 11 percent inflation and rising unemployment.

Partly because of the state of the economy, and partly because of the its strong endorsement of nuclear power, the SDP lost control of the government in 1976. Higher unemployment combined with non-SDP government made workers question whether there would be new jobs if they left their current ones. Workers were unwilling to move, and the active labor policies of the Swedish model that moved workers to high-productivity sectors were replaced with costly subsidies to the ailing steel and shipbuilding industries.

At the same time that political and macroeconomic problems were reducing worker flexibility, the macroeconomic problems relieved much of the labor market pressure that had been driving firms toward use of participation. Turnover rates in manufacturing plants declined by half from their 1960s highs.[80] As the final blow to shopfloor participation, management opposition to several legislated attempts to require co-determination at the plant and corporate levels made shopfloor initiatives less attractive.

Working Life, *Working on the Quality of Working Life* (Boston: Martinus Nijhoff, 1979), pp. 39–40.
    79. Cole, *Strategies for Learning*.
    80. Cole, *Strategies for Learning*, pp. 262, 66.

Recently, several factors have come together to accelerate the spread of participation again. In 1982 the SDP regained power, reducing macroeconomic uncertainty and increasing labor's willingness to be more flexible. A decade of experience has ironed out many of the issues relating to the legislated codetermination, and the return of the SDP to power has increased firms' willingness to carry out legislated representative participation. Unemployment rates have declined from their highs of the late 1970s. Finally, Swedish firms, facing increased competitive pressures, are more concerned about quality. The joint effect of these forces has been an "Efficiency and Participation Agreement" between firms and unions, leading to a host of new workplace experiments.[81]

In sum, the Swedish experience is much in consonance with the theories presented above. When labor markets were tight, firms were unable to motivate workers with fear of job loss. Widespread job redesign throughout Sweden led to a situation where high employment was sustainable. When contractionary macroeconomic shocks hit the system in the early 1970s, the looser labor market reduced firms' incentives to innovate. More recently, because of the return of the SDP to power and the decline in unemployment rates, the incentives for participation are increasing.

Conclusions

In the first part of this paper we presented theoretical and empirical arguments indicating that employee participation can and often does improve productivity. In the second part, we identified four characteristic features of successful participatory firms—profit sharing, long-term employment relations, narrow wage and status differentials, and guaranteed individual rights—and we demonstrated how the product, labor, and capital market conditions in which firms operate influence whether they develop such features. We based our arguments on theoretical considerations, but we illustrated them by reference to the experiences of large Japanese and Swedish firms.

Our arguments suggest that under certain conditions, the market system may be systematically biased against participatory workplaces. Despite the potential efficiency of such workplaces, product, labor, and capital markets can all make participation unprofitable for the individual

81. Cole, *Strategies for Learning,* p. 30; and Bo Sunden, SAF, personal communication, 1988.

firm. As a result, the economy can be trapped in a socially suboptimal position.

To the extent that our theoretical arguments receive empirical support, they have implications for policy. Our analysis of the effects of product market conditions on the firm's industrial relations system implies that policies to maintain high and steady aggregate demand and to ease the transition of resources out of declining industries would enhance the efficiency of participatory workplaces as opposed to workplaces that rely upon fear of dismissal. Granting partial unemployment insurance for partial layoffs (that is, job sharing), increasing the experience rating of unemployment insurance so companies pay higher premiums when they lay off workers frequently, and releasing Jobs Training Partnership Act funds for workers who have not yet been laid off would eliminate the current subsidy that labor-hoarding firms pay to firms that lay off workers. Such policies would stabilize aggregate demand and encourage long-term employment relations to the advantage of participatory workplaces.

Just-cause employment policies lead to adverse selection. In addition, such policies are more important for participatory firms than for traditional firms. Thus participatory firms would be indirectly encouraged if just-cause dismissal policies were required by law for all employers.

The capital market barriers to participatory firms could be reduced by measures that lengthen the time horizons of both managers and investors. A variety of such measures have been proposed in the United States, not in response to growing interest in employee participation, but in response to growing concern about low investment rates. Proposals include introducing a small transactions tax on stock sales to reduce speculation, adjusting stock voting rights so that they increase with length of ownership, removing the tax subsidy on financing with junk bonds, changing the tax laws to encourage long-run remuneration of executives, introducing a graduated capital gains tax that declines the longer an asset is held, and treating training costs as investments on corporate balance sheets.[82]

Finally, if knowledge about the characteristics of successful participation plans were widespread, firms introducing participation would make fewer mistakes. Just as there is a role for the federal government in subsidizing and disseminating scientific research, there is a role for it in subsidizing basic workplace research and disseminating the results

82. Eric G. Flamholtz, *Human Resource Accounting* (San Francisco: Jossey-Bass, 1985).

through publications and conferences.[83] Expanding the Department of Labor's Bureau of Management-Labor Cooperation along the lines of the Agricultural Extension program is one possibility. Such a program could support a wide array of experiments in workplace participation and could serve as an important vehicle for disseminating knowledge.

There is evidence that participation *can* increase firm productivity, but the relationship is affected by the form and scope of participation, the industrial relations system of the firm, and the external environment in which it operates. This paper proposes a new emphasis in the economics of organizations—an emphasis on the interaction of organizations and their environments. We have suggested several theories that address the classic question, Why is work so rarely organized in a participative fashion? To the extent that these theories are empirically supported, the policies we propose constitute a package intended both to improve macroeconomic performance and to raise worker productivity and satisfaction.

Comment by Derek C. Jones

In this stimulating essay the authors draw on an enormous body of work to address two broad questions. First, given certain structural features associated with participation, what are the effects of participation on enterprise performance? Second, what sorts of economic factors affect the incidence of participation? The authors address these complex and difficult issues in an unusually imaginative way, using many disparate sources of information to assemble empirical support for a conceptual framework that is intuitively plausible. In my comment I focus on certain issues that I believe receive short shrift and also elaborate on some of the arguments made in the paper.

The authors begin by providing a useful review of theories of participation. They conclude, as I did in a paper written with Jeffrey Pliskin, that, strictly speaking, theory suggests there are no straightforward relationships between participation and measures of performance, such as enterprise productivity.[1] Such questions can be resolved only empir-

---

83. In Japan, for example, there are on average two conferences on quality cirlces every day. Cole, *Strategies for Learning.*

1. Derek C. Jones and Jeffrey Pliskin, "The Effects of Worker Participation,

ically. To that end, the authors go on to provide an excellent review of the available empirical evidence on the effects of participation on productivity. Furthermore, as an organizing device they develop a threefold typology of conventional firms with different participatory forms—consultative, substantive, and representative. Then they match the available empirical studies for conventionally owned firms with the appropriate participatory type, and undertake a similar exercise for firms classified by type of employee ownership. From this data base, the authors try to draw some general conclusions on the relationships between participatory type and performance. They conclude that the most effective participatory types are those in which participation is direct, those that involve employees in the workplace decisions that most intimately concern workers, and those in which participation results in substantial worker influence.

The final task the authors set themselves in the first half of the paper is to identify characteristics of successful participatory systems. Four features are singled out—profit sharing, long-term employment relations, measures that provide for group cohesiveness, and guaranteed individual rights. Four successful participatory schemes that exhibit these features—Japan, Mondragon, Sweden, and Hewlett-Packard—are chosen as illustrative cases. Taken as a whole, these are important and useful exercises. But though I am sympathetic to the thrust of this conceptual approach, the method is vulnerable to criticism because of its very boldness.

First, when constructing the typology of participatory arrangements, the authors may not have identified all the underlying conditions that are relevant. Many would argue that, for many reasons, the role of labor unions must be taken into account when defining participatory schemes. Information on whether the particular participatory scheme is union based, whether the union was involved in the design and the introduction of the scheme, and the type of the union needs to be included. For example, in the United States unions are sometimes, but not always, involved in the design and implementation of quality circles. Moreover, there is evidence for a variety of participatory forms, including quality circles, that union presence is a crucial factor in influencing economic outcomes.[2] This point could be especially relevant in other industrialized

Employee Ownership and Profit Sharing on Economic Performance: A Partial Review,'' in V. Rus and R. Russell, eds., *International Handbook of Participation in Organization*, vol. 2 (Oxford University Press, forthcoming).

2. Michael A. Conte and Jan Svejnar, ''Productivity Effects of Worker Participation

Western economies, where unions are usually far stronger than they are in the United States.

Furthermore, the three existing participation categories—consultative, substantive, or representative—are so heterogeneous, and the existing evidence sometimes so slender, that the particular inferences may be suspect. For example, representative participation at the board level has been mandated by law in both Sweden and West Germany. But even in formal terms, such as the nature and composition of the board, relationships with participation substructures, and the precise legal basis for employee representation, board-level representation is a very different phenomenon in Sweden and West Germany. In turn, both experiences are very different from more limited attempts to introduce worker directors, such as in the public sector in the United Kingdom and the typical American experience as in Chrysler. Moreover, unlike in West Germany and the United Kingdom, survey evidence for Sweden does reveal some cases where representative participation is associated with substantial employee influence.[3] That is, the same de jure or formal structure can support tremendous variety across the same class of economic agents in different enterprises in their perceptions of their degree of participation in decisionmaking. Although the environmental factors that the authors identify may account for a good deal of this variation across Swedish firms, I suspect they will not explain it all. Also important are such factors as the reason for establishing particular plans and the nature and content of training schemes for worker directors.

In addition, not only has there been little modern econometric work on important forms of representative democracy, but most of the available empirical work on codetermination is necessarily highly aggregative because of limited access to enterprise-level data. Hence the available evidence on this form of representative participation does not yet enable one to reach firm conclusions on its effectiveness.

Similarly, employee ownership includes a vast array of forms. For example, producer cooperatives (PCs) include not only the Mondragon co-ops (which the authors discuss in detail) but many much less successful co-ops, past and present. Although all PCs are "participatory"

in Management, Profit-Sharing, Worker Ownership of Assets and Unionization in U.S. Firms," *International Journal of Industrial Organization,* vol. 6 (March 1988), pp. 139–51.

3. On codetermination in Sweden see, for example, Christian Berggren, "Top Management and Codetermination in Swedish Companies: Greater Union Influence Results in Better Decisions," *Economic and Industrial Democracy,* vol. 7 (1986), pp. 99–108.

firms, the available evidence suggests that not all have exhibited sustained success. Examples include the now defunct U.S. foundry and cooperage PCs and the dwindling number of long-established British PCs. This implies that the list of identifying features for these (and other?) participatory firms may be incomplete. Regarding PCs, theoretical and empirical evidence suggests that issues concerning the eligibility for and benefits of membership need to be addressed. For example, there does seem to be some limited evidence that PCs in which workers are freely admitted to membership are more successful over the long haul than those that restrict entry.[4] Another implication of the diverse nature and scope of participation and employee ownership in PCs is that, contrary to the authors' claims, it may be that lessons for conventional firms can be drawn from empirical work on PCs.[5]

Some of these points carry over to the attempt to determine the characteristics of successful participatory schemes. For example, though all four successful cases may be described as participatory, the differences in the nature and scope of the successful cases are often pronounced. But by focusing attention on structural characteristics *other* than participation, the implication is that all cases are sufficiently similarly participatory to make it possible to analyze incidence within a single conceptual framework. However, if participation is not viewed in this homogeneous fashion, then separate frameworks are needed to explain the incidence of differing forms of participation.

In particular, the Mondragon cooperative case, in which labor hires capital, is quite different from the other schemes like Hewlett-Packard, which ultimately are based on control by capital owners. Although the interests of employees may be considered in successful participatory firms that are capital-controlled, such firms are structured and behave fundamentally differently from firms owned and managed by labor.[6] Moreover, whether the four included cases are representative is prob-

4. Compare, for example, long-established producer co-ops in the United Kingdom or defunct co-ops in the United States with Italian producer co-ops. See Saul Estrin, Derek C. Jones, and Jan Svejnar, "The Productivity Effects of Worker Participation: Producer Cooperatives in Western Economies," *Journal of Comparative Economics*, vol. 11 (March 1987), pp. 40–61; and D. C. Jones, "U.S. Producer Cooperatives: The Record to Date," *Industrial Relations*, vol. 18 (Fall 1979), pp. 342–57.

5. Consider, for example, the case of French PCs. According to law, all are cooperatives. But by adopting various kinds of exclusionary policies in the past, at times some co-ops were much more similar to conventional firms with very modest participation arrangements than to PCs like those in Mondragon.

6. In turn, this has profound implications for the very meaning of "success" in these differing classes of enterprise.

lematical. For example, real-world PCs are a heterogeneous lot. Not only do very few PCs closely resemble the Mondragon co-ops, but PCs have an uneven record. At the moment, therefore, I think the authors may claim too much by focusing on Mondragon. It may be useful, for example, to ascertain the characteristics of PCs that have been less successful.

A related issue is how this framework could be used to tackle the issue of incidence empirically. By focusing on successes alone, the existing conceptual approach entails obvious selection problems. It would be preferable to have a sample of participatory and nonparticipatory firms for which hypotheses about incidence could be tested using an appropriate framework such as Tobit and probit.

Furthermore, there are, as the authors acknowledge in table 2, large differences in the precise meaning of the various conditions for success. For instance, profit- and gain-sharing plans differ in both form (cash or stock) and timing (current or deferred). Because there is theoretical and empirical evidence to suggest that such differences affect economic outcomes, it is an oversimplification to say that "profit sharing" is all that is needed as one of the four ingredients for success in participatory firms. We need to do more work on the particular features of flexible payments schemes that seem to be successful, not only for these four cases but for others too.

In a highly innovative section of the paper, the authors examine the interaction of the firm and its environment. They show how conditions in product, labor, and capital markets affect the choice of industrial relations systems by firms. In particular, they consider how, despite the potential efficiency of participatory workplaces, such factors help to explain the limited extent of participation. I find this section novel and creative, and my comments are mostly minor.

One comment concerns the potential relevance of some theory on labor-managed firms. The recognition of the importance of stability in product demand may be viewed, at least in part, as a generalization of the alleged tendency of such firms to have perverse supply curves. Although most economists now believe that this theoretical chestnut was based on special assumptions and has no basis in fact, most theorists also recognize that labor-managed firms will be characterized by relatively inelastic product supply curves. Since variable product demand would produce significant fluctuations in worker income, it follows that PCs will tend to arise in industries that are subject to smaller demand shocks and that experience slow rates of technical change.

A growing body of theoretical work speaks to the relevance of conditions in the labor and capital for the success of labor-managed firms.[7] For real-world PCs, the effects of capital market conditions seem to be sufficiently important to require successful PCs to establish their own financial institutions. Thus the Caja Laboral Popular is a central feature of the Mondragon complex and also provides a way for workers' portfolio risks to be diversified.

More fundamentally, is it just (or even mainly) a matter of economic or market environment that affects the adoption of participation? Other factors surely count, and if we are to tackle this problem, a broader framework is needed. For example, legal factors need special mention. The existence of laws that relate to the special needs of co-ops seems to have affected the pattern of formation of that kind of participatory firm in the United States.[8]

In the last major section of the paper, the authors examine at length how conditions in Japan and Sweden have facilitated the emergence of participatory firms. Regarding Sweden, I think the authors do not stress enough the resistance to the introduction of the codetermination legislation. That is, though employers may have been "spontaneously" introducing participation at the workplace, frequently they were reluctant to share decisionmaking about strategic issues. Also, with the return to power of the Social Democrats, and the consequent return to an environment that presumably was more hospitable to participation, there was nevertheless tremendous resistance to the introduction of Meidner-type wage-earner plans in 1984—schemes that can be thought of as part of the Social Democrats' commitment to social and economic democracy, that is, part and parcel of the allegedly hospitable environment.

7. Thus some argue that outside labor markets play a crucial role in explaining the allegedly frequently short life cycles of PCs. Also, much theory stresses the problem of physical capital formation in PCs, including the alleged tendency to underinvest. For an excellent review of theory and evidence on some of these issues, see John P. Bonin and Louis Putterman, *Economics of Cooperation and the Labor-Managed Economy* (Harwood Academic Publishers, 1987).

8. Note that to respond to the special environmental problems that beset PCs, theory and evidence argue for the need for a supporting structure. The heart of this (as in the Mondragon co-ops) is often a specialist financial institution. But other institutions serve other needs, such as educational institutions to provide workers with training in ways consistent with the needs of PCs. Other functions of the supporting structure may be viewed as responding to the special product market factors that beset participatory firms, as discussed above. Thus specialists help to choose to establish new firms in product markets that are expected to experience relatively steady demand.

If we were to apply their analysis to American participatory cases like Hewlett-Packard, the interesting problem would be to try to explain the particular pattern of participation that exists in the United States. Why is there participation in Hewlett-Packard (and IBM and others) but not in other firms? And why now and not earlier? Presumably, capital market conditions would not matter much, since those features of the market environment are essentially similar for all large U.S. firms. The explanation would have to draw upon product and labor market factors. At first blush this does seem to do the trick; firms like Hewlett-Packard and IBM have a growing demand for products, highly educated workers, and lots of firm-specific human capital. But often product demand is volatile in these high-tech industries. For such firms, perhaps it is market dominance that is the key market characteristic?

In sum, though I like the general thrust of the approach, I have my doubts about the general applicability of this particular framework. For example, I suspect that, given time, one might think of instances when, using the authors' conceptual framework, the environment is favorable in all respects and yet apparently there is little participation. Is this not true in such small economies as Switzerland, Austria, and the Netherlands? Equally, there are instances in which the environmental factors do not seem to be obviously more propitious and yet participation seems to be growing—the case of Britain in the 1980s. Examples such as these suggest that the framework may be incomplete and that other relevant factors account, at least in part, for the uneven incidence of participation.

Employment and Wage Systems in Japan and Their Implications for Productivity

Masanori Hashimoto

PRODUCTIVITY in a society depends critically on the employer-employee relationship and how conducive it is to economic activity. The relationship between machine and man is superficial and predictable: machines keep producing as long as they are oiled regularly and their mechanisms kept in good repair. In contrast, the relationship between worker and employer is subtle. If workers continue to feel dissatisfied with their work environment, they may deliver less than their full potential productivity. The quality of the work environment is affected by the industrial relations system and labor market institutions. Any study of Japan's high postwar productivity growth would be incomplete, therefore, without an understanding of the key features of the Japanese labor market and of the underlying industrial relations system. The aim of this paper is to contribute to such an understanding.

Japanese industrial relations include a number of notable features that have attracted the attention of interested investigators.[1] The three pillars of the Japanese labor market are said to be the *shushin koyo* system, which guarantees long-term employment, the *nenko joretsu* system, under which earnings grow with tenure in the firm, and enterprise unions, or unions organized within firms and containing workers of diverse skills and ranks. Moreover, many workers receive substantial bonus payments

I thank Yoram Barzel, Barbara Brugman, Hajime Miyazaki, and Donald O. Parsons, as well as seminar participants at the Ohio State University, Yokohama National University, the University of Cincinnati, the Upjohn Institute for Employment Research, and the University of Chicago for their many useful comments on portions of the manuscript. I also thank Reiko Aoki and Tatsuro Ichiishi for valuable mathematical advice and Apurva Mathur for his research assistance. This paper also greatly benefited from the comments made by Alan Blinder and Richard Freeman on an earlier version.

1. Some of the materials contained in this paper were developed while I was also working on a project for the Upjohn Institute for Employment Research. See Masanori Hashimoto, *The Japanese Labor Market in a Comparative Perspective with the United States* (forthcoming), for additional details.

twice a year in addition to their base pay, and their compensation packages are changed annually and synchronously at the time of *Shunto,* or the spring offensive. All in all, labor relations are said to be more harmonious in Japan than in the United States, and the Japanese labor market has been found to show considerable flexibility.[2]

Two points deserve notice. First, many of the so-called unique features of Japanese labor markets became widespread only after the mid-1950s.[3] Cultural and traditional factors alone, therefore, cannot explain their existence. Rather, the maintained hypothesis of this paper is that these features became widespread largely because rapid economic growth, engendered in part by the productivity enhancement campaign (*Seisansei Undo*) launched in 1955, took place in an environment of low costs of transactions relative to the gains. Second, harmonious industrial relations in Japan are not costlessly achieved: management and labor spend a great deal of time, mental energy, and money on smoothing relations with each other.[4] The gains evidently justify these transaction costs. To illuminate these and related points about the Japanese industrial relations system, I present an economic model based on the transaction-cost consideration. It is hoped that this model suggests a promising way of incorporating cultural and traditional considerations into a comparative economic analysis.

Although the focus is on the Japanese labor market, I try to put the analysis in a comparative perspective with the United States as much as

2. See Michio Morishima, *Why Has Japan "Succeeded"? Western Technology and the Japanese Ethos* (Cambridge University Press, 1982); Masanori Hashimoto and John Raisian, "Wage Flexibility in the United States and Japan," in Peter T. Chinloy and Ernst W. Stromsdorfer, eds., *Labor Market Adjustments in the Pacific Basin* (Boston: Kluwer-Nijhoff, 1987), pp. 33–59; Kazutoshi Koshiro, "Labor Market Flexibility in Japan—with Special Reference to Wage Flexibility," working paper, Yokohama National University; and Organization for Economic Cooperation and Development, *Employment Outlook* (Paris, September 1986).

3. Space does not allow a detailed discussion of the prewar Japanese labor market. The literature makes it clear that before World War II many of the contemporary features of Japanese labor markets, such as long-term employment, bonus payments, and enterprise unions, were not common. An excellent glimpse into some aspects of the prewar labor market in Japan can be found in Konosuke Odaka, *Rodoshijo Bunseki* (Labor Market Analysis) (Tokyo: Iwanami, 1984). For an interesting discussion in English, see Koji Taira, *Economic Development and the Labor Market in Japan* (Columbia University Press, 1970). See also Hashimoto, *Japanese Labor Market.*

4. For example, it is well known that workers of various ranks often spend several hours together in the evening drinking and eating. These gatherings are designed in part to promote mutual understanding and to develop a consensus. The famous *nemawashi* procedure, whereby a consensus decision is slowly developed, also consumes time and energy. This procedure is discussed later.

possible. This approach is appropriate, since Japan and the United States are the two most successful free market economies today, with the two highest gross national products. Although the two economies share similarities, they have important differences.[5] Whether these differences are due to cultural, traditional, or economic factors, they inevitably influence how human resources are allocated, how employers and employees interact with one another, and more generally how the institutions of labor relations are organized.

A Profile of the Japanese Employment and Wage Systems

I begin by sketching some representative features of the Japanese employment and wage systems. The prevalence of the shushin koyo and nenko joretsu systems in Japan was documented in 1985 by Raisian and me.[6] This section reviews some of those findings and augments them with additional evidence on productivity, unionism, and institutions of the Japanese industrial relations system. It ends with a discussion of the implications of these features for productivity growth.

Lifetime Employment (Shushin Koyo System)

The term "lifetime employment" should not be interpreted literally, of course, since most Japanese workers are subject to mandatory retirement at younger ages than most U.S. workers. The term does convey the notion of the long-term employment relationship that exists in Japan. To be sure, long-term employment is found in the United States as well, but clearly an average Japanese worker stays longer with the

5. As for the similarities, both countries operate in highly competitive and open markets, both have enjoyed strong positions in manufacturing and high-technology industries, and both have been experiencing significant sectoral shifts in employment since the early 1970s. Because the comparisons are mostly between these two countries, it would be premature to draw any conclusions about which characteristics are "unique" in the international context. A full comparative study, beyond the scope of this paper, would need to draw contrasts among Japan, the United States, and many European countries.

6. Masanori Hashimoto and John Raisian, "Employment Tenure and Earnings Profiles in Japan and the United States," *American Economic Review*, vol. 75 (September 1985), pp. 721–35. To be sure, many employees in the United States also enjoy long-term employment and earnings that rise with tenure in the firm. Clearly, however, the proportion of workers under these systems is greater in Japan than in the United States.

Table 1. Fifteen-Year Job Retention Rates for Male Workers in Japan and the United States

Initial-year conditions		Retention rate (percent)	Terminal-year conditions	
Age (1)	Tenure (years) (2)	(3)	Age (4)	Percent with over 20 years' tenure (5)
Japan, 1962–77				
20–24	0–5	45.1	35–39	9.4
	Over 5	65.3		
25–34	0–5	42.7	40–49	30.9
	Over 5	73.0		
35–39	0–5	37.7	50–54	37.5
	Over 5	75.9		
United States, 1963–78				
20–24	0–5	13.0	35–39	1.5
	Over 5	30.0		
25–34	0–5	22.2	40–49	15.6
	Over 5	47.3		
35–44	0–5	24.4	50–59	29.6
	Over 5	54.5		

Source: Abstracted from Masanori Hashimoto and John Raisian, "Employment Tenure and Earnings Profiles in Japan and the United States," *American Economic Review*, vol. 75 (September 1985), table 1.

same employer than his American counterpart does.[7] Tables 1 and 2 summarize the evidence comparing the prevalence of long-term employment in Japan and the United States.

Column 3 in table 1 reports the job retention rate, calculated as the proportion of male workers in a given age-tenure category in the initial year who had a correspondingly higher age and tenure in the same firm fifteen years later.[8] The computation follows Hall's (see note 7) procedure by which the number of workers is divided by the civilian noninstitutional population, rather than the number of employed persons, to

7. For the extent of long-term employment in the United States, see Kazuo Koike, *Shokuba No Rodo Kumiai To Sanka* (Unions on the Shop Floor and Participation) (Tokyo: Toyo Keizai Shimpo-Sha, 1977); Robert E. Hall, "The Importance of Lifetime Jobs in the U.S. Economy," *American Economic Review*, vol. 72 (September 1982), pp. 716–24; and Hashimoto and Raisian, "Employment Tenure and Earnings Profiles."

8. The 1962 and 1977 issues of *Shugyo Kozo Kihon Chosa* (Basic Survey of Employment Status) fortunately contain information on employment duration, and it was possible to compare Japan and the United States for a similar period of time. At present it is not possible to update these results, since the recent Japanese employment surveys do not always have such information.

Table 2. Distribution of Private Sector Male Employees by Tenure in Progress, by Firm Size, Japan (1982) and the United States (1979)[a]
Percent unless otherwise indicated

	All firms		Small firms		Large firms	
Years	Japan	U.S.	Japan	U.S.	Japan	U.S.
Under 1	7.7	19.4	10.0	22.3	5.2	11.2
Under 5	27.3	50.0	33.9	59.4	19.4	35.6
Under 10	45.5	69.4	53.9	77.9	35.1	57.3
10 and over	54.5	30.6	46.2	22.1	64.9	42.6
20 and over	25.1	12.4	19.9	7.9	30.5	18.8
	Number of years					
Median	10.1	4.0	8.5	3.0	12.9	7.0
Mean	12.6	7.8	10.8	6.1	14.4	10.3

Sources: For Japan, see Prime Minister's Statistical Office, *Basic Survey of Employment* (1982), various pages; for the United States, see Hashimoto and Raisian, "Employment Tenure," table 3.

a. For Japan, small firms have 10–99 employees and large firms have 1,000 employees or more. For the United States, small firms have 26–99 employees and large firms have 1,000 employees or more.

include movements in and out of the labor force as well as among employers.

The retention rates are clearly higher in Japan than in the United States. For example, a little over 45 percent of Japanese male workers aged 20–24 with a tenure of 0–5 years in 1962 were working for the same employer fifteen years later. For the United States the comparable figure is only 13 percent. The same pattern is observed for other age-tenure categories, signifying that the greater prevalence of long-term employment in Japan is not an artifact of a differential in age composition of the labor force between the two countries. (The same point can be made by looking at column 5.) Note also that in both countries workers with higher initial levels of tenure in 1962 or 1963 tend to have higher retention rates. This pattern underscores the tendency in both countries for job hopping to be concentrated in the early years of labor force activity.

Table 2 updates the similar tabulation originally published in Raisian and my 1985 article. It reports for both countries the percent distribution of employed males in the private sector by years of tenure in progress.

In 1982 the Japanese proportion of those with ten or more years of tenure was above 54 percent, in contrast to the U.S. proportion of slightly less than 31 percent in 1979. The same Japan-U.S. contrast continues to hold for those with twenty or more years of tenure. Although a greater proportion of employees have long-term employment in larger firms in both countries, it is clear that long-term employment in Japan prevails even among small firms.[9]

9. In private conversation a manager of a small Japanese firm said he would not

Raisian and I also found that Japanese workers do not change jobs as often as U.S. workers do. A typical Japanese male was found to hold slightly more than 4.9 jobs before retiring, in contrast to his American counterpart, who is projected to hold about 11 jobs. The comparable figures for women are a little over 5 in Japan and a little over 10 in America. These magnitudes suggest that job turnover during the life cycle is notably smaller in Japan than in the United States.

It is useful at this point to take note of various employment categories in Japan, and particularly the relative importance of temporary workers. In Japan workers are classified into four basic categories: self-employed, family workers, regular workers, and nonregular workers. Regular workers have employment contracts without a specified length of employment duration. Most regular workers have long-term employment and nenko wage schedules. Japanese labor law prohibits employment contracts lasting more than one year, and the usual practice is not to specify the employment period. Temporary workers and day laborers, however, are under contracts that have a specified period of employment of less than a year, though such contracts are renewable. There is no direct way of drawing a similar distinction in the U.S. data. A student hired for a summer job, for example, is not distinguishable in the data from a young household head with a permanent job.[10] In recent years in

---

consider dismissing a worker merely because of poor performance or poor economic conditions. It is usually thought that smaller firms have higher failure rates; if so, smaller firms are expected to have on average a shorter duration of employment. A potentially contrary piece of evidence should be kept in mind, however. Cole reported that the proportion of workers in Yokohama who are job leavers because of involuntary discharge, presumably including business failures, tends to be highest in the largest firms and lowest in the smallest firms. Robert E. Cole, *Work, Mobility, and Participation: A Comparative Study of American and Japanese Industry* (University of California Press, 1979), pp. 87–90. No information is available, however, on the proportion of those discharges that are due to business failures. If failure rates were the predominant factor, competition would lead to higher wages in smaller firms. Since wages tend to be lower in smaller firms, there must be more to differences in firm size. As another factor, employees in larger firms have greater opportunities to change jobs without changing employers. Indeed, Cole found that intrafirm mobility increases with firm size in both Yokohama and Detroit. Ibid., pp. 80–81.

10. There is, however, a growing temporary help industry in the United States. This industry is made up of establishments that supply temporary help to businesses and currently accounts for about 1 percent of total nonagricultural employment. Also the U.S. data do categorize employment into part-time and full-time components. In 1983, 81 percent of nonagricultural wage and salary workers worked at full-time jobs, though an additional 2 percent, who usually work full time, worked at part-time jobs for economic reasons. In Japan about 12 percent of employment consists of part-time workers, in contrast to the U.S. figure of 17–19 percent.

Japan, self-employed and family workers—those who work in an unincorporated enterprise operated by a member of the family—amounted to about 20 percent of the total nonagricultural employment, a much larger proportion than the U.S. figure of 8 percent.[11] Moreover, in Japan more than two-thirds of this combined category are self-employed. In other words, self-employment is more prevalent in Japan than in the United States.

Among nonagricultural employees in Japan, about 90 percent are regular workers, with the remaining 10 percent consisting of temporary workers and day laborers. Japanese women are more likely to be family workers than men. In 1983, 14 percent of female workers belonged to the family worker category, as against 2 percent for males. The proportion of self-employed was about the same for both sexes, 12 percent for females and 14 percent for males. Among female nonagricultural wage and salary workers, about 80 percent were regular workers in 1983 as compared with 95 percent of males. In other words, employed Japanese women are more likely than men to be family workers, temporary workers, or day laborers. Also, more than 25 percent of working women, as opposed to 3 percent of working men, worked as part-timers. Thus Japanese women do appear to have a weaker attachment to the labor market, though the notion that few Japanese women are regular workers on a full-time basis is misleading. Temporary and female workers in Japan provide cushions for employment fluctuations in the long-term employment environment. As a result, they experience greater cyclical volatility in employment than male regular workers do.[12]

11. The statistics in this section come from *Japan Yearbook of Labor Statistics,* various years.

12. Raisian and I used the data for Japanese manufacturing to investigate this issue. We regressed year-to-year changes in employment on similar changes in output, separately for regular workers and for temporary workers plus day laborers. The regression coefficients for output indicate the cyclical sensitivity of employment. Not surprisingly, temporary workers and day laborers show greater cyclical sensitivities of employment than regular workers for both sexes. We also found that the cyclical sensitivity of employment for male regular workers is half that for female regular workers (0.2886 versus 0.5779) and less than one-third of that for female temporary and day laborers (0.2886 versus 0.9167). A similar regression for U.S. manufacturing shows a cyclical sensitivity of 0.5802. Interestingly, therefore, output sensitivities for male temporary workers and female regular workers in Japan are rather similar to the output sensitivity for all U.S. workers. Masanori Hashimoto and John Raisian, "Aspects of Labor Market Flexibility in Japan and the United States," revision of a paper presented at the 1986 International Symposium on Employment Security and Labor Market Flexibility, Yokohama National University; and Hashimoto and Raisian, "The Structure and Short-Run Adaptability of Labor Markets in Japan and the United States," in

Table 3. Mandatory Retirement in Japan for Private Sector Firms with Thirty or More Employees, by Firm Size and Age of Retirement

	Percent of all firms with mandatory retirement	Firms with no sex difference in retirement system			
		Percent with mandatory retirement	Percent with retirement age of		
Year	(1)	(2)	55 (3)	60 (4)	Over 60 (5)
All firm sizes					
1974	66.6	65.7	52.0	32.4	35.4
1980	82.2	73.0	39.5	36.5	39.7
1988	88.3	90.1	23.6	55.0	58.8
Extra-large firms (5,000 or more employees)					
1974	100.0	69.9	38.0	11.0	11.0
1980	99.5	79.4	35.3	27.6	27.6
1988	99.1	90.7	3.9	82.4	82.8
Large firms (1,000–4,999 employees)					
1974	99.0	55.8	42.7	19.2	19.9
1980	99.9	70.6	38.9	22.8	24.5
1988	99.9	94.4	12.6	71.1	72.1
High medium-sized firms (300–999 employees)					
1974	94.3	60.9	49.5	22.1	22.8
1980	98.3	70.5	45.1	25.1	26.1
1988	99.0	92.3	18.1	59.1	61.5
Low medium-sized firms (100–299 employees)					
1974	90.4	59.8	53.4	26.9	29.5
1980	93.7	70.3	44.4	30.8	33.2
1988	97.2	90.1	23.7	52.7	55.5
Small firms (30–99 employees)					
1974	55.0	70.1	52.3	37.3	41.0
1980	76.5	74.5	37.1	40.4	44.1
1988	84.3	89.8	24.5	54.9	59.1

Source: *Practical Labor Statistics* (Tokyo: Japan Productivity Center, 1989), table E-15.

Some Issues on Retirement

Increasingly, Japanese firms have been adopting the mandatory retirement system. Larger firms tended to have a higher probability of having mandatory retirement, as seen in column 2 of table 3. This column also shows that the proportion of private sector firms using such a system increased for all firm-size groups except "extra-large firms" (those with 5,000 or more workers). For these very large firms, the proportion with

Robert A. Hart, ed., *Employment, Unemployment and Labor Utilization* (London: Unwin Hyman, 1988), pp. 314–40.

mandatory retirement appears to have dropped since 1974. Column 2 shows that an increasing proportion of firms have moved away from differential treatment by sex in retirement practices. Thus the proportion of firms with a uniform retirement system applying to both sexes, in the population of all firms using the mandatory retirement system, has risen for all firm-size groups. Most mandatory retirement used to take place at age 55, but the retirement age has been advancing (see columns 3 through 5). There is an indication that in 1988 larger firms retired workers at older ages, though a similar firm-size pattern is not observed in earlier years.

There are essentially two explanations for why mandatory retirement takes place.[13] The first argument hinges on the idea that senior workers near retirement receive wages higher than their current productivity. For example, in Lazear's work-effort model, older senior workers are "overpaid" relative to their current productivity to compensate for their having been underpaid when they were junior workers.[14] Such a payment scheme is designed to reduce shirking and other unproductive activities. In effect, workers post bond in earlier years of work, receive the interest payments over the years, and regain the bond at the time of retirement. Alternatively, senior workers may be overpaid as part of the promotion-ladder scheme to reduce inefficient separation of workers who receive training in firm-specific human capital.[15] In this scheme, sometime after the training is completed, workers are promoted to wages that exceed their current productivity simply by seniority. This arrangement eliminates the employer's incentive to dismiss a trained worker prematurely: the employer does not gain from such action because another trained worker will fill the vacated slot on the basis of seniority. Eventually a time comes when it is efficient to separate, either because a worker's productivity has fallen or the value of his leisure time has risen to make it inefficient for him to remain employed. In either model, however, workers have the incentive to continue being employed, since their wages are higher than their productivity. Thus mandatory retirement must be imposed to effect efficient separation.

The second argument, the productivity-dispersion hypothesis, is

13. The discussion here is kept brief to save space. For further details, see Hashimoto, *Japanese Labor Market*.

14. Edward P. Lazear, "Why Is There Mandatory Retirement?" *Journal of Political Economy*, vol. 87 (December 1979), pp. 1261–84.

15. Lorne Carmichael, "Firm-Specific Human Capital and Promotion Ladders," *Bell Journal of Economics*, vol. 14 (Spring 1983), pp. 251–58.

based on the assertion that the dispersion in individual productivity increases with age for health reasons.[16] Since measuring, monitoring, sorting, and reassigning are costly, an investment in such activities for older workers, whose productivity declines and whose remaining working lives are short, becomes unprofitable. It therefore becomes economical to retire all workers when they reach a certain age rather than to ascertain which of these workers are worth keeping.

An evaluation of the merits of these arguments is beyond the scope of this paper. It is noteworthy, however, that the normal U.S. retirement age of 65 is higher than the average Japanese retirement age of about 60. This difference seems to counter the pattern predicted by the argument that Japanese workers invest more in firm-specific human capital than U.S. workers do.[17] As Raisian and I argued earlier (in "Employment Tenure and Earnings Profiles"), the determination of the retirement age reflects many factors, including longevity and worker productivity, so that a comparison of the age level may not be meaningful. That the age of mandatory retirement has been increasing in Japan is consistent with the human capital hypothesis if firm-specific human capital has been increasing there.

Finally, some writers have been concerned with the Japanese redundancy practice, whereby many Japanese firms tend to separate senior and trained workers through discharge and early retirement when demand declines. Koike reported that large Japanese firms have tended to resort to the redundancy measure after continuous losses. This practice has raised the concern that experienced and productive workers are being forced out of employment, thereby causing a large redundancy cost to the economy.[18] It is possible, however, that this practice is an employer's rational response to a decline in demand. Carmichael showed that it is less costly to lay off older, experienced workers than young workers who are receiving training. The reason is straightforward: a layoff does not shorten the time required for training, but it does reduce the total working lifetime of a worker. Thus the productivity loss is always from an experienced worker, whose lost output is evaluated at the current depressed product price. For a young worker in training, lost

16. Walter Oi and John Raisian, "Impact of Firm Size on Wages and Work," University of Rochester, 1985.

17. The evidence could be consistent with either the work effort or the productivity-dispersion hypothesis.

18. Kazuo Koike, "Japanese Redundancy: The Impact of Key Labor Market Institutions on the Economic Flexibility of the Japanese Economy," in Chinloy and Stromsdorfer, eds., *Labor Market Adjustments in the Pacific Basin*, pp. 79–101.

output is evaluated at a price averaged over good and bad times. As a result, the expected value of a young worker's training is less sensitive to current economic conditions than the actual value of an experienced worker's training.[19] Thus, while not ruling out the possibility of wastes caused by the redundancy practice, Carmichael's argument does suggest that it may be a rational practice.

Earnings Profiles
(Nenko Joretsu System)

Another notable difference between Japanese and U.S. labor markets is the shape of the earnings-tenure profile. Earnings typically grow more rapidly with tenure for Japanese workers than for U.S. workers. As workers accumulate years of tenure, they acquire skills and know-how that are useful in the labor market at large (general experience) as well as those that are useful only within the current firm (firm-specific experience). According to the evidence that Raisian and I examined earlier, firm-specific experience has a greater effect on earnings than general experience in Japan, but the pattern is reversed in the United States.

Table 4 documents these patterns. Raisian and I ran cross-sectional regressions of the logarithm of earnings on a number of variables, of which the most relevant ones were years of tenure, total years of experience, and schooling. Using the estimated regression coefficients, we then constructed earnings profiles for typical workers in Japan and the United States, up to the years when the earnings reached their peaks. Interestingly, the peak years, shown in column 1, are not very different in the two countries. Column 2 shows the percentage growth in earnings between the first year of employment and the peak year. Thus a typical Japanese worker who continues to work in a small firm is estimated to experience an almost 236 percent growth in earnings. In contrast, earnings for his U.S. counterpart are expected to grow by only 140 percent.

According to the human capital hypothesis, earnings grow with employment tenure because employees acquire both general and firm-

19. Lorne Carmichael, "Does Rising Productivity Explain Seniority Rules for Layoffs?" *American Economic Review*, vol. 73 (December 1983), pp. 1127–31. Note that an implicit assumption in Carmichael's argument is that there is a prospect of recovery in the future. Without such a prospect, it makes little sense to continue training a worker.

Table 4. Percent Growth of Earnings Associated with Years of Experience,
Male Workers in Japan and the United States

| Size of firm | Peak year of earnings (1) | Percent growth of earnings to peak year due to | | Ratio col. 3/col. 2 (4) |
		Total experience (2)	Firm-specific experience (3)	
Japan (1980)				
Small	24th	235.6	150.4	0.638
Large	27th	242.8	205.2	0.845
United States (1979)				
Small	25th	140.0	57.9	0.414
Large	30th	109.7	52.6	0.479

Sources: Hashimoto and Raisian, "Employment Tenure," table 6.
a. These magnitudes are calculated from regression estimates of earnings profiles, holding constant schooling and union status (for the United States). Small firms are those employing fewer than 100 workers; large firms are those employing more than 1,000 workers. For additional details, see Hashimoto and Raisian, "Employment Tenure."

specific experience. Columns 3 and 4 document the relative importance of firm-specific experience in the total earnings growth. Column 4 shows that for the typical Japanese worker in a small firm, a little more than 150 percentage points out of the 235.6 percentage-point growth in his earnings, or almost 64 percent, are due to firm-specific experience. For his U.S. counterpart, about 58 percentage points out of the 140 percentage-point growth in his earnings, or a little over 41 percent, are attributable to firm-specific experience. Thus firm-specific experience dominates general experience in affecting earnings growth in Japan, but the opposite pattern is true in the United States. The pattern for large firms is similar to that for small firms. Finally, in both countries the relative importance of firm-specific experience is greater in large than in small firms, though the contrast is weak for the United States.

Bonus Payments

As noted elsewhere, many Japanese blue-collar and white-collar workers receive bonuses in addition to their base pay.[20] Typically they are paid twice a year, once in summer, a gift-giving season as well as the time of *obon* (the occasion when the spirits of the deceased are said to

20. Masanori Hashimoto, "Bonus Payments, On-the-Job Training, and Lifetime Employment in Japan," *Journal of Political Economy*, vol. 87 (October 1979), pp. 1086–1104; Hashimoto and Raisian, "Wage Flexibility"; and Richard B. Freeman and Martin L. Weitzman, "Bonuses and Employment in Japan," *Journal of the Japanese and International Economies*, vol. 1 (June 1987), pp. 168–94.

Table 5. Composition of Compensation for Production Workers in Manufacturing, Selected Countries[a]
Percent

Country	Wages and salaries (1)	Bonuses (2)	Total (cols. 1 and 2) (3)
Japan (1978)	56.7	20.3	77.0
Belgium (1981)	56.4	12.0	68.4
West Germany (1981)	57.7	9.1	66.8
Italy (1981)	54.4	8.9	63.3
Netherlands (1981)	57.8	8.8	66.6
France (1981)	56.6	5.4	62.0
United Kingdom (1981)	71.8	0.7	72.5
United States (1977)	74.8	0.4	75.2
Canada (1971)	83.1	0.2	83.3

Source: U.S. Bureau of Labor Statistics, *Handbook of Labor Statistics*, Bulletin 2217 (Department of Labor, June 1985), table 134.

a. Wages and salaries comprise basic time and piece rates, plus overtime premiums and shift differentials. Bonuses are all bonuses and premiums not paid monthly. The remaining components not reported are pay for leave time, sick pay, pay in kind, benefits, and legally required insurance.

visit the living relatives), and in winter, a time to prepare for the new year. Bonus payments may reflect workers' shares in their firm-specific human capital or they may reflect a share economy.[21] Either way, an average Japanese worker counts on bonus payments as a reliable source of income year after year. During the bonus seasons the public media are full of advertisements by banks and retailers trying to attract bonus money. Bonuses usually constitute on average over 20 percent of the annual earnings of Japanese workers; their relative importance is greater for workers in larger firms, and the bonus share tended to increase after 1951, at least until the early 1980s.[22]

The high proportion of bonus payments in worker compensation seems to be unique to Japan among the OECD countries.[23] Table 5

21. For the first interpretation, see Hashimoto, "Bonus Payments"; for the second, see Martin L. Weitzman, *The Share Economy: Conquering Stagflation* (Harvard University Press, 1984); and Freeman and Weitzman, "Bonuses and Employment."

22. In 1985 the proportion of bonus payments in the total annual earnings for manufacturing workers ranged between 14 percent in firms with 5–29 employees to 24.7 percent in firms with 30 or more employees. Regression analyses show that the bonus-earnings ratio increases with the educational attainment of workers, firm size, and tenure in the firm. Regression estimates are remarkably stable for 1967, 1970, 1976, 1980, and 1981. For related discussions, see Hashimoto, "Bonus Payments"; Hashimoto and Raisian, "Wage Flexibility"; and Hashimoto, *Japanese Labor Market*, chap. 2.

23. Korea also has bonus payments. The only research on the Korean bonus system that I am aware of is by Ito and Kang. According to that research, Korean bonuses

summarizes compensation categories for production workers in manufacturing industries for selected countries. The comparisons from this table must be made cautiously: country differences in the importance of bonus payments must be viewed as only suggestive; the inevitable country differences in the concept and definition of bonuses must be addressed before drawing firm conclusions. Even with this limitation, it is interesting that the proportions of the sum of wages and salaries and bonuses reported in column 3 are rather similar among those countries. According to columns 1 and 2, however, the composition of this sum varies greatly among the countries. In particular, the differences in the proportion of bonuses are striking, ranging from 0.2 percent for Canada in 1971 to 20.3 percent for Japan in 1978. Interestingly, the United Kingdom, the United States, and Canada stand out as having rather small proportions of bonus payments compared with continental European countries and Japan.[24]

The importance of bonus payments has increased in Japan over time, but in the United States the trend, if anything, has been downward. There is some indication, though, that the U.S. trend may be reversing as firms increasingly try to tie wages to performance.[25] Thus U.S. bonuses seem to be incentive payments. In contrast, Japanese bonuses do not seem to be incentive payments, since conditions for receiving

---

began to appear about 1971; the bonus-wage ratio is still low compared with Japan's, but it has been increasing since the early 1970s. In the early 1980s the Korean ratio stood at about half the Japanese ratio. Takatoshi Ito and Kyoungsik Kang, "Bonuses, Overtime, and Employment: Korea vs. Japan," paper presented at the January 1989 conference of the National Bureau of Economic Research, the Center for Economic Research, and the Centre for Economic Policy Research.

24. As regards just Japan and the United States, in the 1970s the proportions of total compensation for direct, indirect, and legally required insurance differed little between the two countries. For example, direct payments consisting of wages, salaries, and bonuses amounted to about 75 percent of total compensation in the United States in 1977; that figure for Japan in 1978 was 77 percent. For these same years indirect payments consisting of paid leave, in-kind payments, and other nonpecuniary benefits amounted to about 17 percent in the United States and 16 percent in Japan; legally required insurance, such as unemployment insurance, amounted to about 7 percent in both countries. Clearly, it is in the composition of direct payments—wages and salaries versus bonuses—that one finds a sharp contrast between the two countries. Bonuses are extremely rare in the United States, amounting in 1977 to less than 1 percent of total compensation, whereas in Japan in 1978 they amounted to 20 percent of total compensation and more than 25 percent of direct compensation. Note also that both nonmonetary benefits and legally required insurance grew in importance in Japan as well as in the United States during this period.

25. See, for example, "GM's New Compensation Plan Reflects General Trend Tying Pay to Performance," Wall Street Journal, January 26, 1988.

bonuses are rarely stated in employment contracts.[26] Whatever productivity effects bonuses may have in Japan, it does not appear to be through their direct incentive effects.

One productivity-enhancing effect of Japanese bonuses may be their role in promoting wage flexibility. Wage flexibility based on mutually agreeable contracts increases productivity by allowing labor costs to respond closely to reality, thereby reducing waste and encouraging investments. In my article on "Bonus Payments" I hypothesized that they represent the returns to worker investments in firm-specific human capital and that they contribute to flexible wages in Japan. Flexibility is evident in all components of Japanese earnings, however. For example, the base wage itself is quite flexible, in part because it is renegotiated every spring at the time of *Shunto*.[27] My 1987 study with Raisian on "Wage Flexibility" concluded that the degree of cyclical wage variability is much more pronounced in Japan than in the United States.

Variability of Labor Inputs, Wages, and Bonuses

Japan experienced a rather drastic contraction in the growth rate of its economy after the first oil shock, which started in late 1973.[28] As a result, many firms had to make major, and sometimes painful, adjustments in the utilization of labor. An important public policy response to this situation took place in 1975 with the Employment Insurance Law. This law shifted the emphasis away from the usual concept of an unemployment insurance subsidy directly provided to unemployed workers to a system in which subsidies are given to employers, who, in turn, provide compensation to workers on furlough. A noteworthy aspect of this law was that it enabled the furloughed workers to remain "employed" by the firm; the law also provided for subsidies when employers wished to implement short time schedules.[29]

26. It is worth noting, however, that bonuses in the early years of industrialization, that is, at the turn of the century, tended to be incentive payments. See Hashimoto, *Japanese Labor Market*, chap. 2.

27. See Robert J. Gordon, "Why U.S. Wage and Employment Behavior Differs from That in Britain and Japan, *Economic Journal,* vol. 92 (March 1982), pp. 13–44.

28. In 1974 Japan experienced the first negative growth rate of the postwar period, −1.3 percent. Actually the double-digit growth rate of the Japanese economy in the 1960s lasted only to about 1970. But the slowdown in the growth rate was most dramatic after the oil shock. See Takafusa Nakamura, *The Postwar Japanese Economy: Its Development Structure* (University of Tokyo Press, 1981), p. 168.

29. Cole, *Work, Mobility, and Participation;* Koji Taira and Solomon B. Levine,

Table 6. Cyclical Sensitivity for Male Workers in Japanese Manufacturing Industries, 1959–85[a]

Item	Regression coefficients				
	Intercept	Shipment(Z)	Dummy(D)	$D \times Z$	R^2
	Production workers				
Employment	−0.0472	0.6532	0.0333	−0.5314	0.61
	(−2.59)	(4.66)	(1.67)	(−2.65)	
Hours per month	−0.0334	0.2072	0.0196	0.3069	0.77
	(−4.37)	(3.52)	(2.43)	(3.65)	
Days per month	−0.0075	0.0083	−0.0022	0.2495	0.61
	(−1.46)	(0.21)	(−0.39)	(4.43)	
Bonus earnings	−0.1671	0.6062	−0.0741	−0.6651	0.25
	(−0.49)	(1.63)	(−0.88)	(−0.99)	
	Nonproduction workers				
Employment	−0.0094	0.6505	0.0152	−0.7020	0.55
	(−0.37)	(3.34)	(0.55)	(−2.52)	
Hours per month	−0.0309	0.2060	0.0206	0.1462	0.66
	(−4.17)	(3.62)	(2.54)	(1.80)	
Days per month	−0.0177	0.0931	0.0077	0.1194	0.31
	(−2.23)	(1.53)	(0.88)	(1.37)	
Bonus earnings	−0.2667	0.9836	−0.0124	−0.7917	0.80
	(−2.20)	(7.37)	(−0.41)	(−3.32)	

Sources: Japan Ministry of Labor, Policy Planning and Research Department, *Japan Yearbook of Labor Statistics*, various years; shipment data are from *Practical Labor Statistics* (Tokyo: Japan Productivity Center, 1988), various pages.

a. All variables, except for the dummy variable, are in first difference of logarithms. The dummy variable is unity for the post-1974 years. Contract and bonus earnings are in real terms (using the wholesale price index), and their regressions include a time trend. All variables are for male regular workers in firms with 30 or more employees. The numbers in parentheses are *t*-statistics.

The changes experienced by the Japanese economy in the mid-1970s can be viewed as the emergence of cyclical labor markets. In the regime of high rates of economic growth such as prevailed in Japan before 1970, changes in output demand were likely to be viewed as reflecting long-run, or permanent, changes. After the mid-1970s, however, the rate of growth slowed substantially, and demand changes came to be viewed more as short-run business-cycle phenomena than as permanent changes.

Table 6 documents the emergence of a cyclical economy after the first oil shock. It reports on the regressions of various labor market variables on the demand variable (shipments, Z) and on the dummy variable, D, which is equal to unity for the post-1974 years. The data refer to male

"Japan's Industrial Relations: A Social Compact Emerges," in Hervey Juris and others, eds., *Industrial Relations in a Decade of Economic Change* (Madison, Wis.: Industrial Relations Research Association, 1985), pp. 247–300; and Constance Sorrentino, "Unemployment Compensation in Eight Industrial Nations," *Monthly Labor Review*, vol. 99 (July 1976), pp. 18–24.

workers, separately for production and nonproduction workers, in manufacturing for the period 1959–85. The regression coefficients associated with Z are the elasticities of the labor market variables with respect to demand shocks. Of particular interest are the coefficients on Z and on the interaction variable, $D \times Z$.

For both production and nonproduction workers, employment and hours of work exhibited statistically significant sensitivities to demand changes before 1974, and the elasticities were similar for the two worker categories. After 1974, however, employment became less sensitive than before, and the reduction in the employment elasticity was nominally greater for nonproduction (more skilled) workers. To complement the decrease in the employment elasticity, the hours elasticity increased after 1974 for both worker categories. Thus adjustments in hours of work became more important than adjustments in employment after 1974.

These findings can be seen as reflecting the effects of the Employment Insurance Law, which would have discouraged the use of employment adjustments. They are also consistent with the emergence of cyclical labor markets: it is well known that employment adjustments entail more fixed costs than adjustments in hours of work. Before 1974 demand changes tended to be viewed as permanent changes inducing sizable adjustments in employment, whereas after 1974 they tended to be viewed as short-run changes inducing smaller adjustments in employment, and larger adjustments in hours of work, than before. Interestingly, the elasticity for days worked also seems to have increased after 1974, especially for production workers. Finally, bonus earnings showed a positive response to demand changes, but this finding is statistically significant only for nonproduction workers. The bonus elasticity decreased for both categories of workers after 1974, but again the decrease is statistically significant only for nonproduction workers. These findings could reflect the fact that profit-sharing bonuses, including the sharing of the returns to firm-specific human capital, are more common among nonproduction than production workers.

Output Growth and Labor Productivity

The popular press might have created the impression that the Japanese economy is far more productive than the American economy. Such an impression is misleading when applied to the economy as a whole. As of the mid-1980s—the most recent years for which comparable data are available for the two countries—the United States enjoyed a higher measured labor productivity than Japan. For example, in 1985 the gross national product per labor force member was $33,684 for the United States and $22,268 for Japan (converted to U.S. dollars at the market exchange rate), a difference of 51 percent. The average hourly earnings for a production worker in manufacturing in 1986 were $9.73 in the United States and $6.82 in Japan, a difference of 43 percent. The two measures, therefore, are not very far apart from each other in showing the magnitude of the U.S. productivity advantage over Japan.[30]

One may quibble about the quality of GNP and hourly earnings as measures of productivity, but the conclusions about productivity levels based on those data are supported by other evidence. Abegglen and Stalk, for example, note that high Japanese productivity is limited to certain types of manufacturing processes; the Japanese labor productivity advantage is very large in high-volume assembly processes where a huge number of interdependent steps must be coordinated, but in simpler processes the Japanese advantage is small.[31] In metal refining and simple manufacturing, the authors argue, Japanese labor productivity in comparable plants is no higher than in Western plants. In other sectors as well, "despite all that is said about management style and organizational effectiveness, Japanese organization in such fields as services and distribution have low levels of productivity" (p. 65). Note that the relative importance of the service sector in the economy is growing in both countries. Abegglen and Stalk's comment implies that this development by itself portends a widening productivity gap between the two countries in favor of the United States. Also, the hypothesis of this paper implies that Japanese hourly productivity is lower than indicated by the reported data, which ignore the transaction time spent by labor and management.

At any rate, the difference in the level of productivity between the two countries is dwarfed by the sharp contrast in the growth of measured

30. These figures are from *Practical Labor Statistics* (Tokyo: Japan Productivity Center, 1988), tables I-6, I-7. It is relevant to note that Ellenberger claimed that the U.S. productivity advantage over Japan was 30 percent. James N. Ellenberger, "Japanese Management: Myth or Magic," *AFL-CIO American Federationist*, vol. 89 (April–June 1982), pp. 3–12.

31. In automobile manufacturing, according to these authors, Japanese workers in stamping and assembly plants are twice as productive as U.S. workers; in engine and transmission manufacture they are 50 percent more productive; and in iron foundries 20 percent more productive. They note, however, that only in the late 1970s did Japanese firms achieve higher labor productivity in complex manufacturing. James C. Abegglen and George Stalk, Jr., *Kaisha: The Japanese Corporation* (Basic Books, 1985), pp. 61–62.

productivity in Japan's favor. For the economy as a whole, the Japanese annual growth rate of real GNP fell from double-digit levels during the 1960s to a rate of about 5 percent in the 1970s and 1980s. By comparison, the GNP for the United States grew at a steady annual rate of about 3 percent throughout the same three decades. As a result, the differential in the growth rates between the two countries narrowed considerably during the 1970s and 1980s.

The difference in output growth is especially pronounced in the manufacturing sector. There the Japanese real output grew at an average annual rate of a little over 12 percent during 1951–83, while the U.S. real output grew at only about 3 percent. Although Japan has experienced a persistent decline in the growth of manufacturing output during the last thirty years or so, its annual manufacturing output growth rate of 6 percent in the early 1980s was still much higher than the U.S. growth rate of 2 percent.[32] In fact, this was a wider margin than the difference between the two countries' economy-wide growth rates (5 percent and 3 percent).

Jorgenson and others argue that Japan's higher rates of growth in capital and intermediate inputs were largely responsible for the greater growth in Japan's output between 1960 and 1979. Growth in these inputs, in turn, must have raised labor productivity. In fact, differential growth in labor productivity rather than in labor supply appears to have been the key factor in the difference in output growth between the two countries. The civilian labor force grew steadily in Japan after 1960 at an annual rate of only about 1.2 percent, well below the corresponding U.S. figure of 2.2 percent. As of the early 1980s the growth in real GNP per labor force member was about 4 percent in Japan and 1 percent in the United States. In manufacturing the growth in real output per hour held steady in the United States at about 2.6 percent a year, while in Japan it trended down from about 10 percent in the 1950s to about 7.5 percent in the early 1980s. Even with the declining trend, the growth rate of Japanese labor productivity remains three times as high as the U.S. growth rate.[33]

The data used by Jorgenson and others reveal that during the 1960–

32. The growth rate of Japanese manufacturing output trended downward by 0.4 percentage point a year, while the U.S. rate went down 0.1 percentage point a year.

33. Dale W. Jorgenson, Masahiro Kuroda, and Mieko Nishimizu, "Japan-U.S. Industry-Level Productivity Comparisons, 1960–1979," *Journal of the Japanese and International Economies*, vol. 1 (March 1987), pp. 1–30. The authors also found that differences in the growth rates of labor input were not pronounced between the two countries during the postwar years.

79 period both output growth and productivity growth in manufacturing were on average greater in Japan than in the United States. Moreover, both growth measures fluctuated much more in the United States than in Japan. For this period I calculate the correlation coefficient between these growth measures to be 0.86 in Japan and 0.67 in the United States, suggesting that productivity and output growths were more closely related to each other in Japan than in America.[34]

How closely is the Japan-U.S. difference in output growth related to the difference in the growth of labor productivity? To address this question, I used the data for twenty-eight manufacturing industries reported in Jorgenson and others (table 2) to estimate the following regression of the difference in percentage growth rates of output (ΔY) between Japan and the United States on differences in the growth rates of inputs of capital (ΔK), labor (ΔL), and intermediate inputs (ΔI) (t-statistics in parentheses):

$$(1) \qquad \Delta Y = 0.574 + 0.305\Delta K - 0.041\Delta L + 0.597\Delta I.$$
$$ (2.8) \qquad (-0.2) \qquad (3.3)$$
$$R^2 = 0.72 \, (df = 24)$$

The regression shows that the differences between Japan and the United States in the growth of capital and intermediate inputs had statistically significant influences on the difference in output growth, but that the difference in the growth of labor inputs did not. This finding is consistent with the conclusion reached by Jorgenson and others noted earlier. Since growths of capital and intermediate inputs are expected to have raised labor productivity, the finding suggests that the difference in labor productivity growth significantly influenced the difference in output growth between the two countries.

Japanese Unions

Most Japanese unions are enterprise unions.[35] In 1985, for example, there were almost 12.5 million union members (about 23.4 percent of the

34. This finding is consistent with the earlier finding that productivity is much more procyclical in Japan than in the United States. See Hashimoto and Raisian, "Wage Flexibility," and Hashimoto, *Japanese Labor Market*, chap. 2.

35. Industrial or craft unions are rare in Japan. The only significant craft union is the Zen Nihon Kaiin Kumiai (All Japan Seaman's Union). As the historical precedent of enterprise unions, Aoki cites the Industrial Patriotic Society established in the 1930s

total labor force), of which more than 91 percent were in enterprise unions.[36] An enterprise union is a bona fide trade union rather than a mere company union. It bargains collectively and has the legal right to engage in job actions including strikes.[37] Each firm has its own enterprise union, and basic issues of wages, working conditions, and the like are negotiated on a firm level.[38] Each enterprise union acts independently of others in bargaining with management. Unlike the local of a U.S. industrial union, the Japanese enterprise union is not merely an admin-

---

by the military at all industrial establishments and localities after the independent union movement was outlawed. Masahiko Aoki, *Information, Incentives, and Bargaining in the Japanese Economy* (Cambridge University Press, 1988). The primary purpose of the society was to promote employee morale and increase production. See Hashimoto, *Japanese Labor Market*, for an additional discussion on the historical background of enterprise unionism.

36. The remaining members were divided primarily between craft unions (1.3 percent) and industrial unions (5.5 percent). As is true for the United States, unionism is more prevalent in larger Japanese firms. In 1987, for example, over 58 percent of union members worked in firms with 1,000 or more employees and only about 16 percent in firms with 100 or fewer employees. These magnitudes were calculated from the data contained in *Practical Labor Statistics* (1988), pp. 160–61.

37. Enterprise unions belong to industrial federations, which in turn belong to national confederations. The main functions of federations and confederations are the collection and dissemination of information and political activities. Until November 20, 1987, there were three major confederations—the left-oriented Sohyo (General Council of Labor Unions, founded in 1955 and with almost 4.1 million members in 1987), the right-oriented Domei (Japanese Confederation of Labor, founded in 1964 and with more than 2.1 million members in 1987), and Churitsuroren (Independent Confederation of Unions, founded in 1956 and with more than 1.6 million members in 1987)—and a few minor ones. Both Domei and Churitsuroren were disbanded on November 20, 1987, when Rengo (Japan Private Sector Trade Union Confederation, with almost 5.6 million members) was inaugurated. Sohyo, too, is scheduled to go out of existence in 1990 and join Rengo. These data are from Tadashi Hanami, *Labor Relations in Japan Today* (Tokyo: Kodansha International, 1981); *Japan Times*, Weekly Overseas Edition, December 5, 1987; and *Practical Labor Statistics* (1988), p. 161.

38. Japanese enterprise unions and the works councils (Betriebsräte) in West Germany have certain similarities. For example, both use joint consultation along with collective bargaining. But they also have important differences. For example, Betriebsräte are required by law and are financed by the employers. Japanese unions are not required by law, but are voluntary associations of workers, and are not financed by the employers. Betriebsräte cannot strike and engage in other job actions as Japanese unions do. For more details and informative discussions of the Japanese enterprise unions, see Taishiro Shirai, "A Theory of Enterprise Unionism," in Taishiro Shirai, ed., *Contemporary Industrial Relations in Japan* (University of Wisconsin Press, 1983), pp. 117–43; Kazutoshi Koshiro, "Development of Collective Bargaining in Postwar Japan," in Shirai, ed., *Contemporary Industrial Relations in Japan*, pp. 205–57; and Kazutoshi Koshiro, *Nihon-no Roshi Kankei* (Japanese Industrial Relations) (Tokyo: Yuhikaku, 1983).

istrative unit of a national union. A worker must become an employee of the firm before he can join the union, and a typical union includes white-collar nonsupervisory employees as well as blue-collar workers.[39]

Almost all major collective bargaining in Japan takes place at a specific time of the year that is known to everyone—the spring offensive, or Shunto. The spring offensive must confer economies of scale in information gathering and transacting, since both sides can concentrate on collecting, exchanging, and verifying information at that time.[40] A noteworthy aspect of Japanese collective bargaining is that details are hammered out at the enterprise level rather than at the level of national union federations, as in the United States. Because of the simultaneous wage adjustments that take place annually, Shunto has been considered responsible for the prevalent wage flexibility in Japan.[41]

The fact that Japanese unions are enterprise-based means that both the employer and the employee are interested in the well-being of the same enterprise. The enterprise union may be seen as controlling its members' shirking and malfeasance as well as guarding against the employer's morally hazardous behavior. The union has the incentive to monitor its members within an enterprise so as to uphold their reputation as well as protect their interests from being dissipated by the employer. These monitoring functions may be served more effectively by a union organized within firms rather than across firms. To minimize the moral hazard problem, important decisions are made after close consultations between the management and the unions. It seems plausible that the employer and the employees share more interests in an enterprise union system than they do in industrial or craft unions. The joint consultation system facilitates communication between the employer and employees. As a result, much of the value added that might otherwise be lost in the form of dead-weight loss through externalities is internalized and realized in employment relations. As Taira put it, "The Japanese type of collective

39. Enterprise unionism began to appear during the interwar years among large firms. Pre–World War II unions consisted largely of blue-collar employees. Unlike the locals of American industrial unions, an enterprise union is not merely an administrative component of a national union. Shirai, "Theory of Enterprise Unionism," p. 119. Also, unlike his counterpart in Japanese enterprise unions, a foreman in a U.S. factory is not a member of the local. Koike, *Shokuba No Rodo Kumiai*, pp. 38–40.
40. For an interesting analysis of the effects of the 1986 Shunto on wage increases, see Atsushi Seike, "Analysis of the 1986 Spring Labor Wage Offensive," *Japan Labor Bulletin*, vol. 26, no. 8 (1986). Reprinted in Japan Labor Institute, *Highlights in Japanese Industrial Relations,* vol. 2 (1988).
41. Gordon, "Why U.S. Wage and Employment Behavior Differs"; and Hashimoto and Raisian, "Wage Flexibility."

bargaining necessarily makes the union so conscious of the business conditions of the firm that the enterprise union is, for all practical purposes, just another management in the firm."[42] It should be noted, however, that in Japan, as in the United States, the rate of unionization has been on the decline. The proportion of union members in nonagricultural employment stood at 35 percent in 1970, but by 1985–86 it had fallen to 28 percent.[43]

Institutions of Japanese Industrial Relations

Here I would like to discuss briefly some of the notable features in Japanese industrial relations. The purpose of the discussion is to develop an understanding of how management and labor communicate with each other, how they resolve differences and disputes, how effective these practices are, and how Japanese practices compare with those in the United States.

As noted earlier, work organization and industrial relations in Japan show greater flexibility than in most other developed countries. Flexible work organization is facilitated by the job rotation system whereby a typical worker is rotated among different tasks so that he may acquire a wide range of skills and become multifunctional.[44] In *Information, Incentives, and Bargaining,* Aoki notes, for example, that

The multifunctionality of workers fostered by a wide range of job experience (and job rotation in particular) may enable each shop to

42. Taira, *Economic Development and the Labor Market,* p. 169.

43. Richard B. Freeman, "Business Labor Relations Goals and Practices across OECD Countries," paper presented at the January 1989 Japan MITI conference on Corporate Management and Labor Markets: Implications for International Competitiveness. The decline in union density is partly due to the fact that an increasing number of newly established firms do not have unions. Freeman hypothesizes that the Japanese decline, like the similar decline in the United States, was caused largely by increased management opposition to unionism. A piece of anecdotal evidence for his hypothesis was offered by a Japanese president of a medium-sized firm (about 800 employees), who told me that in the hope of forestalling unionization of his work force, he started a friendship club in his firm to promote the exchange of information between management and labor. For an interesting discussion on the recently emerging issues of Japanese industrial relations, see Machiko Osawa, "Report from the 1988 Conference on Industrial Relations," *Japan Labor Bulletin,* vol. 27 (June 1, 1988).

44. Kazuo Koike, "Skill Formation Systems in the U.S. and Japan: A Comparative Study," in Masahiko Aoki, ed., *The Economic Analysis of the Japanese Firm* (Amsterdam: Elsevier Science, 1984), pp. 47–75; and Aoki, *Information, Incentives, and Bargaining.*

adjust job assignments flexibly in response to the requirements of the downstream operation. . . . Further, workers trained in a wide range of skills can better understand why more defective products are being produced and how to cope with the situation as well as prevent it from recurring. [pp. 36–37]

To be sure, flexible job structures based on cross training have existed in U.S. firms as well. For example, Jacoby views such practices, which prevailed in the late 1920s among some large firms, as a key part of their attempts to stabilize employment. As Aoki notes, however, U.S. firms in the postwar years have tended to emphasize fine task specialization and sharp job demarcation, characteristics that make it difficult to train workers to be multifunctional.[45] In contrast, Japanese firms encourage workers to share knowledge and tasks on the shop floor, thereby enabling workers to cope with local emergencies effectively.[46]

Another source of flexibility is the Japanese collective agreements, which are short, abstract, and even obscure.[47] The brevity of contracts underscores their flexibility, since there must be an implicit understanding among the parties involved that contract terms can be changed easily in response to newly emerging circumstances. This understanding makes it unnecessary to stipulate detailed terms in a contract. Contract flexibility in Japan underlies most economic and other relationships, as Hanami points out:

Westerners consider it important to describe in as precise and detailed a manner as possible the standards which are to be applied in every possible disagreement. They feel that there is no way to settle conflicts without reference to a complete description of the rights and obligations of both parties. Japanese think it is both impossible and unnecessary to provide such an extensive written description and make provisions for every possible eventuality. They believe that no matter how detailed the clauses of a contract may be, some unanticipated developments are bound to occur, and that it is more important to

45. Sanford M. Jacoby, "Pacific Ties: Employment Systems in Japan and the U.S. since 1900," University of California, Los Angeles, 1989; and Aoki, *Information, Incentives, and Bargaining.*

46. For the evolution of the Japanese approach to training, see Solomon B. Levine and Hisashi Kawada, *Human Resources in Japanese Industrial Development* (Princeton University Press, 1980).

47. Tadashi Hanami, *Labor Relations in Japan Today* (Tokyo: Kodansha International, 1981), chap. 2.

establish mutual understanding and trust. . . . Since economic deals in Japan are affected by emotional and sentimental factors, the parties to a contract always expect some flexibility in implementation. The detailed enumeration of specific contact provisions would be fatal to this flexibility.[48]

Clearly, that description applies to employment contracts as well.[49] The brevity of contracts might be taken to show that most decisions are made unilaterally by the employer, as per Hall and Lilien, thereby making it unnecessary to stipulate contractual terms in detail.[50] The Japanese experience does not seem to fit this scenario, however. Rather, major decisions in Japanese firms are made in close consultation with their enterprise unions, and management and labor depend on good faith interactions with each other to resolve disagreements and disputes. (Even firms without unions seem to make efforts to facilitate communications between management and labor.) In this paper, I view this contractual flexibility as a reflection of low transaction costs.

In Japan the management and labor of many firms consult with each other frequently through the joint consultation system and, to a lesser extent, in grievance settlement procedures. Although grievance settlement procedures exist outside Japan, the joint consultation system is often thought to be unique to Japanese employment relations. (But, as noted, work councils in West Germany also use joint consultation.) This practice became widespread after 1955, coincident with the launching of a campaign to raise productivity and international competitiveness by importing modern technologies from the United States and Europe.[51] To coordinate this campaign, the Japan Productivity Center was established in March 1955. Labor unions and leftist politicians initially opposed the

48. Hanami, *Labor Relations in Japan*, p. 53.

49. Thus Hanami goes on to say, "The reluctance to have one's rights and obligations clearly defined is to be found not only in the individual relationship between an employee and his employer but also in the relationship between unions and employers. The situation in industrial relations does not differ markedly from the description of personal or business contracts" (p. 53). For a comprehensive discussion of Japanese labor relations, see also Kazuo Sugeno and Kazutoshi Koshiro, "The Role of Neutrals in the Resolution of Shop Floor Disputes: A Twelve Nation Study—Japan," *Comparative Labor Law Journal*, vol. 9 (Fall 1987, special issue), pp. 129–63.

50. Robert E. Hall and David M. Lilien, "Efficient Wage Bargains under Uncertain Supply and Demand," *American Economic Review*, vol. 69 (December 1979), pp. 868–79. In their model, if supply-side uncertainty is absent, an efficient contract would let the employer determine unilaterally the level of employment.

51. An extensive discussion on the history of this campaign appears in *The Thirty-Year History of the Productivity Campaign* (Tokyo: Japan Productivity Center, 1988).

campaign, fearing that the introduction of modern technologies would displace labor and cause high unemployment. After an extensive debate the campaign eventually gained support from unions and politicians; three principles were agreed on: to prevent the unemployment of workers who would be made redundant (the principle of job security), to promote joint consultations between management and labor regarding the introduction of new technologies and related matters, and to promote a fair sharing of the gains of new technologies among employers, workers, and consumers. It seems evident that these principles, and especially the principle of joint consultations, have become firmly embedded in the Japanese industrial relations system.

The meetings for joint consultations take place according to regularly set schedules for some firms, and for others as the need arises. It is noteworthy that this system exists even in nonunionized sectors, though it is more prevalent in the unionized sector.[52] According to a 1984 survey, of 1,802 unions 1,068, or 59 percent, had joint consultations.[53] Among unions in large firms (1,000 or more employees), the proportion of unions with joint consultation was 71 percent. Even among very small firms (29 or fewer employees), the proportion was 34 percent.

Joint consultation is the primary means of solving problems that are unsuitable for bargaining—recruitment, dismissal, transfer and promotion, changes in production techniques and in management policies, plant closing, industrial safety, and the like.[54] More important, however, is the rationale for this system. In the 1984 survey just mentioned, 86 percent of unions listed expediting communication and 83 percent listed promotion of harmonious relationships as the major objectives of joint consultations.[55]

52. According to a survey taken by the Ministry of Labor in 1977, almost 83 percent of unionized establishments and a little over 40 percent of nonunion establishments had joint consultations. Shirai, "Theory of Enterprise Unionism," p. 143. For informative discussions of joint consultations, see also Koshiro, "Development of Collective Bargaining," and Sugeno and Koshiro, "Role of Neutrals."

53. Hashimoto, *Japanese Labor Market,* chap. 4.

54. Shirai, "Theory of Enterprise Unionism"; Tadashi Hanami, "Conflict Resolution in Industrial Relations: Japan," in Tadashi Hanami and Roger Blanpain, eds., *Industrial Conflict Resolution in Market Economies: A Study of Australia, the Federal Republic of Germany, Italy, Japan, and the U.S.A.* (Deventer, The Netherlands: Kluwer Law and Taxation, 1984), pp. 199–212; and Sugeno and Koshiro, "Role of Neutrals." According to the latter, joint consultation provides the parties with "channels for intimate communication with the result that many matters which might otherwise develop into shop floor disputes are agreed upon in advance and peacefully implemented" (p. 143).

55. Other objectives mentioned were the maintenance and improvement of working

Consensus-based decisionmaking is another uniquely Japanese practice. Here important decisions are made only after a consensus has been achieved through the process known as *nemawashi*. Nemawashi literally refers to the practice of digging around the roots of a fruit plant and trimming excessive roots in order to promote the bearing of abundant fruits. Figuratively it means to take every step necessary to achieve a desired outcome. The nemawashi practice, which prevails throughout the economy and not just in the unionized sector, must be costly in terms of time and energy, but the gains are evidently worth the cost. This cost is a good example of a transaction cost, which plays a central role in the model discussed later. Joint consultation and consensus-based decisionmaking through the practice of nemawashi are the cornerstone of the Japanese industrial relations system.

The proportion of Japanese unions that have formal grievance settlement procedures is lower than the proportion that have joint consultations, which perhaps underscores the preference of the Japanese to solve disputes informally. In 1984, 39 percent of unions had such procedures. The proportion for large firms was 53 percent, and for very small firms 21 percent. These statistics indicate the minor role played by grievance procedures in Japanese industrial relations, perhaps reflecting the effectiveness of joint consultations in reducing the number of disputes.[56] In contrast, grievance procedures seem to be used widely in the United States. An overwhelming proportion of major U.S. labor agreements contain their own grievance and arbitration procedures to resolve disputes over contract interpretations.[57] It should be kept in mind, however, that in both countries many grievances are resolved among the concerned parties rather than through third parties.[58]

---

conditions (77 percent), improvement of productivity (63 percent), participation in management activities (38 percent), and other (20 percent). This information is from Japan Ministry of Labor, *The Latest Status of Labor Agreements* (1984), table 5-3. A case study may be an effective way of appreciating the workings of joint consultations and grievance procedures. An interested reader is referred to an illuminating case study of the Japan Steel Corporation and the postal service in Sugeno and Koshiro, "Role of Neutrals."

56. Sugeno and Koshiro, "Role of Neutrals," pp. 137–40, present additional evidence that in Japan grievance procedures are much less prevalent than joint consultations. In fact, they state that joint consultations reduce the number of grievances.

57. Theodore J. St. Antoine, "Conflict Resolution in Industrial Relations: United States," in Hanami and Blanpain, eds., *Industrial Conflict Resolution*, pp. 251–72.

58. This point is easily established for Japan from published sources. In 1981, for example, over 87 percent of disputes actually settled were between the parties involved. Hanami, "Conflict Resolution," table 1. Comparable data for the United States could

Unresolved grievances are referred to a third party, notably the Labor Relation Commission in Japan and arbitrators in the United States. U.S. arbitrators are selected by the parties involved or are referred by the Federal Mediation and Conciliation Services (FMCS) or the American Arbitration Association (AAA). Decisions by the arbitrators are binding. There are no counterparts to FMCS or AAA in Japan for providing arbitration services.[59] Instead, the Labor Relation Commission usually acts as the third party.[60] Even if a dispute ends up with the commission, most cases—92 percent in 1981—get resolved through reconciliation.[61] In 1980 U.S. arbitrators referred by FMCS issued 7,539 decisions.[62] And as an experienced U.S. arbitrator reported to me, arbitrators referred by AAA issued at least as many decisions as those selected by the parties involved. The sheer magnitude of the U.S. settlements dwarfs the Japanese experience of fewer than 2,000 cases settled, both between the parties and with the help of third parties, in 1980.

The effectiveness of Japanese industrial relations practices may be inferred from the data on labor disputes. The number of labor cases reaching public dispute settlement procedures, that is, labor relations commissions or courts, is much smaller in Japan than in other industrialized countries, and particularly in the United States. In 1976, for example, 0.407 cases per 1,000 labor force members were brought to the U.S. National Labor Relations Board for settlement, but in Japan the comparable figure was only 0.079 cases brought before either the Labor Relation Commission or the courts.[63] Even the courts tend to rely heavily on compromise and conciliation rather than on the issuing of decisions.[64]

---

not be found. My conversation with an experienced arbitrator suggests that the U.S. proportion may also be high.

59. This absence presumably reflects the Japanese aversion to relying on outsiders to make decisions affecting their well-being. In contrast, the United States has experienced an increased use of arbitration in the settlement of labor disputes. St. Antoine, "Conflict Resolution," p. 267.

60. In 1981, of 261 settlements handed by third parties, 249, or over 95 percent, were decided by the Labor Relations Commission. Hanami, "Conflict Resolution," table 1.

61. Japan may not be unique in having mediation and conciliation as the major way to settle disputes. Although comparable data could not be found for the United States, St. Antoine states that mediation and conciliation are the first step to conflict resolution by the arbitrator. St. Antoine, "Conflict Resolution," p. 262.

62. Arthur A. Sloane and Fred Witney, *Labor Relations,* 6th ed. (Englewood Cliffs, N.J.: Prentice Hall, 1988), p. 246.

63. Hanami, "Conflict Resolution," table 9.

64. It is worth noting here that union and management representatives at Chevrolet

Figure 1. Days Lost by Labor Disputes in Japan, 1951–82

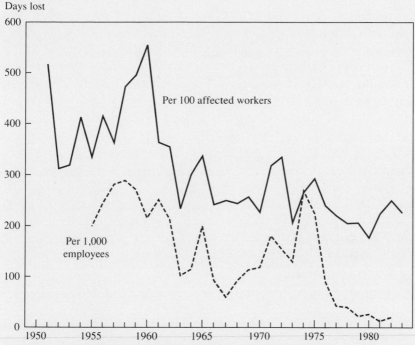

Source: *Practical Labor Statistics* (Tokyo: Japan Productivity Center, 1988), p. 163.

Typically, there are fewer cases of labor disputes, and the resulting productivity loss is smaller, in Japan than in the United States.[65] Figures 1 and 2 show the extent of resource loss, as measured by the number of days lost, caused by labor disputes in Japan and in the United States. Note the difference between the two countries in the scale on the vertical axis. Clearly, labor disputes result in much greater resource loss in the

and Fleetwood once emphasized that one of the best signs of a healthy employment relationship is the willingness to resolve disputes through informal oral discussions instead of resorting to official written grievances. See St. Antoine, "Conflict Resolution," pp. 312–13.

65. Japanese strikes tend to be short lived: they often occur at an early stage in the bargaining process, whether or not negotiations are deadlocked. Thus strikes or other acts of dispute simply demonstrate that the unions disagree with the management. Yasuhiko Matsuda, "Conflict Resolution in Japanese Industrial Relations," in Shirai, ed., *Contemporary Industrial Relations in Japan*, pp. 179–203. Indeed, a distinguishing feature of the mentality of Japanese workers is their reluctance to cause any serious damage to the firm in which they work. Shirai, "Theory of Enterprise Unionism," pp. 135–40.

Figure 2.   Days Lost by Labor Disputes in the United States, 1955–81

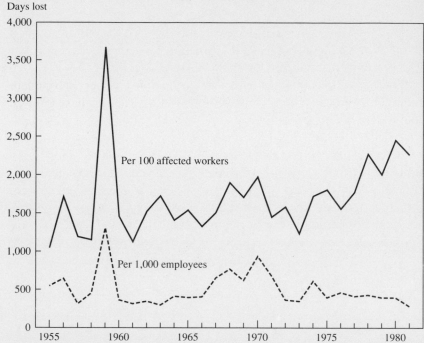

Days lost

Source: U.S. Bureau of Labor Statistics, *Handbook of Labor Statistics*, Bulletin 2175 (Department of Labor, December 1983), table 147.

United States than in Japan. In 1981, for example, there were 955 labor disputes in Japan involving 247,000 workers. These disputes resulted in 554,000 working days lost, or 220 days per 100 affected employees, or 14 days lost per 1,000 employees economywide. In the United States there were 2,568 disputes involving 1.08 million workers, resulting in 24.7 million working days lost. The U.S. experience translates to 2,290 days lost per 100 affected employees, or 276 days lost per 1,000 employees economywide, much higher figures than for Japan.[66] Note in figure 1 that the number of days lost in Japan was rather high in the 1950s, before the

66. The same general conclusion obviously holds for other years as well, as shown in the figures. After 1981 the U.S. data on labor disputes refer only to unions with membership of more than 1,000 workers and are not comparable to the Japanese data. One word of caution is in order when interpreting the Japanese data. The data on disputes used here do not include more subtle forms of work stoppages, such as go-slow or work-to-rule methods. These informal practices are believed to be more widely used in Japan than in the United States. Indeed, these practices are unpopular in America. See, for example, Hanami, "Conflict Resolution," and St. Antoine, "Conflict Resolution."

declining trend set in after 1960. This trend pattern coincides remarkably with the spread of enterprise unionism starting in the late 1950s. Harmonious industrial relations in Japan are a rather recent phenomenon. Figure 2, in contrast, shows an upward trend in the number of days lost in the United States, consistent with the view that U.S. industrial relations tended to worsen during the postwar years.[67]

Finally, no discussion of Japanese productivity issues is complete without mentioning quality control circles (QCs). The Japanese QC was adopted from the concept of statistical quality control pioneered in the United States in the 1950s by W. Edwards Deming.[68] The practice spread widely after the Japanese Union of Scientists and Engineers began publication of a magazine, *Genba to QC* (Quality Control for Foremen) in 1962, and by the early 1980s there were about a million circles there. Quality control circles in Japan are not limited to manufacturing; they exist among department stores, railways, retail shops, auto and television repair services, airlines, hotels, and so on, and even among municipal governments.[69] As discussed later, this practice has been imported to the United States since the mid-1970s with mixed results.

The quality control circle conceptually resembles joint consultation, but in practice there are important differences. Only a handful of production workers doing related work directly participate in a QC. Rather than meet in response to specific problems, the members of a circle engage in a continuous study process involving the issues of quality and productivity.[70] In contrast, joint consultations include both white-and blue-collar workers, not all of them doing related work, and deal

67. For example, Takezawa and Whitehill compare the results of their surveys taken in 1960 and 1976 in Japan and the United States. They infer from these surveys that Japanese management, unions, and workers have come to "share broad mutual goals for the attainment of which the parties are prepared to work together in a spirit of cooperation." They infer that in the United States "workers' commitment to their enterprises has generally decreased; workers have increasingly rejected work as a way of life; and credibility in management has declined." Shin-ichi Takezawa and Arthur M. Whitehill, *Work Ways: Japan and America* (Tokyo: Japan Institute of Labor, 1981), pp. 197, 196.

68. For additional details on the history and practices of quality circles in Japan, see Cole, *Work, Mobility, and Participation*, chap. 5; Robert E. Cole, "Learning from the Japanese: Prospects and Pitfalls," *Management Review*, vol. 69 (September 1980), pp. 22–42; and John D. Blair and Kenneth D. Ramsing, "Quality Circles and Production/Operations Management: Concerns and Caveats," *Journal of Operations Management*, vol. 4 (November 1983), pp. 489–97.

69. Joseph M. Juran, "Quality Control of Service—the 1974 Japanese Symposium," *Quality Progress*, vol. 13 (April 1975), pp. 511–14.

70. Cole, "Learning from the Japanese," p. 26.

with a much broader range of subjects than QCs do. Usually there is more than one quality circle within a firm, and each deals with productivity issues specific to a particular stage of production. However, any worker not belonging to a circle can contribute to improved productivity by passing on his suggestions. Blair and Ramsing note that "Group cohesion and capacity for self control is encouraged through team building exercises, limiting group size (3 to 10), and usually choosing homogeneous membership. The group derives status through the quality and value of its output."[71] Rewards for participating in a quality circle are largely nonfinancial, being stated in terms of contribution to the company and self-development. Such rewards undoubtedly are more effective where a longer-term employer-employee attachment exists.

It should be remembered, however, that quality control circles in Japan have not always been successful. Many firms experienced problems with them for a few years after their introduction. In some firms, as Cole found, workers felt they had been coerced into QCs; in others the emphasis on productivity made the participants doubt the value of circles to them personally, with the result that their participation may have been a mere ritualistic behavior. Moreover, it has not been established that QCs have had a direct effect on productivity and quality: many firms, as Hayes found, already had the reputation for high quality by the time they adopted quality circles.[72]

Implications for Productivity Growth and a Hypothesis

Many of the Japanese labor market phenomena became pronounced after the late 1950s. Although several features, such as the nenko wages, lifetime employment, and enterprise unionism, may have existed in some form in prewar Japan, they do not appear to have been as widespread as in the postwar years. One might insist on historical continuity and argue that the development after the late 1950s reflects a consolidation of what went on before.[73] Even then, one is still left with the question of what factors prompted the consolidation at that particular time. In this paper I argue that the incentives to adopt such practices as bonus payments,

71. Blair and Ramsing, "Quality Circles and Production," p. 492.
72. Cole, "Learning from the Japanese"; and Robert H. Hayes, "Why Japanese Factories Work," *Harvard Business Review*, vol. 59 (July–August 1981), pp. 56–66.
73. For example, Levine and Kawada state that during the 1930s large firms began to institute lifetime employment and nenko wages to retain trained workers. *Human Resources*, pp. 292–96.

long-term employment, enterprise unionism, and joint consultations were *strengthened* by the high rate of economic growth brought about by the introduction of new technologies through the productivity enhancement campaign, launched in 1955. To be sure, the architects of this campaign promulgated joint consultation as one of the basic principles, but its increased attractiveness and widespread adoption hinged on the high rate of economic growth.[74] The prevalence of this and related practices, in turn, contributed to accelerate productivity growth by encouraging investments in firm-specific human capital.

Japanese industrial relations have functioned more smoothly in Japan than in the United States during the postwar years. The harmonious industrial relations encourage, and are encouraged by, investments made in the employment relationship in terms of firm-specific human capital. Besides the technical know-how about the way machines are set up in the firm, an important component of firm-specific human capital is the knowledge that workers acquire about the way they and their employers interact with one another. They cultivate such knowledge through time by working together and sharing in the decisionmaking. This process is an investment in the employment relationship, and the returns to this investment are the improvements in the employer-employee relationship and in the general work environment. These improvements, in turn, raise the returns to investments in firm-specific capital and result in a highly skilled and productive work force.

The amount invested in employment relationships depends on the gains and costs. My hypothesis here is that the costs have been lower in Japan than in the United States. According to this hypothesis, many of the Japanese labor market phenomena, such as bonus payments and long-term employment, are endogenous; therefore, they are not the causes of Japan's high rate of productivity growth. Rather, the low costs of investment in the employment relationship, in terms of both firm-specific human capital and transactions, are the causal variables.[75] Even

74. Along with joint consultations, the other principles agreed upon were no displacement of labor as a result of new technologies and fair sharing of the benefits of new technologies among labor, management, and consumers. See *Thirty-Year History of the Productivity Enhancement Campaign.* It is interesting to note that some high-growth U.S. companies, such as IBM, are said to have long-term employment and other features resembling Japanese practices.

75. One may legitimately go one step further and ask what explains Japan's low costs of investment in the employment relationship. This is an important question, but an analysis must begin somewhere; in this paper I start my analysis by merely asserting the existence of low cost in Japan. See, however, the related discussion at the end of the next section.

the Kanban system, which was not widely adopted in Japan until after the mid-1970s, was feasible because of good employment relations that helped ensure the continuous flow of intermediate parts and components with low or zero defects.[76]

Interestingly, recent efforts to raise productivity in Japanese automobile manufacturing operations in the United States—and, for that matter, in U.S. manufacturing as exemplified by General Motor's Saturn Project—have focused on improving employer-employee relationships. In particular, a major thrust has been to develop a system for including workers in decisionmaking. As discussed later, most of these operations have adopted something resembling joint consultations and related aspects of the Japanese industrial relations system. Available evidence suggests that these efforts have raised productivity considerably.[77] The experiences of these operations are reminiscent of the Japanese experience starting in the early 1960s, when its productivity growth began to take off at about the same time that joint consultations, enterprise unionism, and other related industrial relations practices were becoming popular.

A Transaction Cost Theory of Industrial Relations

In this section I sketch a concrete model representing the hypothesis that the costs of investing in employer-employee relations have been lower in Japan than in the United States. I discuss the model in greater detail in my forthcoming book *Japanese Labor Market;* here I use it to address the issue of the productivity effects of the industrial relations system. Two major costs of interest are the cost of investment in firm-specific technical skills and the cost of transactions. A key result of my analysis is that a lowering of transaction costs encourages the investment in firm-specific technical skills by raising the returns to such investment.

76. The Kanban system was pioneered by Toyota Motor Company in the 1950s, but it became widely adopted by other Japanese manufacturers only after the late 1970s. Under this system, materials, parts, and components are produced and delivered only when they are needed. For an informative discussion of this system, see Abegglen and Stalk, *Kaisha*.

77. For example, at Nummi (New United Motor Manufacturing, Inc.), the joint venture between Toyota and General Motors in Fremont, California, productivity increased considerably over what it was when General Motors alone operated the plant. Also the quality of the products from the Honda plant in Ohio is said to be comparable to the quality of Japanese-made Hondas. Since these operations have existed for only several years, the evidence must be viewed merely as indicative.

In addition, a lowering of the costs of investment obviously increases the amount invested in firm-specific technical skills. Since firm-specific technical skills raise productivity, the analysis identifies the link between productivity and investment in employment relationships.

The main elements of the Japanese industrial relations system—joint consultation and consensus-based decisionmaking—consume resources of time, energy, and money. These transaction costs are incurred presumably because the potential gains justify them. The smooth functioning of joint consultation and consensus-based decisionmaking is the result of the expenditure on transactions. Since transaction costs are high in the United States relative to the gains of transacting, labor relations there tend to be adversarial, and neither joint consultation nor consensus-based decisionmaking has been prevalent. Although recently many U.S. firms have tried to adopt those features, U.S. industrial relations rely heavily on formal grievance settlement and arbitration procedures.

Transaction costs are costs that Robinson Crusoe would not have incurred before he met Friday.[78] Most relevant for this analysis are the costs of communicating and verifying information between the employer and the employee, including the costs of convincing the other party about the information's veracity. The model shows that low transaction costs lead to flexibility in employment contracts. Contract flexibility, in turn, increases the productivity of the employment relationship.

The discussion here is nontechnical, but the technical details will be available in my *Japanese Labor Market*. Although the model is formulated in terms of the choice of flexibility in wages, the analysis of flexibility in such dimensions as task assignments, promotions, and other personnel matters would be similar in spirit. Wage flexibility refers to the degree to which wages are permitted to respond to newly emerging conditions without the contract being rewritten. A fixed-wage (noncontingent) contract stipulates that *none* of these developments be incorporated until the contract comes up for renewal. A flexible-wage (partially contingent) contract allows some automatic adjustments to new developments during the life of the contract.

To simplify the analysis without loss of generality, the model assumes there are two periods in an employment relationship. In the first period

78. I am indebted to Steven Cheung, who offered this succinct definition of transaction costs during a conversation with me several years ago. See also Steven N. S. Cheung, "Transaction Costs, Risk Aversion, and the Choice of Contractual Arrangements," *Journal of Law and Economics,* vol. 12 (April 1969), pp. 23–45.

the employer and the employee decide how much to invest in the relationship and how to share the benefits of such investment. The sharing decision effectively determines the employee's wage in the second period. Investments are made with respect to firm-specific technical skills and to the quality of communications. These constitute the investment in employment relationship. At the beginning of the second period, relevant productivity information is revealed, and the transaction costs become positive.[79] In other words, there is a potential wealth loss caused by postcontractual opportunistic behavior. As Williamson noted in *The Economic Institution of Capitalism,* the value of a transaction that is subject to ex post opportunism will be enhanced by devising ex ante appropriate safeguards (p. 48). In this model the safeguards are the sharing arrangement for the benefits and costs of the employment relationship.[80]

At the beginning of the second period, both the inside and alternative productivities are revealed, but these values are assumed to be private and asymmetrical information. Information asymmetry seems inevitable in employment relationships, since the employer is likely to be better informed about the value of the employee to the firm and the employee to be better informed about his alternative value. The problem is that the parties may have incentives to misrepresent their information. In particular, if the contract calls for sharing the realized returns to the investment, the employer will have the incentive to understate the value of the employee's contribution and the employee to overstate his alternative productivity.

The parties have the incentive to reduce the likelihood of wasteful haggling and inefficient separations by optimally sharing the benefit of the relationship.[81] The parties make relevant decisions in the first period

79. Put another way, there is zero ex ante transaction costs but positive ex post transaction costs, to use Williamson's terminology. Oliver E. Williamson, *The Economic Institutions of Capitalism: Firms, Markets, and Rational Contracting* (Free Press, 1985).

80. The determination of the sharing ratio has been analyzed earlier. Here I incorporate the concept of transaction costs explicitly into the analysis. See Hashimoto, "Bonus Payments"; Masanori Hashimoto, "Firm-Specific Human Capital as a Shared Investment," *American Economic Review,* vol. 71 (June 1981), pp. 475–82; and Masanori Hashimoto and Ben T. Yu, "Specific Capital, Employment Contracts, and Wage Rigidity," *Bell Journal of Economics,* vol. 11 (Autumn 1980), pp. 536–49.

81. This result is the famous sharing theorem in the human capital literature. Gary S. Becker, "Investment in Human Capital: A Theoretical Analysis," *Journal of Political Economy,* vol. 70 (October 1962, supplement), pp. 9–49; and Hashimoto, "Firm-Specific Human Capital." Inefficient separations occur when the parties separate from each other even though both taken together are better off not separating. With a fixed-wage

by comparing the expected values of contracts. It is reasonable to assume that the parties have no difficulty in the first period in agreeing on the probability distributions of the productivity outcomes. This agreement is assumed to be facilitated by common knowledge about the past influence of business cycles and other sources of economic fluctuations. It is useful here to discuss three types of contract: a fully contingent contract (ideal contract), a noncontingent (fixed-wage) contract, and a partially contingent (flexible-wage) contract.

Suppose that the parties could freely agree on the realized productivity values. If so, the ideal (and efficient) wage contract would be feasible, because each party's separation decision would follow exactly the efficient separation criterion.[82] With the ideal contract, all separations are efficient, for they take place only when the employee's value elsewhere exceeds his value with the current employer. Here the distinction between layoffs (dismissals) and quits would be meaningless, since all separations would be mutually desired. The value of entering into the relationship under the ideal contract, M^*, can be computed readily as the sum of the expected value given that the parties do not separate and the expected value if they separate. (See the appendix, available upon request, for an explicit mathematical form for M^*.)

If information is asymmetric, and if transactions are costly between the employee and the employer, the ideal wage contract will not be feasible. The problem is that neither party may have an incentive to reveal his information fully to the other. Assume that the employer knows only the realized value of the inside productivity, and the employee only the realized value of the alternative productivity. The parties therefore face a difficulty when they try to communicate to each other their respective productivity values.

Even with this difficulty, it is in the parties' interest to reach some agreement, however imprecise it may be. The employer wants to persuade the employee of the value of inside productivity, and the employee wants to persuade the employer of the value of his alternative productivity. Each, in turn, wants to verify the other's claim. Persuasion and verification take time and energy and are therefore costly.

If transaction costs between the employer and the employee were prohibitively high, they would be unable to agree and would have to

---

contract, there is bound to be an excess rate of separations. Robert E. Hall and Edward P. Lazear, "The Excess Sensitivity of Layoffs and Quits to Demand," *Journal of Labor Economics*, vol. 2 (April 1984), pp. 233–57.

82. Hashimoto, "Firm-Specific Human Capital."

ignore their realized values in deciding what to do. The result would be a fixed-wage, or noncontingent, contract, because the wage is independent of the realized values of productivities. Here the sharing ratio is critical in determining the efficiency of the contract.

In the fixed-wage contract each party follows his own separation criterion, each being different from the criterion for an efficient separation. As a result, some inefficient separations inevitably occur. When it is efficient to separate, however, a separation will take place through either a dismissal or a quit. The problem is that a separation may take place even when it is inefficient. The resulting efficiency loss reduces the value of this employment contract and thereby reduces the incentive to invest in the relationship.

Under the fixed-wage contract the expected value of the employment relationship, M_1, can be computed as the sum of the expected values under the three mutually exclusive and exhaustive outcomes: no separation, quits but no dismissal, and dismissal.

Although the parties may reduce such a loss by choosing the sharing ratio optimally, they would reduce it further were they to agree on at least the approximate values of the realized productivities.[83] Whatever agreements they reach would contain some inaccuracies, and the extent of the inaccuracies, denoted by σ in this model, would be greater the higher the transaction costs.[84]

A contract that uses such agreements is a partially contingent, or flexible-wage, contract, and the expected value of the employment relationship, M_2, can be computed in a similar way as M_1. An important point is that M_2 equals M^* if σ is zero, but it becomes smaller as σ increases. Under simplifying assumptions, M_2 would decline linearly as follows:

$$(2) \qquad\qquad M_2 = M^* - k\sigma,$$

where k is a positive constant. If σ was endogenous, reducing it would increase M_2, and this increase would be the gains from such a reduction.

Figure 3 depicts the contract frontier implied by the previous discussion. The horizontal axis measures σ, and the vertical axis measures the

83. Hashimoto and Yu, "Specific Capital."

84. For simplicity, the inaccuracy associated with the agreements for inside and alternative productivities is assumed to be the same. This assumption is made to simplify the expression without loss of generality. It in turn implies that the sharing ratio is 0.5. The derivation for this result is available from the author upon request.

Figure 3. Contract Frontier

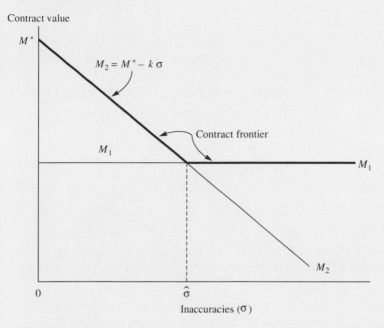

Contract value

M^*

$M_2 = M^* - k\,\sigma$

Contract frontier

M_1

M_1

M_2

0

$\hat{\sigma}$

Inaccuracies (σ)

contract value. Since the contract value for a fixed-wage contract, M_1, is independent of the error variance, it is represented by the horizontal line. As noted above, the contract value for a flexible contract, M_2, is a linearly declining function starting at M^*. For small values of σ, M_2 is greater than M_1, and the flexible contract dominates. As σ increases, M_2 falls. The value of M_2 eventually becomes equal to M_1 at $\hat{\sigma}$. Beyond $\hat{\sigma}$, M_2 is smaller than M_1, and the fixed wage contract dominates. Thus the contract frontier, $\hat{M}$, shown as the thick line, is kinked at $\hat{\sigma}$. (The contract frontier is given by $\hat{M} = \max[M_1, M_2]$.) To summarize, if σ were given exogenously, the choice between the contract types would depend on their magnitudes. The larger the σ, the more likely that a noncontingent contract is chosen over a partially contingent contract.

Optimum Investments in Firm-Specific
Technical Skills and Information
Accuracy

Consider now another decision facing the parties—the amount of investment, h, in firm-specific technical skills. The optimum amount of

Figure 4. Investment in Firm-Specific Technical Skills

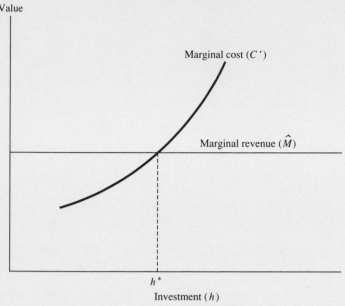

Value

Marginal cost (C')

Marginal revenue ($\hat{M}$)

h^*

Investment (h)

investment is determined by equating the contract value, the larger of M_1 or M_2, with the marginal cost of investment:

$$(3) \qquad\qquad \text{Max}(M_1, M_2) = C'(h),$$

where $C'(h)$ is the marginal cost function.

Figure 4 shows the optimum investment. Obviously, the higher the contract value, or the lower the marginal cost, the larger is the optimum h. With a partially contingent contract, a reduction of σ would raise the contract value and thus increase the optimum h. With a noncontingent contract, however, σ would not affect the contract value and therefore h would be independent of it.

The benefit value from a reduction of σ would take into account the effect of such a reduction on h. What does the schedule of the benefit value look like? As σ increases, the value of the contract, M_2, decreases, and consequently so does h. Therefore, the benefit value declines for two reasons: the decline in M_2 and the decline in h. Figure 5 shows the benefit value as R, which is normalized so that it is zero for σ greater than $\hat{\sigma}$, where M_2 becomes equal to M_1. The reason for this normalization is simple: beyond $\hat{\sigma}$, a reduction in σ does not affect the contract value and, therefore, the optimum investment. Since the benefit value remains

Figure 5. Expenditure on Transactions

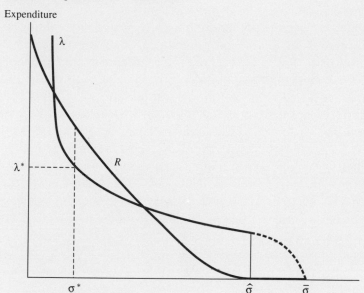

Expenditure

unresponsive to σ in this range, it is normalized to be zero for convenience (see Hashimoto, *Japanese Labor Market*, for technical details).

Figure 5 also depicts a curve labeled λ, which represents transaction costs. To understand it, suppose that a potential employment relationship is characterized by σ̄, which is the value of σ that would prevail if the parties spent no resources on reducing it. Assume that σ̄ is larger than σ̂ to make the analysis interesting. The parties could reduce σ by screening job candidates, by reducing the asymmetry of information on productivity values, and more generally by improving the quality of communication between management and workers. Note that in this case they would move leftward away from σ̄. The cost associated with this movement is the transaction cost, and is shown by the function λ, which depends on technology and input prices. This function would depend on how much σ is reduced, that is, on (σ̄ − σ).

It is obvious that resources are spent to reduce σ only if a contingent contract is chosen. With a noncontingent contract a reduction in σ confers no benefit. The parties select the optimum values of σ and of h to maximize the objective function:

(4) $$\pi = R - \lambda(\bar{\sigma} - \sigma), \quad R \equiv M_2 h - C(h).$$

Assuming that the interior solution exists, figure 5 shows that the parties spend λ^* and choose a partially contingent contract.[85]

To summarize, given the R function, a fully or partially contingent contract is more likely to be chosen the lower is λ. When I state that transaction costs are low in Japan, I refer to a low level of the λ function relative to the R function in that country, but the amount of transaction costs actually incurred refers to the optimized value of λ. Thus it is possible for the Japanese to spend more on transaction costs than Americans—that is, for λ^* to be larger in Japan than in the United States—even though, or because, transaction cost function is lower in Japan. Finally, an important result of this analysis is that the investment in firm-specific technical skills is increased by the lowering of the transaction cost function, which raises the returns to such investment, as well as by the lowering of the cost of the investment (C') itself. Thus the model establishes the link between productivity and the costs of investment in employment relationships.

Implications of the Model

Japanese workers invest more in firm-specific human capital, and they have more flexible wages (partially contingent contracts), than U.S. workers.[86] These differences may result from the differences in the costs of investment and transactions. As discussed earlier, Japanese industrial relations tend to incorporate measures for promoting harmonious relationships between the employer and employees, and Japanese workers of various ranks often spend a great deal of time and money together after regular work hours over drinks and food. (My Japanese friends, both businessmen and academic administrators, told me they tend to spend these resources especially when there is a need to produce a

85. Is the above theory consistent with competition? The answer is yes, for under competition the parties will share the cost of contracting, $C(h) + \lambda$, as well as the benefits to make the respective profit zero in the long run. The employee may pay for his share of the cost either by accepting a lower wage than his productivity in early years of employment or by paying an "entrance fee" at the time of employment. This argument is exactly the same as the one by now familiar in the human capital literature. See, for example, Becker, "Investment in Human Capital"; Masatoshi Kuratani, "A Theory of Training, Earnings, and Employment: An Application to Japan," Ph.D. dissertation, Columbia University, 1973; and Hashimoto, "Firm-Specific Human Capital." The zero-profit theorem states that both the worker's and employer's profits be zero. This condition implies that the worker's share of the costs is given by M_2^w/M_2, where M_2^w is the worker's share in M_2.

86. See Hashimoto and Raisian, "Wage Flexibility"; "Aspects of Labor Flexibility"; and "Structure and Short-Run Adaptability."

consensus on some matter.) These expenditures can be seen as transaction costs, λ, which are investments made to enhance communication among coworkers. In our theory this tendency is consistent with the fact that Japanese employees have partially contingent contracts more often than their U.S. counterparts. Also, there seems to be no reason for the costs of investments in human capital to be higher in Japan than in the United States. If anything, investment costs may be lower there than in the United States if Japanese school graduates are better prepared in basic general skills—reading, writing, and arithmetic—as is often claimed, and if the Japanese on average can be characterized as more *kinben,* or diligent and eager to learn, than Americans.[87] Put another way, the prevalence of contingent contracts in Japan results from the expenditures on transactions to reduce error variances, and the high level of investments in technical skills reflects these expenditures and possibly low costs of investments as well.

Many of the so-called uniquely Japanese aspects of industrial relations became widespread after the productivity enhancement campaign began. Why did the transaction cost effect become visible only after 1955? An answer may be that economic growth after 1955, widespread throughout the economy, increased the incentives to invest in h and to reduce σ. It also increased the attractiveness of contingent contracts. In terms of figure 5, economic growth rotated the R function upward around the original $\hat{\sigma}$, just as in the case of an exogenous lowering of C', thereby increasing the attractiveness of reducing σ.[88]

The relatively homogeneous labor force in Japan, along with an absence of the ethos of individualism, has been cited as being responsible for the harmonious industrial relations there.[89] My model would have to be extended to permit a comprehensive examination of this issue. Let me suggest how such an extension might proceed. Firm-specific human

87. *The Thirty-Year History of the Productivity Campaign* notes that this Japanese characteristic is an important ingredient in producing the successful Japanese-style productivity-enhancement campaign.

88. See the appendix, available from the author on request, for the effects of economic growth. For the evidence on the interaction of technological change and investments in human capital, see Jacob Mincer and Yoshio Higuchi, "Wage Structures and Labor Turnover in the United States and Japan," *Journal of the Japanese and International Economies,* vol. 2 (June 1988), pp. 97–133.

89. Japan is remarkably homogeneous in race, ethnicity, religion, and culture. Cole argues that the Japanese manager views the average worker as being not very different from him, and that this attitude is critical in understanding the willingness of Japanese employers to invest in the training of, and provide responsibility for, blue-collar employees. "Learning from the Japanese," p. 25.

capital is a key factor behind harmonious industrial relations. Suppose that the degree of employee homogeneity refers to how similar $\bar{\sigma}$ and/or the λ function are among the workers. Although my theory has been formulated in terms of a one-on-one employment contract, in reality an employer must negotiate with many employees. If employees were homogeneous, the employer could adopt the policy to reduce σ for all of them. If they were heterogeneous, he would have to take into account individual differences and adopt different policies for different employees. If the employee heterogeneity were large, it might be too costly to devise different policies for different employees for it to make sense to reduce σ for any of the employees.[90] In that case a fixed-wage contract—fixed with respect to the realized productivity values and with respect to individual differences in them—might be chosen for all employees. Since such a contract inevitably reduces the gains from the employment relationship, investment in firm-specific human capital would be discouraged.

The Japanese employer typically screens job applicants with much care, a phenomenon that, I argue, reflects the low cost of screening relative to its gains. The more homogeneous job candidates are to begin with, the lower the cost of screening. A homogeneous labor force is likely to encourage the adoption of policies to reduce σ and fosters investment in firm-specific human capital, thereby encouraging harmonious industrial relations. In this connection, it is interesting to recall that quality control circles usually consist of homogeneous membership.

The transaction cost theory may help us understand how the Japanese economy coped with the two oil shocks of the 1970s. The first shock in late 1973 dramatically reduced the rate of economic growth in Japan. During the 1970–73 period real GNP grew at 8.1 percent a year, but the growth rate fell to a mere 0.6 percent in 1974–75.[91] At the same time,

90. One way to mitigate the problem of employee heterogeneity is to screen job candidates. Japanese employers, particularly those in large firms, are known for the care with which they screen new hires. The screening device includes extensive background checks and exclusive reliance on selected schools from which to recruit. Sorting employees into subgroups may be another way of reducing the number of different policies that must be devised. Sorting is costly, however. A full analysis of this consideration would lead to the issues of hierarchical structures in a firm and of the optimum numbers of departments within an organization.

91. The factual discussion on this experience draws heavily on Yusuke Onitsuka, "The Oil Crisis and Japan's Internal-External Adjustment," Yokohama National University, 1988. That paper contains an informative discussion on the macroeconomic performance of the Japanese economy during the oil crisis.

Japan became plagued with an accelerated rate of inflation. The rate of increase of the consumer price index rose from 9 percent in 1972 to 25 percent in 1974. As is well known by now, the large wage increase demanded by the unions after the first oil shock contributed to the decline of the economy in the 1974–75 period. Unions evidently realized that the wage-hike demand was a mistake, and no such demand was made during the second oil shock in the late 1970s. In fact, the rate of increase of wages dropped from 6.4 percent in 1978 to 6.0 percent in 1979, though the rate rose slightly to 6.3 percent in 1980.[92]

The low transaction cost environment contributed to the performance of the Japanese economy during the two oil crises and after. The key ingredients to the recovery were effective cost-reducing efforts, the low rate of labor disputes, a high productivity growth, and labor market flexibility. As Onitsuka, "Oil Crisis," notes, "workers did not oppose the introduction of robots and other factory-office automation because the lifetime employment scheme guaranteed them job security. Other examples of labor-management cooperation, such as the 'quality circle' and 'zero defect movements,' also tended to reduce costs and improve labor productivity" (p. 21).

As stated earlier, the maintained assumption of this paper is that the transaction cost function is lower in Japan than in the United States, with the gains from transactions differing little between the two countries. The theory is not meant to yield explicit relationships among variables with identifiable parameters that can be estimated. Instead, its testing must rely on qualitative evidence. To this end, I examined, in *Japanese Labor Market,* a prediction from the assumption of lower transaction costs in Japan than in the United States. I found, consistent with the prediction of this theory, that the distinction between quits and dismissals (layoffs) clearly exists in the United States but that in Japan it is ambiguous. Thus quits were found to be distinctly procyclical, and layoffs countercyclical, in the United States, but in Japan neither quits nor dismissals were found to be related to economic fluctuations.

It would be useful to have more direct evidence on the magnitude of transaction costs in Japan and the United States. But transaction costs are difficult, if not impossible, to measure directly, and one would

92. Also at work was the expansion of the money supply. The first oil shock took place against the background of the easy-money policy that preceded it, but when the second oil shock arrived, policymakers responded swiftly with anti-inflationary measures. See Onitsuka, "Oil Crisis."

probably need to rely on anecdotal evidence. For example, the difference in the worker compliance with a foreman's request that the rivet be placed first from the left side rather than from the right is suggestive of a transaction cost difference. As reported to me by a Japanese manager, who operates factories in both countries, Japanese workers comply with such a request without argument, but American workers tend to resist it out of a sheer stubbornness. The task of assembling similar evidence is left for a future study. Finally, the above analysis implies that, for Japanese workers, measured hours of work understate the true hours of work insofar as they do not take into account the expenditure on λ, that is, time spent on smoothing the employment relationship. As a result, the measured productivity per hour is overstated for these workers.[93]

Are the Japanese Practices Importable?

To answer this question, it is important to identify the relevant exogenous variables that are behind these practices. According to my theory, a low transaction cost environment in Japan was the key exogenous variable responsible for the successful adoption of joint consultation and related practices. But the reasons for the low transaction cost environment have been left unexplored in this paper. They must ultimately relate to cultural and traditional factors, the degree of population homogeneity, and other "noneconomic" variables that affect the λ function. Thus without the knowledge of what these variables are and how they affect the λ function, it would be unreasonable to hope for an accurate assessment of the extent to which the Japanese practices can be borrowed successfully.

Consider, for example, the frequently asked question, "Does wage flexibility raise productivity?" My theory suggests that this question is

93. The effect of an adjustment, though approximate, for Japanese hours of work on the productivity comparison may be instructive. Earlier I argued that the difference in the labor productivity was on average 43 to 51 percent in the United States' favor. Suppose that a typical Japanese employee works forty-eight hours a week but that he puts in (conservatively) another five hours a week after work for investing in the reduction of σ. Taking into account the five extra hours, the Japanese hours of work rise by 10.4 percent. Assuming that U.S. workers do not spend any amount of time for similar activities, the adjustment in Japanese hours would widen the productivity gap to somewhere between 58 and 67 percent. Such a calculation must be interpreted with caution, however. In particular, it would be wrong to conclude that Japanese workers are low productivity workers. There is obviously the issue of how to measure productivity. No doubt, the time expenditure by Japanese workers has paid off in terms of their increased competitiveness in the international markets. What is not clear is whether Japanese workers have been overinvesting their time.

posed incorrectly. Wage flexibility is endogenous, and it does not make sense to ask if flexibility affects productivity. Costs of investments in the employment relationship—investments in firm-specific technical skills and in transactions—are the exogenous variables. What is clear is that a low-cost environment for these activities promotes productivity. If an economy is in a high-cost environment, a flexible wage contract may not be efficient, and forcing such a system onto this economy will lower output. A similar consideration applies to other Japanese practices. It is unclear, therefore, if a rush to borrow the "Japanese system" in the United States or elsewhere will always be successful. As Robert Hayes put it:

> U.S. businesses found themselves increasingly displaced in international markets and, more recently, in their home markets as well. This sudden weakness has come as a shock to many American managers who, in searching belatedly for causes and explanations, have often looked for dramatic, easily imitated or purchased solutions: quality circles, government assistance, and the use of intelligent robots. . . . There are no magic formulas—just steady progress in small steps and focusing attention on manufacturing fundamentals. This is why their [Japanese] example will be so hard for American companies—and American managers—to emulate.[94]

The attempt to adopt quality control circles in the United States seems to have met with mixed results.[95] I have not been able to find data that can show the exact degree of success with QC circles in the United States, but the available literature suggests that they have not always been successful. To be sure, QC circles in Japan have not always been successful either, but it seems safe to infer from the literature that the probability of success has been higher in Japan than in the United States. The strong belief in individualism, distrust between employees and management, management's failure to involve unions in setting up quality circles, middle management's fear of being bypassed in decision-

94. Hayes, "Why Japanese Factories Work," p. 65.
95. Quality control circles in Japan were discussed earlier. The first QC circle in the United States started at Lockheed Missile and Space Company, which implemented it in 1974 with subsequent success. Quality circles grew rapidly afterward, and as of the early 1980s there were more than 3,000 circles in U.S. firms. Blair and Ramsing, "Quality Circles and Production." For a list of U.S. firms that have adopted QC circles as well as a discussion of their motives, see Cole, *Work, Mobility, and Participation*, and "Learning from the Japanese."

making processes, all are said to have contributed to the failure of quality circles in some U.S. firms.

The experiences at Nummi, Honda in Ohio, and others do suggest, however, that some of the practices may be importable to the United States, though such a suggestion must be interpreted cautiously.[96] After all, these experiences have been fairly recent, and it is unclear if the phenomena observed so far will persist.[97] At any rate, as discussed earlier, a major thrust at these and other operations has been to develop a sense of teamwork by involving workers in decisionmaking and by improving employer-employee relations. Most firms have adopted something like joint consultation and related Japanese practices, including an elaborate screening of job applicants. As mentioned, some U.S. workers who were hired at Honda in Ohio were reportedly surprised both at the many questions they were asked that seemed unrelated to work and at the length of the interviews, which were attended by executives and vice presidents. As noted in the previous section, careful screening of job applicants is a device for creating an environment of low transaction costs on the shop floor.[98] Once hired, these workers reported attending frequent meetings with the management on production matters. Such frequent meetings at the Honda plant in Ohio are signified by the slogan, "let's Y-gaya," which means in fractured Japanese, "let's have a bull session." In these operations management and workers share the same tables for lunch, thereby creating an informal setting for communication. Finally, layoffs and dismissals have been rare in these operations.

Productivity at Nummi after only one year of operation was reported to have increased by 48.5 percent over what it was at the old Fremont plant under GM management.[99] Absenteeism and drug use, which

96. For the facts regarding the U.S. operations of Japanese automobile manufacturing, see Haruo Shimada, *The Economics of Humanware* (Tokyo: Iwanami, 1988).

97. Nummi was established in 1984; Honda in Ohio started production in 1978. Since Nummi inherited the old Fremont plant operated by General Motors as well as many of the same workers, its experience seems particularly useful for ascertaining the effects of Japanese-style operations in the United States.

98. Shimada, *Economics of Humanware*, chap. 2, states that American workers who were hired at Honda in Ohio also reported having gone through lengthy interviews in the presence of executives and vice presidents. For similar evidence on an intensive screening at Mazda in Michigan and the Diamond-Star (joint venture between Chrysler and Mitsubishi) in Illinois, see William J. Hampton, "How Does Japan Inc. Pick Its American Workers?" *Business Week*, October 3, 1988.

99. What is noteworthy is the fact that the productivity improvement occurred even though the plant and equipment were largely inherited from the old Fremont operation and many of the workers were the same as those who worked at the old plant. See Shimada, *Economics of Humanware*, p. 32.

plagued the old Fremont plant, dropped dramatically after Nummi took over. Nummi's efforts at productivity enhancement continue with the slogan "let's kaizen," or "let's improve."[100] Also, in contrast to the old Fremont plant, the quality of the automobiles produced at Nummi has been rated highly.[101] What little evidence there is on productivity at Nummi indicates that in the first year of operation it ranked in productivity somewhere between the old Fremont plant and a Toyota plant in Japan.[102]

Honda's operation in Ohio is another interesting example. Honda in Japan is known for its emphasis on nurturing the sense of cooperative teamwork among its workers. This emphasis was imported to Honda's operation in Ohio. At the Ohio plant workers, referred to as associates, are encouraged to acquire skills and training by continual interactions with one another on the shop floor rather than through formal training sessions. Productivity at the plant reportedly approaches that of Honda's plants in Japan, and the quality of the automobiles produced in Ohio is said to equal that of Japanese-made Hondas.

These recent experiences do suggest that some of the practices of Japanese industrial relations may be imported successfully, but it is too early to tell what is the effective way to do so. My theory suggests that a key to the successful borrowing of any of the Japanese practices is to create an environment of low transaction cost. Such an environment encourages investments in the employment relationship, and the resulting long-term commitment to and identification with the employment relationship promote productive behavior. Put another way, a low transaction cost environment generates what Cole terms the harmonization of worker and organizational goals.[103] Only after a low-cost environment is created does it become feasible to adopt joint consultations, quality control circles, and the like. Clearly, the borrowing must be done very selectively to fit American needs and circumstances. After

100. The "kaizen" also underlies the philosophy at Mazda in Flat Rock, Michigan. See Hampton, "How Does Japan Inc. Pick Its American Workers?" p. 88.

101. *Consumer Reports* in 1986 rated the Nova produced at Nummi somewhere between 3.6 and 3.8 out of the maximum attainable of 5, whereas other U.S.-made automobiles averaged 2.0 to 3.0. Shimada, *Economics of Humanware*, p. 42.

102. In terms of hours of labor, including production and nonproduction workers, it took 29.1 hours at the GM Fremont plant (1978), 19.6 hours at Nummi (1986), and 18.0 hours at a Toyota plant in Japan to produce a car. Shimada, *Economics of Humanware*, table 1. This type of comparison obviously must be interpreted with caution, if only because automobile models differ among plants.

103. Cole thinks that such harmonization is the heart of the distinctiveness of the Japanese approach. See *Work, Mobility, and Participation*, chap. 9.

all, that is what the Japanese have done in modernizing their economy after the Meiji restoration of 1868 and more recently with the productivity enhancement campaign and related activities.

Comment by Richard B. Freeman

In this well-written, carefully thought-out paper, Hashimoto describes the distinctive features of the Japanese labor market and develops a "transactions cost" interpretation of Japanese labor market institutions and their relation to Japanese economic growth. In contrast to studies that focus on a single feature of the Japanese labor system—such as bonuses, job rotation, tenure and nenko wages, enterprise unionism, or mandatory retirement—the paper offers a quick tourists' guide of the features of the Japanese system. Then it makes its contribution by developing a transactions cost interpretation of the "whole schmear," in which good employee relations are linked with productivity growth.

The virtue of this approach is that the author can present a broad and sweeping interpretation of the Japanese labor market experience that is more appealing than a more detailed analysis of a particular institution. The problem with the approach is that, lacking data on transactions costs, he cannot put the interpretation to any test.

His analysis has three elements:

—that good employee relations raise productivity;

—that lower costs of investing in employee relations lead firms to make such investments; and

—that costs of investing in the employment relationship are lower in Japan than elsewhere, inducing greater investments and increased productivity.

Hashimoto postulates that the first relation operates through greater investments in specific technical skills. But that is not critical. Good employee relations could also operate through increased worker effort or cooperation with other workers. The key is that the labor relations practices have a productivity payoff.

Considerable evidence in U.S. studies supports the author's claim that good employer-employee relations are associated with high productivity. For example, in a detailed study of GM plants, Katz, Kochan, and Gobeille found that plants where managers and union officials rated labor relations as good had higher output per worker and lower grievance rates.[1] Many other studies find similar patterns.[2] The problem is how to create such good relations.

No labor economist will argue with the second element of Hashimoto's analysis. If there is one thing we all believe, it is that lowering the price of a factor of production will increase its usage. If we didn't believe that, we would be in another business.

It is the third point, however, on which the analysis turns, and here supporting data are hard to find. The author correctly notes that one cannot measure the costs by determining how much is spent on good employee relations (Japan spends a lot, he tells us), since that reflects the outcome of the system. What one needs is the price of investments in good employee relations—a price not given on the Tokyo stock market.

Hashimoto offers some reasons why the price or transactions cost of investing in good employment relations might be lower in Japan—the work force is more homogeneous and better educated in basic skills— but he does not make a big point of them, presumably because he finds the arguments only a bit less unconvincing than I do. Ultimately he leaves the reasons for the low cost of investing in good employee relations unexplored in favor of deriving the implications of the low costs for outcomes. That is probably about as much as one can do with existing data and analytic tools. And Hashimoto does it well. His paper is an important and valuable piece, one of the most insightful interpretations of Japanese labor relations I have seen.

But it leaves the big question still open: *how do we create good employer-employee relations, or, in Hashimoto's terminology, a low-cost transaction environment?* Unfortunately, conventional economics offers little insight here.

1. Harry C. Katz, Thomas A. Kochan, and Kenneth R. Gobeille, "Industrial Relations Performance, Economic Performance, and the Quality of Working Life Efforts: An Interplant Analysis," *Industrial and Labor Relations Review,* vol. 37 (October 1983), pp. 3–17.

2. For a summary of the relationship between unions and productivity, see Dale Belman, "Unions, the Quality of Labor Relations, and Firm Performance," draft paper for the Economic Policy Institute, Washington, D.C., May 31, 1989.

Contributors

JOSEPH RAPHAEL BLASI
*Professor, Institute of Management
and Labor Relations
Rutgers University*

ALAN S. BLINDER
*Gordon S. Rentschler Memorial
Professor of Economics
Chairman of the Department of Economics
Princeton University*

DAVID CARD
*Professor of Economics
Rutgers University*

MICHAEL A. CONTE
*Professor of Economics
University of Baltimore*

RONALD G. EHRENBERG
*Professor of Economics
Director of School of Industrial
and Labor Relations
Cornell University*

RICHARD B. FREEMAN
*Professor of Economics
Harvard University*

MASANORI HASHIMOTO
*Professor of Economics
Ohio State University*

DEREK C. JONES
*Professor of Economics
Hamilton College*

DOUGLAS L. KRUSE
*Assistant Professor of Industrial Relations
and Human Resources
Rutgers University*

EDWARD E. LAWLER III
*Professor of Management and Organization
Director of Center for Effective Organization
School of Business
University of Southern California*

DAVID I. LEVINE
*Assistant Professor
Haas School of Business Administration
University of California at Berkeley*

DAVID LEWIN
*Professor of Business
Columbia University*

DANIEL J. B. MITCHELL
*Director of the Institute
of Industrial Relations
University of California at Los Angeles*

JAN SVEJNAR
*Professor of Economics
University of Pittsburgh*

LAURA D'ANDREA TYSON
*Professor of Economics
University of California at Berkeley*

MARTIN L. WEITZMAN
*Professor of Economics
Harvard University*

Index